# THE COMPUTER AS A PRODUCTIVITY TOOL IN EDUCATION

*This book belongs to*

Darlene Van Tiem
1310 Kensington Rd.
Grosse Pointe Park, MI 48230

**Richard C. Forcier**
**Western Oregon State College**

Merrill, an imprint of Prentice Hall
Englewood Cliffs, New Jersey    Columbus, Ohio

**Library of Congress Cataloging-in-Publication Data**

Forcier, Richard C.

    The computer as a productivity tool in education / Richard C. Forcier.

      p. cm.

    Includes bibliographical references and index.

    ISBN 0-02-338702-5 (pbk.)

    1. Education—Data processing—Study and teaching (Higher)
2. Computers—Study and teaching (Higher) 3. Computer managed
instruction. 4. Computer-assisted instruction. I. Title.

LB1028.43.F67   1996

371.3'334'071'2—dc20                        95-23760

                                                  CIP

Cover art: Majory Dressler
Editor: Debra A. Stollenwerk
Production Editor: Julie Anderson Peters
Photo Editor: Anne Vega
Design Coordinator: Julia Zonneveld Van Hook
Text Designer: Anne Flanagan
Cover Designer: Retter/Pattons & Associates, Inc.
Production Manager: Deidra Schwartz

This book was set in Palatino by Carlisle Communications, Ltd. and was printed and bound by R.R. Donnelley & Sons Company. The cover was printed by Phoenix Color Corp.

 © 1996 by Prentice-Hall, Inc.
A Simon & Schuster Company
Englewood Cliffs, New Jersey 07632

Photo credits: All photos supplied by the author except pp. 60, 135, 166, 207, 303, 308, and 312, by Scott Cunningham/Merrill/Prentice Hall, and p. 306, by Tom Watson/Merrill/Prentice Hall.

Printed in the United States of America

10 9 8 7 6 5 4 3 2

ISBN: 0-02-338702-5

Prentice-Hall International (UK) Limited, *London*
Prentice-Hall of Australia Pty. Limited, *Sydney*
Prentice-Hall of Canada, Inc., *Toronto*
Prentice-Hall Hispanoamericana, S. A., *Mexico*
Prentice-Hall of India Private Limited, *New Delhi*
Prentice-Hall of Japan, Inc., *Tokyo*
Simon & Schuster Asia Pte. Ltd., *Singapore*
Editora Prentice-Hall do Brasil, Ltda., *Rio de Janeiro*

# Preface

*The Computer as a Productivity Tool in Education* was written after seventeen years of teaching undergraduate and graduate computer education courses to education majors and to inservice teachers who found themselves interacting with a computer in their classroom. Some of those teachers had chosen to bring the computer into their classrooms, whereas others had the interaction forced upon them. Most had one thing in common, a desire to better understand how the computer could help them in their professional and personal lives. They were not as interested in what the computer was, nor in step-by-step instructions on how to use it, but rather, wanted to know what they could do with it. Those students have unknowingly become significant contributors to this text because they have asked pertinent questions, accepted the challenge of understanding and applying a new technology to teaching, and challenged this instructor to better explain and illustrate the computer's use.

Changes have occurred in how educators approach the teaching of the application of computers in the classroom. Gone is the overriding concern with programming. It has been replaced by a focus on application software as a solution to a productivity problem in an instructional or management function and increasingly places the student in an authoring role. Gone is the fascination with equipment for equipment's sake. It has been replaced with a better understanding of selection and use of equipment. Gone is the memorization of historical facts. It has been replaced with an appreciation of the development of computing and the application of the computer as a *problem solving tool* to better understand the present state of the art and better predict successful future developments.

The task of this book is to lead teachers and those aspiring to be teachers to become proficient at applying the computer to solve problems, to infuse the computer into the curriculum, and to integrate it into their professional and personal lives. Those who are successful in doing this will indeed come to see the computer as an extension of their human capability. The computer will allow them to do more, to do it faster, and to do it better and more accurately.

## A Problem Solving Focus

*The Computer as a Productivity Tool in Education* provides a current comprehensive look at the computer's role in education, stressing task analysis, problem solving, and the application of the computer as a *tool of the mind*.

As the text examines the computer's various roles in education, the topics of school management, research, instruction, and learning are broken down into specific areas of interest to encourage an understanding of the computer's contribution to solving problems. Inclusive in the text are problem solving models, addressing the needs of both linear and nonlinear thinkers, to encourage an increase in computer productivity and clarify the application of the computer in a thoughtful and deliberate manner, reinforcing the concept of the computer as a mind tool.

## Text Organization and Special Features

Woven throughout this text is the use of the computer as a personal productivity tool for the teacher in both an instructional and a management role as well as for the student in a learning role. The text therefore is organized with the following thematic frameworks.

- *Learning theory and instruction.* Theoretical structures are established to look at the computer's role in teacher-centered instruction and to examine student-centered learning. Both behaviorist and constructivist perspectives are examined. Underlying principles and theories of education and communication are reviewed and applied to discussions of computer-assisted instruction (CAI) and computer assisted learning. Implications of emerging technologies are discussed.
- *Strategies for computer use.* The computer as a productivity tool is applied to drill and practice, tutorial, and simulation formats. Technologies such as CD-ROM, videodisc, computer interactive desktop video, and multimedia are examined and their roles in education are discussed.
- *Selecting, evaluating, and managing a software collection.* A unique examination of the process of developing and sustaining a software collection is included to meet the information needs of teachers and students. By identifyng the processes involved in the evaluation, selection, acquisition, and maintenance of software, its effective use is more readily established. In addition, after examining evaluation instruments pertinent to software referenced in the text, readers are encouraged to develop their own evaluation forms. The management of a software collection on FileMaker Pro is discussed.
- *Issues in information technology.* A number of issues are examined including copyright from both a legal and ethical perspective, information ownership, equitable computer access, and gender equity. The computer's role in the educational reform movement is discussed as well as its place in current and future trends in information technology.

Furthermore, the text is ordered to provide thorough coverage of computer knowledge and educational applications including:

- *The computer itself and its user interfaces.* An explanation of computer hardware commonly found in schools is presented. A look at current and emerging user interfaces is examined.

- *Word processing.* Concepts of word processing are explored and examples are given. Applications are suggested and examples are used to illustrate various applications.
- *Graphics.* The concepts of bit-mapped and vector or object graphics are explored and examples are given. Proper selection of chart types and the interpretation of data represented by graphs is analyzed. Information on the use of the computer to generate display graphics for charts and graphs, signs, posters, bulletin boards, and overhead transparencies is presented.
- *Spreadsheets.* Problem solving models are applied to the development of spreadsheets. Applications are suggested and examples are used to illustrate those applications.
- *Databases.* The organization and retrieval of information is examined. Problem solving models are applied to the development of databases. Applications are suggested and examples are used to illustrate those applications.
- *Telecommunications.* Networking schemes are explored as well as fundamental concepts of telecommunications. Applications are suggested and examples are used to illustrate those applications. An introduction to the Internet is presented.

## Chapter Features

This book provides the student with information in a highly readable format. The following sections are included in each chapter.

- *Chapter Introduction.* Each chapter begins with a goal statement and a list of advanced organizers for the chapter.
- *Charts and line drawings* are used to illustrate concepts in a concrete manner.
- *Screen displays* illustrate concepts and application software in, as much as possible, a nonspecific hardware platform. Users of Macintosh, MS-DOS, and Windows platforms should be able to profit equally from the illustrations.
- *Chapter Exercises.* Exercises address the topics discussed in the chapter and are designed to allow the student the opportunity to process the information presented in the chapter and apply it in a practical manner.
- *Chapter Glossary.* Important terms are printed in boldface when they are introduced to the reader. They are then defined in the chapter glossary and are included in the index at the end of the book to facilitate reference.

## Appendices

The appendices serve as a ready reference to the student. They include sample software evaluation forms, a sample parental permission form for telecommunications, a practical listing of telecommunications resources, field definitions for a software database, a list of software publishers with a statement of each one's sales and support policies, and a selected list of journals and professional associations.

## Acknowledgments

I would like to acknowledge the significant contributions that the following people made to the creation and development of this text:

Peggy Forcier, manager of the Washington County (Oregon) Cooperative Library Services, as well as my wife and best friend, for her unflagging support, thoughtful consideration of every idea expressed, and careful reading of every word written.

Dr. Edward Wright, a colleague with whom I co-authored a previous text and whose contributions appear throughout this one.

Melanie Wallis, an elementary library media specialist in McMinnville, Oregon, for her significant contributions to Chapter 12 and the delightful story that concludes this text.

Nancy Powell, an international consultant on collection assessment, for her thoughtful review and many suggestions that contributed greatly to the strength of Chapter 11. Figure 11.1 is an adaptation of a model she suggested.

Janet Murray, a co-founder of K-12 Net and a library media specialist at Wilson High School, Portland, Oregon, for her assistance with Chapter 8 and description of K-12 Net.

Dr. Richard Jensen and Paul Yeiter, colleagues who provided thoughts, suggestions, and inspirations on the human side of computer applications.

All of my graduate students, especially Sylvia Sandoz for her clever design of a model representing virtual reality and the related discussion of it; Susan May for her help on Big Books and cooperative writing ideas; and Don Price and Karl Paulsen for their thoughtful discussions on new and emerging technologies.

Last, but certainly not least, S. Evangeline Dufault, my eighth grade teacher, who instilled in her students a sense of intellectual curiosity and who taught us never to accept things without asking the question, WHY?

I would also like to express my gratitude to the reviewers who so thoughtfully read and offered constructive criticism to the work in progress. Their expertise contributed greatly to the strength of this book and to its potential usefulness in a course dealing with computers in education. They include:

Doris Dale, Southern Illinois University
Carol Dwyer, Penn State University
Kim Foreman, San Francisco State University
Patricia K. Freitag, University of Wisconsin—Madison
Jack Garber, University of Wisconsin—Eau Claire
Gail F. Grejda, Clarion University
Hilary McLellan, Kansas State University
David Moursund, University of Oregon
Gregory C. Sales, University of Minnesota
Janice R. Sandiford, Florida International University
Mary C. Ware, State University of New York, Cortland

*Rich Forcier*

# Brief Contents

# Contents

## 11    MANAGING A SOFTWARE COLLECTION                    271

# 1

# COMPUTER APPLICATIONS IN EDUCATION

*All media are extensions of some human faculty.*
Marshall McLuhan (1967)

The word *media* has been defined in many ways. Its most popular definition in our culture refers to the mass media of communications: radio, television, newspapers, and magazines. Some teachers see media as new *audiovisual aids;* some see media as relating to library and **information technology.** A definition gaining favor in recent years identifies media as a *tool.* Consider the word media itself. Media is a plural form of the word medium, a term broadly understood as being in the middle. Something is medium if it is neither hot nor cold, neither fast nor slow, neither large nor small. Medium implies *in the middle or between* two extremes or two points. This understanding is the ideal foundation for defining medium as a *tool* between the user and information to be created, received, stored, manipulated, or disseminated. A tool is the middle between the user and the task being addressed.

Tools are what McLuhan was referring to as extensions of our human capability. From the study of archeology, we know that humans have always been tool makers and tool users. Consider, during our existence on this planet, how we have created and adapted *physical tools* such as the lever, the wheel, and the engine to amplify our physical abilities and *figurative tools* such as language and mathematics to enhance our cognitive abilities. Some would define technology as this deliberate ingenious effort to create, select, adapt, and apply tools to a task or problem at hand. Among our ancestors, women were some of the earliest technologists as they fashioned agricultural and homemaking tools.

1

The computer is one of our most recent tools in education. "When the only tool you have is a hammer, every problem looks like a nail" (Greene, 1988). When we consider technology in education we include, among other things, the application of the computer as a multifaceted tool. Not being limited to a single tool, we select from a variety of tools, perhaps adapt, and then apply the tool to the problem at hand. We, as teachers, do not create the computer itself, the **hardware,** but we may, in rare instances, create the **software.** More often, we select the computer hardware and software and adapt it to fit our curriculum. We apply the computer system to the instructional, management, or research task at hand.

The way we view computing has shifted in at least four significant areas. Figure 1–1 illustrates this shift radiating outward from the past, shown in the innermost circle, to the present and to the near future, represented by the outermost circle. Beginning in the upper left quadrant and progressing in a clockwise fashion, the areas represented may be summarized by the words *Where, How, Who,* and *What.*

The *Where* has been a transition from a computer room to the users' desktops in the classroom, in the office, or at home. The transition has now progressed to users themselves as they transport computers with them wherever they go as personal assistants in the form of **laptops, palmtops, and personal digital assistants (PDAs)** The *How,* or under what conditions, has been a shift from a tightly controlled, centralized and institutionalized environment such as a school district office or a service bureau providing computer services to the school to a highly personalized one with the user in command of the computer and increasingly to a truly interpersonal one that lets users interact with one another. In addressing the *Who* of computing we have seen a distinct move from the **computer oper-**

**FIGURE 1–1**

*Shift in computer paradigms*

(Adapted from Greene, *Apple Viewpoints*, 1988)

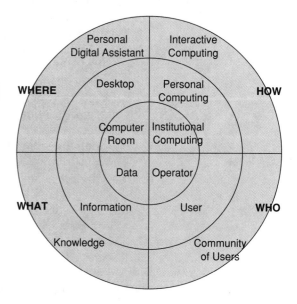

**ator** (often a technician somewhat remote from the problem) to the **end user** (the person deriving direct benefit) interacting directly with the computer. The near future will witness a **networked community of users** interconnected electronically with one another. Teachers and students will communicate with peers around the globe. Finally, the *What* demonstrates a move from a fascination with huge amounts of stored **data** to a concern for the value of the **information** that can be extracted from it. Teachers and students alike are developing increasingly sophisticated skills in the creation of, access to, and manipulation of information. The move to knowledge is a bit more difficult to describe. Information answers questions while knowledge seeks to frame and explore new ones (Greene, 1988).

Keeping in mind these shifting paradigms of the student or teacher personally exchanging information with another user in the same neighborhood or around the world, the goal of this chapter is to present an overview and classification of computer applications in education to gain a better perspective of the breadth of applications and to better understand their relationships. The classification proposed is hierarchical with three main divisions according to function. Classification schemes, no matter how well reasoned, are somewhat arbitrary. Some applications may not neatly fit in the pigeonholes of the structure but may cross boundaries and overlap.

Recognizing that there are many theories of teaching and learning, that classroom practice is often based on one or more of these theories in combination, and that this text does not purport to be a learning theory textbook, we review some theories in modest detail that are covered in depth in courses dealing with the psychology of learning. The intent of this chapter is to demonstrate that the computer can be a practical tool used by the student and by the teacher in concert with various teaching/learning strategies.

## Advanced Organizers

1. What are some functional categories of computer applications in education?
2. How do the categories in school management relate to tasks you might commonly perform as a teacher, school library media specialist, or administrator?
3. How does the application of the computer in instruction and learning relate to teacher- or student-centered strategies?
4. What is computer literacy and what is its future?
5. What does computer-managed instruction offer you as a teacher?
6. How can the computer enhance your capability as a teacher to design teaching materials?
7. How can the computer be used as an information tool by the student?
8. How is the computer a research tool?
9. How is the computer broadly defined as a productivity tool?

## COMPUTERS IN EDUCATION

Any classification is an attempt to group like items together in order to study them, noting their similarities and their differences. Early software classification attempts derived **computer-assisted instruction (CAI)** and **computer-managed instruction (CMI).** They, by themselves, are no longer adequate. The software classification model proposed in Figure 1–2 emphasizes function. It places primary emphasis on how software is used.

In this model, the functional use of computers in education has been divided into three categories: *management, instruction and learning,* and *educational research.* The *management* category includes school and classroom applications in budgeting, accounting, record keeping, printed and electronic communication, and information retrieval. The category of *instruction and learning* has been subdivided into *teacher-centered instruction* to take in software functions interacting directly with students under the teacher's control in the design, development, and delivery of instruction as well as *student-centered learning,* recognizing functions related to the student involved in constructive activities that lead to learning. Categories are further subdivided to recognize common computer applications. The *educational research* category including applications in statistical analysis and information retrieval must be recognized for the contribution it makes to teaching and learning. It is an area with unique tools designed for specific purposes. It is not, however, within the scope of this text except to acknowledge its existence and its role in education.

Software classification permits the identification and comparisons of like programs. Organization schemes other than the one proposed in this chapter are of course possible and should be encouraged if they will facilitate the study of software and its application.

The development and use of classification methods to identify software will facilitate the task of teachers who ultimately decide which material to use in the classroom. It will promote a better understanding of software selection, evaluation, and software collection management.

Classification methods also promote better communication between teachers and publishers. Teachers can more clearly explain their needs to publishers and publishers can better describe their available products. The software classification must reflect accepted theories and practices in education.

The emphasis in this text will be on the management category and on the instruction and learning category. The elements of teacher-centered instruction have been the most widely addressed and will continue to receive attention. Learning theories and the continued evaluation of new technologies are increasingly placing strong emphasis on the growth and development of student-centered learning.

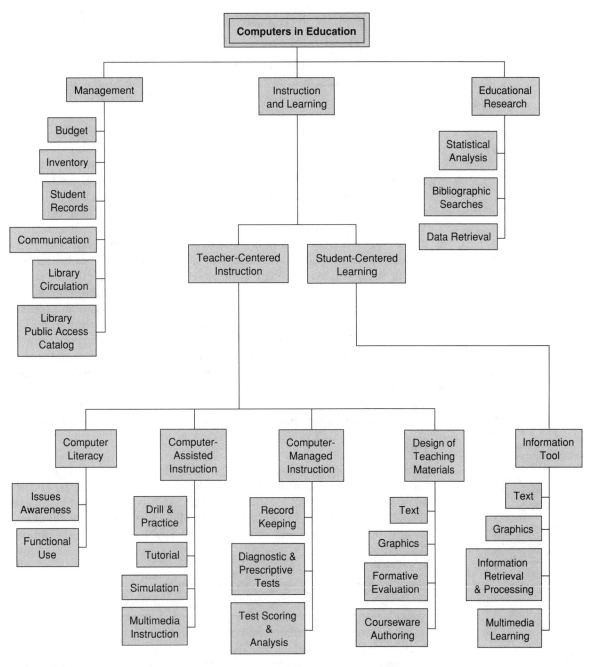

**FIGURE 1–2**
*Classification of computers in education*

## MANAGEMENT

The chart presented as Figure 1–3 suggests that there are several areas in the realm of school and classroom management that are well suited to computer applications. In each area, the computer used as a tool can save the user some time, improve the accuracy of information, and efficiently handle large amounts of data.

### Budget

Budgets must often be built by teachers, department heads, and other administrators to deal with instructional materials, field trip costs, student club activities, personnel, and departmental needs. In preparing a budget, school administrators and teachers depend on records of historical information. With the exception of zero-based budgeting (a technique that assumes that every budget category begins at zero each year), past budgets form the foundation for future budget development. It is necessary to understand past practices, allocations, and expenditures. It is equally important to be able to project ahead in areas of school and program enrollment, staffing needs, curriculum changes, and inflation. Computer-based **file managers** and **spreadsheets** are particularly useful tools to accomplish tasks relating to budget preparation and management. On the one hand, they provide the user with current accurate records in a timely fashion and on the other, with the ability to reflect changes dynamically as the user manipulates variables to look at projections. Spreadsheets have earned their well-deserved reputation as being "what if. . ." tools. They immediately reflect the results when the user asks "What if this amount were changed? What impact would this have?"

### Inventory

School personnel are accountable for a wide variety of items ranging from food and janitorial supplies to textbooks, curriculum materials, and instructional equipment. A computer-based file manager can record use, track inventory levels, record the location of items and their condition easily and accurately, and make information available at a moment's notice.

### Student Records

A school is required to keep many different records concerning students. Health and immunization records begin in the primary grades. Information about home and parents/guardians is recorded. Attendance is closely followed. Grades are calculated and stored, then grade reports are generated. Individual Education Plans (IEPs) are tracked and students' growth in ability and performance levels is monitored. Participation in athletics, music programs, talented and gifted programs, and extracurricular activities is noted. In the past, manual record-keeping systems were used. They worked but they were time consuming and yielded limited additional information since cross-referencing was difficult. Well-designed computer-based systems again prove to be quicker, more efficient, and yield more potentially useful information by creating a more complete profile of the student.

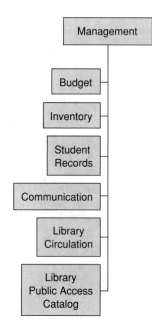

**FIGURE 1–3**
*Computers in school and classroom management*

## Communication

Parental involvement can increase student achievement and improve the parents' relationship with the school. Written and electronic communication is greatly facilitated by the computer. Personalized letters to parents generated by a word processor save a great deal of clerical time and tend to increase the amount of correspondence between school and home. A **desktop presentation** program allows teachers and administrators to enhance their presentations to students as well as to parent and community groups by projecting text and graphics on a screen. Modems allow schools throughout a district to communicate by exchanging memos, notices of important events, and attendance data. Teachers can access lesson plans stored on electronic bulletin boards. Students, sitting at computers with modems, can reach across the miles to others and can begin to truly understand the term "global village."

## Library Circulation

Manual library circulation systems have existed for a long time in schools and public libraries. A manual system, though acceptable for recording the checkout and return of books and other materials, is time consuming and provides little additional information of benefit to the user. An automated circulation system employing a computer and bar codes on the circulating materials can record the checkout and return of materials and can also generate lists of the library's holdings, record borrowers' transactions quickly and efficiently, generate lists of overdue materials, provide inventory control to a level that was never before possible, and calculate use statistics. A computerized library circulation system performs existing tasks quicker and more accurately than a manual system and provides the user with information not easily acquired in the past.

## Library Public Access Catalog

Just as an automated library circulation system can enhance the distribution of materials, an on-line **public access catalog (PAC)** of a library media center's materials collection can greatly improve access to information (Figure 1–4). Such a system should allow a user to browse the collection electronically and to perform author, title, subject, and keyword searches. Most sophisticated systems allow the use of the Boolean operators AND, OR, and NOT to facilitate more complex searches. Beside supporting direct queries, an automated system can generate highly specialized bibliographies. Computers serving as PAC terminals can also give the user access to external databases.

## INSTRUCTION AND LEARNING

The category of instruction and learning is separated into *teacher-centered instruction*, dealing with those functions that directly include the student in either an individual or group setting and take into account teacher planning, preparation, and delivery of instruction, and *student-centered learning*, including the functions that deal with the student involved in constructive activities that lead to learning.

**FIGURE 1–4**

*Public access catalog (PAC)*
*screen*

(Photo courtesy of Western
Oregon State College)

```
                    **** WOLF ****
     WESTERN OREGON STATE COLLEGE LIBRARY CATALOG
                  *** MAIN MENU ***
        SELECT ONE OF THE FOLLOWING OPTIONS:

     K > KEYWORDS in title or subject
     T > TITLE
     J > JOURNAL TITLE
     A > AUTHOR
     S > SUBJECT

     C > CALL NUMBER
     N > NUMBER search (ISBN, ISSN, other)
     R > RESERVE lists

     U > Search Orbis UNION Catalog
     H > HELP and Library Information

     Q > QUIT
       Choose one (K,T,J,A,S,C,N,R,U,H,Q)
```

## Teacher-Centered Instruction

As seen in Figure 1–5, teacher-centered instruction can comprise the areas of computer literacy, computer-assisted instruction (CAI), computer-managed instruction (CMI), and design of teaching materials. Computer literacy is a relative newcomer to the school curriculum. The presentation of information through computer-assisted instruction under the control of the teacher and the management of the student's performance and interaction with that information through computer-managed instruction, though viewed separately for the purpose of functional examination, sometimes overlap. Some management features of CMI are sometimes incorporated into CAI software. As a design tool, the computer has become widely used by teachers to create hard copy as well as projected instructional materials.

### Computer Literacy

The subject of **computer literacy** focuses on the computer as the object of instruction. This topic is not to be confused with computer science instruction, which studies hardware, operating systems, and computer languages. In computer literacy, a scope and sequence of curriculum goals is usually developed within a school district that specifies what is to be learned about the functional use of the computer and about its role in society. Computer literacy often examines the history of computing and computer awareness and functional use as well as the broader role of the computer as it relates to societal issues such as computer access, gender relationships, software copyright, rights of privacy, data security, and information ownership. We will examine a number of these issues in a later chapter.

**FIGURE 1-5**
*Computers in teacher-centered instruction*

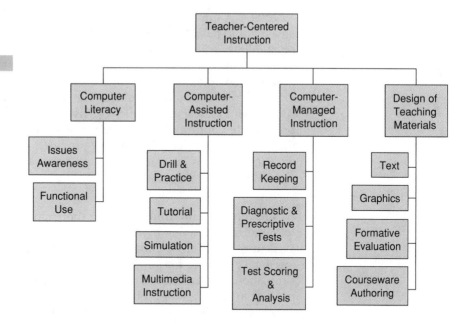

Some educators argue that as computers become commonplace items in homes and schools, the need for computer literacy will be diminished in the curriculum. Some feel that while teaching scope and sequence of skills may no longer be necessary, computer-related issues will still need to be discussed.

### Computer-Assisted Instruction (CAI)

Computer-assisted instruction is a term applied to a teaching/learning situation that involves the direct instructional interaction between computer and student. In this teacher-centered approach, the teacher, ultimately having responsibility for all instruction in the classroom, sets up the learning environment through careful selection and analysis of the instruction material; ensures that each student has the necessary entry-level knowledge, skills, and attitude to engage in a particular activity; monitors the learning activities, adjusting them according to the students' needs; and follows up with activities designed to promote retention and transfer of learning.

Drill and Practice.    **Drill and practice** is a time-honored technique used by teachers to reinforce instruction by providing the repetition necessary to move acquired skills and concepts into long-term memory. It assumes that the material covered has been previously taught. In the past, teachers have used flash cards, worksheets, board games, and verbal drills to achieve the desired results. Computer programs present an additional and, if used well, a more powerful alternative.

Tutorial.    A **tutorial** program exposes the student to material that is believed not to have been previously taught or learned. Tutorial instruction often follows a linear programmed instruction model mainly because it is difficult, time consuming, and therefore expensive to write branching programs that would attempt to remediate incorrect responses. A tutorial program often includes a placement test to ensure student readiness and sometimes a pretest on specific objectives to validate the placement test. It presents new information to students and questions them on that information. New material is commonly provided in small increments replete with instructional guidance and appropriate feedback to encourage correct student response.

Simulation.    **Simulation** is another time-honored teaching strategy used to reinforce instruction by the teacher. It can also function effectively in a student-centered environment by providing a climate for discovery learning to take place or for newly acquired skills and concepts to be tested. A simulation can present a sample of a real situation and can offer genuine practice at solving real problems unhampered by danger, distance, time, or cost factors. Simulations call for decisions made by the student. In the past, teachers have used board games, drama, and role playing to implement the simulation technique. The computer is a useful tool to manage this technique. A sophisticated simulation can present the facts and rules of a situation in a highly realistic manner without the limiting factors of time, distance, safety, and cost and then adjust these factors to respond to interaction by the student.

Multimedia Instruction.    Few, if any, pieces of software are "pure" drill and practice, or tutorial, or simulation. Some are predominantly one type but embody elements of other approaches. **Multimedia instruction,** more than any other category of software, blurs these lines of distinction. It is also closely related to multimedia learning.

If you refer to Figure 1–2, you will notice that multimedia learning is a subcategory of information tool under the category of student-centered learning. The two multimedia categories differ primarily in the manner in which the roles of the teacher and student are viewed. These categories will be further examined in a later chapter.

As suggested by the simple schematic in Figure 1–6, multimedia programs are often used to control the presentation of video information from external sources such as video tape or **videodisc** as well as graphic, audio, or textual information from **CD-ROM.** Although the majority of these programs are designed for individual instruction, they may be adapted for group use by the instructor. Typically, audio and video material (still frames, sounds, and/or moving images with sound) is presented to the viewer accompanied by computer-generated text in a true multimedia fashion. The instructional designer uses the computer to select the video

**FIGURE 1–6**
*Multimedia system*

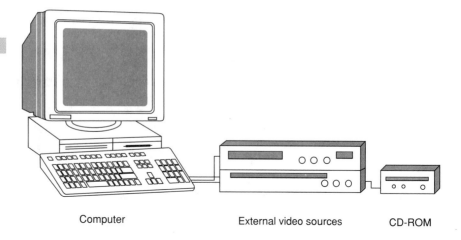

Computer                    External video sources          CD-ROM

segment and present it on the screen, often interspersed with computer-generated question frames. Depending on the response to the question, the designer can program the computer to repeat the segment, present another one in a remediation mode, or move on to new information. Responses are often stored by the computer for later use by the teacher or student.

Multimedia instruction in a computer-assisted instruction format is blossoming rapidly in business and industry as an effective and efficient training tool. It is receiving a good deal of attention at the college and university level and is making rapid inroads in K-12 education as better software becomes commercially available and as teachers develop increasing confidence and skill in designing their own lessons. In an information tool format, multimedia allows students to create their own visuals and incorporate them into their products or to create their own navigation through existing resources.

### Computer-Managed Instruction

Although computer-assisted instruction (CAI), especially tutorial software, sometimes includes some management and record-keeping function, its emphasis is on the presentation of information or instruction. Computer-managed instruction (CMI), on the other hand, stresses the management of student performance in a direct on-line approach with the student working directly at the computer or in an off-line approach, as suggested by Figure 1–7. The CMI category includes programs that are *diagnostic and prescriptive tests*, programs that *analyze test scores*, and programs that *keep student records*. Spreadsheet and database management software is playing an increasing record-keeping and analysis role in CMI. Management opportunities also increase as computer networks become more prevalent.

Most teachers believe in the concept of individualized instruction. With great effort, many succeed. Individualized instruction is not to be

**FIGURE 1–7**
*Two approaches to CMI*

| Computer-Managed Instruction | |
| --- | --- |
| **On-Line Approach** | **Off-Line Approach** |
| Database of goals and performance indicators is established. | Database of goals and performance indicators is established. |
| Test items are stored in computer. | Printed tests are constructed. |
| Student takes a test "on-line" at the computer. | Student responds to test on optical scored cards. |
| | Optical scanner records student responses. |
| Computer analyses student performance on test items related to established goals. | Computer analyses student performance on test items related to established goals. |
| Computer presents tutorial, drill and practice, simulation, or interactive video instruction to student. Supplementary "off-line" activities may also be suggested. | Computer directs student to learning activities based on the performance analysis. |
| Teacher retrieves a student profile from the computer. | Teacher retrieves a student profile from the computer. |

confused with independent study. Individualized instruction means that a teacher knows all students well on the basis of their personal, cultural, experiential, and academic background, scholastic ability, and learning style. It further signifies that knowing the students in this manner the teacher is capable of providing for this diversity in the classroom. Given the typical student/teacher ratio involved, this is a monumental management task. It is, however, a task well suited to the computer. Student progress can finally be tracked effectively and efficiently.

### Design of Teaching Materials

Many teachers have relied heavily on commercially prepared teaching materials in the form of bulletin board materials, overhead transparency masters, duplicating masters for worksheets, and other handouts. At times this has resulted in an accommodation between the teacher's perceived needs and the materials available designed by a third party. This reliance on commercial materials could at times be attributed to teachers' lack of confidence in their own creative ability as well as to the time demanded for the production of original materials. Teachers are learning that the computer can significantly increase their ability and dramatically decrease production time demands.

Text.    The computer is ideally suited to create display materials and users are presented with a wide variety of software from which to choose. A word processor can be used to prepare practice exercises for the student to complete in school or at home. By selecting a large type size, this same program can prepare an overhead transparency master. Color can be used to highlight key words by separating the components of the transparency into two masters and printing them in different colors. A similar procedure can result in "overlay" transparencies, that is, transparencies where items are added in a progressive fashion to develop the finished product or complete idea. Special attention might be paid to programs that allow the easy integration of graphics and the selection of a variety of text typefaces, styles, and other attributes.

Graphics.    Many individuals do not have a high degree of confidence in their artistic drawing ability. Graphics programs level the playing field. They allow the creation of respectable illustrations and often serve to bolster the self-esteem of self-proscribed non-artists. Programs such as Corel Draw, ClarisDraw, Harvard Graphics, Kid Pix, MacBillboard, PC Paint, Print Shop, Super Paint, and others facilitate the creation of bulletin board and display graphics and text. Aldus Persuasion and PowerPoint allow the creation and projection of a series of images containing both text and graphics. Crossword Magic permits the creation of crossword puzzles to drill students in vocabulary, terminology, and definitions in any subject area. Programs such as ClarisWorks, CricketGraph, DeltaGraph, Excel, and Works generate line graphs, bar graphs, or pie charts from numeric data.

Programs and video boards are available that allow computer screens to be recorded on videotape to serve as titles, credits, animated graphics, or instructional text screens. A variety of *wipes* and *dissolves* that allow one image to fade or merge into another lends sophistication to the recording. Desktop presentation software permits the projection of computer screens by either a video projector or a video display panel placed on the stage of an overhead projector. Either projection can be in black and white or in color depending on the equipment used. Software that supports the design of teaching materials serves as an extension of the creative teacher. Although these materials can be created in other ways, the computer makes it easier and less time consuming and thereby stimulates teachers to maximize their creative efforts.

Formative Evaluation.    The computer in the CMI testing mode passes judgment on whether the student is right or wrong on a particular item. **Formative evaluation,** on the other hand, does not focus on the performance of the learner but rather, assesses the quality of the instruction and deserves consideration in a discussion of the design of materials. In a formative evaluation mode, the computer can perform an item analysis on the data collected in the testing mode and can reveal information that is used to shape or *form* instruction. It can collect data on one student and many items, on one item and many students, and on many items and many students. It can affect both content and process of instruction by revealing

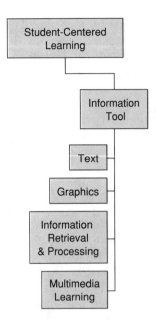

**FIGURE 1–8**
*Student-centered learning*

poorly selected, designed, or executed learning activities and materials, poorly constructed test items, or improper assignments based on level of difficulty or on poor student placement. Information thus presented allows the teacher to correct errors or discrepancies and to refine teaching strategies and materials.

## Student-Centered Learning

Student-centered learning is an approach that views the computer as an information tool for the student to use to create, access, retrieve, manipulate, and transmit information. One or more students can approach a computer on a needs basis in a classroom, school library, or computer lab environment. As can be seen in Figure 1–8, student-centered learning encourages students to view the computer as a tool similar to a pencil, brush, or calculator in order to solve a problem. The techniques embodied in student-centered learning are found in subsequent chapters dealing with the computer as a word processing, spreadsheet, database, or graphics tool. The computer is not only a productivity tool for the teacher but also a tool that enhances the productivity of the student.

### Text

The word processor allows the student to express ideas and, with the teacher's guidance, refine the quality of that expression with a reasonable amount of effort in a short period of time. Inquiry strategies can be mapped, content outlines prepared, and detailed reports written. Simple skill-building exercises can become pleasurable. Classroom and school newspapers can be published with word processors and desktop publishing software. Students of all ages can become authors and their books placed in the school library for others to read.

### Graphics

Paint and draw programs not only allow the students artistic expression but also nonverbal communication as they prepare signs relating to a cocurricular activity, maps for a social studies project, posters promoting a candidate in a school election, and banners proclaiming significant events. They allow students to explore the spatial relationships of an idea. Graphing programs allow students to examine abstract numeric relationships in a more concrete manner.

### Information Retrieval and Processing

Database managing and spreadsheet tools allow a student to investigate information. By developing powerful search strategies, a student can find answers to perplexing questions, connect related facts, and derive new information. By sorting information, a student can examine precedence and develop a better understanding of linear relationships or hierarchical order.

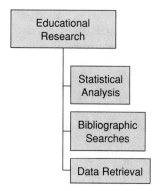

**FIGURE 1-9**
*Computers in educational research*

## Multimedia Learning

**Multimedia learning** gives the student control of powerful tools in the exploration and creation of information. Multimedia tools allow a student to compose a complex statement that might include computer-generated sound, graphics, and animation along with sound and visual forms stored in another medium such as videodisc, videotape, or CD-ROM.

## Educational Research

The functional application of the computer to educational research, as addressed in Figure 1–9, includes statistical analysis, bibliographic searches, and data retrieval. Once again the computer is seen as a tool. It is a tool that supports **action research**, placing the teacher in the role of the researcher, usually examining some aspect of classroom practice. Action research is applicable to the setting in which it is conducted and not generalizable to other settings. Riecken and Evans discuss collaborative action research conducted by university and public school personnel (1993). They point out that the range of acceptable techniques for data collection and analysis has broadened (1993, p. 122). The personal computer is one of these new tools. It behaves as a number cruncher, providing for the storage and analysis of data. It replaces paper indexes and provides better and faster electronic access to information.

### Statistical Analysis

For many years educational researchers at colleges and universities have had access to statistical analysis programs on mainframe computers in campus computing centers. The advent of powerful statistics programs available on personal computers has now provided access to educators at all grade levels in their offices and in their classrooms. This ready access will especially encourage the growth of educational research at the K-12 level. Numbers plugged into spreadsheets can yield a chi-square analysis. Even a simple grade book designed on a spreadsheet can reveal mean, range, and standard deviation of scores. As teachers move toward new product-oriented, criterion-based methods of assessment they are also attempting to understand and compare student performance through means such as **quartile analysis,** which examines four groups of students based on their performance on a measure. Statistics will become a more meaningful tool for the teacher as easier to use programs are written. This does not, however, alleviate the need to understand how to interpret the statistical output.

### Bibliographic Searches

A large number of bibliographic databases have been available on-line through Dialog™ and other vendors. Educational pricing policies regarding access and computer costs have been established that make these databases feasible for use by faculty and students in secondary schools and colleges. Many of the databases available on-line, such as the ERIC database, are now available on CD-ROM on a subscription basis. New curriculum-related databases such as *Science Helper K-8*, a compendium of science lessons plans produced by the University of Florida, are now published on CD-ROM. A teaching resources database called *A-V Online*, published by Silver Platter, gives a brief descriptive annotation, subject matter classification, and grade level and identifies sources of films, filmstrips, videotapes, and other media produced between 1900 and the present. CD-ROM databases mounted on a **network file server** become readily accessible to many users in a school building, or within a school district for that matter.

### Data Retrieval

Data retrieval integrates with other functions mentioned in the management of information. Schools that store data accumulated from CMI programs can run statistical correlations on SAT scores, GPA, and individual student performance. With the help of a personal computer and appropriate software, researchers probing a specific topic can perform a survey of existing related literature from remote and local databases, generate bibliographies of locally available materials by searching their library's public access catalog, and analyze data collected on their sample populations and gleaned from student records. Although this certainly could have been done before the advent of the personal computer, now it can be done more easily and cost effectively.

### A Productivity Tool

A tool is a medium for completing some work and extends the user's ability. We either create a tool or select from a variety of existing ones and apply it to the task at hand (e.g., screwdriver to fasten something, sewing machine to assemble clothing, automobile to transport us swiftly and comfortably, word processor to record our thoughts in a quick, flexible manner, etc.). Accepting this definition of a tool allows us to see its intervention between the user and the information to be created, received, stored, manipulated, or disseminated. The student who uses a database to search for information, then uses a word processor to write a report and a graphics program to draw a map for inclusion in the report is using the computer as a productivity tool to enhance efficiency and effectiveness.

The shifting paradigms described in the chapter introduction describe a transition from a computer room to the users' desktops and even to users themselves as they carry their personal computers wherever they go. A shift is occurring from a centralized environment to a personalized one with the user in command of the computer and to an interpersonal one where users interact with one another. There is a distinct move from the computer operator to the end user interacting directly with the computer and to a networked community of users interconnected electronically with one another. Finally, we have moved away from a fascination with huge amounts of stored data to a concern for the value of the information and development of knowledge.

Every one of these paradigm shifts addresses the issue of productivity. This concept as it applies to the computer has been broadened in recent years to get us past the notion of simply accomplishing menial tasks. Productivity relates to both efficiency and effectiveness. Rather than limiting our view to developing a product often associated with the performance of clerical tasks, we have begun to see productivity as maximizing or extending our innate capabilities. Is the computer a productivity tool for the secretary? Absolutely! It enhances the performance of repetitive clerical tasks. It is also a productivity tool for the administrator to make projections, find information, and communicate it effectively. It is a productivity tool for the teacher who selects appropriate drill and practice, tutorial, simulation, multimedia, or utility software and adapts it to the instructional, management, or research task at hand. Students are increasing their productivity by developing increasingly sophisticated skills in the creation, access, manipulation, and transmission of information in order to solve a problem. Keep in mind that we are witnessing the adaptation of some time-tested teaching and learning strategies along with new innovations to a medium that gives students a wider variety of education experiences than has ever been offered before.

## Summary

This chapter examined a framework for software in three major categories: school management, instruction and learning, and educational research.

School management was divided by data processing and information retrieval functions into six functional categories: budget, inventory, student records, communication, library circulation, and library public access catalog.

Instruction and learning was divided into two major areas, teacher-centered instruction and student-centered learning. Teacher-centered instruction examined the computer as the object of instruction as well as a tool of instruction and the management of instruction. It was subdivided into the categories of computer literacy, CAI, CMI, and design of teaching materials.

Computer literacy was recognized as addressing both issues awareness and functional use. As the computer becomes easier to use and more commonplace, less time and effort will go into teaching how to use it. Societal issues related to the computer such as access, copyright, rights of privacy, data security, and information ownership may well continue to command attention in the classroom.

Computer-assisted instruction was subdivided into categories that parallel learning theory. Drill and practice software supports the practice of newly introduced concepts and reviews others. Tutorial software deals with the initial introduction to concepts. Simulation software supports the problem-solving learning that all students must go through to connect concepts into major clusters of knowledge. It was suggested as a means of helping to hold a student's attention while being careful not to interfere with the lesson's intent. Multimedia instruction examined combining the computer with other instructional devices to control the presenting, analyze the responses, and store the results of instructional events. The distinguishing characteristics that separate the different categories of computer-assisted instruction are beginning to blur, because strategies are being combined to achieve a wider range of objectives. We must keep in mind that we are witnessing the adaption of time-tested teaching strategies to a different medium. This adaptation gives students a wider variety of educational experiences than has ever been offered before.

Computer-managed instruction was discussed as a category of software that helps the teacher track students' progress. If this time-consuming work can be done more efficiently with the aid of the computer, then the teacher will have more time to help students. This alone can make for a more effective learning environment.

Design of teaching materials deals with the design, development, and creation of teaching materials. It also deals with the evaluation of the impact of materials and techniques on the content and process of instruction. A vast array of tools are available to the creative teacher to design and produce materials that communicate effectively. The computer's record-keeping capability allows the teacher to examine the effectiveness of instruction.

Student-centered learning views the computer as a tool for the student to use to create, access, retrieve, manipulate, and transmit information in order to solve a problem. Understanding the concept of the computer as an information tool relies on accepting the fact that the computer is a productivity tool for the student and the teacher alike.

Educational research includes functions relating to information gathering and processing. The teacher/researcher may examine student performance data in new and revealing ways. Bibliographic citations of studies performed by educators around the world can be acquired and perused from the desktop.

The complexity of hardware and software design will increase because of technological advances, greater sophistication in programming, and innovative discoveries. As this happens, programs will address multiple skills embedded in more intriguing activities that may change the way we learn.

## Chapter Exercises

1. Describe your personal use of any tool outside of the educational setting. Now describe how you might use the computer as a tool. Compare your two examples and demonstrate how a tool extends your human capability.
2. Create a mock budget for a student activity club in an area of personal interest. List income and expenditures. How could a computer assist you in managing this budget?
3. Identify as many tasks as you can that are included in library circulation. Which of these tasks might be facilitated by a computer? Which would not?
4. Compare the instructional intent of drill and practice, tutorial, and simulation software and describe how a teacher might employ all three types of programs within a unit of instruction.
5. Review a drill and practice program on a computer and explain in detail how it employs that technique.
6. Review a simulation program on a computer such as *Oregon Trail* by MECC or *Where in the World is Carmen Sandiego?* by Broderbund. What does the program simulate and how does it do it? Does it employ any drill and practice techniques? Explain.
7. Reviewing catalogs of instructional materials publishers, list ten titles of materials available in videodisc and/or CD-ROM formats and identify their subject area, grade level, systems requirements, and cost.

## Glossary

**action research**   The teacher as a researcher investigates a problem usually arising from some classroom practice. Results are applicable only to the setting in which the research was conducted.

**CD-ROM**   Compact disk–read only memory. An optical storage device connected to a computer that reads or plays back text, graphics, and sound.

**computer-assisted instruction (CAI)**   The direct instructional interaction between computer and student designed to produce the transmission of information.

**computer literacy**   The study of the development and functional use of the computer as well as related societal issues.

**computer-managed instruction (CMI)**   Use of the computer as a diagnostic, prescriptive, and organizational tool to gather, store, manipulate, analyze, and report information relative to the student and the curriculum.

**computer operator**   A technician trained in the operation of large computer system who is interposed between the user and the computer.

**data**    Vast amount of stimuli than can be perceived in any given environment. We are constantly inundated with data in our daily lives, most of which we tend to ignore until we perceive a need.

**desktop presentation**    The display of screens (images or text) of information stored in a computer. The display device is often a video projector or flat panel overhead projection device.

**drill and practice**    A teaching strategy that consists of presenting problems to students and then providing feedback on their responses.

**end user**    The individual who ultimately benefits from the computer application.

**file manager**    Software that is designed to create and manage data files. Current usage employs this terms synonymously with database manager.

**formative evaluation**    Assessment of the efficacy of instructional materials, strategies, and techniques.

**hardware**    A term used to describe physical equipment (e.g., computer, monitor, printer).

**information**    Data selected and organized in order to produce meaning.

**information technology**    The process of creating, storing, organizing, accessing, and displaying information.

**laptop**    Portable, lightweight, battery-operated computer with LCD screens that usually fold down onto the keyboard for ease of carrying.

**multimedia instruction**    The technique of accessing and displaying information stored in electronic, magnetic, or optical form under the control of a computer to meet objectives specified by the teacher.

**multimedia learning**    The technique of accessing, organizing, and displaying information stored in electronic, magnetic, or optical form under the control of a computer to meet needs felt by the student.

**network file server**    A computer to which other computers are connected by various means (telephone wire, cable, etc.) that provides access to files or documents stored in its external memory.

**networked community of users**    Computer users who have the ability to transfer information between and among each other.

**palmtop**    Lightweight, battery-operated computer considerably smaller than a laptop.

**personal digital assistant (PDA)**    Very small battery-operated computer, usually with limited but very specific built-in functions.

**public access catalog (PAC)**    A computer-based system that provides user access to examine a library's holdings.

**quartile analysis**    The ranking of performance measures from high to low and the separation of the measures into four groups to study performance by high, medium, and low achievers.

**simulation**    A teaching strategy based on role playing within structured environments.

**software**    Computer program(s) preserved on some type of recording medium and usually distributed on floppy disks or CD-ROM.

**spreadsheet**   Software that accepts data in a matrix of columns and rows with their intersections called cells. One cell can relate to any other cell or ranges of cells on the matrix by formula. Often used with numeric data to forecast results of decisions.

**tutorial**   A teaching strategy that assumes no prior mastery and presents leading questions and offers instructional guidance based on the responses.

**videodisc**   A twelve-inch disk capable of storing 54,000 frames of information on each side read by a laser on a videodisc player. It can display text, still images, or full motion video sequences.

# Notes & Suggested Readings

Bankhead, B. (1991,October). Through the technology haze: Putting CD-ROM to work. *School Library Journal*, 44–49.

Goodson, B. (1989, September). Looking into the 1990s. *Teaching and Computers*, 7(1), 18–21.

Greene, S. (1988, September 26). Redwoods and hummingbirds. *Apple Viewpoints*, 1–3.

Ensor, M. (1990, September). The media center online catalog: A modern day instructional tool. *Wilson Library Bulletin*, 26–30.

McLuhan, M. (1967). The medium is the message, New York: Bantam Books, 26.

Meyers, J. K. (1991). What's new with the news? *Tech Trends*, 36(6), 43–46.

Pitsch, B. & Murphy, V. (1992, March). Using one computer for whole-class instruction. *The Computing Teacher*, 19(6), 19–21.

Riecken, T. & Evans, R. (1993). Building practical and theoretical knowledge about HyperCard through collaborative action research. *Journal of Technology and Teacher Education*, 1(2), 121–131.

Selby, C. C. (1993, May). Technology: From myths to realities. *Phi Delta Kappan*, 74(9), 684–689.

Transforming American education: Reducing the risk to the nation. (1986, August). *T.H.E. JOURNAL*, 14(1), 58–67.

Waetjen, M., & Bellisimo, Y. (1992, March). Down from the ivory tower. *The Computing Teacher*, 19(6), 16–18.

White, M. A. (1989, September). Educators must ask themselves some important questions. *Electronic Learning*, 9(1), 6–8.

# 2

# EXAMINING THE TOOL

A discussion of computer equipment can never be truly current, for as this is being written a new product is undoubtedly entering the market. The goal of this chapter is to acquaint you with fundamental concepts related to equipment, or hardware, and to describe in modest detail the equipment that has found some measure of acceptance in schools.

This chapter offers a brief look at the evolution of computer hardware and an explanation of the various components of a computer system. It will show how their interrelationship allows a user to put data into a system, manipulate those data, and retrieve information in an appropriate manner, and then highlights particular applications in school settings. It also introduces you to the concept of a **disk operating system.** The Macintosh computer is used for purposes of illustration. The majority of references, however, can be generalized to all other major brands of microcomputers.

## Advanced Organizers

1. How has computer technology evolved and what is its potential impact on you as a user?
2. What are the primary processes involved in a computer system (input of data, operations performed on the data, and output of information)?
3. The input process: What hardware exists today to facilitate your entering data?
4. What is a CPU?
5. What are the different types of memory and how do they differ?
6. The output process: What hardware exists today to facilitate your extracting information?

7. How has the user interface evolved and what is the potential impact on you as a user?

## EVOLUTION OF COMPUTER TECHNOLOGY

Rapid changes in computer technology have resulted in greatly improved and expanded applications. Early applications were computational in nature and early programming was done in a numbering system other than our familiar decimal one. Thus, a misconception arose that in order to be a programmer or even a competent user, one had to have an extensive mathematical background. This idea was also believed in schools, where math teachers were among the very few who used computers in the classroom at first. We now realize that the computer is a tool for everyone.

As we review the history of computer technology, we become aware of a tremendous simplification in operation: a vast improvement of the machine/human interface and a dramatic reduction in equipment size. Both of these elements contribute significantly to the expanding computer utilization in society in general and in education in particular. Six significant occurrences are identified in Figure 2–1 and discussed in the following sections.

### 1890

The 1880 census took seven years to process manually and, with a growing population, the 1890 census posed a serious problem. It appeared that it would take more than ten years to process the census information unless some new method were employed. Herman Hollerith solved the problem with a machine that stored data printed as holes punched on cards. The machine sorted and counted the cards. The 1890 census was processed in just three years. Hollerith manufactured his invention, then merged with another company. The new firm was called International Business Machines (IBM).

### 1945

The first general-purpose electronic **digital** computer was introduced in 1945. The **ENIAC** occupied 3000 cubic feet of space, weighed 30 tons, con-

**FIGURE 2–1**
*Significant events in computer evolution*

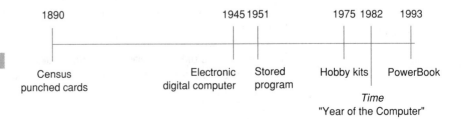

tained over 18,000 vacuum tubes, and drew 140,000 watts of power when it was running. The **vacuum tube** resembled a light bulb in appearance. It acted like a gate, passing or blocking an electric current in a digital circuit. As current was passed or blocked it was translated into a binary code of 1s and 0s. The operating principle of the vacuum tube was that a filament was designed to burn itself up in order to emit necessary radiation. Imagine the army of technicians scurrying about this electromechanical monster looking for burned-out tubes to replace.

The ENIAC could do only simple addition, subtraction, multiplication, and division but it performed these operations in a programmed sequence. In order to change the sequence to perform a different process and address a new problem, the ENIAC had to be rewired by hand.

## 1951

The first electronic computer to use a stored program entered the market in 1951. The early vacuum tubes were replaced by scaled-down versions and then by the **transistor.** One transistor, a half-inch square, replaced the vacuum tube and the computer itself was reduced from building size to room size and then to the size of several large file cabinets.

Programs stored in computers were written in machine language as **binary** code. Think of the vacuum tube for a moment. It can be "on" and passing current or it can be "off" and blocking current. This on or off state could be represented by a 1 or by a 0. Examine the set of binary codes, the zeros and ones, in Figure 2–2.

Notice that the zeros and the ones in Figure 2–2 are gathered in groups of eight. As shown in Figure 2–3, eight **bits** in this case form one **byte,** representing an alpha or numeric character. For fun, try to spell out your name in binary code by using the table in Figure 2–2.

Imagine yourself seated in front of an ENIAC or a UNIVAC I computer. In place of a keyboard, your input controls consist of eight switches and an enter button. Since, as we have just seen, the computer understands a binary code, you must throw each of the eight switches either on or off and then press the enter button to enter each letter or number into the computer.

Fortunately, although today's computer still understands only binary code, we do not have to use this code to communicate with it. Computer languages have been developed that allow us to employ English-like words, which are then translated into a binary form. These are called "higher level" languages because they resemble English as opposed to the "lower level" languages at the machine level of 0s and 1s.

## 1975

Microcomputers marketed in kit form for the hobbyist were introduced in 1975. Within two years, Apple and Radio Shack microcomputers were on the market and the microcomputer explosion was under way. Remember

**FIGURE 2-2**
*Binary representation of single digits and the alphabet*

| Character | Bit Representation | Character | Bit Representation |
|-----------|-------------------|-----------|-------------------|
| 0 | 00110000 | A | 01000001 |
| 1 | 00110001 | B | 01000010 |
| 2 | 00110010 | C | 01000011 |
| 3 | 00110011 | D | 01000100 |
| 4 | 00110100 | E | 01000101 |
| 5 | 00110101 | F | 01000110 |
| 6 | 00110110 | G | 01000111 |
| 7 | 00110111 | H | 01001000 |
| 8 | 00111000 | I | 01001001 |
| 9 | 00111001 | J | 01001010 |
|   |          | K | 01001011 |
|   |          | L | 01001100 |
|   |          | M | 01001101 |
|   |          | N | 01001110 |
|   |          | O | 01001111 |
|   |          | P | 01010000 |
|   |          | Q | 01010001 |
|   |          | R | 01010010 |
|   |          | S | 01010011 |
|   |          | T | 01010100 |
|   |          | U | 01010101 |
|   |          | V | 01010110 |
|   |          | W | 01010111 |
|   |          | X | 01011000 |
|   |          | Y | 01011001 |
|   |          | Z | 01011010 |

the vacuum tube and the transistor that replaced it? The **integrated circuit,** or **chip,** is approximately one-quarter inch square and may contain millions of transistors.

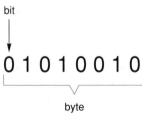

**FIGURE 2-3**
*Byte composed of eight bits*

## 1982

*Time* magazine proclaimed 1982 as "The Year of the Computer," not because of new and different uses of institutional computers, but because of the significant contributions that personal computers made in complementing human abilities. For 55 years *Time* magazine had published an annual "Man of the Year" cover. In explaining its departure from past practice in 1982, the editors said, "A new world beckons, created by a

**FIGURE 2–4**
*The Macintosh PowerBook 540c*
(Courtesy of Apple Computer, Inc.)

technological upheaval that is bringing computers to millions. Since no one person dominated this process, *Time*'s Man of the Year for 1982 is not a man but the computer itself" (Friedrich, 1983). The personal computer can not only do the automated tasks necessary to keep a business operating efficiently, but, being small (desktop size and smaller) and operated by the person responsible for a given task, it is performing as an extension of that person. It can serve as a high-powered calculator, a word processor, a filing and retrieval system, a means of generating graphics from tabular information, and much more. All of these applications are immediately and directly accessible to the user.

## 1993

Unlike the thirty-ton ENIAC that occupied 3000 cubic feet of space, Apple's laptop Macintosh PowerBook 540 (Figure 2–4) weighs about seven pounds and occupies less than one-seventh of a cubic foot of space. The ENIAC had an internal memory capacity of 12K, that is, it could store about 12,000 characters in its memory. The Macintosh has a 4 **megabyte** (MB) memory, expandable to 36**MB** (about 36 million bytes), which is about 3,000 times greater than the ENIAC and is 100,000 times more reliable. This development has taken place in fifty years. What will the size, capacity, and power of computers be twenty years from now?

### Shifting Paradigms

Once again the shift in computer paradigms identified in Chapter 1 becomes apparent as we trace the development of the technology and in particular the development of computer hardware. Now the mobile user employing a personal computer is able to interconnect to a network of other users in order to search a labyrinth of databases to access valuable information.

## WHAT IS HARDWARE?

Hardware is a term commonly used to designate the equipment components of a computer system. A monitor, a keyboard, a mouse, a joystick, a printer, a disk drive—all would be examples of **hardware.** Not all tangible objects are encompassed by this term, however. For instance, floppy disks, which are tangible real objects, are usually termed "magnetic media" or just "media" and are considered consumable supplies. Recording a program on a floppy disk changes the terminology of the **disk** to **software.** More precisely, the actual magnetic recording of the program itself on the magnetic medium is the software but you can see that at some point it is impossible to separate the two. To unravel the confusion related to equipment specification, this chapter is organized according to the three processes involved in a computer system and examines hardware related to each.

### What Processes Are Involved in a Computer System?

When we refer to a computer system, we are taking into account all components necessary to perform a designated task. The actual pieces of hardware may vary but a computer system, as illustrated in Figure 2–5, has three basic processes: input, operation, and output.

**FIGURE 2–5**
*Computer processes*

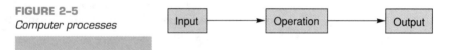

The **input** is the process of entering data into the computer system. The **operation** is the process of manipulating the data in a predetermined manner by the computer itself or, more precisely, by the central processing unit (CPU) under the control of a program. The **output** is the process of retrieving the information once it has been acted upon by the CPU. All hardware other than the computer itself is referred to as peripheral equipment.

The computer system as illustrated in Figure 2–6 groups equipment in clusters that parallel the input, operation, and output processes.

**FIGURE 2–6**
*The computer system*

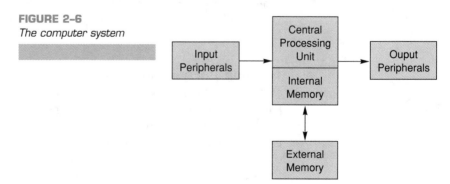

## Input Peripherals

**Input peripherals** are all the hardware items whose function is to enter data into the computer through tactile, audio, video, or electronic means (Figure 2–7). Specialized cables and connectors are used to transfer electronic impulses between the peripheral devices and the computer. Keep in mind the relationship of the various hardware elements so that you will more easily understand the functioning of the computer system.

The **keyboard** is the primary device through which data are entered into a personal computer system. This typewriter-like device's function is to generate a digital code that can be entered into the computer's memory and be understood by the microprocessor. The binary code used in personal computers is **ASCII** (American Standard Code for Information Interchange, pronounced "askee").

The computer keyboard resembles most closely in layout and design the one typists are accustomed to using. Most full-keystroke computer keyboards have good spring tension on the keys for a positive tactile response. The use of multiple keystrokes, the Option, Command, Escape, and Function keys, as well as unique software features serve to differentiate between keyboarding and typing. Basic keyboarding skills are being introduced in schools at an early age.

A **mouse** is a small hand-held input device that a user moves left, right, up, or down on a flat surface such as a desk. It depends on a software interface (a program) to move a cursor on the screen, replicating the motion of the mouse. The software constantly monitors the position of the cursor on the screen. Pressing a button on the mouse results in one of several actions depending on the program being used. For example, to delete a file in the computer's external memory, a user would move the cursor to an icon (a graphic representation of the file) and while holding the mouse button would drag that file icon to another icon of a trash can located on the bottom edge of the screen and then release the mouse button. The file would be deleted (discarded into the trash can). The Apple Macintosh™ as well as computers operating under Microsoft Windows™ use the mouse to move a cursor.

**FIGURE 2–7**

*A schematic indicating input peripherals*

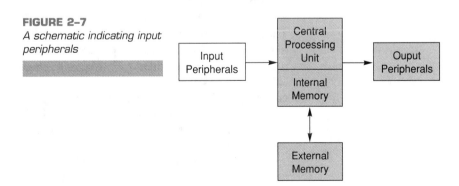

Printed bar codes similar to the **UPC** (Universal Product Code), found on many products make data entry extremely fast and accurate. The codes are read by devices such as the one shown in Figure 2–8 that sense the sequence of thick and thin lines and their spacing. Two commonly used **bar code readers** are the hand-held wand and the stationary reader similar to those commonly employed at grocery checkout counters. The bar code readers generate light that reflects from the bar code in a light and dark pattern. The reader, sensing the pattern, generates the appropriate matching digital code, thus eliminating the need for time-consuming keyboard entry with its inherent typing errors.

A school library's circulation system could be based on a bar code applied to each student's identification card with appropriate bar codes placed on book spines or card pockets. Information can be read into a computer by a bar wand and in seconds the checkout procedure is completed. Imagine how easy it would be for a library media specialist to take a book inventory at the end of the school year if each book on the shelves had a bar code label affixed to its spine. To enter the books into a database in the microcomputer, one would just walk down the library aisles and pass a bar wand over each book's spine label.

**FIGURE 2–8**
*A bar code reader*
(Courtesy of Worthington Data Solutions)

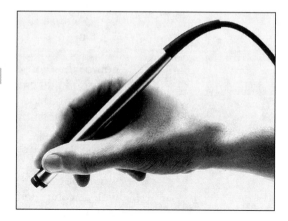

**Optical scanners,** as shown in Figure 2–9, are available in hand-held models and as flatbed scanners somewhat resembling small photocopiers. They operate by reading light reflected from the surface of an object such as a photograph, line drawing, or printed page of text. The scanner is accompanied by software that allows it to exercise some degree of control over the scanned image. It is often possible for the user to vary the image's size by **cropping** (adjusting only the outside dimensions) or **scaling** (proportionally enlarging or reducing the entire image) and to adjust brightness and contrast.

**Graphics tablets** similar to those depicted in Figure 2–10 are input devices that allow you to create or trace figures or drawings of any kind. A student can draw a picture with a stylus provided on the surface of the tablet and see it replicated on the monitor screen. The stylus allows the

**FIGURE 2-9**
*Optical scanner*
(Courtesy of Apple
Computer,Inc.)

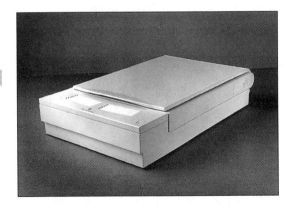

user far greater control than the mouse in drawing intricate designs. The
accompanying software translates the stylus' position and displays it as a
point on the monitor screen. The series of points are the representation of
a straight or curved line segment making up a total picture. You can also
fill in solid areas of color, as well as enlarge or reduce your drawing. Again
using the software, the user can select certain shapes, shadings, and line
widths or "paintbrush" effects. An art teacher might choose to have students use this device to execute lessons in perspective, line, or contour
drawing. With its inherent ability to trace existing material, the graphics
tablet is an excellent device to facilitate the production of maps.

Although **voice entry devices** have been available for a few years to interface with the IBM Personal Computer and the Macintosh, it is only recently that they have gained ready acceptance. Most current applications
allow command words (e.g., NEW, BOLD, ITALIC, SAVE, etc.) to be spoken into a microphone that, through the appropriate software, conveys the
command to the computer. Broader applications are on the horizon, however. Voice entry has the advantage of eliminating the need to learn keyboarding skills. It offers speed, ease of use, and the potential for voice recognition security. A great deal of research and development is occurring in
this area and dramatic new software product announcements are expected.

**FIGURE 2-10**
*Graphics tablets*
(Courtesy of Kurta®)

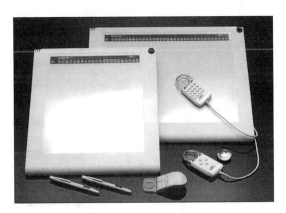

**FIGURE 2–11**
*A modem*
(Courtesy of Supra
Corporation®)

The telephone **modem** (modulator-demodulator) is both an input device and an output device. It translates digital computer information into **analog** signals of varying frequency that can be transmitted over telephone lines and analog signals into a digital form that can be processed by a computer. The relatively inexpensive modem is playing a major role in making the information revolution a reality. It is a vital link allowing computers to exchange information. The modem shown in Figure 2–11 has a cable with a modular plug that connects directly into a phone jack. Depending on their speed of transmission, modems are now most commonly available in 14,400 or 28,800 bps. **Bps** (bits per second) has replaced the former designation of **baud rate.**

With telefacsimile (fax) machines becoming so commonplace in businesses and schools, the advent of the **fax-modem** came as no surprise. It allows a computer to communicate with another computer or with a fax machine. Fax machines send and receive information in a type of graphic format so that pages of text are transmitted as images. Faxes received by fax-modems are stored in the computer as graphic documents unless software is used to convert them into text files that can be edited.

Daily attendance figures could be gathered at each school, entered into a microcomputer, and transmitted by modem to a computer at a central office where the data could be analyzed and stored. With the use of modems, electronic mail within a school district is a reality. Modems facilitate the sharing of computer resources among schools and school districts, as well as public schools and colleges.

## Central Processing Unit

A computer program is a series of executable instructions and related information conveyed as a digital signal in binary form. The heart of the computer system through which all instructions and information flow is the **Central Processing Unit (CPU)** (see Figure 2–12). This term is a throwback to large mainframe jargon when the CPU was in fact a separate piece of equipment. The CPU is now often referred to as the microcomputer chip or the **microprocessor.** It is usually the largest chip on the computer's cir-

**FIGURE 2–12**
*A schematic indicating the central processing unit*

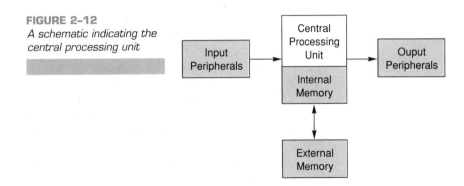

cuit board. The two predominant families of microprocessor chips are manufactured by Intel (e.g., 80386, 80486, Pentium), used by the computers operating under MS-DOS and Windows, and by Motorola (e.g., 68030, 68040), used by Macintosh computers. A new type of microprocessor called a reduced instruction set chip (RISC), with greatly increased power and speed, may well become the microprocessor of choice.

## Internal Memory

The **internal** or working **memory** of the computer (Figure 2–13) can be examined in two basic categories, *constant* and *temporary*. The manufacturer stores instructions that govern the fundamental operations of the computer in the constant memory. The Macintosh operating system, for instance, resides in the computer's constant memory. The constant memory cannot be changed by the user employing ordinary means nor is it dependent upon a supply of power to maintain itself. The acronym **ROM** (read-only memory) is commonly used when referring to constant memory. A fairly large integrated circuit or chip contains the ROM, which consists of instructions that, once encoded by the manufacturer, cannot be erased, written to, or modified in any way. The amount of constant memory needed in a computer is governed by the power and sophistication designed into it by the manufacturer.

**FIGURE 2–13**
*A schematic indicating internal memory*

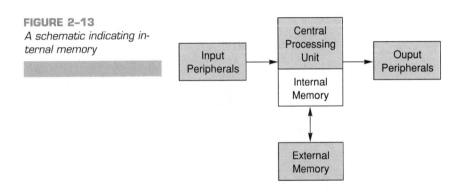

The **temporary memory** is that category of internal memory available and accessible to the user. When you write an original program, load a prepared program from a diskette, type a letter using a word processor, or enter information into a database management program, you are in fact entering instructions or information and placing it in temporary memory called random-access memory or **RAM.** RAM is often called **volatile memory** because it requires a constant source of power to maintain itself. Should power fail for even a brief moment, the contents of RAM are lost forever. Users who are concerned about power outages or interruption usually connect their computer to a backup or uninterruptible power supply **(ups).** Figure 2–14 is a reminder of the different types of internal memory.

There are times when the user is employing the computer (and its internal memory exclusively) in a direct, immediate mode, perhaps to write a letter to a friend or as a supercalculator to solve a mathematical problem. In most other instances, however, it is important to save work done on the computer. When the program being written or the information being entered should be preserved, RAM is really only a temporary holding area where the ideas are manipulated and the data organized before being passed on and stored permanently in external memory. In the case of RAM, bigger is indeed better. The more temporary memory available (RAM), the larger and more sophisticated is the application program that can be run and the larger is the file that can be processed. Graphics files, for instance, can consume a very large amount of RAM. The amount of RAM is measured by counting the potential bytes of information. Remember that a byte is the amount of memory required to represent one alphabetic or numeric character. The amount of RAM may be expressed in units of one thousand bytes represented by the symbol **K** as in *kilo.* Thus a computer with 64K of RAM is capable of storing 64 **kilobytes** (approximately 64,000 bytes) in its temporary memory. For those of you who are offended by the simplicity of this explanation of K, yes, it is true that 1K of RAM can indeed store 1024 bytes (2 to the 10th power) and that 64K of RAM is therefore 65,536 bytes. For practical purposes, however, let us accept what most of the world has agreed on, namely, the convention that 1K stands for 1000. Computers today are sold with over a million bytes of RAM and the convention of **MB** is used to designate **megabyte.**

**FIGURE 2-14**
*A schematic identifying internal memory*

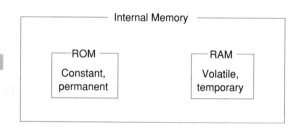

## External Memory

The **external memory** apparatus (Figure 2–15) can really be considered as both input and output devices. Information such as programs and files are saved (output) to this hardware to be later retrieved (input) from it. External memory, as its name implies, is not located on the main internal circuit board of the computer. It is the auxiliary storage of programs and data, often on a removable medium such as magnetic disk, housed in a piece of equipment sometimes separate from the computer cabinet itself. In most instances, the preferred form of external storage is on magnetic disk.

**FIGURE 2–15**
*A schematic indicating external memory*

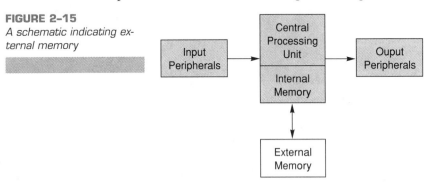

The type of external storage widely available in the past was the **floppy disk,** a small wafer of flexible polyester film about 5 inches in diameter and coated with an emulsion having magnetic properties similar to audio or video tape. It is encased in a 5 1/4" square flexible protective plastic jacket that is lined with a nonwoven fabric liner designed to clean the diskette as it rotates smoothly. It has a large center hole designed to accept a spindle, which spins the disk at high speed within its protective jacket. The small adjacent hole is used as a registration point for the operating system encoded magnetically on the disk. The jacket's oval cutout running from the center toward one edge allows a read-write head (similar to a record/playback head on a tape recorder) to travel over the disk surface. The write-enable slot is a quarter-inch notch cut out of one edge of the jacket. When the notch is open (uncovered), programs and data can be recorded to and erased from the disk. Covering the notch with a tab or piece of adhesive tape prevents recording to or erasing from the disk.

The 3 1/2" **microdiskette** format (Figure 2–16) has gained wide acceptance because of its smaller size, improved protection against dirt and physical damage, and increased storage capacity. The microdiskette is not only much smaller than the original 5 1/4" floppy, it is housed in a rigid plastic protective case; nevertheless, the term "floppy disk" has persevered. The hub opening is nearly covered by the metal hub piece and the read-write head access slot is protected by a spring-loaded sliding metal cover. Write protection is accomplished by sliding a small plastic tab located near

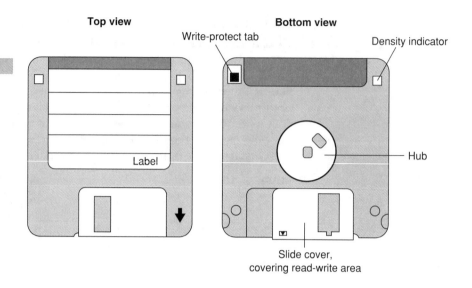

**FIGURE 2–16**
*A 3 1/2 inch
microdiskette*

Top view

Bottom view

Write-protect tab

Density indicator

Label

Hub

Slide cover,
covering read-write area

one corner on the bottom of the diskette toward the edge of the case. When the slot is open, the disk is protected. When the tab covers the hole, information can be stored on the disk or erased from it. Microdiskettes are recorded in such a way as to store much more information than the larger 5 1/4" floppies.

The disk drive's function is to save information to and retrieve information from the floppy disk. It does this by engaging the disk and rotating it at high speed on a motor-driven spindle while the magnetic read-write head scans the surface sensing or creating magnetic domains (Figure 2–17). This aspect is in fact similar to audiotape recording and playback. When a song is played from a tape it is not removed from the tape. Likewise, when a program is read from a disk, it is only copied into RAM and not removed from the disk. The actual process of searching for and loading a program (copying it into RAM from external memory) is much more analogous to playing an LP album than an audiotape, however. Both are random-access devices having multiple access points. Many different programs can be stored on the same diskette. Each program has a unique identifier stored in a diskette directory or catalog track. When selecting a song to play from a record album, you can physically move the tone arm

**FIGURE 2–17**
*Disk read-write access*

As disk rotates . . .

. . . head moves
back and forth

**FIGURE 2-18**

*Tracks and sectors estab-lished by formatting*

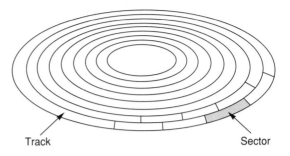

Track                                                          Sector

to a particular spot over the record as the turntable is spinning and lower the arm to the record. When you instruct the computer to load a particular program from a diskette, the spindle rotates the disk while the read-write head scans the surface looking for the beginning of the program you selected, which it then loads into RAM. Using current operating systems, most drives read and write 1.4 MB on the 3 1/2" microdiskette. Combining the two factors of spinning the disk at high speed and quickly moving the read-write head in and out across its surface results in rapid random access to any information on the disk.

Disks are offered as *double-density* (720K of storage in the IBM format and 800K in the Macintosh format) or *high density* (1.44 MB in the IBM format and 1.40 MB in the Macintosh format). Both types of disks are double-sided and are manufactured to support the recording on both surfaces by double-sided drives. They rotate in only one direction within their jackets but are read by two different heads.

It is necessary to prepare a blank floppy disk to receive data. This **formatting** or **initializing** process allows you to later save your programs onto the disk. In preparing a disk, the computer lays out an indexed map on the disk so it will know where to write the programs and files to be saved.

Programs on floppy disks are indexed by *track* and *sector* number. When the disk is formatted a directory is created and concentric circles called **tracks** are laid out on the surface of the disk (Figure 2–18). These are the major divisions of the disk. Each circular track is divided into units called **sectors.** Each sector is capable of storing a certain number of bytes of information. Newer operating systems allow much greater storage density than previous ones.

This format directory or computer-created map on the disk can be compared to a road map. You can find a city on a map by looking up its horizontal and vertical location coordinates in the map index. The index may also tell you the population of that city. The disk map or directory tells the computer where to find a specific file and its memory size.

Figure 2–19 gives pointers on the care and handling of floppy disks.

Another form of external memory that has gained in popularity is the **hard disk.** It is a rigid platter coated with a magnetic emulsion similar to

**FIGURE 2-19**
*Care and handling of disks*

**Care and Handling of Floppy Disks**

- Do not place the disk on a dirty or greasy surface.

- Keep the disk away from liquids or excessive chalk dust.

- Do not store disks in direct sunlight or next to a heater. Protect them from extremes of temperatures.

- Keep all magnets away from the disk. Do not place a disk on a TV or monitor. The picture tube's magnetic field may destroy the information on the disk.

- Do not retract the metal shutter and touch the resulting exposed disk surface

that used on a floppy diskette. The hard disk is often enclosed in the computer's case and is then called an internal hard disk. It is referred to as an external hard disk if it is enclosed in its own separate case and connected by cable to the computer. It is usually fixed, whether inside or outside of the computer, but may also be removable for portability, a new popular trend. The read-write head rides just above the disk surface, floating on a cushion of air. The entire apparatus is sealed in an airtight container, creating a dust-free environment.

The hard disk's main advantage over the floppy diskette is its far greater memory storage capacity. Secondary advantages are faster access time when loading programs and the ability to network a number of computers to the same disk drive to share information. Hard disks typically store from 40 megabytes (40 million characters) to 500 megabytes and more. Advances in technology allow in excess of a gigabyte (one hundred million bytes) of storage on a hard drive. This allows users to place programs permanently on the hard drive rather than having to work from floppies. A school might choose to install a central hard drive of this size in order to serve the needs of a number of simultaneous users on a network of all the computer stations throughout the school.

The **laser videodisc** is making a growing contribution in school applications. The recording is stored on a rigid platter either 8 or 12 inches in diameter and is read by a laser. It is used mainly to store text, pictorial information along with audio information, and moving images to be presented under the control of a computer. By taking advantage of its two separate audio tracks, recordings can be presented in English and also in a second language; the user can select which track to listen to. This feature has drawn considerable attention in bilingual education. Thanks to the laser disk's growing success in the consumer entertainment market as a medium for

**FIGURE 2-20**
*A schematic indicating out-put peripherals*

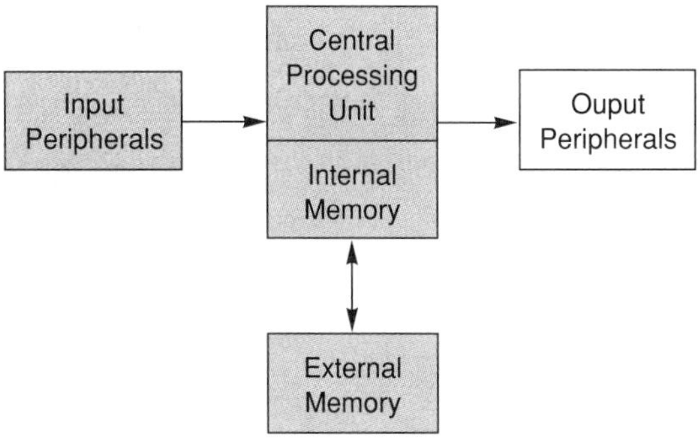

feature films, players are now readily available and reasonably priced. It is important to recognize that at the present it is strictly a playback medium. Teachers must depend on the commercial availability of recorded laser disks. Laser disk recorders would significantly improve this situation.

Another laser-read medium with application in the consumer market shows great promise for mass storage of data. **CD-ROM** is currently available as a 5″ diameter disk. The acronym CD-ROM stands for compact disk–read only memory. Grolier Inc. has released their Electronic Encyclopedia in this format. Other encyclopedia publishers have followed suit. Connecting a CD-ROM player to an IBM-PC–compatible or Macintosh computer and using the software provided, the user can perform rapid and sophisticated searches of the encyclopedia. Many new products ranging from specialized databases to titles of works in children's literature have been introduced in this format.

## Output Peripherals

**Output peripherals** (Figure 2–20) are all the hardware items whose function it is to display information from the computer through audio, video, print, or electronic means. Specialized cables and connectors are used to transfer electronic impulses between the peripheral devices and the computer.

Once again, it is important to keep in mind the relationship of the various hardware elements in order to understand the functioning of the computer system. Without one or more output peripherals, the computer system would be incomplete and of little value.

The **video monitor** accepts a video signal directly and is capable of displaying a picture of much higher resolution than a television receiver; therefore it is the standard for computer applications. Monitors are available in either monochrome or in color. The color monitors commonly accept a composite video signal containing information for the colors red, blue, and green as well as black and white. The monitor deciphers these color signals and displays the appropriate mix of color on the screen.

Although one or two interconnected large screen (25″ or larger) video monitors may suffice when presenting information to a small group of

**FIGURE 2-21**
*A video projector*
(Courtesy of Sharp
Electronics Corp.)

viewers, they are not adequate in front of a large group. **Video projectors** such as the one shown in Figure 2–21 are capable of displaying a large (10 foot diagonal or larger) projected image. They accept a video signal directly from a computer. Their main drawback is the need for better light control than is the case when using monitors. The projected image's lack of brightness demands a darkened room to maximize the impact of the projected image.

This entry into the field of presentation technology holds great promise for large group applications. The **overhead display panel** as shown in Figure 2–22 is a portable lightweight liquid crystal display **(LCD) panel** that is designed to sit on the stage of an overhead projector. Many panels are multiscan and accept video signals of different bandwidths from computers like the Macintosh and IBM compatibles. One model, PC Viewer, even has its own internal battery-supported RAM to store up to 75 screen images so that the computer doesn't even have to be connected during the presentation. Screen brightness is very good and image size is a function of the overhead projector and screen placement.

The most popular type of printer in schools is the **dot matrix printer** that prints on regular bond paper. Most models accept cut sheets such as letterhead, as well as continuous form fan-fold tractor paper, and are available with friction feed as well as adjustable tractors. The printing at a resolution of 72 dots per inch (dpi) is somewhat jagged and is recognizable as being computer

**FIGURE 2-22**
*An overhead display panel*
(Courtesy of InFocus, Inc.)

**FIGURE 2–23**
*A dot matrix print head*

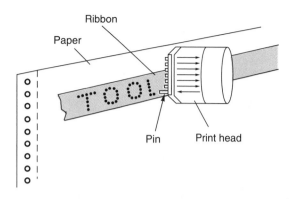

generated, but great strides have been made in enhancing the overall appearance of the letters. Some dot matrix printers achieve greater than 72 dpi resolution and are advertised as being "near letter quality." Print size and density can easily be manipulated, achieving compressed, expanded, darkened, and emphasized print. This is achieved by sending commands from the computer to the printer. Dot matrix printers are also capable, through dot-addressable graphics, of printing pictures, charts, and other graphics on paper.

The dot matrix print head (Figure 2–23) consists of one or more columns of pins, which are activated or fired separately to strike an inked ribbon, printing dots which when viewed at a normal distance appear to form a letter. With each firing of the pins, the print head forms part of the letter as it travels across the paper. Most printers use nine pins but a few employ twenty-four smaller pins to enhance the detail quality and resolution of the print.

The **ink jet printer** shown in Figure 2–24 prints on regular bond paper. Most models accept cut sheets such as letterhead, as well as continuous form fan-fold tractor paper, and are available with friction feed as well as adjustable tractors. Rather than firing pins to strike an inked ribbon, the print head of an ink jet printer squirts a dot of quick drying ink through precisely controlled nozzles onto the paper. Ink jet printers can achieve a resolution of 300 dpi and are much quieter in their operation than dot matrix printers.

**FIGURE 2–24**
*An ink jet printer*
(Courtesy of Hewlett-Packard Co.)

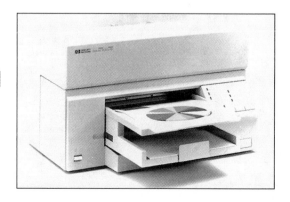

FIGURE 2–25
*A laser printer*
(Courtesy of Hewlett-Packard
Co.)

At the high end of the printer cost scale are **laser printers** (Figure 2–25) that employ a laser beam to create an image on a photosensitive drum surface. The image is transferred by means of a carbon toner to produce letter-quality printing (approaching typeset quality) of text and graphics onto plain bond or letterhead paper at a very high resolution of 300 to 600 dots per inch (dpi). This technology is very similar to the one employed by sophisticated photocopiers. As the price continues to drop, this may well become the printer of preference for many school applications.

A laser printer receives information from a computer and stores it temporarily in its internal memory. It transfers this information as a code that governs the operation of a laser that strikes a photosensitive drum, as illustrated in Figure 2–26, setting up electrical charges on its surface. The

FIGURE 2–26
*How a laser printer works*

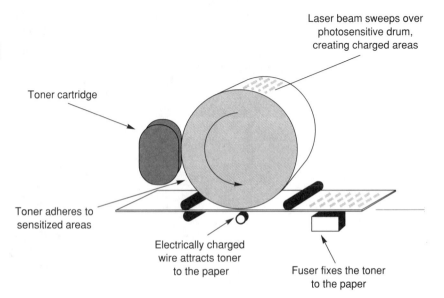

Laser beam sweeps over
photosensitive drum,
creating charged areas

Toner cartridge

Toner adheres to
sensitized areas

Electrically charged
wire attracts toner
to the paper

Fuser fixes the toner
to the paper

drum rotates past a carbon particle toner reservoir where toner is attracted to the charged areas. A sheet of paper is pressed against this toner-bearing drum and the toner transfers to the paper. Before exiting the printer, the paper passes through a thermal fuser section that hardens and fixes the toner on the paper.

When considering printers, we must also consider interfacing, or the ability to transmit information from the computer to the output device. An interface is a two-part device; one part is built into the peripheral device and the other part into either the computer or a firmware card that plugs into one of the expansion slots on the computer's main circuit board. A cable attaches the card to the printer or plotter.

Interfaces are available in either *parallel* or *serial* mode (Figure 2–27) depending on the particular printer used. A **parallel interface** sends the seven or eight bits of data comprising the byte simultaneously along eight different wires in a flat ribbon cable. In addition, other wires in the cable carry communication signals between the computer and the printer. This cable is limited to a short length of only a few feet.

**FIGURE 2–27**
*Comparison of serial and parallel modes*

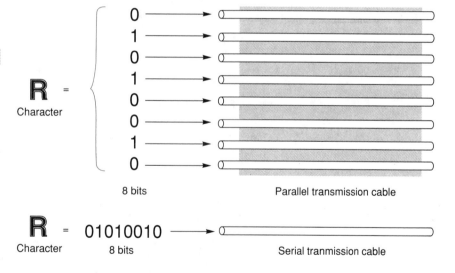

The **serial interface** sends one bit at a time in a continuous sequence along one wire, inserting a code to separate the bytes. The cable may be a simple **twisted pair** of wires and may run for many, many feet. The important thing to remember is that the printer used determines the interface mode. A parallel printer will not accept serial transmission and vice versa. Some printers have both serial and parallel ports built in and can therefore communicate in either mode.

Figure 2–28 outlines steps you can take if your computer is having problems operating properly.

**FIGURE 2–28**

*Ideas for troubleshooting
simple problems*

**Troubleshooting Guide**

Never plug or unplug anything inside a computer with the power turned on.
If you must reach inside the computer, touch the power supply before you
touch any other component.

1. No light on the screen:
   - Is computer turned on?
   - Is monitor turned on?
   - Check contrast and brightness controls.
2. No image on the screen:
   - Check cable connecting computer and monitor.
3. Double letters on screen:
   - Commonly called key bounce. Identify the faulty key(s).
     Individual keys may be replaced on some keyboards but not on others.
     Refer problem to a technician.

4. Printer does not operate:
   - Is printer turned on?
   - Is printer on-line, in a mode ready to receive information from the
     computer?
   - Check connecting cable.
   - On Macintosh, refer to *Chooser* to make sure you have selected the
     printer.
   - Refer to printer manual and run its self-test. If test is unsatisfactory,
     refer problem to a technician.

Most other problems should be referred to a competent technician. Be
careful not to do anything that would void your warranty.

## USER INTERFACE

The **user interface** can be thought of as the interaction between human
and machine. It is receiving a good deal of attention in the design of new
operating systems. Early interfaces progressed from mechanical (throwing
switches) to text based (typing command words). In the late 1970s, the
Apple II included the text-based disk operating system (DOS) in ROM so
that when turning on the computer, the user was prompted to enter a command word. The most widely used operating system of all time,
Microsoft's MS-DOS, uses a text-based command line interface. It is powerful in that it gives the user a great deal of control over the functions of
the computer. It is complex, requiring the memorization of command
words and demanding absolute typing accuracy. Some users find it intim-
idating. It is certainly not for the faint of heart.

Apple Computer introduced a computer called the Lisa, the predecessor to the Macintosh, in the early 1980s. It capitalized on research done by Xerox and was the first commercially successful computer to substitute a **graphic user interface (GUI)** for the command line interface. Graphics have become much more important to the manner in which humans interact with computers. Microsoft introduced a graphic interface called Windows that runs once MS-DOS is loaded. Operating systems for the IBM computer and its clones are following the lead of the Macintosh and substituting the use of **icons,** or pictorial representations, for complex verbal commands. Instead of typing a command to retrieve a file from external memory, you might simply move a screen arrow to point to the icon of a file folder and click the mouse button to open the folder. The file can be opened immediately by pointing to it and double clicking the mouse button. Should you decide later that the file is no longer needed, you can drag its icon to an icon of a trash can, thus "throwing away" the file. Here the screen action replicates kinesthetic behavior associated with everyday occurrences in the work environment.

In examining Figure 2–29, it is easy to see that folder icons look very much like manila file folders used in a filing cabinet. Software publishers

**FIGURE 2–29**
*Various types of icons*

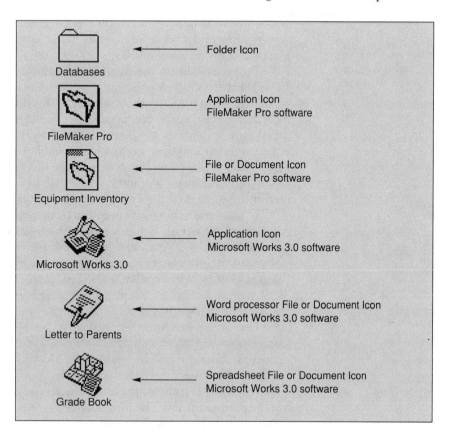

**FIGURE 2–30**

*Overlapping windows and icons on the Macintosh*

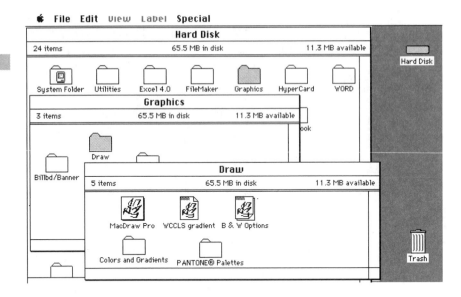

design their own unique icons to represent their software and the files or documents created by their software. Program and document icons can be dragged to folder icons in order to store them in that folder. Folders may be placed inside other folders.

Figure 2–30 illustrates overlapping windows, open folders, and icons. The Hard Disk window is in the background on the patterned desktop. The pattern on the Graphics folder indicates that it is open and its window is therefore also open, overlapping the Hard Disk window. The pattern on the Draw folder indicates that it is open and its window is therefore also open, overlapping the Graphics window. Notice that in the Draw window, the program MacDraw Pro, two files and two additional folders are found. Two icons, one representing the hard disk drive and one representing the trash, are located on the desktop to the right of the open windows.

In September 1993, Apple Computer released its first personal digital assistant (PDA), called the Newton MessagePad. This small hand-held computer (the size of a paperback book and weighing one pound) organizes information in an interactive manner in an address book, a list of things to do, and a calendar. It also communicates information to the outside world by modem, fax, radio pager, infrared beam, a serial port, and a LAN connection.

One of the most exciting features of the Newton, however, is its pen-based operating system that recognizes cursive handwriting. It borrows concepts from the graphics tablet. As illustrated in Figure 2–31, the user writes with a plastic stylus that presses against a protective cover layer. This pressure is transmitted to conductive layers that allow current flow at the pressure point. The information is transferred to an LCD pixel matrix layer that creates shapes in what is being called *digital ink*. The op-

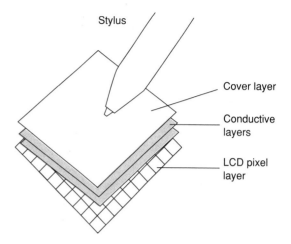

**FIGURE 2–31**
*How a pen-based system works*

Stylus

Cover layer

Conductive layers

LCD pixel layer

erating system attempts to recognize the shapes as letters or common objects. Users can increase the likelihood of the system recognizing letters by teaching it their handwriting. It recognizes shapes and transforms roughly drawn circles, for instance, into perfect ones of an equivalent diameter.

Just as the GUI and pen-based systems have revolutionized the use of the computer, the next generation user interface may take us into brand-new territory. The next interface may revolve around voice entry, allowing the user to speak command words to the computer. The new interface may be able to recognize many different voices and, depending on the voice recognized, would allow or deny certain operations or access to certain files.

The research and development in improving the user interface is focused on making the use of the computer as natural and as easy as possible so that the hardware use becomes transparent to the purpose at hand. Rather than being overly conscious of the hardware and concerned with how to perform a computer task, the user should be allowed to concentrate on the content and nature of the problem being addressed. The most significant question posed by teachers and students will become, not "How do I use this computer?" but "What can I do with a computer?"

## Summary

Rapid changes in computer technology have resulted in greatly improved and expanded applications as well as a tremendous simplification in operation, a vastly improved user interface, and a dramatic reduction in equipment size.

When we refer to a computer system, we are taking into account all hardware components necessary to support the processes of input, operation, and output. The input is the process of entering data into the computer system. The operation is the process of manipulating the data in a predetermined manner by the computer itself under the control of a software program. The output is the process of retrieving the information once it has been acted upon by the CPU.

The internal memory of the computer can be examined as constant or read-only memory (ROM) and temporary or random-access memory (RAM). The manufacturer stores instructions that govern the fundamental operations of the computer in the constant memory. The ROM cannot be changed by the user employing ordinary means nor is it dependent upon a supply of power to maintain itself. The RAM is available to the user and is often called volatile memory because it requires a constant source of power.

External memory is the auxiliary storage of programs and data, often on a removable medium, such as magnetic disk, housed in a piece of equipment sometimes separate from the computer cabinet itself. In most instances, the preferred form of external storage is on magnetic disk. The formatting or initializing process prepares a blank floppy disk to receive data, allowing the user to save programs or files onto the disk. In preparing a disk, the computer lays out an indexed map of track and sector numbers on the disk so it will know where to write the programs and files to be saved.

Output peripherals are all the hardware items that display information from the computer through audio, video, print, or electronic means. Specialized cables and connectors are used to transfer electronic impulses between the peripheral devices and the computer.

A parallel interface sends the seven or eight bits of data comprising the byte simultaneously along eight different wires in a flat ribbon cable that is limited to a short length of only a few feet. The serial interface sends one bit at a time in a continuous sequence along one wire, inserting a code to separate the bytes. The cable may be a simple twisted pair of wires and may run for long distances. Some printers have both serial and parallel ports built in and can therefore communicate in either mode.

Hardware, whether the computer itself or input and output peripheral devices, represents a substantial investment of a school district's financial resources and is constantly in a state of flux. Today's new and exciting item may be old next year. A careful analysis of computer applications in the curriculum will allow a school to develop an acquisition program and build on its established equipment base without having to replace everything and start from scratch as new technological developments occur.

Early user interfaces progressed from mechanical to text-based ones. Graphic user interfaces (GUI) that substitute the use of icons for complex verbal commands have now become the norm for human interaction with computers. Pen-based operating systems recognize cursive handwriting, allowing the user to write with a plastic stylus. The GUI and pen-based systems have revolutionized the use of the computer. The next generation user interface may revolve around voice entry, allowing the user to speak command words to the computer, and allowing or denying certain operations or access to certain files. Each progressive improvement in user interfaces makes the use of the computer as natural and as easy as possible so that the hardware use becomes transparent to the purpose at hand.

## Chapter Exercises

1. Examine computer magazines, journals, and catalogs. List advertisements for the various entry devices available for the computer. Discuss briefly the features that are being promoted.
2. List the different types of external storage devices for the microcomputer. Discuss the advantages and disadvantages of each in a school setting.
3. Examine computer journals and magazines and list, by brand names, the variety of external storage devices available for the type(s) of computer(s) found in your school.
4. What two computer output devices are essential in a classroom setting? What other device would be useful? Discuss how this other device would be particularly useful.
5. Many programs in the school setting currently use keyboard input from students. At what grade level would you begin teaching keyboarding skills? Defend your position.

## Glossary

**analog**   Signals of continuous nature that vary in frequency and amplitude. Analog signals can be transmitted over telephone lines.

**ASCII**   Acronym for American Standard Code for Information Interchange. A code in which the numbers 0 to 127 represent alphanumeric, symbolic, or control characters.

**bar code reader**   A device that translates the sequence of spaced thick and thin lines to the computer, enabling it to identify a specific object.

**baud rate**   A term that has been replaced by bps (see below).

**binary**   Consisting of two parts; limited to two conditions or states of being. Computer memory is designed to store binary digits symbolized by 0s and 1s in a code. The computer circuitry is designed to manipulate information in an on/off state.

**bit**   The single digit of a binary number, either 0 or 1; derived from the words *binary digit*.

**bps**   A measure of data transmission speed between computers in *bits per second.*

**byte**   Usually a grouping of eight bits (*by eight*); the code representing one character of data.

**CD-ROM**   A five-inch optical disk usually used to store text, graphics, and sound.

**central processing unit (CPU)**   The point (a chip) in the computer where all parts of the system are linked together and where the calculations and manipulation of data take place (may be referred to as a microprocessor).

**chip**   A small piece of silicon housing an integrated circuit that may contain tens of thousands of transistors and other electronic components.

**CPU**   See *central processing unit*.

**cropping**   Controlling the size of an image without affecting the size of any of its components. Cropping an image smaller than the original eliminates some of the content.

**digital**   Pertaining to a single state or condition. A digital circuit controls current in a binary on or off state.

**disk**   An external storage medium consisting of a rigid platter (hard disk) or a flexible one (floppy disk) coated with a magnetic emulsion.

**disk operating system**   An operating system that enables the computer to control and communicate with one or more disk drives. Usually referred to as DOS.

**dot matrix printer**   An impact printer that uses a series of electrically hammered pins to create characters composed of a pattern of dots.

**ENIAC**   The first general-purpose electronic digital computer; it was introduced in 1945.

**external memory**   The auxiliary storage of programs and data, often on a removable medium such as magnetic disk or tape, housed in a piece of equipment usually separate from the computer cabinet.

**fax-modem**   A device that allows a computer to communicate by phone lines with a facsimile (fax) machine or with another modem-equipped computer.

**floppy disk**   An external storage medium made of flexible polyester film with magnetic properties similar to audiotape.

**formatting**   Preparing a blank disk to receive information.

**graphics tablet**   A peripheral input device used with accompanying software that allows the user to create or trace figures, maps, graphs, or drawings with a finger, a stylus, or other instrument on the tablet and see it replicated on the screen.

**graphic user interface (GUI)**   The on-screen use of pictorial representations (icons) of objects. The user can move a screen pointer onto an icon and click a mouse button to issue a command to the computer.

**hard disk**   An external storage medium consisting of a rigid platter coated with a magnetic emulsion and not removable from the disk drive; three to five times larger than a floppy disk, it has far greater memory storage capacity.

**hardware**   Equipment components of a computer system.

**icon**   A pictorial representation of an object.

**initializing**   See *formatting*.

**ink jet printer**   A printer that uses a series of electronically controlled nozzles to create characters composed of a pattern of dots squirted on the paper.

**input**   The process of entering information into the computer system.

**input peripherals**   Equipment whose function is to enter data into the computer.

**integrated circuit**   An electronic component made up of circuit elements constructed on a single piece of silicon.

**internal memory**   The storage facilities in a computer system where data and programs are placed immediately before execution; usually the highest-speed memory in the system.

**K**   Symbol for kilo, equated with one thousand (actually 1024 in computer terms).

**keyboard**   The primary input device for the computer; it generates a digital code that can be understood by the microprocessor.

**kilobytes**   One thousand bytes, used as a reference to memory capacity.

**laser printer**   A printer that employs a laser beam to create an image on a photosensitive drum and transfers this by means of carbon toner to paper.

**laser videodisc**   A laser-read rigid platter in either 8" or 12" diameter mainly used to record pictorial and moving images as well as accompanying sound.

**LCD panel**   Liquid crystal display panel (see also *overhead display panel*).

**MB**   Symbol for megabyte, equated with approximately one million.

**megabyte**   One million bytes, (actually 1,048,576 in computer terms) used as a reference to memory capacity.

**microdiskette**   A three and one-half inch format that houses a magnetic disk in a rigid plastic protective case. It typically has much higher storage capacity than the larger five and a quarter-inch floppy disk.

**microprocessor**   See *central processing unit*.

**modem**   A device that translates digital computer information into analog signals that can be transmitted over telephone lines and analog signals into a digital form that can be processed by a computer.

**mouse**   A hand-held device connected to the input port of a computer which, if moved up, down, left, or right on a flat surface, moves a pointer on the screen that selects functions or options.

**operation**   The process of manipulating information in a predetermined manner by the central processing unit of the computer system.

**optical scanner**   An input peripheral that reads an image by reflecting light from its surface.

**output**   Information that a computer sends out to a screen, printer, or mass storage device.

**output peripherals**   Equipment whose function is to display information from the computer.

**overhead display panel**   A liquid crystal panel designed to sit on the stage of an overhead projector allowing a computer image to be projected to a screen.

**parallel interface**   A method of transmitting data a byte at a time, using a separate line for each bit being transferred to achieve a high rate of speed.

**RAM**   Random-access memory; temporary internal memory that is erased if power to the computer system is interrupted.

**ROM**    Read-only memory; constant memory contained in an integrated circuit or chip that cannot be modified by the user.

**scaling**    Controlling the size of an image and in direct proportion all of its components; scaling an image reduces or enlarges all of its elements.

**sector**    Segment of a track as determined by the disk operating system.

**serial interface**    An input or output device that affects both data transmission and reception, transforming parallel output data into a sequential string of pulses and transforming input data from a sequential string of pulses into parallel binary words.

**software**    A computer program (information and directions to control the computer) preserved on a recording medium (e.g., floppy disk) and usually accompanied by written documentation.

**temporary memory**    Internal memory that is available and accessible to the user and requires a constant source of power to maintain itself; also called RAM or "volatile" memory.

**track**    Path followed by a disk drive read/write head on which data is recorded to or read from a disk.

**transistor**    A small electronic device that controls current flow and does not require a vacuum to operate.

**twisted pair**    A cable consisting of one or more pairs of conductors running side by side.

**UPC**    *Universal Product Code*, a sequence of thick and thin lines on consumer products spaced to identify a specific item, read by an optical bar code reader.

**ups**    An *uninterruptible power supply* is a device that provides emergency power from batteries in the event of an AC power failure.

**user interface**    The interaction between human and machine.

**vacuum tube**    A sealed electronic device designed to regulate current flow.

**video monitor**    A television set that has been manufactured to accept a video signal directly and is capable of displaying a picture of much higher resolution than a standard television receiver.

**video projector**    A device that accepts a video signal and projects an image on a screen.

**voice entry device**    A computer input peripheral that converts human voice or sounds into a digital signal.

**volatile memory**    See *temporary memory*.

## Notes & Suggested Readings

Bortman, H. (1992, February). Is there a pen in your future? *MacUser*, 144–148.

Brady, H. (1992, March). IBM raises the bar. *Technology and Learning, 12*(6), 34–37.

Davis, F. (1992, December). Electrons or Photons? *Wired, 1*(1), 30–32.

Friedrich, O. (1983, January 3). The computer moves in. *Time, 121*(1), 12–24.

Lu, C. (1993, September). A small revelation. *Macworld, 109*(9), 102–106.

Malfitano, R., & Cincotta, P. (1993, May). Network for a school of the future. *T.H.E. Journal, 20*(10), 70–74.

McMullen, (1993, September). Unleash your LAN. *Macworld, 10*(9), 209–212.

Pittelkau, J. (1989, January). Through the liquid glass. *MacUser, 5*(1), 213–221.

Schultz, E. (1991, January). Putting it all together. *Teacher Magazine, 2*(4), 44–49.

Tessler, F. (1992, April). Review: Voice express and voice navigator II. *Macworld,* 180–182.

# 3

# WORD PROCESSING

There are different resource managers in a school. The classroom teacher manages grades, test files, and teaching materials. The library media specialist manages the print and nonprint collection of materials and equipment. The counselor manages class scheduling and certain student records. The special educator manages students' Individual Education Plans (IEPs), specialized teaching materials, and progress reports. The principal manages supplies, budget records, health records, attendance reports, teacher schedules, and teacher personnel records, and forecasts next year's needs. All of these activities require a substantial investment of time and attention. Using the computer, a tool that has gained wide acceptance in the business world, greatly decreases the amount of time required to perform various management tasks.

When asked where they would really like some help, teachers often respond "with the paperwork," the evaluation of students' work, the preparation of supplementary materials and tests, the recording of scores, the preparation of grades, and the finding and filing of resource materials. These activities do not involve students directly and are often done outside actual class time. If the time required to perform these tasks could be decreased, the teacher would have more time to devote to planning and preparing lessons or to working directly with students.

A teacher creates some classroom material that does not change substantially from one year to the next. An exercise sheet used once in a unit plan may be used the following year with only slight modification. Every teacher maintains a set of resource materials. Yet each time these materials are used, they seem to require a little revision.

Classroom teachers obviously are not the only educators who can make use of word processors. Library media specialists can use them to maintain bibliographies of the print and nonprint materials available.

Special educators can use word processors to maintain individual student correspondence files that are continually updated. They can build a student's IEP and later recall the IEP to update it easily.

Principals and administrative office staff can use word processors in many of their tasks, since they maintain the ongoing records and reports for the school. Some documents must be updated every year, yet only parts of each form are actually changed. A document kept on the computer can be amended at any time and reprinted when needed without having to reconstruct it in its entirety.

Word processing has also become a powerful tool in the hands of students. Research studies in computer applications consistently show that the use of word processing improves students' attitude toward writing by making them want to write more and making then feel better about their writing (Roblyer, 1988). Studies have shown a positive relationship between word processing and a desire to write (Woodruff, Bereiter, & Scardamalia, 1981). According to Riedesel and Clements (1985), students are also more eager to write, claiming it is "easier to get down ideas with a word processor" and they use a larger vocabulary because they find it easy to correct spelling.

## Advanced Organizers

1. What is a word processor?
2. What are some common features of word processors?
3. What are some editing functions found in word processors?
4. Why is lettering important and what are some guidelines for its effective use?
5. How might the word processor be a productivity tool for you as a teacher or administrator?
6. How is the word processor a productivity tool for the student at different grade levels?

## WORD PROCESSORS

The term **word processor** is used to denote a whole category of software whose primary purpose is to facilitate written communication. As indicated in Figure 3–1, word processing is a systematic organization of procedures and equipment to display information efficiently in a written form and to preserve it electronically. This section focuses on computer software available to assist in the creation of written material.

Word processing programs usually consist of two basic interacting parts, a text editor and a print formatter and, depending on the individual software, several additional parts such as a spell checker, a dictionary, a thesaurus, and even a grammar checker. The **text editor** is the most visible

**FIGURE 3-1**
*Word processing*

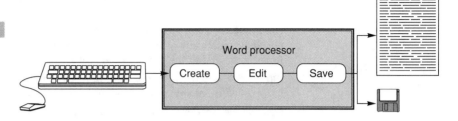

part of the program and is the one that allows the user to manipulate text on a screen display. It is used during the text entry phase to help you add, change, and delete text as well as to locate words or phrases and to embed the format commands needed to control the print formatter. From the editor you can insert the commands to determine the print font, margins, and line spacing. The editor also contains the means to save, merge, copy, and insert text from one file to another.

The **print formatter** delivers the text file to the printer and ensures that it is printed correctly on paper. A good word processing program will accommodate many different printers. Different word processors will use different procedures to specify the print control characters that govern the margin settings, lines per page, length of page, and the special commands to enhance the printed text.

## Word Processor Features

There are many good word processors from which to choose. Selecting the one that is best for you depends on your computer and printer, and most of all on your individual needs. Figure 3–2 presents a list of features that might be considered when choosing a program. Selection of a word processor will be explored in Chapter 11.

The following is a brief discussion of features found in word processing programs.

**column formatting**   In addition to specifying top, bottom, and side margins, some word processors allow the user to format a page in more than one column. Multiple columns yield shorter line lengths that may at times improve the readability of the text.

**FIGURE 3-2**
*Features found in word processing programs*

| Column Formatting | Orphan/Widow Control |
|---|---|
| Dictionary | Outlining |
| Footnotes | Pagination |
| Glossary | Preview Document |
| Header/Footer | Save as ASCII text files |
| Help Screens | Spell Checking |
| Hyphenation | Style Sheets |
| Index | Table of Contents |
| Mail Merge | Thesaurus |

**dictionary**   This feature provides word definition and syllabication as well as allowing the user to confirm spelling.

**footnotes**   Some programs allow the user to mark words in the text to be referenced automatically as footnotes at the bottom of the page, or more often, as endnotes at the end of the chapter or article.

**glossary**   Often-used words and phrases can be created and stored in a glossary to be called up at any time by a simple keyboard command.

**header**   A **header** is a brief message that may include a date, time, or page display that is automatically added to the top of each page. Usually the header can be suppressed on a title page.

**footer**   Similar to a header, a **footer** is automatically added to the bottom of each page and can also be suppressed on a title page.

**help screens**   Help screens are designed into some programs to present information to the user about the operation of the word processor and its functions as the need arises. The better ones are context sensitive, which means that the information presented applies closely to what the user has been attempting to do.

**hyphenation**   Since word wrap can leave lines of varying lengths, thereby creating a ragged right margin, some word processors allow the user to turn on a hyphenation feature that will generate a hyphen at the most appropriate syllable break in a word at the end of a line. This function can also be turned off at will.

**index**   The creation of an index can be greatly facilitated by a feature that allows a user to mark words that are then automatically copied to an index at the end of the document.

**mail merge**   An almost indispensable feature when sending form letters that appear to be personalized with appropriate names and addresses is the ability to merge data from one file to another at the proper place in the document.

**orphan/widow control**   **Orphans** are single lines of text that occur at the bottom of a page. **Widows** are single lines of text that occur at the top of a page. Some word processors will not allow these to occur but instead will force the appropriate page break so that at least two lines of text will appear together.

**outlining**   Some of the more powerful word processors have integrated outliners built into them, allowing the user to create an outline of the document and to expand or collapse various levels.

**pagination**   Once a user sets the page length of the document by prescribing top and bottom margins on a specified size of paper, this feature allows a word processor to automatically generate page breaks and indicate them on the screen and to number pages and renumber them when editing is performed.

**preview document**   All worthwhile word processors allow the user to see the document on the screen as it will look when printed. The better programs allow document editing in this page view and closely approach a **WYSIWYG** (What You See Is What You Get) state.

**save as ASCII text file**   Word processors usually save documents created in their own native format. Saving them also in an **ASCII text** format allows the documents to be transported between word processors produced by different publishers.

**spell checking**   Contrary to a dictionary, a spell checker does not display definitions but rather compares all words found in the document against its master list. Any word not matching is called to the user's attention and if possible, a replacement word is suggested. Most allow the user to add frequently used unusual words (proper nouns, acronyms, etc.) to a custom list.

**style sheets**   A **style** is a set of format characteristics (left aligned, 10 point, Times, .5 inch first line indent, for example) that can be applied to text. A **style sheet** is a collection of styles used in a document.

**table of contents**   This feature facilitates the creation of a table by allowing a user to mark words that are then automatically copied to a table of contents at the beginning of the document.

**thesaurus**   This feature soon becomes a writer's favorite tool. A selected word is compared to a list in the thesaurus and a number of synonyms are suggested to avoid undue repetitions or to adjust a subtle nuance in the writing.

A grammar checker is another feature that has drawn some interest. It is often a separate add-on program to the word processor. It attempts to identify wordiness, awkward constructions, singular/plural agreement, and the use of passive voice. Some writers feel that grammar checkers have rather limited capability. Another stand-alone program favored by some is a program that contains famous quotations that a user is allowed to search in a variety of ways.

Word processors are available either as individual programs or as integrated software that may also contain a spreadsheet, a file manager, and even graphics and telecommunications components. Word processors may be categorized into the following three major functional categories.

### Short, Simple Documents

Programs in this category are for people who do not do much writing or for users who are willing to sacrifice power because they need only limited functions. They often stress well-designed ease of use rather than a wealth of complex features. Some programs aimed at the grade school student also fit this category. Programs in this category are usually used to write letters, memos, brief reports, and simple handouts. Features normally found in this category include format ruler, search and replace, spelling checker, and perhaps graphics placement.

### Longer, Complex Documents

Some programs in this category are for the serious user who does not, however, need (or want) the full, extended features of the page layout programs. For example, programs in this category may not be able to allow for multiple document editing with a split screen and for text wrap around graphic images. These programs do contain all of the necessary functions for work on full reports, position papers, and article manuscripts. In addition to the features mentioned in the first category, these programs include headers and footers, a thesaurus, and usually include the ability to build a table of contents, index, and footnotes automatically as well as mail merge, so that form letters personalized with names and comments can be printed.

## DESKTOP PUBLISHING

The term **desktop publishing** infers the ability to create documents locally that once were in the domain of publishing companies. Programs in this category contain the most extensive set of commands and include advanced page layout capabilities. They are usually designed for people who publish printed material or whose job primarily involves complex written communication. These sophisticated programs require an investment of time and/or training to take full advantage of their many features, as well as continual use to maintain skill level. They contain all of the necessary functions for work on full reports, newsletters, brochures, and documents that include **text-wrapped graphics.** In addition to the features mentioned in the first two categories, these programs include the ability to create a master page layout or design that is repeated on every page, to format variable-width columns, and to import and format graphics as well as to wrap lines of text around their irregular edges.

Full-featured, sophisticated desktop publishing programs can be expensive and quite complex for the average user. Less expensive desktop publishing programs are available with a reduced set of features making them easier to use. These have found favor with teachers and students who use them to prepare newsletters or bulletins and even lay out yearbooks.

*Desktop publishing programs are used as tools by students to prepare newsletters lay out yearbooks, among other activities.*

Once you have determined your word processing needs in general, consider the major features that will affect your usage and minimize the problems you may encounter. If you intend to use a word processor to create a document at home and then wish to print it at school, you will need word processing programs that are able to read the same file format. Also consider that some word processors are considerably more difficult to use than others. With some you need the reference manual at hand until you have become thoroughly familiar with the program through many hours of use.

## Editing Functions

A sample of representative editing functions is presented in Figure 3–3. The user can navigate through the document, adding, deleting, finding, replacing, or moving information at will. Operating in the Macintosh or Windows environments, many editing features are invoked through pull-down menus but most have shortcuts that are keyboard equivalents or double key presses so that the program can distinguish a command from text entry. A double key press simply means that the user holds down a designated key such as the Command or Alt key and presses a second key.

Let's briefly review the most significant functions that make the word processor the powerful tool it is. Most word processors allow you to create a document by invoking the New command. As you enter text you realize that a word that cannot completely fit at the end of a line is automatically moved down to begin a new line. This feature is called **word wrap.** It requires you to type a return only at the end of a paragraph or to create a blank line. As you reach the bottom of the screen, the program automatically *scrolls* your text upward to allow you to continue typing without hesitation. The following are the most often used editing functions.

**block moves**    The selection of any amount of text and/or graphics to reposition it elsewhere in the existing document or in another document as explained in the Cut, Copy, and Paste commands.

**copy**    The Copy command allows the duplication or copying of selected text or graphics. The duplicated item is stored in temporary memory, however. In the Macintosh, this area of temporary memory is called the **clipboard.**

**cut**    This command allows the removal of selected text or graphics. This removed item is also stored in temporary memory.

**delete**    The removal or erasure of text can be accomplished in a number of ways. Placing the cursor immediately following a text character and pressing the key

**FIGURE 3–3**

*Some word processor editing functions*

| Block moves | New |
| --- | --- |
| Copy | Open |
| Cut | Paste |
| Delete | Save |
| Find and Replace | Save As |
| Insert | Word wrap |

usually labeled Delete or Backspace erases the character to its immediate left one character at a time. Many word processors allow the user to easily select and delete an entire word or even an entire line at a time. The remaining text is automatically rearranged properly with word wrap and page breaks taken into account.

**find and replace**   This feature allows one to find a particular word or phrase by searching for it from the beginning of the document. Once found, the item can be replaced with a new word or phrase if desired.

**insert**   Placing the cursor anywhere in a line of text; additional typing spreads apart the existing text to accommodate the new entry. The material being inserted may be as little as a single letter or may be many paragraphs in length.

**new**   The command that allows the creation of a new document.

**open**   The command that allows a previously created document to be accessed for possible reading, editing, and printing.

**paste**   This command allows whatever is stored in temporary memory to be duplicated and inserted in the document at the location of the cursor.

**save**   Allows a document to be recorded to a hard disk or to a floppy diskette.

**save as**   Allows a renamed, modified document to be saved alongside the original.

**word wrap**   Automatically moves a word to the next line without splitting the word.

In addition to the editing commands, there is a set of commands to determine the format of the printed output. These print commands, of course, are not printed out as text; they are the embedded control commands giving instructions to the printer being used. These allow the user to describe paper size; margins; character typeface, size, and style; right, left, center, or full line justification; and more.

## Lettering

Word processing has added a new graphic dimension to communicating in print. It's not only what you say and how you say it but *how it looks on the page*. Word processing has placed at our disposal the ability to affect the appearance of the printed word easily yet markedly. Reflecting on the adage that "A picture is worth a thousand words," word processing has now added somewhat of a "picture" quality to the text medium and requires us to attend to some terms and some guidelines concerning the appearance of text.

### Typeface

A **typeface** is the design of the letter and the name given to the design. New designs are constantly emerging and are usually copyrighted by the creator. Typefaces affect the feeling imparted by the message as well as its content. Some employ harsh angular lines while others use soft curves. Some are narrow and condensed, others are round or broad. Some use thick lines and convey a heavy or dark impression to a body of text while others use thin lines resulting in a light text. Sample typefaces are illustrated in Figure 3–4.

**FIGURE 3–4**
*Sample typefaces*

Bookman
Geneva
Linotext
New Century Schoolbook

**FIGURE 3–5**
*Point sizes*

9 point
10 point
12 point
18 point
24 point

## Size

The *height* of a letter is expressed in points (1 point = 1/72″). Figure 3–5 illustrates a progression from 9 to 24 point. Different typefaces vary in letter width and thickness of line, sometimes giving the appearance of a variation in **size.**

## Style

Style refers to the appearance of a particular typeface as visual modifications are applied, as illustrated in Figure 3–6.

## Font

The collection of characteristics applied to typeface in a particular size and style is called a **font.** Sample fonts are illustrated in Figure 3–7.

Serif typefaces, such as those illustrated in Figure 3–8, have fine lines that finish the major strokes of the letters. These serve as decorative yet

**FIGURE 3–6**
*Styles of a typeface*

| | |
|---|---|
| Plain Text | Underline |
| **Bold** | Outline |
| *Italic* | Shadow |

**FIGURE 3–7**
*Fonts*

**Bookman in 14 point Bold**
*Palatino in 12 point Italic*
Zapf Chancery in 18 point Plain Text

| Palatino 10 pt. | An analysis of factors that influence typeface sel |
| **Palatino 10 pt.** | **An analysis of factors that influence typeface s** |
| Palatino 12 pt. | An analysis of factors that influence typ |
| **Palatino 12 pt.** | **An analysis of factors that influence ty** |

## 24 point Plain text

| Times | An analysis of fact |
| Palatino | An analysis of fac |
| Bookman | An analysis of f |

## 24 point Bold text

| **Times** | **An analysis of fa** |
| **Palatino** | **An analysis of f** |
| **Bookman** | **An analysis o** |

functional connectors that appear to join adjacent letters, thereby helping the reader to perceive groups of letters as words. Therefore, serif typefaces enhance the speed and ease with which text can be read. This text is printed in a serif typeface.

As you study Figure 3–8 and Figure 3–9, notice that some typefaces occupy more line length in the same point size because of the rounder shapes of their letters. The rounder shape of the lowercase letters in Bookman make this most apparent in Figure 3–8. Notice also the effect that a bold-face style has on line length.

Sans serif typefaces, such as those illustrated in Figure 3–9, should not be used in body text. Their clean lines and lack of connectors make them somewhat difficult and tiring to read. Sans serif typefaces should be used primarily in a bold style and larger size as headlines and titles. As you study Figure 3–9, notice that although applying a bold style to a typeface doesn't change its height or point size, it might change its width; therefore it occupies more line length. Notice also that different typefaces in plain text use a thicker line, thereby making a stronger statement.

Ornate typefaces, such as those illustrated in Figure 3–10, are certainly attention getting and effective if used sparingly. They are as much graphic as they are text. The message embodied in the ornate design should support the written words.

The Macintosh provides some special-purpose typefaces that are, in fact, line drawings. Each drawing represents a letter. Young children enjoy deciphering the "code" of the images in order to derive meaning from the encrypted message. A letter may be substituted for the word represented by the image or one or more of these images/letters may be inserted into a sentence for dramatic effect. At times these letters/images can be useful as outline "bullets" in text.

**FIGURE 3–9**
*Some common sans serif typefaces*

| | |
|---|---|
| Futura 10 pt. | An analysis of factors that influence typeface s |
| **Futura 10 pt.** | **An analysis of factors that influence t** |
| Futura 12 pt. | An analysis of factors that influence ty |
| **Futura 12 pt.** | **An analysis of factors that infl** |

## 24 point Plain text

| Helvetica | An analysis o |
| Avant Garde | An analysis |
| Futura | An analysis of |

## 24 point Bold

| **Helvetica** | **An analysis** |
| **Avant Garde** | **An analysis** |
| **Futura** | **An analysi** |

**FIGURE 3–10**
*Some ornate typefaces*

24 Point Canterbury (first letter) followed by 18 Point Linotext

An analysis of factors that influence type

Party

An analysis of factors that influence typeface selecti

Brush Script

An analysis of factors that influence typeface selecti

Umbra

AN ANALYSIS OF FACTORS THAT INFLUENCE

Castellar

AN ANALYSIS OF FACTORS THAT INFL

Every text example shown thus far has been a **proportional-spaced** typeface. That is to say, its design attempts to achieve **optical spacing** by allowing the surface area of the space between each letter to be roughly the same. The distance will, therefore, vary between each letter depending on its shape. A **monospaced** typeface such as Courier is sometimes referred to as achieving **mechanical spacing.** Its design allows each letter to be equally distant from the next regardless of the letter shape. As you examine Figure 3–12, which illustrates the difference between the two types of spacing, pay particular attention to the letters "i" and "I" and their adjacent letters.

**FIGURE 3–11**
*Special-purpose typefaces*

Cairo

Davy's Dingbats

## Lettering Guidelines

- Select a suitable typeface to enhance readability and the expression of your words.

**FIGURE 3-12**
*Proportional and mono-
spaced typefaces*

New Century Schoolbook (proportional):
Analysis of factors that influence typeface select

Courier (monospaced):
Analysis of factors that influence ty

- Use sans serif typefaces for headlines or titles. Used sparingly they have a simplicity that commands attention. Large amounts, such as in body text, are difficult to read. Sans serif typefaces are best used in a large size.
- Use serif typefaces for body text. The decorations on the letters help to guide the reader's eye movement from one letter to the next, thereby helping the reader to perceive words rather than letters.
- Use ornate text sparingly for special visual effects.
- Avoid mixing typefaces within the same document except for a distinct purpose.
- Select a letter size appropriate to the message and its intended impact. Consider that not all output is intended for 8 1/2" × 11" paper. Consider the optimum viewing distance and the medium (e.g., a minimum of 18 point size should be used for overhead transparencies).
- Use style (plain, bold, italic, outline, shadow, underline) for emphasis.
- Use two letter spaces between sentences.
- Allow plenty of space around a block of text. A block of text takes up space, so be sure to consider it in your overall design.

## WORD PROCESSOR APPLICATIONS

As stated in the introduction to this chapter, teachers want help in alleviating the paperwork demands made on them. They want help in accomplishing activities that do not involve students directly and are quite often done outside of actual class time. If the time required to perform these tasks could be decreased, teachers would have more time to devote to working with students.

Teachers create some written classroom material that changes very little from one year to the next. An exercise sheet or other resource material such as a game or puzzle used once in a unit plan may be used the following year with only slight modification. Material, once designed, can be easily modified to serve a similar purpose in another unit of study. The word puzzle in Figure 3-13 is one of many different worksheets a teacher could create in any subject area where terminology is important. It might present the student with an interesting and challenging drill and practice exercise. By using a word processor, the teacher could develop a few standard templates and change the vocabulary words as appropriate.

**FIGURE 3–13**
*Worksheet example*

> ## Find the Hidden Terms
>
> Underline all the words in this puzzle that come from the unit we are studying.
>
> B I R D B N W T F R O A
>
> E D E A R E I B E A K S
>
> E R C L A W N I A T R M
>
> S O N G K S G L T O I S
>
> W B L T I D O L H E S M
>
> A I D O W N I F E M O P
>
> A N E A T H E E R A M E
>
> Have you found all ten terms?

In addition to the preparation of instructional materials, consider the writing that is expected of a teacher. Ask yourself how a teacher might save time and effort and still accomplish the writing tasks effectively. One example of these writing tasks might be asking parents to allow their child to participate in a school-sponsored field trip. The task might be accomplished by sending home an impersonal request form and asking the parents to fill in the name of their child and sign the form. Using a word processor and merging information from a data file, this process can be personalized as shown in Figure 3–14. Labels in curly brackets { }indicate an item to be inserted from the data file.

In addition to appearing as a more personal communication to the parents, the form letter could be used as **boilerplate** for any other field trip permission form with a minimum of retyping. *Boilerplate* is a term that comes from the legal profession and signifies material that can be used repeatedly without modification. The term **template** is becoming a popular replacement for boilerplate.

We often think of a word processor as a tool that enhances an individual's personal productivity, and indeed it is. Collaborative writing, however, is a technique that allows more than one student to engage in a writing activity together. The technique often calls for students to agree on an outline and then to parcel out the writing tasks. The written documents are then merged together and the students edit each other's work and rewrite

**FIGURE 3–14**
*Sample personalized form letter*

Sunrise Elementary School
P.O. BOX M78J
Sherwood, OR 97140

{TODAY'S DATE}
Dear {PARENTS' NAMES},

{CHILD'S NAME}'s class will be going on a field trip to the Oregon Museum of Science and Industry next Tuesday, February 17th to view the exhibit of computer technology and robotics. Two parent volunteers will assist me in supervising the field trip. Transportation will be by school bus departing at 10:00 a.m. and returning to the school by 2:00 p.m. We ask that you provide your child with a sack lunch and, if you wish, money to purchase a beverage. Please sign, date, and return the lower portion of this notice giving permission for your child to participate.

Sincerely,
{TEACHER'S NAME}

-------------------------------------------------------------------

{CHILD'S NAME} has permission to participate in the field trip to the Oregon Museum of Science and Industry next Tuesday, February 17th.

(signed): _____

(today's date): _____

the composition. If the writing is done in a computer lab, students can brainstorm a story idea and then begin drafting the story on their own computers. After fifteen to twenty minutes, students can exchange places and continue writing where the previous student ended. New software allows students sitting at computers on a network to write and to edit each other's documents in real time.

For many years teachers have promoted the teaching of writing as a process of drafting, revising, editing, and publishing. The word processor makes this process less tedious, thereby encouraging a far more positive attitude toward writing.

Figures 3–15 through 3–27 depict activities to illustrate how a word processor might be used as a tool by students to explore creative writing, to write reports, compositions, and poetry. These examples can be modified to

*"When students write using the word processor, they tend to examine their work and 'fix things that are broken'. It really encourages them to rewrite."*

Becky Benjamin, 7th Grade Language Arts Teacher
Carrollton Junior High, Carrollton, GA

```
...He had told all hands that they ought to see
to their equipment; once they got on the trail,
opportunities for repair work might be scarce.
The Spettle brothers, for example, had no equip-
ment at all, unless you called one pistol with a
broken hammer equipment.  Newt had scarcely
more; his saddle was an old one and he had no
slicker and only one blanket for a bedroll. The
Irishmen had nothing except what they had been
loaned.



                                   "Lonesome Dove"
                                   Larry McMurtry
```

**Suggested Use**

Using a word processor, the teacher types a selection from a popular novel, eliminating the first topic sentence and running two or more paragraphs together,
then saves it as a word processing file.

Class discussion reviews topic sentences and getting the main idea of a
paragraph. Students are assigned to load the teacher's file, create a topic sentence, and separate the paragraphs. They then print out their modified file.

Discussion follows in which the teacher indicates the correct paragraph
breaks and students listen to each other's topic sentences, discussing their merits. The teacher then reads the original selection from the book.

**FIGURE 3–15**
*Topic sentence*

Billie, Billie, what do
you see?
I see a white bunny
rabbit looking at me.

**Suggested Use**

Children use "Big Books" in primary grades to acquire simple language skills. Following the pattern of a "Big Book," children could dictate one page of a story to the teacher or to a parent volunteer who would enter it into a word processor file leaving space for an illustration. In this example, children were asked to name an animal and a color along with their name in a rhyme.

Children would be encouraged to draw a picture illustrating their words. Drawn on a simple graphics paint program, the image could be then inserted into the word processor file. If it were drawn by hand on paper, the drawing could be scanned into an electronic form and then this image inserted into the word processor file. Stories could be bound and placed in the school library media center to be read by others.

**FIGURE 3–16**
*"Big Book" authored by students*

**FIGURE 3–17**
*Student authors*

Frog and toad swam in the pond.

Later they rode bikes.

"Would you like to come to my house for dinner?" said frog.

"Sure,. . .," etc.

serve in a variety of subject areas and grade levels. Word processing objectives, writing objectives, and subject matter objectives often dovetail. If students are to capitalize on the power of the word processor as a tool and employ it with confidence, they must develop an understanding of its application and a reasonably high level of skill in its use. Using this tool, they will enhance their written communication as they acquire and construct knowledge in various content areas.

Commercially published "Big Books" are in a large format that lends itself to being read and displayed in front of a group of students. They usually contain one story with some of them having repetition on each page as illustrated in Figure 3–16. The example in Figure 3–17 is a continuous story with each child responsible for writing and illustrating one page. Books created by children can range over a wide variety of topics and can integrate a number of subject matter disciplines. Consider the following ideas.

- Endangered animals:
    An illustration and facts about the animal that would require some research.
- Alliteration with names from your home town or state to foster recognition of place names, cities, towns, rivers, and so on.
    "Suzy Smith from Seaside sings in the shower."
    "Terrific Terry from Troutdale Travels along the Trask River."
- Report on a classroom activity:
    "What I learned about raising quail chicks in school."
- Read a story such as "Alexander and the Magic Pebble" and respond to it.
    "If I had a magic pebble, I would . . ."
- Wonderful word problems. Write and illustrate math word problems. Place answers to the student-written problems on the last page.

```
    I have a 1978 Chevrolet Caprice station wagon
to sell. Considering its age and its 178,000
miles, it's in good shape.  The 400 cu. in.
engine runs very well, no doubt because I have
changed its oil and filter faithfully every 3000
miles. It averages 12 to 14 miles per gallon of
gas. The automatic transmission is original and
had been serviced at regular intervals. The body
has no rust on it and only a few minor scratches
and small dents.  The fuel pump, rear wheel
bearings, universal joints and all four brakes
are about one year old. The water pump is
original. I would estimate that the tires have
at least a good year of wear left on them.  The
car has a heavy-duty load-equalizing trailer
hitch attached to its frame.  I am asking $350 in
cash but would not refuse any reasonable offer.
You must see it to fully appreciate it.
```

**Suggested Use**

The teacher prepares a lengthy and verbose paragraph describing an article for sale and saves it as a word processing file.

Class discussion reviews topic sentences and getting the main idea of a paragraph.

Students are assigned to load the teacher's file and to (1) underline the main idea, (2) eliminate extraneous elements, and (3) prepare a succinct classified advertisement from it. Students then print the teacher's modified file and their original advertisement. Discussion would follow to select the best ads.

A follow-up activity would be to select classified ads from the newspaper, improve them, and write more descriptive paragraphs.

**FIGURE 3–18**
*Classified advertisement*

*Mrs. Prosser's Classroom News*
May 21, 1995

## School Built on Site of Indian Village

Mr. Claude Smith showed his collection of arrowheads to Mrs. Prosser's fifth grade class. He grew up here in Chicopee Falls and started his collection when he was a young boy. He found his first arrowheads in what is now the school playground years before the school was built. He found some small arrowheads that he thinks were used to hunt birds.

Mr. Smith also showed some broken pieces of pottery that he found down on the river bank. The pottery shards, the arrowheads, and pictures of what the playground area looked like before the school was built will be placed in the display case in the school library.

**Suggested Use**

The teacher serves as guide and advisor as students publish a class newspaper. They discuss events of the past week and decide which to report. They focus attention on the importance of the headline and take turns writing the stories. They edit each other's stories for content, spelling, grammar, and creative expression.

In an extension of this activity, the teacher encourages students to interview local business and civic leaders, examine local occupations, or record stories told by old-timers in the community.

Student photographs and drawings could be scanned and inserted in the document. Modest page layout software could eventually replace the word processor and give the publication a more sophisticated look as the students gain skills and experience.

**FIGURE 3-19**
*Classroom newsletter*

'Twixt optimist and pessimist
_____

The optimist sees the doughnut;
   The pessimist sees the hole.


   The pedigree of honey
   Does not concern the bee;
   A clover, any time, to him
   _____ .


    Dogs in the country have fun.
    _____

    But in the city this species
    Is dragged around on leashes.

### Suggested Use

Using a word processor, the teacher types selections from several poems, eliminating one line from each poem, then saves the document as a word processor file.

Class discussion reviews rhyme and meter. Students are assigned to load the teacher's file and create the missing line. Each student then prints a copy of the completed poems.

Discussion follows in which the students listen to the poems, discussing their merits. The teacher then reads the original selection.

**FIGURE 3–20**
*Poem*

What would the Oregon Country be like, she wondered as she gazed at her child burning with fever.  Would this interminable trek ever end? Would they find the answer to their prayers? Would she, Abner and their children ever see the green valleys and rushing streams they had heard about?

The parching heat and blowing dust make every mile seem like ten.  The slow creaking of the wagon wheels and plodding of the oxen add to the monotony.  The scout says there's a river an hour away where we will make camp for tonight.  The thought of water and some rest lift my spirits  and give me the energy to keep going.

**Suggested Use**

Students agree on a story outline. Using a word processor, they develop some ideas as they write paragraphs into a file. Students merge their separate files into one document.

The example above shows two students' files merged together. Each student then takes a copy of the document and rewrites the entire segment to give the paragraphs coherence and unity of expression.

Students print their own file when they are finished and exchange papers to compare writing styles. Students are then given the opportunity to modify their own document.

**FIGURE 3–21**
*Collaborative exercise*

**WORD PUZZLE**

| | | | |
|---|---|---|---|
| ITEM | CALM | LARK | TIME |
| STEM | PALM | MARK | |
| STEP | PALE | | |
| STOP | | | |
| SLOP | | | |
| SLIP | | | |
| FLIP | | | |
| FLAP | | | |
| FLAT | | | |
| FLIT | | | |

**Suggested Use**

Using a word processor, the teacher prepares a file consisting of four columns of words.

Starting with the first word in each column, students change one letter only to create a new word until ten different words appear in each column. The students display the changed letters in boldface and underlined.

Students print the file when they are finished and exchange papers to check the correctness of the spelling.

In a follow-up activity, students write the preferred definition for each word.

**FIGURE 3–22**
*Spelling vocabulary*

A student approached Mrs. Alderson after class with a request for help. She said that she was confused between the terms latitude and longitude. She couldn't remember which was which.

Mrs. Alderson responded with a comparision of the similarity in the words latitude and altitude pointing out their North-South or "up-down" and height relationship.  She concluded by suggesting that latitude be thought of as a ladder that she would climb up and down and pointing out the alliteration, ladder and latitude.

**Suggested Use**

The purpose of the lesson is to rewrite sentences eliminating the gender-specific pronouns "he" and "she" when they do not refer to an identifiable person in the story.

Using a word processor, the teacher prepares a paragraph using several pronouns and saves the document as a word processor file.

Class discussion reviews pronouns and antecedents. Students are assigned to load the teacher's file and to rewrite the paragraph replacing gender-specific pronouns where appropriate. Students print the modified file. Discussion would follow in which the modified paragraphs were examined.

**FIGURE 3-23**
*Gender-neutral style*

1. The child enters the classroom.
   The <u>child</u> enters the classroom.

2. The kitten loves to chase the ball of yarn.
   The <u>kitten</u> loves to chase the <u>ball</u> of yarn.

3. The man waits patiently for the store to open.
   The <u>man</u> waits patiently for the store to open.

4. The woman sits quietly while eating her lunch.
   The <u>woman</u> sits quietly while eating her lunch.

**Suggested Use**

Using a word processor, the teacher prepares a file containing sets of sentence pairs and distributes it on disk or by a file server to student workstations.

Students read the sentences on the computer screen. Using the editing capabilities of the word processor, students modify the second sentence in each pair by replacing the underlined words with a plural form.

Care must be given to making appropriate changes to assure correct verb forms and pronoun agreements.

Students print the modified copy and either check each other's work or submit it to the teacher.

**FIGURE 3–24**
*Plural forms*

It was a  *  and  *  night. The moon was  *  hidden behind a  *  cloud and a  *  wind was blowing from the North. It was a night when imaginations could  *  run  *  .

 *  , Jim and Gwenda heard an  *  sound coming from just outside their campground. They wondered if their  *  sister, Margaia, had heard it too. They heard it again. This time it seemed  *  .

**Suggested Use**

Using a word processor, the teacher prepares a file consisting of a selection with missing modifiers replaced by asterisks.

After reading the selection, students replace the asterisks with one or more adjectives or adverbs. Students underline the modifiers that they inserted, rename the file, and save it to a diskette or to a folder assigned to them on a hard disk or file server.

In a follow-up activity, students load each other's files and substitute other modifiers for all underlined words in order to change the mood or meaning of the selection. A discussion should follow on how modifiers can alter the meaning of a story.

As a further creative writing activity, students could be asked to complete their story.

**FIGURE 3–25**
*Modifiers*

```
I  predict for America, not despair but
rather great hope. I believe  that anything
is possible if people want it badly enough.




I see America, not in the setting sun of a
black night of despair  ahead of us, I see
America in the crimson light of a rising
sun fresh from the burning, creative hand
of God. I see great days ahead, great days
possible to men and women of will and
vision . . .

                              —Carl Sandburg
```

**Suggested Use**

The teacher finds a quotation that illustrates expressive language. Using a word processor, the teacher paraphrases the quotation in a direct style and, after spacing down the page, enters the quotation. Using a large monitor or an overhead display panel, the teacher shows the first section to the class.

After reading the first section, students rewrite the selection using a more expressive style. They may then read their selection aloud or display it for the class to read. The teacher then displays the original quotation and leads the class in analyzing the style.

In a follow-up activity, students load each other's files and edit each other's work in an attempt to influence the mood of the selection.

**FIGURE 3–26**
*Whole-class writing exercise*

The state of Oregon was founded.

John Jacob Astor established a flourishing fur trade.

Andrew Jackson became president.

Wagons completed the first journey over the Oregon Trail.

The Oregon Territory was created.

The Civil War ended.

The first missionaries arrived in the Willamette Valley.

Lewis and Clark reached what is present-day Astoria, Oregon.

**Suggested Use**

Using a word processor, the teacher prepares a file consisting of a series of historical events in a scrambled chronological order.

Students read the statements on the computer screen. Using the cut and paste function of the word processor, students arrange them in the correct chronological order and print the file. Using reference tools in their classroom and in the library, students verify the correctness of their printout.

In a follow-up activity, students assign dates to each event and identify names of important people and places related to the events where appropriate.

A slight variation of this activity might mix local, state, national, and world events in the file prepared by the teacher. Another variation might mix events from social studies, science, and the arts in order to foster cross-curriculum integration.

**FIGURE 3–27**
*Chronological order*

## THE WORD PROCESSOR AS A PRODUCTIVITY TOOL

The computer is a tool and word processing is one of the most popular and powerful tool uses. Seat work, homework, exercise sheets, lesson plans, bibliographies, class notes, reports, essays, compositions, memos, letters to parents—the list of practical word processing applications goes on and on. It is easy to understand why most people purchasing a personal computer do so to use it as a word processor.

The argument can be built that the word processor and not the computer itself is in fact the productivity tool. Software indeed transforms the hardware. Using the best software appropriate for a given task makes the computer far more effective or productive than using poorly designed or inappropriate software. Once software is loaded into the hardware perhaps we should no longer refer to it as a computer but rather call it a word processor, database manager, drawing table, etc.

To gauge its value as a productivity tool, the following questions must be answered. Does using the word processor increase my accuracy? Does it ease my task? Does it increase the speed at which I can complete a task? Does it allow me to accomplish something that I might otherwise find impossible? In other words, does it contribute to my efficiency or effectiveness?

## Summary

This chapter addressed the value of using a word processor in the classroom as a tool to facilitate written communication. Studies have shown the use of word processing by students increases their motivation to write and expands their vocabulary. Applications by students, teachers, library media specialists, administrators and clerks were discussed.

Features that might be considered when choosing a word processor were examined. The more sophisticated, and usually more expensive, programs are expected to contain a greater number of features. After writing needs are determined, a program can be selected that has an appropriate set of features.

Representative editing functions were examined that allow the user to navigate through the document, adding, deleting, finding, replacing, inserting, or moving information at will. In addition, print commands were acknowledged that allow the user to describe paper size; margins; character typeface, size and style; right, left, center, or full line justification. Lettering guidelines were suggested in order to take full advantage of the visual impact of print generated from a word processor.

Teacher applications were explored using the word processor as a tool to save time and effort and to personalize communications. A process called mail merge integrates information from a data file into a word-processed document. Material that is used repeatedly without modification is known as boilerplate and can be incorporated into documents, thereby saving a good deal of time.

Collaborative writing, a technique that allows more than one student at a time to engage in a writing activity, is greatly facilitated by a word processor. New software allows students sitting at computers on a network to write and to edit each other's documents as they write them.

Examples of student applications were presented in a cross-disciplinary fashion in order to stimulate the reader's imagination and encourage unique creative applications. Instructional or teacher-centered applications were differentiated from student-centered applications of the word processor as a learning tool.

## Chapter Exercises

1. Many programs in the school setting currently use keyboard input from students. There has been a good deal written in the last several years on the subject of keyboard instruction. Write a two- to three-page paper discussing the issue of teaching typing starting at an early level. Cite your sources.
2. Describe at least five examples of how you might use word processing in your work as a teacher. Develop a sample of one of them.
3. Using a word processor, write a two- to three-page reaction paper to the concept of collaborative writing. Include a bibliography listing at least three sources.
4. Using a word processor, write a few paragraphs about the motivation that is prompting you to enter the teaching profession and save the file. Exchange your file with a friend who has written a similar one. Finish the document you have received by adding a few paragraphs of your own describing what you hope to accomplish as a teacher. Edit the entire document for consistency of style. Once again exchange it with your friend and compare the documents.
5. Pick a partner and together choose a topic on which to write. After agreeing on an outline, divide the writing task between yourselves. After completing your independent writing assignment, merge your files. Edit the entire document for consistency of style.

## Glossary

**ASCII text**   A format that allows text files or documents to be transported between word processors produced by different publishers.

**boilerplate**   A paragraph or section of a document that is used repeatedly with little or no modification when inserted into word-processed documents.

**clipboard**   An area of temporary computer memory capable of storing a single item that has been cut or copied.

**desktop publishing**   Usually refers to the use of software that contains an extensive set of text and graphics manipulation commands and includes advanced page layout capabilities.

**font**   The collection of characteristics applied to a typeface in a particular size and style.

**footer**   A brief message that may include a date, time, or page display that is automatically added to the bottom of each page.

**header**   A brief message that may include a date, time, or page display that is automatically added to the top of each page.

**mechanical spacing**   Letter spacing that requires letters within a word to be equally distant from each other regardless of the letter shape. This results in unequal surface areas in the spaces between letters.

**monospacing**   See *mechanical spacing.*

**optical spacing**   Letter spacing that requires letters within a word to have equal surface areas in the spaces between each other, thereby taking letter shapes into account. Distances between letters will vary.

**orphans**   Single lines of text that occur at the bottom of a page.

**print formatter**   The part of the word processing program that delivers the text file to the printer and ensures that it is printed correctly on paper.

**proportional spacing**   See *optical spacing.*

**size**   The height of a letter expressed in points (1 point = 1/72 of an inch).

**style**   (1) A set of format characteristics (left aligned, 10 point, Times, 0.5 inch first line indent, for example) that can be applied to text in a word processor. (2) When dealing strictly with the appearance of text, style pertains more narrowly to the appearance of a particular typeface (plain, bold, italic, outline, shadow, and underline).

**style sheet**   A collection of styles used in a document.

**template**   See *boilerplate.*

**text editor**   The part of the word processing program that allows the user to manipulate text on a screen display. It is used during the text entry phase to help add, change, and delete text as well as to locate words or phrases.

**text-wrapped graphics**   The format feature that allows the program to wrap lines of text around the edges of graphics.

**typeface**   The design or appearance of a particular letter type and the name given to that design (Bookman, Geneva, Times, New Century Schoolbook, Palatino, etc.).

**widows**   Single lines of text that occur at the top of a page.

**word processor**   Software, with accompanying hardware, used primarily to facilitate the creation, editing, formatting, saving, and printing of information in electronic and hard copy form.

**word wrap**   A process of monitoring the entry of words so that words are not split on the right side of the screen. If a complete word will not fit on the current line, the complete word is moved to the next line.

**WYSIWYG**   (What You See Is What You Get, pronounced WHIZ-EE-WIG.) The exact screen replication of what will be printed on paper.

# Notes & Suggested Readings

Aker, S. Z. (1992, June). Key words. *MacUser, 8*(6), 18–28.

Beaver, J. F. (1992, February). Using computer power to improve your teaching. *The Computing Teacher, 19*(5), 5–9.

Griest, G. (1993, April). You say you want a revolution: Constructivism, technology, and language arts. *The Computing Teacher, 20:*(7), 49–51.

Koppelman, J. (1988, October). Introductory computer literacy skills for students and faculty through word processing. *Tech Trends, 33*(5), 34–36.

Landau, T. (1992, September). The right word processor. *MacUser, 8*(9), 101–110.

Marcus, S. (1991, May). Word processing: Transforming students' potential to write. *Media and Methods, 27:*(5), 8.

McCain, T. D. E.(1993, March). There's more to reading than reading. *The Computing Teacher, 20*(6), 5–9.

Riedesel, C. A., & Clements, D. H. (1985). *Coping with computers in the elementary and middle schools.* Englewood Cliffs, NJ: Prentice-Hall.

Roblyer, M. D. (1988, September). The effectiveness of microcomputers in education: A review of the research 1980–1987. *T.H.E. Journal,* 85–89.

Woodrow, J. F. J. (1991, Summer). Teachers' perceptions of computer needs. *Journal of Research on Computing in Education, 23*(4), 475–493.

Woodruff, E., Bereiter, C., & Scardamalia, M. (1981). On the road to computer assisted compositions. *Journal of Educational Technology Systems, 10*(2), 133–148.

Wresch, W. (1990, October). Collaborative writing projects: Lesson plans for the computer age. *The Computing Teacher, 18:*(2), 19–21.

# 4

# GRAPHICS

The adage "A picture is worth a thousand words" is an appropriate beginning to any basic discussion about graphics. Teachers appreciate the value of this statement because pictorial representations have always been an important means for communicating ideas and concepts to students quickly and accurately.

Many different graphics tools have been employed in instructional situations. The chalkboard, drawings, flowcharts, diagrams, print of different sizes, underlining, and arrows are common methods of enhancing the communication of ideas to students. Other tools such as film projectors, video recorders, overhead projectors, slide projectors, photographs, posters, maps, textbooks, video, and television have added different dimensions to our capabilities in using visuals to affect the learning experience. Each tool expands the user's ability to refine the presentation of ideas and emphasize key parts through motion, color, size, or blank space. The computer is a visual tool that can present many of these capabilities interactively, adding more power to graphic communication.

An extensive use of computer graphics can be found in engineering, where drafting and designing are rapidly performed on video screens and transformed to blueprints for production. Three-dimensional graphic images can be turned and rotated in ways that traditional two-dimensional drawings can never duplicate.

The advertising industry has made a science of using graphics. Computers have emerged as devices to manipulate visual images and to create forms of video animation. Having recognized the power of visuals to communicate ideas and to persuade the viewer, this industry remains at the forefront of computer graphics applications.

Schools have recognized the uniqueness of visual literacy and many include visual literacy skills training as part of their curriculum. A scope and sequence of visual literacy skills as they apply to still images often proceeds along the following continuum.

Naming—recognizing objects or elements and labeling them or calling them by name

Describing—sorting out details and delineating them verbally or in writing

Interpreting—studying details; deciphering visual clues; inferring probable past, present and future actions and the relationships between people, objects, or events

Music and language have discrete systems of notation. Visuals have a complex code system composed of color, texture, size, medium, realism, etc. These codes combine to make visuals powerful tools. Teachers have recognized that students are surrounded and constantly bombarded by visual stimuli and, often as part of a visual literacy skills curriculum, have attempted to teach them effective **decoding** skills in order to derive accurate meaning from these stimuli. Computer-generated graphics also provide students the opportunity to learn powerful **encoding** skills as they analyze the symbols they choose in order to communicate effectively.

Still images can stimulate interest and assist the understanding of verbal materials. Line drawings, easily prepared in a computer graphics program, can sometimes simplify a complex visual reality. Projected as an overhead transparency, these graphics can reach a large group through conventional delivery methods or through the electronic projection process called desktop presentations.

## Advanced Organizers

1. What are some tools you might use for creating computer graphics?
2. What are bit-mapped graphics?
3. What are vector or object-oriented graphics?
4. What is clip art and how can it be used?
5. What is a practical application of computer graphics that you might use as a teacher in designing instructional materials for your classroom?
6. What are some basic rules to follow when designing overhead transparencies on the computer?
7. What are desktop presentation programs and how might you use them?
8. What are some tools you might find useful for displaying computer-generated graphics?

## TOOLS FOR CREATING GRAPHICS

MacPaint®, PC Paint™, ClarisDraw®, CorelDRAW, MacBillboard™ and other graphics programs are available for Macintosh computers and for computers running Windows to facilitate the creation of bulletin board and display graphics and text. Crossword Magic simplifies the creation and printing of crossword puzzles to drill students in vocabulary, terminology, and definitions in any subject area. Programs such as Microsoft®, Excel, DeltaGraph™, ClarisWorks®, and Microsoft® Works automatically generate line graphs, bar graphs, or pie charts from numeric data. Software in this category serves as an extension of the creative teacher. Although these materials can be created in other ways, the computer makes it easier and less time consuming and thereby stimulates teachers to reach out and maximize their creative efforts.

Programs and video boards are available that allow computer screens to be recorded on videotape to serve as titles, credits, animated graphics, or instructional text screens. A variety of wipes and dissolves that allow one image to fade or merge into another lends sophistication to the recording. Various input peripherals were discussed in Chapter 2. They were defined as those hardware items that enter data into the computer. Of those discussed, the ones most important as graphic tools are optical scanners and graphic tablets.

Remember that optical scanners are available in hand-held models and as flatbed scanners somewhat resembling small photocopiers. They operate by reading light reflected from the surface of an object such as a photograph, line drawing, or printed page of text. The hand-held scanner is priced considerably lower than the flatbed scanner and is most useful for scanning (copying) small images, up to four inches wide. Wider images can be scanned but the process becomes more complex as image parts must be joined. Flatbed scanners, depending on the model, accept originals with dimensions up to 11 in. by 14 in. Both types of scanners are usually accompanied by software that allows some degree of control over brightness, contrast, and image size.

The graphics tablet was discussed as an input device that allows the user to create or trace figures or drawings. The user can draw a picture on the surface of the tablet with a stylus that provides far greater control than a mouse. Using the software that accompanies the tablet, certain shapes, shadings, and line widths or "paintbrush" effects may be selected by the user. With its inherent ability to trace existing material, the graphics tablet is an excellent device to facilitate the production of state, regional, and even local maps that can then be projected and are so often in demand in the classroom.

Employing the video digitizer, it is possible to record still images through the use of digital cameras such as the Apple® QuickTake 100 shown in Figure 4–1 and video camcorders. By using appropriate firmware cards in the computer and accompanying software, recorded im-

**FIGURE 4–1**
*Digital still video camera*
(Photo courtesy of Apple
Computer, Inc.)

ages can be transmitted into the computer, manipulated, and stored on disk as graphic files.

## BIT-MAPPED GRAPHICS

There are two basic ways in which graphics are created by the computer. One type of computer graphic is called **bit-mapped.** The computer-generated image is composed of bits or screen picture elements called pixels that are turned on (black or colored) and bits that are off (white or clear). A pixel is the smallest dot a computer can display. Most programs that incorporate the name "Paint" in their titles produce bit-mapped graphics. This has led to the practice of calling bit-mapped programs paint programs. Programs such as MacPaint, PC Paint, and Kid Pix often were the user's first introduction to computer graphics and as such should not be disparaged even though more powerful programs certainly exist.

A simplified bit-mapped drawing of the side view of a child's wagon created in a paint program is presented in Figure 4–2, with a dot pattern applied to the body and a solid pattern applied to the wheels.

Figure 4–3 shows that same wagon with a section of the drawing enlarged. Horizontal or vertical lines are smooth, but notice the jagged edges of the circle (wheel) and of the diagonal line (handle shaft). The square shape of the pixel becomes apparent. One of the inherent drawbacks of bit-mapped graphics is that the size of the pixel limits the sharpness or reso-

**FIGURE 4–2**
*Wagon in bit-mapped
graphics*

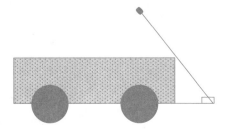

**FIGURE 4–3**
*Enlargement showing low resolution of bit-mapped graphics*

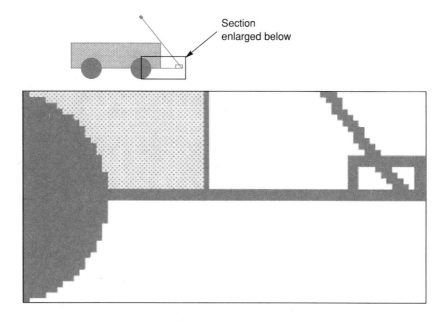

lution of the drawing regardless of the resolution of the monitor or printer used to display the graphic. Normally, bitmaps are created at a resolution of 72 dots per inch (dpi). One pixel is 1/72 of an inch. Phosphor dots on a video tube are much smaller and many are required to make up a pixel. Laser printers frequently found in schools are capable of printing at 300 or 600 dpi. Unfortunately, bit-mapped images cannot take advantage of either the higher screen display or higher printing resolution.

In order to modify an existing image in a paint program, the user must turn pixels on or off individually or erase larger segments, as shown in Figure 4–4. Notice that the eraser (the white square) is turning bits off, that is, it is turning black or colored pixels white against a white background, virtually making them disappear. Whenever text is inserted, as in Figure 4–3 and Figure 4–4, the art also becomes a bit-mapped graphic. Think of it as a picture of the words. Once text is fixed in position, it cannot be edited. Pixels composing the letters can be erased like any other graphic element, thereby allowing entire letters and words to be erased. Once text is inserted into a "paint" document, typing errors cannot be easily corrected, nor can typefaces, sizes, or styles be changed.

## VECTOR OR OBJECT-ORIENTED GRAPHICS

The other type of computer graphic is called **vector** or **object oriented.** The computer-generated image, instead of being composed of bits or screen pixels that are turned on and off, is determined by formulas that create discrete objects of a certain size and position. Most programs that incorporate the

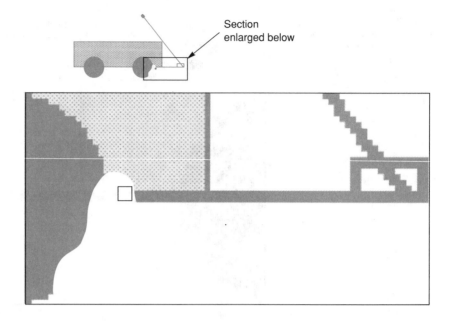

Section
enlarged below

name *draw* in their titles, such as ClarisDraw and CorelDRAW, produce object-oriented graphics. This has led to the practice of calling object-oriented programs draw programs. Integrated packages, such as Microsoft Works, include a draw program or module.

In Figure 4–5, the front wheel has been moved away from the rest of the drawing. Each picture element is a separate object and can be changed independently. It can be enlarged, reduced, moved, or have its pattern changed. Creating an image in a draw program is conceptually very different from creating one in a paint program. Rather than drawing freehand with a pencil or a paintbrush, the user of a draw program creates objects of different shapes (e.g., lines, circles, rectangles, and polygons), adjusts line thickness and applies patterns to the objects, then organizes or groups them into new, more complex objects.

**FIGURE 4–5**
*Wagon in object-oriented graphics*

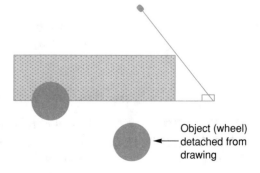

Object (wheel)
detached from
drawing

Many draw programs allow the use of **gradient fill** patterns similar to those shown in Figure 4–6 that begin with a certain density of pattern or opacity at a determined point and gradually fade to a less dense pattern or increase to a denser one. Gradient fills can create the appearance of a third dimension on an object and are a dramatic background for text.

**FIGURE 4–6**
*Sample uses of gradient fill*

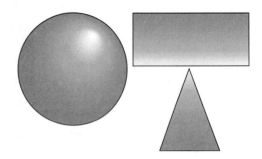

Once objects are created in draw programs, their shape, size, and position can be changed. Two or more objects may be linked or grouped together to form a new object. Text inserted in a drawing remains an editable text object. Typing mistakes can be easily corrected and typefaces, sizes, and styles can be changed at any time. Being a discrete object, text may also be repositioned at will.

Count the objects making up the wagon in Figure 4–7. There are seven objects: (1) the shaded body of the wagon, (2) the rear wheel, (3) the front wheel, (4) the steering plate, (5) the handle tongue, (6) the handle shaft, and (7) the handle. Since the drawing is composed of independent objects, they may overlap or be layered on top of one another. Notice that the rear wheel is placed underneath the body of the wagon in this illustration. Some graphics programs include both bit-mapped and draw layers so that the user can take advantage of what each approach has to offer.

Figure 4–8 illustrates tools that are common to a number of paint and draw programs. Notice that a number of tools are common to both types of

**FIGURE 4–7**
*Objects making up the drawing*

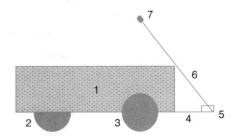

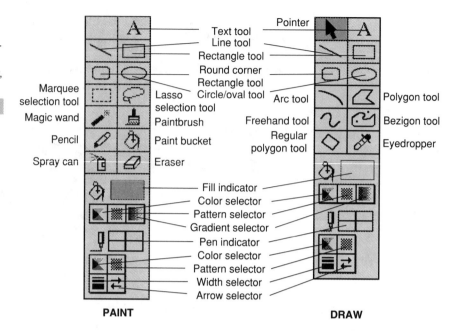

**PAINT**                                                    **DRAW**

programs. If a paint or a draw program is truly to become a productivity
tool, the user must become comfortable with the individual program and
adept at using it. The following lists and descriptions help to introduce you
to these tools.

### Paint Tools

Paint tools are those that create bit-mapped images in paint programs.

**marquee selection tool**   Selects a rectangular area including any white background present.

**lasso selection tool**   Selects an irregular shape without any extraneous background.

**magic wand**   Selects adjacent pixels of the same color.

**paintbrush**   Paints strokes of various sizes and shapes.

**pencil**   Paints fine lines in a freehand manner. One of the first tools people learn
to use in a paint program.

**paint bucket**   Used to fill an enclosed shape with color, pattern, or gradient.

**spray can**   Used to create a spray-painted effect.

**eraser**   Erases part of an image, pixel by pixel.

### Draw Tools

Draw tools are those that create objects in draw programs.

**pointer**   Selects, moves, and resizes objects.

**arc tool**   Draws an arc curving between two points.

**polygon tool**   Draws closed shapes made up of straight lines and angles.

**freehand tool**   Draws irregular lines in the manner similar to a pencil.

**bezigon tool**   Draws shapes with the user selecting specific points. The tool draws smooth curves through those points.

**regular polygon**   Draws polygons of equal sides.

**eyedropper**   Picks up colors, patterns, or gradients from any object drawn and adjusts the proper selection tool. The result appears in the Fill indicator.

## Common Tools

These tools are employed by both types of programs though they behave somewhat differently in each.

**text tool**   Inserts text on the screen in a selected font.

**line tool**   Creates straight lines.

**rectangle tool**   Creates rectangles and squares.

**round corner rectangle**   Creates rectangles and squares with round corners.

**circle/oval tool**   Creates ovals and circles.

**color, pattern, and gradient fill selectors**   Allow user to select specific color, pattern, or gradient to fill a shape or object.

**color, pattern, width, and arrow pen selectors**   Allow user to select specific color, pattern, width, and arrow style for the pen.

**fill and pen indicators**   Display the specific fill and pen characteristics that have been selected.

## CLIP ART

For many years graphic artists have subscribed to services that have provided them with black and white or color line drawings and half-tone images. The artists *clipped out* any illustration that suited their needs and incorporated it into their own original work. **Clip art** files on disk are also available for use in computer graphics programs. The files are specifically available in the draw or paint format. Purchase of clip art entitles users to copy images or parts of images to use in their own drawings.

Examine the various illustrations in Figure 4–9. Some clip art files are composed solely of borders such as those shown in the upper and lower left-hand corners. There are clip art files of the flags of every nation. The chick and would-be ballplayer are simple line drawings. Notice the effective use of shading in the eagle, the kitten, and Santa. Clip art is a great time saver for all and an exceptional resource for those of modest or limited artistic skills and talents.

**FIGURE 4–9**

*Various samples of clip art*

(Courtesy of T/Maker, Magnum Software Corp., and Miles Computing, Inc.)

## DESIGN OF INSTRUCTIONAL MATERIALS

In designing any communication, whether it be oral, written, or graphic, the sender of the message must know the anticipated audience that is to receive it and design the communication appropriately. The user must know what will capture the audience's attention and get the information across clearly and convincingly.

Line drawings are the most common type of graphics created on the computer. When considering line illustrations, a few simple rules apply.

- Present one topic or main idea per illustration.
- Use thick (bold) lines.
- Keep the use of text to a minimum and use a bold style.

Desktop presentation software permits the projection of computer screens by either a video projector or by a video display panel placed on the stage of an overhead projector. Either projection can be in black and white or in color depending on the equipment used. Some view these desktop presentation tools on the computer as "high tech overhead or slide projectors." Computer graphics allow the user to enhance "low tech" presentations as well. Signs, posters, maps, and banners can be created easily; so can overhead transparency masters.

Although equipment for other forms of projected media require some effort and setup time, the overhead projector sits ready to use in the front of most classrooms. This availability and its ease of use have contributed to its widespread popularity with teachers and increasingly with students. Unfortunately, the medium has not always been used most effectively. Computer graphics present a tool for improving the preparation of transparencies and increasing the effectiveness of their use.

### Basic Design Rules

When designing overhead transparencies, keep in mind the following six design rules.

1. Use landscape (horizontal) rather than portrait (vertical) orientation for your layout.
2. Lettering must be at least 1/4" high (18 point) and should be simple, bold, and easy to read. This will allow the projected screen image of the text to be viewed comfortably from the rear of a typical classroom.
3. Lettering and drawings should fill most of the overhead frame, leaving enough blank or unoccupied space to emphasize the design elements.
4. Color should be used where appropriate. Different colors can be used to highlight keywords by separating the components of the transparency into two masters and printing them in different colors of thermal film.
5. Text should be kept to a minimum and should present only an outline or key points rather than specific details. Remember that this is an

ephemeral medium in that once a projector is turned off the projected information is gone. Significant text and detail require a printed hard copy in the hands of the students.

6. Divide complex topics into "overlay cells" so that the concept may be presented in a logical sequence "Overlay" transparencies allow items to be added in a progressive fashion to develop the finished product or complete idea.

For many years, teachers have created thermal transparencies using the 3-M Thermofax™ copier. This heat process uses thermal film that is chemically treated on one side with an emulsion that will produce a black, red, green, blue, or purple line. It is a line medium in that it will not re-produce solid areas, fine patterns, or photographic half-tones well.

The original or master being copied must have a significant amount of carbon in its ink in order to reflect the heat to the film's emulsion in the copier. Prints from laser printers work well as transparency masters but those from dot-matrix printers must be photocopied. The copies then serve as transparency masters.

Designing transparency masters in computer graphics is a fairly straightforward task. The first step requires the user to create the entire drawing and save the document. In Figure 4–10, the process depicting plant growth was drawn in its entirety as a file named Master. The second step involves deciding what elements of the total drawing should be pre-sented first. All other elements are deleted from the drawing and the file is saved under a different name. This file was saved as Base Cell in Figure 4–10. The files should be saved in such a way that the user will easily rec-ognize the contents. The third and subsequent steps require the user to open the original complete document (e.g., Master in Figure 4–10), delete unwanted elements, and save the results as a new file with a different name (e.g., 1st Overlay and 2nd Overlay in Figure 4–10).

**FIGURE 4–10**
*Design of an overlay trans-parency*

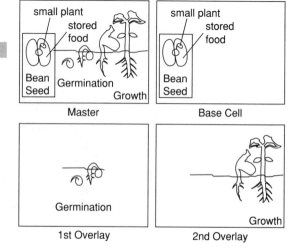

**FIGURE 4–11**
*Mounting base cell*

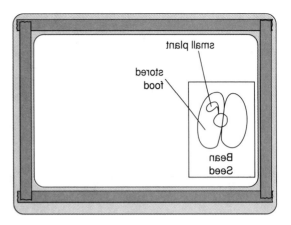

Multiple cell transparencies should be mounted on a cardboard frame. The first or base cell is securely fastened with masking tape on all edges on the underside of the frame, as shown in Figure 4–11.

Overlay cells should then be mounted on the top surface of the frame as illustrated in Figure 4–12. They may be mounted all on the same edge or on different edges.

If the concept being presented calls for information to be added in the same order (e.g., fixed sequence, progressive growth, sequential development of a idea), then overlay cells may be mounted all on the same edge of the frame so they can never be shown in the wrong order. If, on the other hand, an overlay cell is placed, adding information to the base cell, and then removed to allow a subsequent overlay cell to be placed showing contrasting information, the cells must be mounted on different edges of the frame to allow for this flexibility.

In examining the process just described, it is apparent that the user, once having acquired a certain degree of skill and comfort level with a

**FIGURE 4–12**
*Mounting overlay cells*

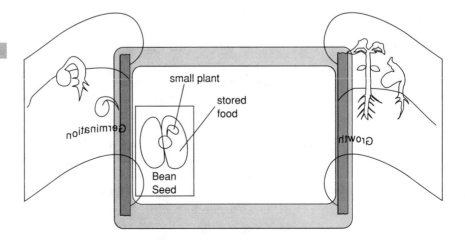

**FIGURE 4–13**
*A tiled graphic*

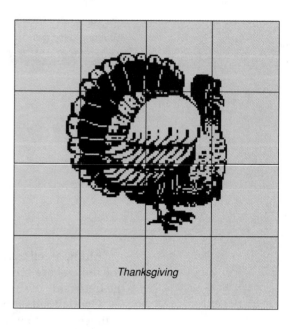

*Thanksgiving*

computer graphics program, can use it as a tool that extends abilities in a low tech environment. Other examples include banners that can be created on continuous-form computer paper by programs such as Print Shop.

Some programs take an original (either scanned into the computer or created in a paint program) and allow the user to enlarge it to huge dimensions. The image is printed in segments on four to sixteen (or more) standard 8 1/2 in. by 11 in. sheets of paper that are tiled or assembled into the finished product. The example in Figure 4–13 shows an image printed on sixteen sheets of paper. The sheets are assembled and fastened to each other to form a poster approximately 34 in. by 44 in. . Graphics programs such as these enhance the creative ability of students and teachers and facilitate visual communication.

## DESKTOP PRESENTATION

**Desktop presentation** signifies the design, creation, and display of textual and graphic information under the control of a personal computer. It has gained favor in boardrooms, business meetings, civic luncheons, as well as in elementary, secondary, and college classrooms. It is gradually replacing traditional overhead transparencies and slide shows as a medium of projected visual information. To take advantage of this new electronic medium, the user must have access to software that permits the creation or import of text and graphic images and its subsequent organization and display. The medium also requires appropriate hardware to project the images for viewing by the selected audience.

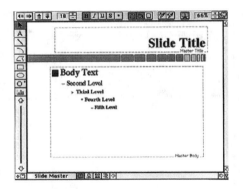 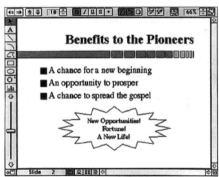

**FIGURE 4–14**
*Master slide and slide view*

### Presentation Software

A number of presentation software packages are available. Microsoft PowerPoint and Aldus Persuasion are among the most popular ones available for both the Macintosh and Windows platforms. These programs provide the user with word processing, outlining, drawing, graphing, and presentation management tools. They also readily accept existing material originally prepared by other word processor, spreadsheet, and graphics programs. In addition to projecting visuals on a screen under software control, the user can print outlines of the presentation, speaker's notes, and handouts.

The software usually allows the user to switch among four different views as the presentation is being created. The illustration of those four views, shown in Figure 4–14 and Figure 4–15, were prepared by Microsoft PowerPoint and are representational of those created by other desktop presentation programs.

The *slide view* shows a single visual and allows the user to type text and draw shapes, as illustrated in the right-hand panel of Figure 4–14. Material created with word processors, graphics programs, and spreadsheets can be imported into most desktop presentation programs. Professionally designed templates including borders, bullets, and gradient fills are provided to the user. Graphics elements such as the starburst shown in the right-hand panel of Figure 4–14 can be easily created to draw the viewer's attention. The presentation management tool is a unique element provided by this software. This tool allows the user to create a slide master, shown in the left panel of Figure 4–14, to format all of the visuals in the presentation. It saves the user considerable time in that the slide master eliminates the need to recreate repetitive elements such as the patterned border composed of gradient bars used in both panels of Figure 4–14.

The *outline view*, shown in the left panel of Figure 4–15, displays all of the title and body text of the entire presentation. As the user types in titles

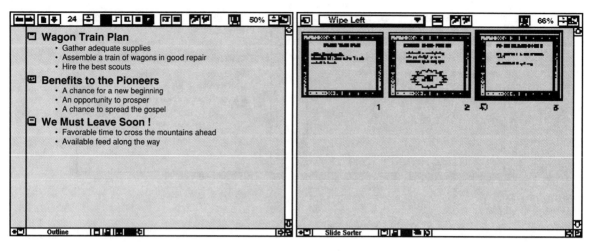

**FIGURE 4–15**
*Outline view and slide sorter view*

and text the software creates the visuals. As in any outline, the user can move paragraphs and headers up or down a level.

The *slide sorter view,* shown in the right-hand panel of Figure 4–15, allows the user to view miniature replicas of the visuals and arrange them in any desired order. Notice the visual titled "Benefits to the Pioneers," shown in Figure 4–14, was created as the second slide and labeled as such in the lower part of its screen. Examining Figure 4–15, notice that it is the second slide in the sequence. While in the slide sorter view, it could be moved to any other position. Visuals can also be easily copied in this view to be used in other presentations.

The presentation management tool allows the user to select transition effects from a wide variety of **wipes** and **dissolves** between visuals. A wipe is a transition effect that allows a second visual to gradually replace the first visual being viewed. The visuals in the presentation shown in Figure 4–15 employ a *Wipe Left* as indicated at the top of the right-hand panel. The following visual will enter the screen at the right and move leftward across the preceding visual. Other common wipes include a *scroll,* acting either vertically from top or bottom of the screen or from side to side; a *barn door,* acting horizontally from or toward the center of the screen; a *venetian blind,* acting as its name implies by breaking up the image in horizontal slats and introducing the new one; and an *iris,* which is a circular effect acting from or toward the center of the screen.

The *notes view* permits the user to create speaker's notes as the rest of the presentation is being created. These notes, as shown in Figure 4–16, contain a reduced image of the appropriate visual and can be printed.

**Wagon Train Plan**

■ Gather adequate supplies
■ Assemble a train of wagons in good repair
■ Hire the best scouts

Remember to include spare wagon parts along with ammunition, food, medical supplies and light weight items to barter with settlers and indians along the way.

Don't accept a wagon in the train that looks like it won't make the trip.

Try to find at least one scout who has crossed the trail before.

**Wagon Train Plan**

• Gather adequate supplies.
• Assemble a train of wagons in good repair.
• Hire the best scouts

**Benefits to the Pioneers**

• A chance for a new beginning.
• An opportunity to prosper.
• A chance to spread the gospel.

**We Must Leave Soon!**

• Favorable time to cross the mountains ahead.
• Available grazing along the way

**FIGURE 4–16**
*Notes and handouts printed from the presentation program*

Handouts can be printed with usually one, three, or six visuals per page. The right-hand panel of Figure 4–16 shows that printing three visuals per page leaves ample room for the audience to take their own notes.

Following the guidelines in Figure 4–17 will ensure a more effective presentation. Remember that the visual is an important part of the presentation but you, as the presenter, are the most significant element.

## Display Devices

Display devices for desktop presentations must be appropriate to the size of the audience. A twenty-five-inch color monitor may be adequate for viewing by a small group of a dozen or less viewers. Larger group sizes call for devices such as video projectors or overhead display panels capable of displaying larger images.

Video projectors capable of handling data transmitted from computers range from large, expensive devices usually permanently mounted to

**FIGURE 4-17**

*Guidelines for preparing*
*effective presentation*
*graphics*

- Begin and end your presentation with a blank screen.
- Use of generous margins will help focus attention on content.
- Use of a single background or frame will unify the presentation.
- Limit yourself to two or three colors on one screen.
- Use bright colors to emphasize important points.
- Use color contrasts effectively (e.g., yellow on blue is highly visible, while red on black is barely readable).
- Limit yourself to two typefaces in one presentation.
- Use an attention-grabbing title screen.
- Use single words and short phrases on the screen to focus attention on the details provided orally.
- Check carefully for spelling/typing errors.
- Use all uppercase letters only in major headings and make them a slightly larger size.
- Place headings at the same location in successive screens.
- Use **dingbats** (bullets, check marks, or other symbols) to organize lists.
- Use drop shadows and gradient fills for interesting visual effects.
- Use transition effects (wipes and dissolves) that add a graceful style to your presentation and help your audience to follow your train of thought.

the ceiling to small, portable, fairly inexpensive ones often fastened for the sake of security to a rolling equipment cart. In a school setting, these are often housed in a library media center and circulated from there. Most video projectors are capable of accepting an R-G-B signal or an NTSC composite signal, which is a common standard. Many are capable of accepting both. Just as printers are configured to accept parallel or serial transmissions (or both), video display devices accept a certain signal transmission.

Overhead display panels, often called LCD panels, are fast becoming one of the large image display devices of choice. They are reasonably priced and new ones, such as the one shown in Figure 4–18, employ an active matrix, capable of displaying high resolution, color, and full motion. They are placed on the stage of the overhead projector. They require a considerably stronger light source than the typical overhead transparency and, in fact, may require the dimming of room lights for the projected image to be fully appreciated.

### Desktop Presentation as a Tool

Conforming to the tool definition explored earlier, desktop presentation, with its ability to design, create, and display information under the control of a personal computer, extends the capability of the user to communicate. This new electronic medium requires users to access software that permits

**FIGURE 4–18**
*An LCD display panel on an overhead projector.*
(Photograph courtesy of InFocus Systems, Inc.)

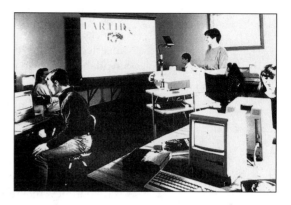

them to design and create the message and to use appropriate hardware to display the message effectively. The presentation, once created, may be saved in a single file on disk, making it a very portable presentation indeed. Once again as we note decreasing equipment size and increasing portability, we see evidence of the paradigm shifts described in Chapter 1 as we compare a presenter carrying file folders full of overhead transparencies or carousel trays full of slides to one carrying a floppy disk in a pocket or purse.

## Summary

Some graphics programs facilitate the creation of graphics for bulletin boards and other displays. Some generate drawings, others automatically generate line graphs, bar graphs, or pie charts from numeric data. Programs and video boards are available that allow computer screens to be recorded on videotape to serve as titles, credits, animated graphics, or instructional text screens. Although these materials can be created in other ways, the computer makes it easier and less time consuming and thereby stimulates teachers to maximize their creative efforts.

Optical scanners read light reflected from the surface of an object to be copied. Graphics tablets allow the user to create or trace figures or drawings on the surface of the tablet with a stylus that provides far greater control than a mouse. A video digitizer accompanied by a digital camera or a video camcorder allows the user to record still images that can be transmitted into the computer, manipulated, and stored on disk as graphic files.

In bit-mapped graphics, the computer-generated image is composed of bits or screen picture elements called pixels that are turned on and bits that are off. One of the inherent drawbacks of bit-mapped graphics is that the size of the pixel limits the sharpness or resolution of the drawing regardless of the resolution of the monitor or printer used to display the graphic.

In vector or object-oriented graphics, each picture element is a separate object and can be changed independently. The user of a draw program creates objects of different shapes, adjusts line thickness and applies patterns to the objects, then organizes or groups them into new, more complex objects. Text inserted in a drawing remains an editable and movable object. Clip art is available as files in paint or draw formats on disk for use in computer graphics programs.

In designing any communication, whether it be oral, written, or graphic, the sender of the message must know the anticipated audience that is to receive it and design the communication appropriately in order to capture attention and get information across clearly and convincingly.

Signs, posters, maps, banners can be easily created; so can overhead transparency masters. There are six basic design rules to keep in mind when creating overhead transparencies. For many years, teachers have created thermal transparencies using a process employing thermal film that is chemically treated on one side with an emulsion that will produce a black, red, green, blue, or purple line. It is a line medium in that it will not reproduce solid areas, fine patterns, or photographic halftones well. The original or master being copied must have a significant amount of carbon in its ink in order to reflect the heat to the film's emulsion in the copier. Prints from laser printers work well as transparency masters but those from dot-matrix printers must be photocopied.

The first step in designing transparency masters in computer graphics requires the user to create the entire drawing and save the document. The second step involves deciding what elements of the total drawing should be presented first. All other elements are deleted from the drawing and the file is saved under a different name. The third and subsequent steps require the user to open the original complete document, delete unwanted elements, and save the results as a new file with a different name.

Desktop presentation signifies the design, creation, and display of textual and graphic information under the control of a personal computer. The software provides the user with word processing, outlining, drawing, graphing, and presentation management tools. In addition to projecting visuals on a screen under software control, the user can print outlines of the presentation, speaker's notes, and handouts. Display devices for desktop presentations, such as large color monitors, video projectors, or overhead display panels, must be appropriate to the size of the audience.

Conforming to the tool definition explored earlier, desktop presentation, with its ability to design, create, and display information under the control of a personal computer, extends the capability of the user to communicate. The presentation, once created, may then be saved in a single file on disk, making it a very portable presentation. Once again as we note decreasing equipment size and increasing portability, we see evidence of the paradigm shifts described in Chapter 1.

# Chapter Exercises

1. Using a paint program, create a cover page for a report. How does the graphic you created heighten the reader's interest in the report?
2. Write a brief report on a topic of current national interest and use a graphic captured from a scanner to illustrate your report.
3. Using the draw component of an integrated package or a stand-alone draw program, create a set of informational or directional signs for a school lunchroom.
4. Using the same program, create a set of bookmarks that might be placed in a school library to promote books worth reading.
5. Using a paint program, draw the outline map of your state. Add the major cities and other significant geographical features such as rivers and mountains. Print the results as a base cell and two overlays. Explain why you divided the elements the way that you did.

# Glossary

**bit-mapped graphics**   Computer-generated images composed of bits or screen pixels that are turned on (black or colored) and bits that are turned off (white or clear).

**clip art**   Prepared files of black and white or color line drawings and half-tone images available on disk in the draw or paint format for use in computer graphics programs that are intended to be incorporated into the user's own original work.

**decoding**   The process of giving meaning to data being communicated.

**desktop presentation**   Software that facilitates the organization of text and graphics into computer screens with the intention that the user will project them to an audience.

**dingbats**   Symbols such as bullets or check marks used to organize lists.

**dissolve**   A transition effect between visuals. The original visual fades into another one and is replaced by it.

**encoding**   The process of selecting symbols and other elements to communicate desired information.

**gradient fill**   A pattern that begins with a certain opacity or density of pattern at a determined point and gradually fades to one that is less dense or increases to one that is more dense.

**object-oriented graphics**   Computer-generated images determined by formulas that create discrete objects of a certain size and position.

**vector graphics**   See object-oriented graphics.

**wipe**   A transition effect between visuals. One visual appears to slide over another, replacing it.

## Notes & Suggested Readings

Duren, P. (1990–91, December–January). Enhancing inquiry skills using graphics software. *The Computing Teacher, 18*(4), 23–25.

Kinnman, D. E. (1993, March). LCD panels: The next generation. *Technology & Learning, 13*(6), 44–50.

Lake, D. (1990, May). Patrick's visual: A book report using presentation software. *The Computing Teacher, 17*(8), 54–55.

Mathis, J. (1988, October). Turning data into pictures. *The Computing Teacher, 15*(2), 40–48.

Metzler, B. (1990, April). Who can draw with a Macintosh? *The Computing Teacher, 17*(7), 21–23.

Robinson, P. (1993, March). How to warm up a crowd: Desktop presentation software. *New Media, 3*(3), 60–69.

Williams, S. K. (1991, January). Something for everyone. *Teacher Magazine,* 40–43.

# 5

# INCREASING PRODUCTIVITY THROUGH PROBLEM SOLVING

All educators are decision makers. Administrators are involved in the planning and implementation of curriculum decisions. They help to select and provide continuing education and training opportunities for their staff. They take part in establishing rules and regulations that affect students' safety and welfare as well as their education. They manage the physical plant of the school. In many school districts throughout the country site-based management teams or committees composed of administrators, teachers, classified staff, parents, and in some instances students are empowered to make decisions in areas that were formerly the exclusive province of school administrators.

Teachers are constantly faced with the management of instructional units and the creation of teaching materials. They must analyze their student population and match student needs with instructional materials. They must then track the students through the learning material and assess their progress. Each of these tasks requires the teacher to solve problems, many of which could be performed with the assistance of a computer. If the computer is to be an effective tool in increasing productivity, fundamental questions to be answered by the teacher are, "When do I use a computer?" "Will using a computer save time?" "Will it allow me to perform tasks that might otherwise be beyond my skills?" "Can I get better, more complete, and more accurate information by using a computer or will it just complicate my life?"

Using computers in education implies that software will be used. It is indeed the effective use of that software that can increase productivity. Viewing a computer program as a potential solution to a problem, we need to understand the application of computer programs and how they function so that we can better select, evaluate, and use available programs. As computer users, we need to be thoroughly familiar with the process of problem solving. Most of us will never choose to become computer programmers, but as educators we do need to be good users of computer programs, and we do need to acquire skill in the development of problem-solving specifications.

Problem-solving activities are part of everyday life. Many of us, however, do not approach this process systematically, and as a result, solutions may often be hit or miss. This chapter will examine two different approaches to the problem-solving process. We should be able to apply a systematic technique when confronted with the need to solve a problem, whether it be to prepare a lesson plan, develop a study guide, give a demonstration, design a test, or effectively use application software. The processes discussed in this chapter are appropriate for the analysis of most decisions that teachers and administrators make on a regular basis.

Looking beyond our own needs as educators, problem-solving skill is an essential skill that we must help our students develop. The constructivist point of view (Bagley & Hunter, 1992) holds that students interact with the real-life experiences that surround them and construct mental structures that provide an understanding of their environment. If students are to build these mental structures, they must refine skills needed to solve problems they will encounter whether they are working individually or in cooperative learning groups.

If problem solving is examined from the aspect of learning, the application of the computer is truly multifaceted. A balance of work and play must be achieved if learning is to be enjoyable. The childhood refrain of "All work and no play makes Jack a dull boy!" is appropriate to how we view the applying the computer. Restricting our use of the computer only to work is a sure way to promote drudgery and boredom. Restricting it only to play will get very little accomplished. A balance, on the other hand, will allow us to accomplish tasks, to experiment with ideas, to test our intuition, to marvel at some of our accomplishments, and to solve problems in an enjoyable manner.

Not all people approach problem solving in the same fashion. There is no single best approach. Extensive work done by Anthony Gregorc in the development and application of his Learning Style Delineator (Tompson & O'Brien, 1991) suggests that individuals' thinking patterns and learning styles can be measured along two continua, *abstract* to *concrete* and *sequential* to *random*, yielding the four polar attributes of *abstract random*, *abstract sequential*, *concrete random*, and *concrete sequential*. In reality most individuals possess all four traits to some extent, though they usually exhibit a predominant tendency toward one or more. Linear-thinking, sequential individuals feel comfortable with problem-solving strategies that follow a neat, orderly process. Divergent-thinking randoms feel stifled by those strategies and tend to employ some that are less confining. Both approaches are valid and should be valued. In either case, problem-solving skills and strategies are important. This chapter will suggest strategies to appeal to either type of individual.

When examining tasks to be carried out at least in part on a computer, we need to determine what the computer must do to produce the solution. After deciding what must be done, we can select the appropriate software to carry out the tasks.

## Advanced Organizers

1. What is problem solving?
2. How do problem-solving strategies relate to your learning style?
3. How might different strategies be implemented?
4. What is task analysis?
5. How should a task be analyzed?
6. How can a task be translated into an algorithm or a set of algorithms?
7. How is a flowchart constructed?
8. How can you as a teacher or administrator apply computer programs to solve problems?

## PROBLEM SOLVING

When examining problems for which the solution may be partly carried out on a computer, we must first be sure that we truly understand the task and then determine what the computer and the software must do to address the solution. Only then can we select the appropriate program and apply it effectively.

### A Nonlinear Approach to Problem Solving

The process of problem solving might be approached by an individual with a **random** learning style in a manner similar to the simple three-part process illustrated in Figure 5–1. "Given" is the information in my possession. What do I know about the situation or job at hand? What are its component parts? What are the restrictions or limitations with which I must cope? "To Find" is the information I am seeking. What output do I need? What are the results I am trying to achieve? When will I know that I have

**FIGURE 5–1**

*A random-style individual's approach to problem solving*

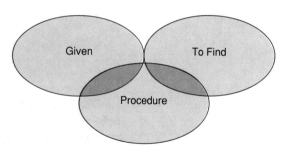

achieved them? "Procedure" is the method I am going to employ to reach my goal. How will I achieve results? What strategy should I develop? What tool should I use?

Apply the process just described to the following simple word problem: A boy takes home $4.00 an hour from a weekend job. How many hours must he work in order to be able to purchase a $300 bicycle?

| | |
|---|---|
| Given: | Individual is male (not relevant to solving problem). |
| | Take-home pay is $4.00 per hour. |
| | Work is on weekend only (not relevant to solving problem). |
| | Cost of the bicycle is $300. |
| To Find: | Number of hours of work required to earn enough to purchase the bicycle. |
| Procedure: | Divide the cost of the bicycle ($300) by the hourly take-home rate of $4.00 (300 / 4.00 = ?). |

Consider another example, writing an article on a particular topic. What are the tasks related to writing a successful article?

| | |
|---|---|
| Given: | Identification of the target audience. |
| | Background information on the topic. |
| | Range of thoughts on the topic. |
| | Viewpoint or bias on the subject matter. |
| | Writing skills. |
| To Find: | Clear, concise, and convincing article. |
| Procedure: | Choose a presentation format and style. |
| | Organize thoughts clearly. |
| | Prepare a draft copy. |
| | Revise draft until satisfied. |

Now consider another example, the creation of a computerized grade book to report student progress in your classroom. What is involved in this problem? What are the related tasks?

| | |
|---|---|
| Given: | Student names. |
| | Student performance on a variety of measures. |
| | Target audience of students and their parents. |
| To Find: | Complete, accurate report of student progress in a timely manner. |
| Procedure: | Select presentation format. |
| | Choose software that facilitates the selected presentation format. |
| | Organize relevant data clearly. |
| | Summarize performance measures appropriately. |

This approach to problem solving allows divergent-thinking individuals room to determine their own pattern without having a hierarchical structure imposed on them. They can contemplate the information in their possession and examine it in light of what they understand to be the desired goals. They can then consider an alternative from several options. They can reject an alternative that at first seems appealing and go on to another one.

## A Linear Approach to Problem Solving

A problem-solving strategy that might appeal more to a **sequential** learner is illustrated in Figure 5–2. It consists of two phases, the *analysis* phase and the *synthesis* phase. In the analysis phase we develop a clear definition and understanding of the problem and of the component tasks that relate to the problem. In the synthesis phase we plan our strategy and carry out the solution to the problem. Evaluation provides feedback that could modify decisions made in both the analysis and synthesis phases.

If the problem is to give a speech on computer literacy, the analysis phase would consist of defining computer literacy within the context of the speech, assessing the knowledge level of the audience, determining what points must be made and how to make them. The synthesis phase would be the writing, polishing, and delivery of the speech. Audience reaction or feedback would be a measure of whether or not the goal was reached.

### Analysis Phase

To more clearly understand the process, let's take a look at both phases in greater detail. **Analysis** is defined as the separation of a whole into its component parts for the purpose of examination and interpretation. As shown in Figure 5–3, we need to clearly examine the problem, define *what* must be done, and clearly identify the specific tasks involved during the analysis phase.

Defining the Problem.   The first step in solving a problem is making sure that you understand the nature of the problem and exactly what is

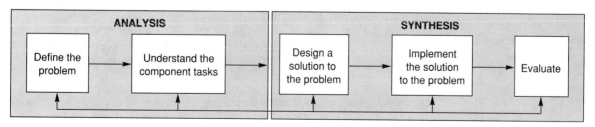

**FIGURE 5–2**
*A sequential-style approach to problem solving*

**FIGURE 5–3**
*Analysis phase of problem solving*

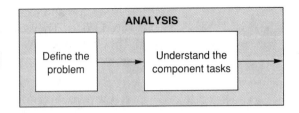

expected in its solution. Be sure that you have a reasonable basis for making and proceeding on your assumptions. One of the biggest mistakes made in solving problems is to make assumptions about what is supposed to happen and to neglect the verification of those assumptions. In defining the problem you will establish a need. A need is the discrepancy between the present state and the desired state. It is an evaluation of the "what is" and the "what ought to be."

Imagine a person saying, "It's springtime! I guess I'll have to get the soil in my garden ready for planting." What does this statement signify to you? What need is expressed? Careful—don't jump to unwarranted conclusions! Do you know anything about the person's physical characteristics? Are there other unstated limitations that might affect the conditions suggested in the statement? Often we formulate a solution without even understanding the problem. We have an answer before really understanding the question.

In the statement above, the implication is that the soil is not in a proper state. The soil has probably become too compacted over the winter and must be loosened and its texture smoothed in order to facilitate planting. If that is indeed the case, we *need* to till the soil in some manner to change its present undesirable state to a desired state. To achieve this goal, we must analyze the task at hand.

A reasonable knowledge of gardening would tell us that the person intends to grow plants and that some form of soil preparation is in order. We don't know much else. Is the garden a window flower box, a 2 ft. by 4 ft. flower bed on a city lot, or a half-acre vegetable garden? Without being able to determine this, we certainly could not select the proper tool to till the soil prior to planting. Try turning over a half-acre of soil using nothing but a hand trowel! How about tilling a 2 ft. by 4 ft. flower bed with a 7-hp power tiller! In order to select the proper tool, we must understand the task that it is being called upon to perform. We must assess the need and perform a task analysis.

**Understanding the Component Tasks.**   When first examined, many problems seem to be so complex that they defy solution. Should you find yourself in this situation, start by examining the output required and determine what is necessary to produce this result. An outlining strategy is often helpful in reaching a better understanding of component tasks. The top-down outlining approach is one that proceeds from global to specific

| Problem Statement |
| :--- |
| 1. **Task 1** |
| • Subtask 1 |
| • Subtask 2 |
| • |
| 2. **Task 2** |
| • Subtask 1 |
| • Subtask 2 |
| • |
| 3. **Task 3** |
| • Subtask 1 |
| • Subtask 2 |
| • |

**FIGURE 5–4**

*Using an outline to under-stand component tasks*

concerns and facilitates systematic analysis. In order to better understand a complex task, attempt to simplify the problem and to break it down into subtasks. If possible, simplify each of the subtasks. When you have achieved what you believe to be the subtask's simplest form, proceed to the synthesis phase and design a solution to address that simple task. Expand the solution to cope with the relationships between the subtasks until you are effectively addressing the complex problem.

Let's apply the outlining method shown in Figure 5–4 to better understand the statement, "It's springtime! I guess I'll have to get the soil in my garden ready for planting." The following questions would be addressed: Is the soil ready to till? Has debris been removed? Is the soil dry enough so that it will turn over in a fine, smooth consistency? What size is the garden and are there any time considerations? What are the physical limitations of the gardener, if any? What tools are available? Considering answers to the previous questions, what is the proper tool to use? The component task analysis might resemble Figure 5–5.

The most difficult task a student faces in organizing a term paper is where to begin, how much to say, and where to end. The initial struggle is one of defining the problem. Once the beginning and ending parameters have been identified, a topic outline similar to the task outline suggested in Figure 5–4 should be prepared to ensure that the important points will be covered in a logical manner. At this stage, attention should be focused on *what* to say and not be overly concerned with *how* to say it.

In an effort to bring the problem-solving process into sharper focus and to understand component tasks, let's consider the management of an instructional area such as a classroom. Dealing effectively with such a broad problem calls for making a list of all the aspects of a classroom management system. The emphasis should be on identifying the tasks that a teacher must do, not on how to do them.

Following is a list of some of the management tasks that classroom teachers routinely encounter:

**FIGURE 5–5**

*Analyzing component tasks*

| Till the Garden |
| :--- |
| 1. Prepare the soil |
| • Remove any debris |
| • Test moisture content of the soil |
| 2. Select the tool |
| • Determine time constraints |
| • Evaluate physical limitations of gardener |
| • Assess area of garden |
| • Choose from available tools |

- Keep inventory of materials for which they are accountable
- Create lesson plans
- Design worksheets
- Develop tests
- Record attendance
- Record student progress
- Devise a means to communicate effectively with parents

For each of those tasks, a more detailed list of subtasks must be created in order to determine the structure of the input data and to determine the form of the output. We might phrase these subtasks in the form of questions. Consider once again the task of recording student progress, for example. The recording system might well take the form of a computerized grade book. The following questions must be answered *before* you can sit down at a computer and begin to solve the problem:

- How many different classes will be entered in the grade book?
- How many students will be in each class?
- How will student names be entered? (last name first?)
- How many different activity types will be allowed for each class? (e.g., quiz, test, project, portfolio, lab, etc.?)
- How many different grades will be entered into each activity type?
- How are grades to be calculated? (will they be weighted?)
- How are grades to be reported?

The tasks listed above could certainly be further expanded, refined, and organized in an outline fashion similar to the one suggested in Figure 5–4. As you attack the problem of preparing a computerized grade book, you must make sure that you understand what is required of the software *before* you attempt to solve the problem. You may otherwise select the wrong software or spend a lot of time and effort producing something that will not meet expectations.

### Synthesis Phase

**Synthesis** is constructive and is defined as combining elements to form a coherent whole. As indicated in Figure 5–6, the primary purpose of the synthesis phase of problem solving is to help ensure that solutions designed to address the identified tasks are carried out in an effective and efficient manner and that the results are evaluated. When solutions involve

**FIGURE 5–6**

*Synthesis phase of problem solving*

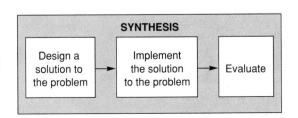

use of the computer, you must ascertain that the software chosen will meet the specified need and that it will be applied in such a way as to produce the necessary results. Having defined *what* must be done and identified tasks, we can now determine *how* each task can be carried out. Any solution to a problem should be examined to see if the solution is practical. Almost every problem can be solved in more than one way. The user must decide on the best way for the given situation.

Designing a Solution to the Problem.    Top-down design requires that having identified your broad goal, you formulate the execution of each identified task and subtask that relates to the goal and prescribe the proper sequence of action. Develop each task fully and tie the tasks together in a fashion that effectively addresses the major goal.

The solution to the problem consists of a sequence of actions. There are certain tasks that must be done first, second, third, and so on. Develop a list and check out alternate sequences of actions. A common mistake made in solving problems is the tendency to neglect to check perceptions and to jump to conclusions without the proper examination of alternatives and the proper analysis of the preferred solution. Except for the simplest of problems, the solution will not be composed of a single task but of many interrelated ones. Your responsibility is to outline an acceptable sequence of actions. Your primary concern is to establish an order of events that will lead to the solution of the stated problem.

The Algorithm.    Since infancy, we have been learning how to act, how to do things. We learn to "expect" certain behavior. Much of what we do unconsciously, we once had to learn. Tasks such as how to talk to each other, how to dress, how to walk, how to recognize colors, have for most of us been reduced to "automatic" actions. We have formed in our mind a **program** that takes care of these tasks without conscious thought. However, each of the tasks we do unconsciously requires that we have certain primitive abilities. If we are color-blind, we cannot learn how to recognize colors. Each tasks must be carried out through the sequencing of the **primitive actions** we are capable of doing. These primitive actions are fundamental ones that cannot be further broken down into yet simpler components.

An **algorithm** is simply a description of a structured sequence of clear and effective actions that will produce a result. Cooking recipes, operating instructions for appliances, directions for assembling an item, instructions for leaving a building during a fire drill—all are examples of algorithms.

In education many of the subject area divisions of the curriculum are based on learning how to solve problems. Mathematics could never have been developed without logical sequences of steps for solving problems or proving theorems. Music requires a definite sequence of notes to be recognizable. Any structured action or product is dependent on a sequence of steps. The sequence of steps, or program, for the event that occurs may or may not require that we consciously think through the component series of required procedures, processes, or facts. In effect, when we do consciously think through a process, we are reloading the program stored in our long-term memory that will carry out the task.

The computer is a machine that is capable of the sequential performance or execution of commands to perform certain tasks, providing that those tasks can be defined in terms of basic primitive actions. The computer, having both programmed logic and memory, might be considered an "intelligent" machine.

After you have described the order of tasks to be accomplished, you have a good idea of *what* must be done, but you may not know *how* to carry out the tasks in order to achieve the desired result. You must now break down each task into individual steps. Two excellent outlining tools, the **written algorithm** and the **flowchart,** are at your disposal. Let's first examine the use of the written algorithm, a tool for the development of a sequence of executable steps that can be used to solve the tasks. Although both outlining tools are sequential in nature, the less formally and tightly structured written algorithm may be more appealing to individuals with random learning styles.

The Written Algorithm.    In writing the proper algorithm(s) to accomplish your task, you must carefully examine alternatives. Most tasks that you will assign to the computer (e.g., entering course names, student names, student grades and sorting lists) can be done in a number of different ways. You need to select the best choice. Referring to the definition of an algorithm, in choosing a plan for solving a problem, you must state the plan in a sequence of steps. This implies a defined starting point, a prescribed means of moving to the next step in the sequence, and a defined ending point.

Each operation must be written in a *clear and effective* manner. *Clear,* used in this context, means that the operation must be understandable to the person and/or the machine executing the algorithm. *Effective* means that some distinct method exists for performing that operation:

> Multiply 17 by 2
> Go to the principal's office
> Get on the school bus

These are all effective operations. We could easily carry them out. On the other hand, examine the following operations, which are not effective:

> Divide 14 by 0
> Wait −5 minutes
> Paint the perfect sunset

These are not effective operations because they either do not exist, cannot be done in a finite amount of time, or we have no idea how to assess the result.

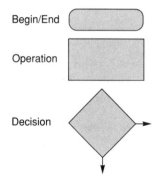

Begin/End

Operation

Decision

**FIGURE 5–7**
*Some common flowchart symbols*

The Flowchart.    A flowchart is a visual representation of the problem-solving process. It is often referred to as a logic diagram. Being visual, it is constructed out of symbols of various shapes. Each symbol represents a unique function within the diagram. It is not the purpose of this chapter to teach you all there is to know about either written algorithms or flowcharts. You are simply being introduced to a few flowchart symbols in Figure 5–7 so that you may gain a better understanding of problem synthesis. A starting point as well as the ending point, both represented by an oval symbol, must be identified for the process. The operation, denoted by the rectangular symbol, describes an action. At any point in the process where a decision must be made, the diamond is used to indicate that decision point. Arrows emanating from different points of the diamond allow for multiple paths reflecting the decision made. Figure 5–8 demonstrates the use of both outlining techniques. It offers a side-by-side comparison of their application to solve the problem of preparing soil for planting.

Once you have satisfactorily completed the outline and have written algorithms for each task, you are ready to select the appropriate application software. Excellent software can be found to accomplish most communication and management tasks. After the software has been chosen the data input routines, processing procedures, and output requirements can be developed according to your design.

Error Trapping.    **Error trapping** is a process of designing safeguards into your solution. In tilling the garden, you might pause after every second pass to check the soil consistency. In writing the article, you might periodically check your writing against your outline. You might verify the accuracy and authenticity of your citations. If certain values must be excluded when using the computer, then a technique must be employed to ensure that the unwanted data cannot be entered into the program. In error trapping, a designer makes sure that entry of incorrect data is either refused or ignored by the program. An example of common error trapping in drill and practice software would be a program asking the student to press the Y key to indicate yes or the N key to indicate no in response to a question and not accepting any other key press but the Y or N. This prevents potential errors that could cause the program to execute incorrectly. An example of error trapping data entry in a student records database would be to designate a range of values from 4 to 0 in a field designed to store a numerical equivalent of an A to F course grade. Limiting data entry to this range would catch typing errors such as a double key press that might attempt to enter a nonsensical value of 33, for example.

Implementing the Solution to the Problem.    Having analyzed the problem and then designed an acceptable solution to the problem, we must now execute the tasks to solve it. We must till the garden, write the article, or enter grades in our computerized grade book and print reports.

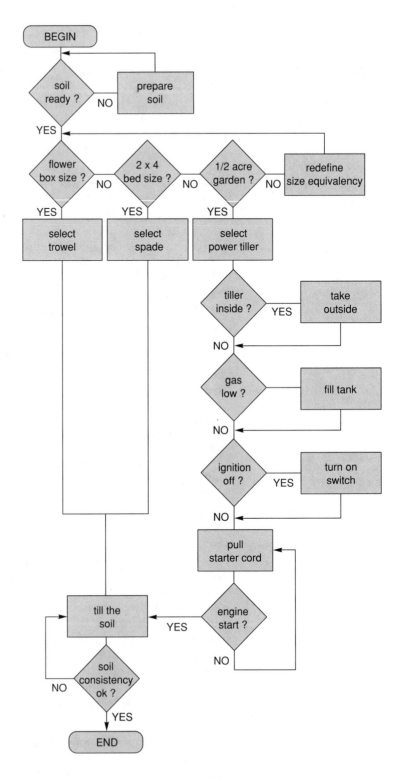

IF soil not ready
THEN prepare soil

IF flower box size
THEN select trowel, ELSE
IF 2'x4' bed size
THEN select spade, ELSE
IF 1/2 acre size
THEN select power tiller, ELSE
redefine size equivalency

IF tiller inside
THEN take it outside

IF gas level is low
THEN fill gas tank

IF ignition is off
THEN turn switch on

REPEAT pulling starter cord
UNTIL engine starts

REPEAT tilling soil
UNTIL soil consistency acceptable

**FIGURE 5–8**
*The written algorithm (left-hand column) and the flowchart (right-hand column) represent outlining techniques*

Debugging the Solution.    **Debugging** is the process of correcting logic and construction errors. In editing the first draft of a term paper, you are in fact debugging it. As you till the garden you make minor adjustments to the depth of the tilling tines or decide to pass over the same area a number of times. After the paper is written, you proofread the document, noting all errors. Then you revise and reprint the paper in a final correct form. Sometimes, under the press of time, you may be satisfied with a less than perfect paper because you know that your reader can overlook a few minor errors and still decipher your meaning. Computers, on the other hand, cannot understand what is not there. The software cannot determine what you have written unless it is expressed in exactly the correct form. An often used debugging procedure is to give the program some test data that will produce known output over the entire range of use. Before entering your students' actual scores into your grade book, you might enter score values that you can compute easily and verify that the computer results are as expected. If the results are other than expected, debugging allows you to verify the correctness of your formula, the appropriateness of the functions you employed, and the logic of your design. This testing determines whether or not the program will always run correctly.

Evaluating the Results.    In tilling the garden, you now examine the soil and determine if it has reached the consistency desired for planting. If the consistency is not yet acceptable, you till once more. In writing an article, this is the review or criticism phase. You might ask a friend, who hopefully has some knowledge of the subject covered in your article, to read your paper and to criticize it. Reacting to the criticism, you might decide to make additional modifications to the article. Once the computer program has been debugged, in a form the software can execute, you must verify that the program produces the desired output. You must determine if your logic was correct.

Documenting the Application.    Although it is unlikely that you would write a procedure manual for tilling the garden or for writing an article, **documentation** that accompanies a computer application provides valuable information for the user. The user of the application must be briefed concerning the intent of the program to prevent false assumptions being made. With software, this could result in using a program in the wrong setting or using it with students who are not prepared. The documentation should clearly point out the intent of the program. Detailed written instructions relative to the utilization of the program can better ensure that the program is used effectively. The instructions supplied with the program must clearly tell the user where data are to be entered, the expected results of that data entry, what needs to be done to get the program to run correctly, and what can and cannot be done with the program.

# Summary

There is no single best approach to problem solving. Individuals' thinking patterns and learning styles can be measured along the continuum *sequential* to *random*. In reality most individuals possess traits that place them somewhere between the extremes, though they usually exhibit a predominant tendency toward one end of the scale or the other. Linear-thinking, sequential individuals feel comfortable with problem-solving strategies that follow a neat, orderly process. Divergent-thinking randoms feel stifled by those strategies and tend to employ some that are less confining.

A nonlinear "Given—To Find—Procedure" approach to problem solving was suggested to allow divergent-thinking individuals room to determine their own pattern without having a hierarchical structure imposed on them. A linear problem-solving strategy that might appeal more to a sequential learner, consisting of two phases, the *analysis* phase and the *synthesis* phase, was examined. The analysis phase supports the developing of a clear definition and understanding of the problem and its component tasks. The synthesis phase is the planning of strategy and carrying out of the solution to the problem. Evaluation provides feedback that could modify decisions made in both the analysis and synthesis phases.

In defining a problem, a need is established as the discrepancy between the present state and the desired state. An outlining strategy is often helpful in reaching a better understanding of a problem's component tasks. The top-down outlining approach is one that proceeds from global to specific concerns and facilitates systematic analysis. In order to better understand a complex task, attempt to simplify the problem and to break it down into subtasks.

In the synthesis phase an algorithm is defined as a description of a structured sequence of clear and effective actions that will produce a result. The written algorithm and the flowchart were examined as two excellent outlining tools.

Error trapping is a process of designing safeguards into a solution. It is often accomplished by controlling data entry in computer programs. Debugging is the process of correcting logic and construction errors. An often used debugging procedure consists of giving the program some test data that will produce known output over the entire range of use.

Software documentation provides valuable information for the user. The documentation describes the intent of the program and should provide detailed written instructions relative to its effective use.

# Chapter Exercises

1. Using the nonlinear model suggested in Figure 5–1, analyze the following case: Given a grade book with students names and scores already entered, write a report showing students' progress.

2. Using the linear model suggested in Figure 5–3, perform the task analysis for the following case: Given a grade book with students' names and scores already entered, write a report showing students' progress.
3. Using the linear model suggested in Figure 5–6, perform the task synthesis for exercise 2.
4. Explain why you feel more comfortable with the linear or with the nonlinear model.
5. Using either the linear or nonlinear model as a guide, design your own grade book.
6. "Debugging" is a natural, nonthreatening step in using some computer application software. Discuss the transfer of this process to the regular curriculum process of evaluating and revising student work.
7. What is error trapping?
8. Choose an activity that you are familiar with. Design a flowchart that represents the steps you follow to complete this activity. See if a partner can improve your chart and complete the activity.
9. Using either the linear or nonlinear model as a guide and a word processor as a tool, write a report on the computer's impact on the curriculum.

## Glossary

**algorithm**   A structured sequence of clear and effective operations that will always reach a definite conclusion and produce a result.

**analysis**   The separation of a whole into its component parts for the purpose of examination and interpretation.

**debugging**   The process of removing all logic and construction errors.

**documentation**   Written explanations supporting program maintenance and use.

**error trapping**   The provision for the treatment of incorrect data entry in such a way that it is either refused or ignored by the program.

**flowchart**   A visual representation of the problem-solving process. It is often referred to as a logic diagram.

**primitive action**   The fundamental action that the person or machine performing the operation is capable of directly understanding and executing. An action that does not require being further broken down into component parts.

**program**   A planned sequence of instructions describing steps to be followed in order to perform a task.

**random**   An attribute that allows your mind to perceive and organize information in a nonlinear, holistic manner.

**sequential**   An attribute that allows your mind to perceive and organize information in a linear, methodical, step-by-step manner.

**synthesis**   Combining elements to form a coherent whole.

**written algorithm**   A written sequence of clear and executable steps leading to the solution of a problem.

## Notes & Suggested Readings

Bagley, C., & Hunter, B. (1992, July). Restructuring constructivism and technology: Forging a new relationship. *Educational Technology,* 22–27.

Fagella, K. (1992, January). Solid gold problem solving. *Instructor, 101* (5), 35–37.

Foucar-Szocki, D. L. (1992). *Beyond training: A field test of the American Society for Training & Development's workplace basics.* Staunton, VA: Education and Training Corp.

Gregorc, A. F. (1982). *An adult's guide to style.* Columbia, CT: Gregorc Associates.

Samples, B. Charles, C., & Barnhart, D. (1977). *The wholeschool book: Teaching and learning late in the 20th century.* Reading, MA: Addison Wesley.

Tompson, M. J., & O'Brien, T. P. (1991, April). *Learning styles and achievement in post-secondary classrooms.* Paper presented at the annual conference of the American Educational Research Association, Chicago, IL.

Wheeler, P. J. (1991, April). *Style mismatch or learning disability: A case study.* Paper presented at the annual conference of the American Educational Research Association, Chicago, IL.

Zelazek, J., & Lamson, S. (1992, February). *Action research and the student teacher: A framework for problem solving and reflective thinking.* Paper presented at the annual meeting of the Association of Teacher Educators, Orlando, FL.

# 6

# SPREADSHEETS

The term **spreadsheet** originated in the accounting world to refer to data entered in a column on a large, wide sheet of paper and related, component, or derivative data "spread" across columns in the same row. This ledger sheet or spreadsheet, as it became known, was in fact a two-dimensional paper matrix of rows and columns. Spreadsheets can be used for a wide variety of activities, but most applications of spreadsheets focus on generating numeric information from other numeric information such as creating budgets and income projections, and forecasting needed amounts of equipment or supplies based on a number of factors.

In 1979, Daniel Bricklin and Robert Frankston developed the first electronic spreadsheet for computers. They looked upon it as a visible calculator and thus named their product VisiCalc. Because the accountants who saw VisiCalc demonstrated recognized it as a highly efficient 63 column by 254 row electronic simulation of their favorite paper and pencil tool, they began putting computers on their desks. VisiCalc became known as the program that sold computers. The present-day electronic spreadsheet or simply spreadsheet, as we will now refer to it, has greatly increased its power, size, sophistication and ease of use. It lets the user enter text or values and create formulas that set up relationships between values, which may be governed by the simple arithmetic operators of $+$, $-$, $*$, and $/$ or by sophisticated functions that are expressions of more complex mathematical and statistical formulas. The spreadsheet automatically recalculates all values as the data entries are made, thereby revealing relationships instantaneously.

Why would a teacher use a spreadsheet? One of many classroom applications of spreadsheets is to manage grades. Why not use a commercial grade book program? Teachers manage grades in many different ways. All too often the adoption of a grade book program forces teachers

| | A | B | C | D | E | F | G |
|---|---|---|---|---|---|---|---|
| 1 | Name | Lab 1 | Lab 2 | Test | Midterm | Portfolio | Grade |
| 2 | | 10 | 10 | 100 | 100 | 100 | 100 |
| 3 | Adams, Laura | 9 | 7 | 78 | 75 | 80 | 78 |
| 4 | Alderson, Kathy | 10 | 9 | 98 | 90 | 95 | 95 |
| 5 | Alvarez, Manuel | 10 | 8 | 85 | 80 | 85 | 85 |
| 6 | Drexler, Richard | 9 | 8 | 80 | 80 | 90 | 84 |
| 7 | Kersey, Clyde | 6 | 7 | 75 | 70 | 80 | 73 |
| 8 | Prosser, Peggy | 10 | 10 | 98 | 90 | 95 | 96 |
| 9 | Prosser, Walt | 8 | 8 | 90 | 80 | 80 | 83 |
| 10 | Williams, Andrea | 9 | 9 | 80 | 85 | 80 | 83 |
| 11 | Highest Score | 10 | 10 | 98 | 90 | 95 | 96 |
| 12 | Lowest Score | 6 | 7 | 75 | 70 | 80 | 73 |
| 13 | Average | 8.88 | 8.25 | 85.50 | 81.25 | 85.63 | 85 |

**FIGURE 6–1**
*A spreadsheet used as a grade book*

to change their grading methods to adapt to the software purchased. A spreadsheet, on the other hand, can be custom-designed to the teacher's system.

Consider the example in Figure 6–1. As the classroom teacher uses this grade book spreadsheet, it will continually calculate the student's total point accumulation and display a final score in column G. It is also designed to keep the statistics on each class activity, identifying the highest, lowest, and average score on the activity, giving the teacher information by which to assess the activity. The rows may be sorted in alphabetical order by the student names in column A at any time so as new students are added, the grade book is sorted once again.

## Advanced Organizers

1. What is a spreadsheet and how does it work?
2. How are text and values entered in a spreadsheet?
3. How are formulas created?
4. How can a spreadsheet be used to sort information?
5. How could the problem-solving strategies discussed in Chapter 5 be applied to designing spreadsheets?
6. How might you as a teacher use a spreadsheet as a productivity tool to keep and sort records, calculate numerical data, forecast results of decisions, and analyze information?
7. How can charts be generated from spreadsheet data?

8. Following a linear problem-solving approach, how can a grade book system be developed on a spreadsheet?
9. How can a school library budget be developed on a spreadsheet?

## USING A SPREADSHEET

The illustrations used to explain the operation of spreadsheets are actual screens of Microsoft Excel 3.0 for the Macintosh. It is important to note that most spreadsheets, regardless of program or operating system platform, look and act very much alike. To help visualize the capability of a spreadsheet, consider a grid or matrix made up of many columns and many rows. A spreadsheet is this matrix of lettered columns and numbered rows. As illustrated in Figure 6–2, the intersection of a column and a row is called a **cell** and is named by first the column and then the row designation. The cursor can be moved around through this grid and positioned in any cell. When you click in a cell, an outline appears around it indicating that it has been selected as the **active cell.** In the illustration, the active cell is B2. Notice that the name of the cell also appears in the upper left-hand corner. The primary task when working with spreadsheets is specifying the relationship between the cells.

When an entry (text or a value) is made from the keyboard, it appears in an area at the top of the screen called the **formula bar.** As illustrated in Figure 6–3, B2 is identified as the active cell and the value that has been typed in that cell, 17, also appears in the formula bar, the area across the top of the screen. For obvious reasons, this area is sometimes also referred to as the data entry bar.

Once text, a value, or a formula is entered into a cell, the program must know that you are finished working in that cell and some signal must be given denoting that entry has ended. Fortunately, most programs adhere to the same conventions. In Figure 6–3, the Enter key was pressed. Notice that this action, while denoting the end of data entry in the cell, does not move the cursor from the active cell.

**FIGURE 6–2**
*A cell named B2*

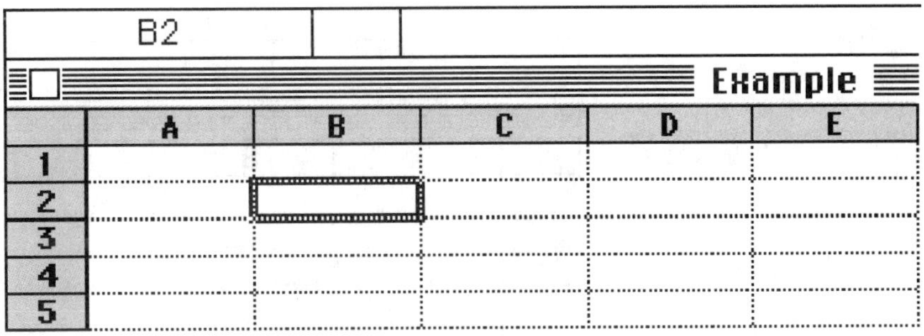

FIGURE 6-3
*Data displayed in the
formula bar*

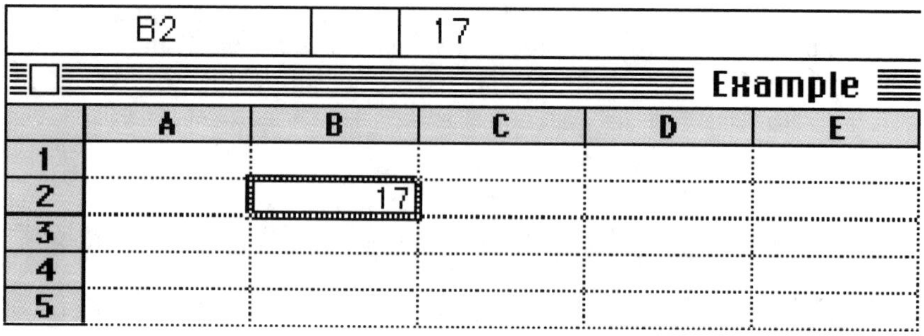

A second way to indicate that you have finished entering data or a formula in the cell is to press the Return key. As shown in Figure 6–4, this will also move the cursor to the next cell down in the same column. Notice that the active cell is then B3 and that its name appears in the top left-hand corner.

A third way to indicate that you have finished working in the cell is to press the Tab key. As shown in Figure 6–5, this will also move the cursor to the next cell to the right in the same row. Notice that the active cell is then C2 and that its name appears in the top left-hand corner. In addition to using the Enter, Return, and Tab keys, you may also press one of the arrow keys to indicate that you have finished working in a cell and wish to move the cursor to one of the four adjacent cells.

One of the real strengths of spreadsheets is the ability to relate cells to each other.

- The data in one cell can be automatically replicated in another by making cells equal to each other.
- Data in one cell can be added to, subtracted from, multiplied or divided by data in another cell.
- Complex mathematical relationships can be expressed in a group of cells.

Formulas are created to express this ability to relate cells.

In Microsoft Works, Excel, or ClarisWorks, formulas always begin with the *equal* sign and reference cells by their name. As you saw in Figure 6–3, the value 17 was entered in cell B2. Figure 6–6 shows the formula =B2 entered in cell A4. This formula will replicate in cell A4 any entry occurring in cell B2.

FIGURE 6-4
*Pressing the Return key to
signify end of entry*

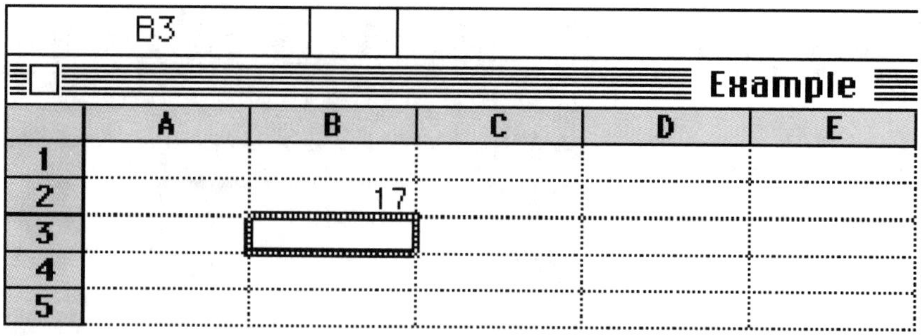

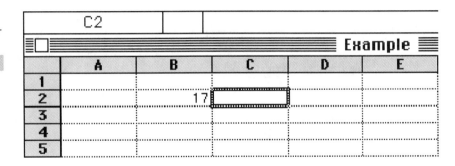

As we see in Figure 6–7, the value 17 was entered in cell B2 and the value 2 was entered in cell C2. An additional cell, D2, was selected as the active cell and the formula entered in it was =B2*C2 [cell B2 (containing the value of 17)*(multiplied by) cell C2 (containing the value of 2)]. Notice that the result of the formula is displayed in cell D2 while the formula itself appears in the formula bar.

Formulas may contain the arithmetic operations of addition, subtraction, multiplication, division, and exponentiation. These are represented by $+$, $-$, $*$, $/$, and $^$, respectively. The operations are performed in the following order: (1) perform all operations inside parentheses, working from inside out if parentheses are nested within each other; (2) compute exponents; (3) perform all multiplications and divisions in order from left to right; (4) perform all additions and subtractions in order from left to right; and finally, (5) perform order operations ($<$, $>$, and $=$).

In the example shown as Figure 6–7, both B2 and C2 are known as *relative* references in the formula since they actually relate to cells one position and two positions to the left of the active formula cell, D2. If, on the other hand, the formula is meant to always refer to an exact cell regardless of the placement of the formula cell within the spreadsheet, the reference is called *absolute* or *fixed*. For example, if the formula must contain a reference to the top cell in the second column, the cell would be entered into a formula as a fixed reference and in most spreadsheets would be typed as $B$1. The dollar signs indicate that the column and row will not change. Should the formula be cut or copied to any other cell, no matter where it is located in the spreadsheet, the fixed reference would remain to cell B1.

FIGURE 6-7
Manipulating the contents
of two other cells in a formula

| D2 | | =B2*C2 |

**Example**

| | A | B | C | D | E |
|---|---|---|---|---|---|
| 1 | | | | | |
| 2 | | 17 | 2 | 34 | |
| 3 | | | | | |
| 4 | 17 | | | | |
| 5 | | | | | |

To assist the user, the spreadsheet program contains a wide variety of built-in functions that can be used simply by referencing them in the desired formula as well as the cells containing the related data. The following are common mathematical functions often used in formulas:

Sum (of values within a cell group)
Average (of values within a cell group)
Minimum (value of the values within a cell group)
Maximum (value of the values within a cell group)
Standard deviation (of values within a cell group)

Spreadsheets are in fact highly specialized databases. They can store and manipulate text and numeric values and are sometimes used instead of database managers when their two-dimensional matrix format (columns and rows) lends itself to convenient data entry and when printed report requirements are minimal. The illustration in Figure 6–8 demonstrates the use of text both as **labels** in row 1 and as data to be manipulated. Spreadsheets are often used as powerful sorting devices to examine information grouped in a variety of ways. Each row in Figure 6–8 contains information about one dinosaur. A multilevel sort has arranged the information by (1) DIET in ascending order, then within that first sort by (2) LENGTH in descending order, and then within those two levels of sort by (3) WEIGHT in descending order. This ability to nest one sort within another adds versatility to the spreadsheet.

FIGURE 6-8
Using a spreadsheet to
sort text

| | A | B | C | D |
|---|---|---|---|---|
| 1 | **NAME** | **LENGTH** | **WEIGHT** | **DIET** |
| 2 | Tyrannosaurus | 50 ft. | 8 tons | Carniverous |
| 3 | Allosaurus | 25 ft. | 4.5 tons | Carniverous |
| 4 | Brachiosaurus | 70 ft. | 80 tons | Herbivorous |
| 5 | Triceratops | 20 ft. | 7 tons | Herbivorous |
| 6 | Stegosaurus | 20 ft. | 4 tons | Herbivorous |

*"I teach research skills by grouping my fifth graders into cooperative learning groups. Each group collects data from the* Sports Illustrated *CD-ROM, then enters the data into a spreadsheet in order to sort it, analyze it, and draw conclusions."*

Doris Holman, 5th Grade Teacher
Fuqua School, Farmville, VA

## PROBLEM SOLVING WITH SPREADSHEETS

Consider the process of problem solving discussed in Chapter 5 that might be approached by an individual with a random learning style. Let us review the nonlinear method and the illustration that was presented. "Given" is the information in your possession. "To Find" is the information you are seeking. What are the results you are trying to achieve? "Procedure" is the method you are going to employ to reach your goal. How will you achieve results? This approach is illustrated in Figure 6–9.

Apply the problem-solving process just reviewed and illustrated in Figure 6–9 to the following simple word problem: A boy takes home $4.00 an hour from a weekend job. How many hours must he work in order to be able to purchase a $300 bicycle?

| | |
|---|---|
| Given: | Take-home pay is $4.00 per hour.<br>Cost of the bicycle is $300. |
| To Find: | Number of hours of work required to earn<br>enough to purchase the bicycle. |
| Procedure: | Divide the cost of the bicycle ($300) by the hourly<br>take-home rate of $4.00 (300 / 4.00 = ?). |

In Figure 6–10, the cost of the bicycle ($300) is entered in cell A2 and the hourly take-home rate ($4.00) is entered in cell B2. The formula = A2 / B2 (cost divided by hourly rate) is entered in cell C2. Upon completing the

**FIGURE 6–9**

*A nonlinear approach to problem solving*

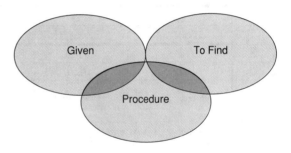

**FIGURE 6–10**

*Using the spreadsheet as an organizer and calculator*

| C2 | | =A2/B2 | |
|---|---|---|---|

**Weekend Job**

| | A | B | C | D |
|---|---|---|---|---|
| 1 | Cost of bicycle | Hourly Rate | Hours to work | |
| 2 | $300 | $4.00 | 75 | |
| 3 | | | | |
| 4 | | | | |
| 5 | | | | |

formula entry, the formula is displayed in the formula bar and the value resulting from the formula as hours to work (75) is displayed in the cell.

Having discovered the number of hours necessary to earn the required amount, the boy might now wish to see the effect of moving to a higher paying job. He could play "what if" and forecast the results of change. As shown in Figure 6–11, by changing the data under "hourly rate" he could immediately see the impact on the number of "hours to work."

**FIGURE 6–11**

*Using the spreadsheet as a forecasting tool*

| C2 | | =A2/B2 | |
|---|---|---|---|

**Weekend Job**

| | A | B | C | D |
|---|---|---|---|---|
| 1 | Cost of bicycle | Hourly Rate | Hours to work | |
| 2 | $300 | $4.50 | 67 | |
| 3 | | | | |
| 4 | | | | |
| 5 | | | | |

Accuracy in measurement may be encouraged by having pairs of students measure a cube. The measurements from each pair may be entered in a spreadsheet as illustrated in Figure 6–12. Even a slight difference in length, width, or height can result in a considerable difference in volume.

| | A | B | C | D | E |
|---|---|---|---|---|---|
| 1 | Group # | Length | Width | Height | Volume |
| 2 | 1 | 4.3 | 3 | 5 | 64.50 |
| 3 | 2 | 4.4 | 2.8 | 4.7 | 57.90 |
| 4 | 3 | 4.8 | 2.9 | 5.1 | 70.99 |

**FIGURE 6–12**

*Using a spreadsheet to promote accuracy*

The following formula would yield the necessary calculation in Figure 6–12:

$En = Bn * Cn * Dn$ [$n$ represents the number of the row]

Once the formula is entered in cell E2, students could be shown how it can be replicated down the column by first beginning in E2, then selecting the group or range of cells down the E column where the formula was to be repeated and invoking the *Fill Down* command.

Adapting a recipe to a different number of servings is a common problem faced in preparing a meal. Figure 6–13 illustrates how a recipe designed for a set number of servings can be adapted for any number. The illustration deals with servings of 20, 24, and 30 but in reality any number may be used.

The formula must first calculate the unit measure by dividing the amount by the serving size given in the recipe. It then multiplies the unit measure by the number of servings desired.

**FIGURE 6–13**
*Using the spreadsheet to calculate portions*

| | A | B | C | D | E | F |
|---|---|---|---|---|---|---|
| 1 | Ingredient | Measure | Serving | | | |
| 2 | | | 12 | 20 | 24 | 30 |
| 3 | Wheat flour | Cup | 2 | 3.3 | 4 | 5 |
| 4 | Baking Powder | Tsp | 2 | 3.3 | 4 | 5 |
| 5 | Salt | Tsp | 0.50 | 0.8 | 1 | 1.3 |
| 6 | Egg | | 1 | 2 | 2 | 3 |
| 7 | Vegetable Oil | Cup | 0.25 | 0.4 | 0.5 | 0.6 |
| 8 | Honey | Cup | 0.25 | 0.4 | 0.5 | 0.6 |
| 9 | Milk | Cup | 0.50 | 0.8 | 1 | 1.25 |

The following formulas would yield the necessary calculations in Figure 6–13:

$Dn = (C3/\$C\$2) * \$D\$2$

    [$n$ represents the number of the row and the $ indicates an absolute reference]

$En = (C3/\$C\$2) * \$E\$2$

$Fn = (C3/\$C\$2) * \$F\$2$

Students could design a spreadsheet to record information about the weather and to calculate high, low and average temperatures as well as amount and average precipitation and days of precipitation. In the example in Figure 6–14, the daily high temperature would be entered in column

B; the daily low temperature would be entered in column C; and the amount of precipitation would be entered in column E. The average *daily* temperature would be calculated in column D. Whether or not precipitation occurred during the day would be calculated in column F. The total amount of precipitation would be calculated in cell E32. The total number of days in which precipitation occurred would be calculated in cell F33. The highest temperature for the month would be calculated in cell B34. The lowest temperature for the month would be calculated in cell C35. Averages for the month would be calculated in row 36.

In May of 1843, 1,000 emigrants in 120 wagons left Independence, Missouri, on a five-month journey to the Oregon Country. This was the be-

**FIGURE 6–14**
*Using the spreadsheet to calculate sums and averages*

| | A | B | C | D | E | F |
|---|---|---|---|---|---|---|
| **1** | City : Portland, OR | | | | | |
| **2** | Date | High | Low | Mean | Am't | Days |
| **3** | | Temp | Temp | Temp | Precip. | Precip. |
| **4** | 1-Feb-93 | 61 | 46 | 54 | 0.75 | 1 |
| **5** | 2-Feb-93 | 64 | 48 | 56 | 1.00 | 1 |
| **6** | 3-Feb-93 | 56 | 44 | 50 | 0.25 | 1 |
| **30** | 27-Feb-93 | 42 | 36 | 39 | 0.00 | |
| **31** | 28-Feb-93 | 48 | 40 | 44 | 0.10 | 1 |
| **32** | Amt. Precip. | | | | 2.10 | |
| **33** | Days Precip. | | | | | 4 |
| **34** | High for month | 64 | | | | |
| **35** | Low for month | | 36 | | | |
| **36** | Average | 54.2 | 42.8 | 49 | 0.42 | |

The following formulas would yield the necessary calculations in Figure 6–14:

D4 = AVERAGE (B4:C4) to average between the day's high and low temperature

F4 = IF (E4>0,1,"") [If there is a value greater than 0 in cell E4, then enter 1 in cell F4, else leave blank] to count the day as having precipitation or not

E32 = SUM (E4:E31) to add the total precipitation for the month

F33 = SUM (F4:F31) to add the total days in which there was precipitation

B34 = MAX (B4:B31) and C35 = MIN (C4:C31) to calculate highs and lows

B36 = AVERAGE (B4:B31) to calculate averages

*This student is applying this spreadsheet as a tool in keeping track of his favorite teams' progress*

ginning of the largest unforced mass migration in history. From 1843 to 1860, over 10,000 lost their lives along the trail, but over 300,000 successfully made the trip to Oregon. Stories written in pioneer diaries have contributed to making the Oregon Trail a romantic adventure in the minds of many young people. The study of the Great Migration presents a wonderful opportunity for the development of problem-solving skills in more than one discipline. Using a spreadsheet such as the one illustrated in Figure 6–15, a student could study the geography of the trail and locate

|   | A | B | C | D | E | F | G | H |
|---|---|---|---|---|---|---|---|---|
| 1 | | Starting Date: | 5/10/43 | | Estimated days for the trip: | | | 150 |
| 2 | Date | Milestones | Current | Distance | Speed | Days | Days | % of trip |
| 3 | | | State | from prior | (mph) | from prior | elapsed | |
| 4 | 10-May | Independence | MO | 0 | 0 | 0 | 0 | 0% |
| 5 | 27-May | | | 400 | 1.5 | 17 | 17 | 11% |
| 6 | 23-Jun | | | 400 | 1 | 27 | 44 | 29% |
| 7 | 14-Jul | | | 300 | 1 | 21 | 65 | 43% |
| 8 | 8-Aug | | | 300 | 1 | 25 | 90 | 60% |
| 9 | 5-Sep | | | 250 | 0.75 | 28 | 118 | 79% |
| 10 | 27-Sep | | | 180 | 0.75 | 20 | 138 | 92% |
| 11 | 10-Oct | Oregon City | OR | 140 | 1 | 12 | 150 | 100% |

**FIGURE 6–15**
*A cross-disciplinary spreadsheet use*

The following formulas would yield the necessary calculations in Figure 6–15:

A5 = $C$1+ G5 [remember that the $ indicates a fixed reference]

F5 = (D5/E5) / 16 [16 = the hours traveled in a day. This quickly changes to 12]

G5 = G4+F5

H5 = G5 / $H$1

landmarks identified by the mileage markers in column D. By studying the topography and climate conditions along the trail, one could adjust the speed in column E and in fact shorten the trip to about 130 days as the pioneers in 1849 did. When using the popular MECC simulation *Oregon Trail,* students could be encouraged to develop their own spreadsheets to record information and to help them make decisions.

The ability to generate graphs from the numerical data entered is a powerful feature of spreadsheets. The graph shown in Figure 6–16 comes from a slight manipulation of the data displayed in Figure 6–15. Data were taken from that figure and entered into a new spreadsheet, a calculation was done to establish one-month intervals, an area of the spreadsheet was selected, and invoking the *New* command and specifying a chart, the spreadsheet then produced a graph. A line graph was selected as being the best way to display this particular information. Looking at a progression over time, it demonstrates at a glance that better progress was made at the start of the trip. The going got slower as the wagon train encountered the formidable mountains of the West and sickness and fatigue set in.

**FIGURE 6–16**
*Progress graph*

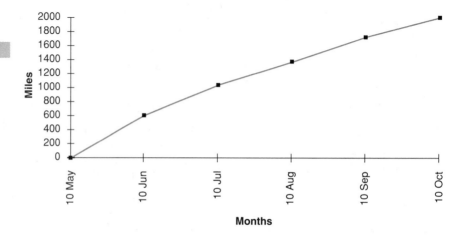

## CHARTS AND GRAPHS

Abstract numerical data can be presented in a concrete, clear, and interesting manner by line or bar graphs, pie charts, and other pictorial means. Prompted in part by the significant increase in graphs in the popular media (newspapers, magazines and television news), graphing is now being introduced to students at a much earlier age. Graphs can display relationships that would be more difficult to convey in a text or verbal mode. As visuals, they capture attention and promote greater retention of information.

Although graphs can certainly be informative, they have the potential of expressing a bias by the manipulation of scale. Thus, the analysis and interpretation of graphs has become an important subject in the K-12 curriculum. Students can be presented data and led through exercises designed to promote an understanding of those data. They can then be asked to select the most informative and accurate presentation of the data. They may discover that, depending on the data, numeric tables show the most accurate but also the most abstract and difficult to understand relationships.

*Line graphs*, as shown in the upper left section of Figure 6–17, are ideal for displaying a continuous event or trends over time (e.g., growth or decline over time). Notice the steady increase in sales over the first four weeks portrayed on this graph. The rise and fall of the line on a graph easily portrays the fluctuations in value. Multiple trends can be compared simultaneously by plotting more than one line on the graph. *Area graphs* are variations of line graphs that are successful at depicting amount or volume. A line is plotted and the area below it is filled in with a selected pattern. Each data set creates a band or area with each area being stacked on the preceding one. These graphs can be eye-catching, but since they show cumulative results they can, at times, be more difficult to understand.

*Column graphs* (vertical columns), as shown in the upper right section of Figure 6–17, and *bar graphs* (horizontal bars) present changes in a dependent variable over an independent variable and are excellent ways of comparing multiple variables to a common variable (e.g., different performances during the same time frame), but lack the feeling of continuity displayed by a line graph. Notice how the individual weeks stand out in this graph, making it easy to determine that the first and fourth weeks were the sales leaders. At times column graphs and line graphs can be combined effectively, as shown in the lower left section of Figure 6–17, to present both discrete and incremental views of the data. More elaborate graphs adding another variable (e.g., different performances at different locations during the same time frame) can be created by stacking the columns/bars.

*Pie charts* are the ideal way to display part-to-the-whole relationships or percentages. The size of each slice shows that segment's share of the entire pie. As shown in Figure 6–18, a segment (pie slice) may even be dragged away from the center for emphasis and the chart displayed in three dimensions. Other, more esoteric charts and graphs can be created to

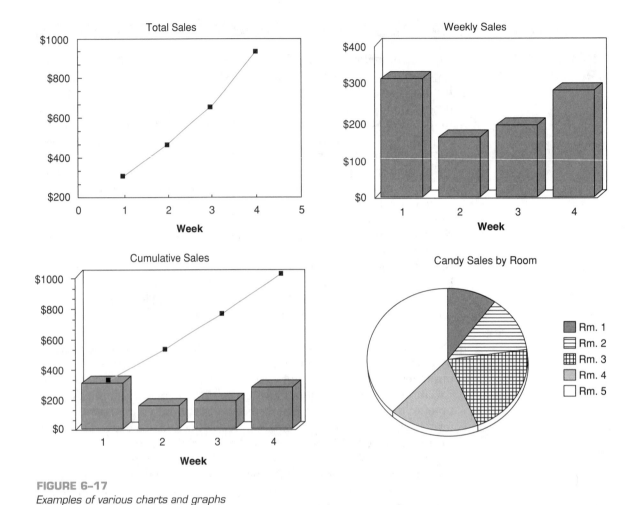

**FIGURE 6–17**
*Examples of various charts and graphs*

display central tendencies, shared variables, and relationships to a common constant.

Several integrated software packages include a built-in graphing function. A number of other computer programs exist that allow a student to enter data directly or input them from a text file, determine the appropriate scale, and select the type of graph or chart to be generated by the computer. This allows the student the opportunity to examine several graphic representations of the same data and choose the most accurate and informative one.

## Graph Components

Graphs are composed of certain common basic components. Note the components as they are labeled in the column graph in Figure 6–19. The

**FIGURE 6–18**
*Pie chart in an exploded
three-dimensional view*

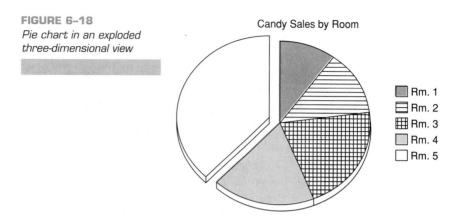

**FIGURE 6–18**
*Pie chart in an exploded
three-dimensional view*

*title* announces what your graph is all about and often hints at the conclusion you want your viewer to draw. In Figure 6–19 the title *Weekly Sales Are Climbing* is more suggestive of the conclusion you want drawn than merely titling the graph *Sales*.

Data *elements* are the major component of the graph that represent the quantity of the data being portrayed. The elements in Figure 6–19 are columns. As we have seen, elements can also be bars, lines, areas, and wedges.

The *axes* are the vertical and horizontal dimensions of the graph. The horizontal axis is usually used to display the independent variable such as the *Weeks* shown in Figure 6–19.

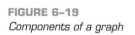

**FIGURE 6–19**
*Components of a graph*

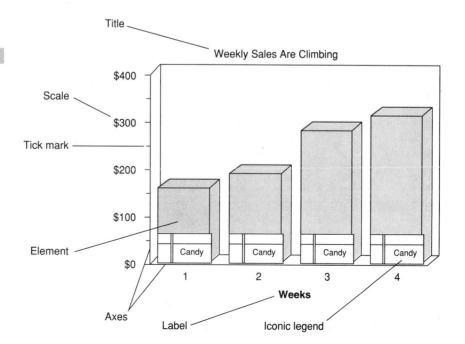

The *scales* located along the axes indicate to the viewer how the data are measured. Scales usually begin at zero at the intersection of the $x$ and $y$ axes. The user can select the range, zero to the maximum amount, and the unit increments within the range. The graph in Figure 6–19 uses increments of 100.

*Tick marks* are short lines located on the axes to serve as visual reference points dividing the axes into evenly spaced units. They may be located on either side of the axis line or may cross through it. They are located at each major unit of scale and evenly distributed between them.

*Labels* may be applied wherever the are needed to identify other components. The word *Weeks* in Figure 6–19 designates the number of weeks along the horizontal axis.

The *legend* is usually a separate area of the graph that identifies the patterns or textures of columns, bars, or wedges and what they represent. The iconic legend may, however, be used as pictorial elements, similar to the candy boxes used in Figure 6–19, to strengthen the graph's message.

## Graphs and How They Communicate

Let's explore graphs in a bit more detail. Figure 6–20 depicts population data in two different graphs, the line graph and the column graph. Both graphs use the same scale, represent data changing over time, and compare three quantities. The line graph clearly shows that population growth is leveling out in North America and in Europe while it is increasing dramatically in Latin America. The column graph, though depicting the same data, does not show the trend as readily.

In 1950 North America and Latin America each had a population of approximately 165 million. In 1990, North America's population was 278 mil-

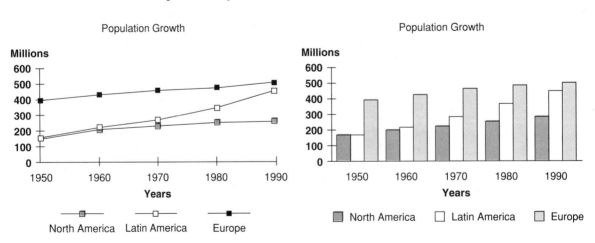

**FIGURE 6–20**
*Line graph and column graph representing the same data*

lion and Latin America's was 447 million. Examine the line graph and area graph shown in Figure 6–21 that portray these changes in populations.

The line graph on the left of Figure 6–21 clearly demonstrates the regions' population trends. The area graph on the right effectively displays change in amount but notice that the top sloping line represents the sum of the population in both regions and the scale of the graph, therefore, has changed. Does it allow you to better understand the change within each region or is it more difficult to decipher? Which of the two graphs in Figure 6–21 is the most effective at communicating its information at a glance?

An inappropriate choice of scale can be very misleading. Consider the following hypothetical example. Five students receive grades on an assignment; a perfect score would be 10 points. Marci scored 8 out of 10, Kristin 9, Dick 7, Jerry 6, and Katie 9. The user must decide on the most accurate scale when graphing the data. Examine the two examples presented in Figure 6–22.

As demonstrated in Figure 6–22, selecting the wrong scale may be misleading. Since the perfect score on the assignment was ten, a scale of 0 to 10 was chosen for the graph on the left side of Figure 6–22. When this scale is employed, the differences between the students' scores on the assignment are accurately portrayed. It is easy to see at glance that scores for Kristin and Katie were 50% better than Jerry's score. The graph on the right shows the same data on a scale of 0 to 100. Notice how close all scores appear. The scale is too great to clearly show much differentiation and conveys the misleading impression at first glance that all scores were approximately the same.

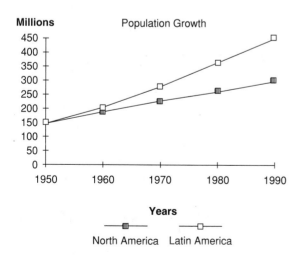

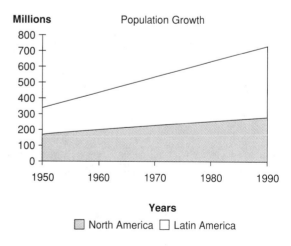

**FIGURE 6–21**
*Line graph and area graph representing the same data*

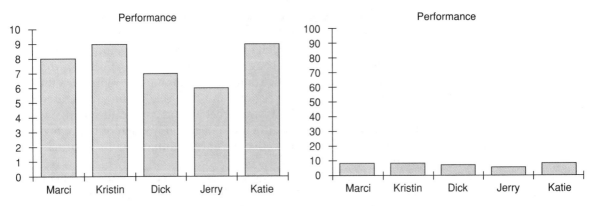

**FIGURE 6-22**
*Column graphs demonstrating the impact of scale*

Capitalizing on student interest in the Oregon Trail topic, English to metric relationships can be explored as well as the relationship of speed and time. As illustrated in Figure 6–23, the comparisons can be dramatic. A student can play "what if" by changing the speed or the hours traveled during a day or both variables and immediately see the impact of those decisions. Students could be asked to justify both the speed they selected and the length of the travel day.

Following the procedure previously described, an area of the spreadsheet shown in Figure 6–23 was selected and invoking the *New* command, the chart shown in Figure 6–24 was generated by the spreadsheet. Since a feeling of continuity was not important, a column graph was selected to

**FIGURE 6-23**
*Using the spreadsheet to calculate conversions*

|   | A | B | C | D | E | F | G | H |
|---|---|---|---|---|---|---|---|---|
|   | **Mode** | **Miles** | **MPH** | **Kilometers** | **KPH** | **Hrs/Day** | **Hours** | **Days** |
| **1** |  |  |  |  |  |  |  |  |
| **2** | Covered Wagon | 2000 | 1.1 | 3200 | 1.76 | 12 | 1818 | 152 |
| **3** | Bike | 1750 | 6 | 2800 | 9.6 | 8 | 292 | 36 |
| **4** | Automobile | 1750 | 50 | 2800 | 80 | 10 | 35 | 4 |
| **5** | Airplane | 1200 | 450 | 1920 | 720 |  | 3 |  |

The following formulas would yield the necessary calculations in Figure 6–23:

D2  =  B2 * 1.6[1.6 kilometers in a mile]

E2  =  C2 * 1.6

G2  =  B2 / C2

H2  =  G2 / F2

**FIGURE 6–24**
*Time comparisons*

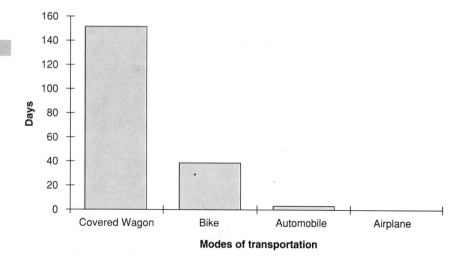

show direct comparisons in time among the various modes of transportation used in the spreadsheet.

## Activity Management

A teacher may at times supervise some activity to raise funds through a class project. Before deciding on a specific project the teacher may want to consider alternatives with the hope of finding a project that will generate the maximum income for time and effort spent. The fundamental criterion for the analysis would be money raised for effort spent. For example, suppose one of the projects under consideration is the sale of candy. The list price, number of available students, and target earnings could be set. The use of the spreadsheet would let the teacher explore the required total sales volume and the number of units each student would need to sell at each list price. With a spreadsheet such as the one in Figure 6–25, the teacher could play "what if" and immediately see the results. Selling a more expensive product would reduce the required sales volume and therefore require a lower minimum sales target per student in order to achieve comparable results.

After the initial values are placed in columns A, B, and C, all of the remaining cells are filled in automatically by the spreadsheet.

**FIGURE 6–25**
*Using the spreadsheet to forecast sales*

|   | A | B | C | D | E | F |
|---|---|---|---|---|---|---|
| 1 | **Profit** | **# of** | **List** | **Profit** | **Total Boxes** | **Boxes per** |
| 2 | **Goal** | **Students** | **Price** | **Margin** | **To Sell** | **Student** |
| 3 | $500.00 | 30 | $5.00 | $2.00 | 250 | 8 |
| 4 | $500.00 | 30 | $6.00 | $2.40 | 208 | 7 |
| 5 | $500.00 | 30 | $7.00 | $2.80 | 179 | 6 |

The following formulas would yield the necessary calculations in Figure 6–25:

D3 = C3 * .40 (40;pc discount)

E3 = A3 / D3

F3 = E3 / B3

> "The business class at our high school runs a concession stand. The students use a spreadsheet to track sales, profits, and inventory. Purchase and pricing decisions are made on a spreadsheet projection of sales."
>
> Fred Ross, Bering Strait School District
> Unalakleet, AK

## Account Ledger

A spreadsheet might be used to keep an expenditure journal. Many school accounts have day-to-day activity, but the general ledger print-out only comes out once a month. A spreadsheet set up along the lines of the one suggested in Figure 6–26 would reveal the current status of each account.

Once the labels and formulas are designed, the template described above may be saved to disk; called up each month and the beginning balance entered; and resaved to disk under a new name corresponding to the current month. The beginning account balance can be entered in cell D1. Information can then be entered on a new line whenever a purchase order is written and the current balance would be displayed in cells E4 . . . E*n*. The formula calculating the balance on the first transaction is in Cell E4. For every subsequent transaction, the formula calculating the balance is in column E.

At the end of the month this account can be reconciled against the school district's printout for the account and any differences noted and addressed.

**FIGURE 6–26**

*Using the spreadsheet to keep an expenditure journal*

| | A | B | C | D | E |
|---|---|---|---|---|---|
| 1 | | Beginning Account Balance: | | $1,000.00 | |
| 2 | Date | Purchase | Transaction | Expense | Current |
| 3 | | Order # | | Amount | Balance |
| 4 | 2/17/95 | B950012 | Powell's Bookseller | $105.50 | $894.50 |
| 5 | 3/1/85 | B950023 | F&J Deli | $28.00 | $866.50 |

The following formulas would yield the necessary calculations in Figure 6–26:

E4 = D1 − D4 (beginning balance − expenditure)

E5 = E4 − D5 (prior balance − current expenditure).

## Equipment Replacement

A spreadsheet could be used to help project the cost of replacing existing instructional equipment based on the projected life of equipment, purchase date, original cost, and inflation.

In the spreadsheet shown in Figure 6–27, values would be entered in the cells in columns A, B, C, D and H. Some spreadsheets could post the expected life figure in column E from a look-up table containing the life expectancy of various types of equipment based on available research; otherwise, this value would also be entered manually.

The following formulas would yield the necessary calculations in Figure 6–27:

AGE (Column F)

F4 = (TODAY() − D4) 365.25

[TODAY() is a function that reads the computer's internal clock/calendar and dividing by 365.25 converts the number of days into years]

REPLACE DATE (Column G)

G4 = D4 + (E4 * 365.25)

DEPRECIATED VALUE (Column I)

I4 = C4 * ((E4 − F4) / E4)

REPLACEMENT COST (Column J)

J4 = (C4 * (F4 * H4)) + C4

| | A | B | C | D | E | F | G | H | I | J |
|---|---|---|---|---|---|---|---|---|---|---|
| 1 | Serial | Item | Purchase | Purchase | Expected | Age | Replace | Inflation | Depreciated | Replace |
| 2 | Number | Type | Cost | Date | Life | | Date | Factor | Value | Cost |
| 3 | | | | | | | | | | |
| 4 | 10023 | OH | $279 | 3/1/90 | 7 | 3 | 8/31/97 | 0.03 | $159 | $304 |
| 5 | 10036 | VCR | $485 | 3/1/89 | 5 | 4 | 3/1/94 | 0.03 | $97 | $543 |

FIGURE 6-27

*Using the spreadsheet to manage an equipment inventory*

## Grade Book

Consider the creation of a computerized grade book to report student progress in your classroom. Employing the nonlinear problem-solving process reviewed earlier in this chapter, how might we proceed?

| | |
|---|---|
| Given: | Student names. |
| | Student performance on a variety of measures. |
| To Find: | Complete, accurate report of student progress. |
| Procedure: | Choose software that facilitates the selected presentation format. |
| | Organize relevant data clearly. |
| | Calculate and summarize results on performance measures. |

As was also pointed out in Chapter 5, a problem-solving strategy that might appeal more to a sequential learner consists of two phases, the *analysis* phase and the *synthesis* phase. In the analysis phase we need to clearly examine the problem, define *what* must be done, and clearly identify the specific component tasks that relate to the problem. In the synthesis phase we plan our strategy and carry out the solution to the problem. Evaluation provides feedback that could modify decisions made in both the analysis and synthesis phases.

In an effort to bring that linear problem-solving process into sharper focus, let's review the illustration in Figure 6–28 and consider once again the task of recording student progress in a computerized grade book.

### Define the Problem

Develop a system to record grades given to student work and then to calculate an equitable and accurate score representative of the student's performance within the class.

### Understand the Component Tasks

The following questions must be answered *before* you can sit down at the computer and begin to solve the problem:

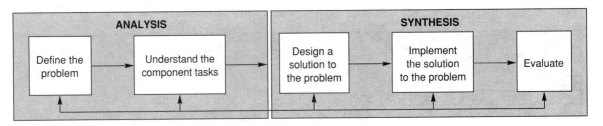

**FIGURE 6–28**
*A linear approach to problem solving*

- How will student names be entered? (last name first?)
- How many different activity types will be allowed for each class? (e.g., quiz, test, project, portfolio, lab, etc.?)
- How many different grades will be entered into each activity type?
- How are grades to be calculated? (will they be weighted?)
- How are grades to be reported?
- What information will be calculated concerning class performance?

## Design a Solution to the Problem

The primary purpose of the synthesis phase of problem solving is to help ensure that solutions designed to address the identified tasks are carried out in an effective and efficient manner and that the results are evaluated. Having defined *what* must be done and identified tasks, we can now determine *how* each task can be carried out. The solution to this problem consists of designing labels as identifiers, creating appropriate formulas, and then entering accurate data.

Each operation must be written as an **algorithm** in a *clear and effective* manner.

- Student names will be entered in one column, last name first.
- Grades for two labs, one test, one midterm project, and one cumulative portfolio will be entered.
- Maximum raw scores are established for each activity as follows:
  Labs will have a maximum score of 10
  The test will have a maximum score of 100
  The midterm project will have a maximum score of 100
  The cumulative portfolio will have a maximum score of 100
- Grades will be weighted as follows:
  Labs will be equally weighted and will together account for 20%
  The test will be weighted 25%
  The midterm project will be weighted 25%
  The cumulative portfolio will be weighted 30%
- The final grade will be reported on a scale of 1–100 (a percent)
- The highest and lowest scores will be identified and an average calculated on all activities as well as on the final grade.

## Implement the Solution to the Problem

As illustrated in Figure 6–29, student names were entered in column A, last name first. They may be entered in any order and then sorted alphabetically by the spreadsheet. Grades for two labs with a maximum score of 10 each and a weighting of 10% each were entered in columns B and C, one test with a maximum score of 100 and a weighting of 25% was entered in column D, one midterm project with a maximum score of 100 and a weighting of 25% was entered in column E, and one cumulative portfolio with a maximum score of 100 and a weighting of 30% was entered in column F. The final grade will be calculated on the basis of 100 in column G.

| | G3 | | | =B3+C3+(D3*0.25)+(E3*0.25)+(F3*0.3) | | | |

| | A | B | C | D | E | F | G |
|---|---|---|---|---|---|---|---|
| | | | | | | **Grade Book** | |
| **1** | **Name** | **Lab 1** | **Lab 2** | **Test** | **Midterm** | **Portfolio** | **Grade** |
| **2** | | 10 | 10 | 100 | 100 | 100 | 100 |
| **3** | Adams, Laura | | | | | | 0 |
| **4** | Alderson, Kathy | | | | | | |
| **5** | Alvarez, Manuel | | | | | | |
| **6** | Drexler, Richard | | | | | | |
| **7** | Kersey, Clyde | | | | | | |
| **8** | Prosser, Peggy | | | | | | |
| **9** | Prosser, Walt | | | | | | |
| **10** | Williams, Andrea | | | | | | |
| **11** | **Highest Score** | 0 | | | | | |
| **12** | **Lowest Score** | 0 | | | | | |
| **13** | **Average** | #DIV/0! | | | | | |

**FIGURE 6-29**
*Creating the grade book/spreadsheet*

Examine the formula showing in the formula bar in Figure 6–29 that calculates this final grade. Functions named MAX, MIN, and AVERAGE were invoked in rows 11, 12 and 13 to calculate the highest and lowest scores and an average on all activities as well as on the final grade.

> The following formulas would yield the necessary calculations in Figure 6–29:
>
> G3  =  B3 + C3 + (D3 * 0.25) + (E3 * 0.25) + (F3 * 0.30)
>     This formula is then replicated down column G
>
> B11  =  MAX (B3:B10) to calculate the highest score in rows 3 to 10
>
> B12  =  MIN (B3:B10) to calculate the lowest score in rows 3 to 10
>
> B13  =  AVERAGE (B3:B10) to calculate the average score of rows 3 to 10

The formulas that calculate the maximum, minimum, and average scores are then repeated in columns C through G. Spreadsheets will allow the user to replicate the contents of a cell (text, value, or formula) automatically to the right across a row or down a column, thus often saving appreciable time. When a formula is created that has a blank (empty) cell as a divisor, many spreadsheets will generate a #DIV/O! message, indicating that they cannot divide by zero. As soon as a value is entered in the divisor cell the message will disappear.

Having first analyzed the problem and then designed an acceptable solution to the problem, we must now execute the tasks to solve it. We must enter grades in our computerized grade book and print reports.

### Evaluate

As previously discussed, **debugging** is the process of correcting logic and construction errors. An often used debugging procedure is to give the program some test data that will produce known output over the entire range of use. Before entering your students' actual scores into your grade book, you might enter score values that you can compute easily and verify that the computer results are as expected. In Figure 6–30, zero is entered as the score in each item for the first student and the maximum (10 or 100) is entered for the second student. If the results are other than expected, debugging allows you to verify the correctness of your formula, the appropriateness of the functions you employed, and the logic of your design. A look at column G and at rows 11, 12, and 13 verifies our expected results.

**Documentation** that accompanies a computer application provides valuable information for the user. The user of the grade book must clearly understand the intent of the program. Detailed written instructions relative to the actual utilization of the program can better ensure that the program is used effectively. The instructions supplied with the grade book must clearly tell the user where and how to enter student names, the maximum

|  | A | B | C | D | E | F | G |
|---|---|---|---|---|---|---|---|
| 1 | Name | Lab 1 | Lab 2 | Test | Midterm | Portfolio | Grade |
| 2 | | 10 | 10 | 100 | 100 | 100 | 100 |
| 3 | Adams, Laura | 0 | 0 | 0 | 0 | 0 | 0 |
| 4 | Alderson, Kathy | 10 | 10 | 100 | 100 | 100 | 100 |
| 5 | Alvarez, Manuel | | | | | | |
| 6 | Drexler, Richard | | | | | | |
| 7 | Kersey, Clyde | | | | | | |
| 8 | Prosser, Peggy | | | | | | |
| 9 | Prosser, Walt | | | | | | |
| 10 | Williams, Andrea | | | | | | |
| 11 | Highest Score | 10 | | | | | |
| 12 | Lowest Score | 0 | | | | | |
| 13 | Average | 5 | | | | | |

FIGURE 6–30
*Debugging the grade book/spreadsheet*

scores allowed, where to enter the scores, how the scores will be weighted, and how the final grade will be calculated and reported.

As the classroom teacher uses the grade book/spreadsheet, it will continually calculate the students' total point accumulation and final scores and keep the statistics on each class activity. The rows may be sorted in alphabetical order by the data in column A at any time so as new students are added, the grade book is sorted once again.

The grade book stores data about individual students but also reveals information about their progress and their comparative performance within the group. The results in Figure 6–31 also reveal that students had a bit more difficulty with the second lab and that grades were lower on the midterm project than on either the test or the portfolio.

The grade book **template** (blank form) can be saved after labels and formulas are created but before any names or scores are put into the gradebook. By loading the template, naming it with the course name, and resaving it, the teacher may use the same grade book template for many classes.

## Commercially Available Grade Books

Now that you have examined the process of building an electronic grade book on a spreadsheet program, it would be worth your while to evaluate commercially available grade book software. The fundamental question you must ask is, "Is the commercial product flexible enough to meet my needs?" Can you adapt the software to meet your requirements or will you have to change your grading system? Another question to ask, "Does it

|  | A | B | C | D | E | F | G |
|---|---|---|---|---|---|---|---|
| 1 | Name | Lab 1 | Lab 2 | Test | Midterm | Portfolio | Grade |
| 2 |  | 10 | 10 | 100 | 100 | 100 | 100 |
| 3 | Adams, Laura | 9 | 7 | 78 | 75 | 80 | 78 |
| 4 | Alderson, Kathy | 10 | 9 | 98 | 90 | 95 | 95 |
| 5 | Alvarez, Manuel | 10 | 8 | 85 | 80 | 85 | 85 |
| 6 | Drexler, Richard | 9 | 8 | 80 | 80 | 90 | 84 |
| 7 | Kersey, Clyde | 6 | 7 | 75 | 70 | 80 | 73 |
| 8 | Prosser, Peggy | 10 | 10 | 98 | 90 | 95 | 96 |
| 9 | Prosser, Walt | 8 | 8 | 90 | 80 | 80 | 83 |
| 10 | Williams, Andrea | 9 | 9 | 80 | 85 | 80 | 83 |
| 11 | Highest Score | 10 | 10 | 98 | 90 | 95 | 96 |
| 12 | Lowest Score | 6 | 7 | 75 | 70 | 80 | 73 |
| 13 | Average | 8.88 | 8.25 | 85.50 | 81.25 | 85.63 | 85 |

**FIGURE 6–31**
*Using the updated spreadsheet as a grade book*

provide me with information about my students' performance beyond what is available in a grade book that I would create on a spreadsheet?"

David Stanton (1994) reviewed six of the best known grade book programs. Most are available for the Macintosh, MS-DOS, and Windows platforms. Along with publisher contact information and cost, Stanton presented information dealing with class size, grading categories and activities, linkage to other administrative systems, and the programs' ability to generate graphs, make seating charts, and track attendance. Most of the programs rated offered password protection. He found some more intuitive and easier to use than others; some were extremely rich in features but required an investment of time and effort to learn. Some were easy to customize and presented a wide variety of useful reports with some programs printing optional reports in Spanish, French, or German.

Whether creating your own personalized grade book or purchasing one that is commercially available, it would serve your interests well to review the analysis phase of the problem-solving process suggested in Figure 6–28. Clearly define the requisites of your grading system, understand all of its component tasks, and proceed as your grade requirements, time, budget, and personal preferences dictate.

## School Budgeting

A spreadsheet could be used in any budget matter, doing cost projections for changes in operations and investigating costs of alternate school operation plans. As an example, consider the planning of a school library media budget in which past expenditures, inflation, special curriculum needs, and per pupil expenditure are factors. Note that the illustration provided by Figure 6–32 is not meant to suggest that indeed school budgets should be prepared in this manner, but rather it is meant to demonstrate the use of the spreadsheet as an analytical and forecasting tool. The impact of changes entered in student enrollment figures and inflation rate is revealed immediately.

The actual and projected student enrollment is entered in B4, C4, and E4. The projected inflation rate is entered in F4 as 1.xx (1.03 in the example given). Actual expenditures are entered in the appropriate cells in columns B and C. Projected special program expenditures (e.g., curriculum changes that would have a direct impact on the library collection) are entered in column E.

In the illustration in Figure 6–32, once the labels are defined and the proper formulas are created, you can project the impact on the total budget of decisions you make.

Many more examples could be given. Any calculations that are done repeatedly on a regular basis are prime candidates for spreadsheet applications. The user needs only to set up a form that replicates the types of calculations that would have to be done by hand and then save the template. Whenever the calculation has to be done again, the template can be loaded and the problem addressed.

| | A | B | C | D | E | F | G |
|---|---|---|---|---|---|---|---|
| 1 | 2220 | Library Media Services | | | | | |
| 2 | | | | | | | |
| 3 | | 1994-95 | 1995-96 | | 1996-97 | Inflation | |
| 4 | #Students | 490 | 545 | | 565 | 1.03 | |
| 5 | | | | Average | Special | | 96-97 |
| 6 | | Spent | Spent | Spent | Programs | Real $ | Budget |
| 7 | 2222-School Library | | | | | | |
| 8 | 410-Supplies | $823.12 | $697.87 | $660.50 | | $742.62 | $743 |
| 9 | $/Student | $1.27 | $1.28 | $1.28 | | $1.31 | |
| 10 | 430-Library Books | $2,837.28 | $2,638.41 | $2,767.85 | $250.00 | $3,125.53 | $3,376 |
| 11 | $/Student | $5.79 | $4.95 | $5.37 | | $5.53 | |
| 12 | 432-Reference Books | $946.50 | $885.23 | $915.87 | | $1,034.68 | $1,035 |
| 13 | $/Student | $1.93 | $1.62 | $1.78 | | $1.83 | |
| 14 | 440-Periodicals | $870.42 | $715.92 | $793.17 | | $899.11 | $899 |
| 15 | $/Student | $1.78 | $1.31 | $1.54 | | $1.59 | |
| 16 | 541-Equipment, New | $2,285.00 | $1,310.00 | $1,797.50 | $600.00 | $2,056.30 | $2,656.30 |
| 17 | $/Student | $4.66 | $2.40 | $3.53 | | $3.64 | |
| 18 | 542-Equipment Repl | $552.00 | $980.00 | $766.00 | | $851.01 | $851 |
| 19 | $/Student | $1.13 | $1.80 | $1.46 | | $1.51 | |
| 20 | | | | | | | |
| 21 | TOTAL | $8,114.32 | $7,287.43 | | | $8,709.25 | $9,559 |
| 22 | $/Student | $16.56 | $13.37 | | | $15.41 | $17 |
| 23 | | | | | | | |

**FIGURE 6-32**
*Using the spreadsheet as a budgeting tool*

The following formulas would yield the necessary calculations in Figure 6–32:

Expenditures per student in columns B and C

  B9 = B8 / $B$4 and C9 = C8 / $C$4

Two year average expenditures in column D

  D8 = AVERAGE (B8:C8)

Average expenditure per student in column D

  D9 = AVERAGE (B9:C9)

Expenditure per student adjusted for inflation in column F

  F9 = D9 * $F$4

Real dollars adjusted for inflation in column F

  F8 = F9 * $E$4

Projected budget figures in column G

  $Gn$ = $En$ + $Fn$

Budget total in cell G21

  G21 = SUM (G8:G19)

# Summary

An electronic spreadsheet is a two-dimensional matrix of columns and rows. The intersection of a column and row is called a cell. The power of this software lies in the fact that cells relate one to another, allowing the contents of one cell to affect another cell. Cells may contain text, values, or formulas. Complex mathematical, statistical, and logical relationships can be described as formulas. Powerful functions are embedded in the software and can be called up by the user. Since the results of cell relationships are displayed and changing one cell immediately affects the results of the relationship, spreadsheets are often referred to as "what if" tools and are often used to make projections or forecast results.

Reviewing a nonlinear problem-solving approach introduced in Chapter 5 and applied in this chapter allows us to appreciate this approach to problem solving that permits divergent-thinking individuals to determine their own pattern without having a hierarchical structure imposed on them. A linear problem-solving strategy that might appeal more to a sequential learner was reviewed. It consists of two phases, the *analysis* phase, including defining the problem and understanding component tasks, and the *synthesis* phase, including designing a solution to the problem, implementing the solution, and evaluating. It was applied to the design of a grade book.

A number of examples were given in which the spreadsheet was used to predict results, promote accuracy of the calculation of whole numbers and fractions, calculate sums and averages, generate graphs, convert time and speed measurements, and functioning as a database, to sort text.

Graphs can represent abstract numerical data in a concrete, clear, and interesting manner. They can display relationships that would be more difficult to convey in a text or verbal mode. As visuals, they capture attention and promote greater retention of information. The analysis and interpretation of graphs has become an important subject in the K-12 curriculum.

Debugging is the process of correcting logic and construction errors. The debugging procedure employed with the grade book consisted of entering the minimum and maximum scores as test data, which produced the expected results of grades of 0 and 100. The documentation of the grade book should provide detailed written instructions relative to its effective use.

Ideally a spreadsheet would become a tool for the teacher to examine options and to forecast results. It would be taught to a student who could use it to answer "what if" questions in any academic discipline in which the act of problem solving dealt with the examination of comparisons. Along with graphics programs, word processors, and database managers, spreadsheets are programs that truly exemplify the concept of using the computer as a tool to extend our human capabilities.

# Chapter Exercises

1. Design a spreadsheet to record performances on a softball team. Calculate individual and team batting averages and on-base percentages for each game and for the season.

2. Design a spreadsheet to calculate a budget for the first Thanksgiving. From a reference source, identify the food items that were most likely present. Estimate the number of portions needed. Calculate the cost in terms of today's prices.

3. Design a spreadsheet to convert your weight in pounds to kilograms and your height in feet and inches to centimeters.

4. You are responsible for raising $2000 in income for each home football game played. Explain your problem-solving strategy and design a spreadsheet to accomplish your goal.

5. Take a poll of your classmates to determine the five cities in which they would prefer to live. Assign a weighting of 5 for their first choice, 4 for their second choice, etc. Design a spreadsheet to record their preferences and identify an overall ranking for the cities chosen.

6. Replicate the spreadsheet shown in Figure 6–15. Change the rate of travel for the wagon train and then modify the spreadsheet to show miles traveled in a one-month interval. Generate a graph showing progress on the one-month interval.

7. Record the gender of each student in your class and the length of time they have lived at their current address. Rank order the data from shortest to longest occupancy for each gender. Using the graphing capability of an integrated package or a stand-alone graphing program, create a line graph showing the occupancy ranges for each gender. Describe the results to a classmate.

8. The following problem is derived from an article entitled "Can You Manage?" (Hastie, 1992). Suppose you are a biologist responsible for managing a healthy, stable deer population in a given area. You must regulate the size of the deer herd according to the habitat that supports it. In other words, you must determine an annual deer harvest so as not to exceed the carrying capacity of the habitat and ultimately destroy it.

   Design a spreadsheet to manage four populations of deer. For Group One, hunters will be allowed to harvest 25% of the summer population; Group Two, 50%; Group Three, 75%; Group Four, 0%. Allow all groups to reproduce at a rate of 50% (new fawns equal one-half of the number of deer in the group each year.)

   For each group, (a) start with 20 deer the first year, (b) for year 2, remove number harvested, (c) and add the yearly fawn crop. Continue this process for three more years for a total of five years.
   Answer the following questions.

   • Which populations decreased in size? Which increased? Which remained the same?

- Suppose you determine the winter carrying capacity of each habitat to be 20 deer. Which harvest rate would allow you to do this and still maintain a reasonably stable population?
- Could you continue to harvest at the same rate each year or would you have to adjust the harvest rate in some years? If so, what rate would you use?

# Glossary

**active cell**   The cell that is selected and ready for data entry or editing.

**algorithm**   A structured sequence of clear and effective operations that will always reach a definite conclusion and produce a result.

**cell**   The intersection of a row and a column in a spreadsheet.

**debugging**   The process of removing all logic and construction errors.

**documentation**   Written explanations supporting program maintenance and use.

**formula bar**   The area at the top of the screen that displays the content of the active cell and can be edited.

**label**   The text descriptor related to adjacent data.

**spreadsheet**   Software that accepts data in a matrix of columns and rows with their intersections called cells. One cell can relate to any other cell or ranges of cells on the matrix by formula.

**template**   A blank form in a spreadsheet or file manager program.

# Notes & Suggested Readings

Albrecht, B., & Firedrake, G. (1993, March). Elements of the human body. *The Computing Teacher, 20*(6), 49–51.

Beare, R. (1992, December). Software tools in science classrooms. *Journal of Computer Assisted Learning, 8*(4), 221–230.

Beaver, J. (1992, March). Using computer power to improve your teaching, part II: Spreadsheets and charting. *The Computing Teacher, 19*(6), 22–24.

Berghaus, N. (1990, April). Teach spreadsheet proficiency with personal money management projects. *The Computing Teacher, 17*(7), 54–55.

Chesebrough, D. (1993, March). Using computers: Candy calculation. *Learning, 21*(7), 40.

Crisci, G. (1992, January). Play the market: Curriculum connection. *Instructor, 101*(5), 68–69.

Harrison, D. (1990). *The spreadsheet style manual.* Homewood, IL: Dow Jones-Irwin.

Hastie, B. (1992, May–June). Can you manage? *Oregon Wildlife,* 9–10.

Kellogg, D. (1993, November). Spreadsheet circuitry. *Science Teacher, 60*(8), 12–23.

Killen, R. (1993–94, December/January). Using magic squares to teach spreadsheet fundamentals. *The Computing Teacher, 21*(4), 10–11.

North Carolina State Department of Public Instruction. (1992). *Voteline: A project for integrating computer databases, spreadsheets, and telecomputing into high school social studies instruction* (ED350243). Raleigh.

Parker, O. J. (1991). *Spreadsheet chemistry.* Englewood Cliffs, NJ: Prentice Hall.

Ramondetta, J.(1992, April–May). Using computers: Learning from lunchroom trash. *Learning, 20*(8), 59.

Stanton, D. (1994, September). Gradebooks, the next generation. *Electronic Learning, 14*(1), 54–58.

# 7

# DATABASES

Data are everywhere. Fortunately, we are very selective in attending to them and we can ignore most of them. Our conscious and subconscious mind filters data, accepting some and rejecting the rest. We have the ability to organize the data we accept and give it meaning. Only then do data become information. Information is purposefully structured data. A database manager is software designed to structure data in order to produce information.

We commonly use databases in our everyday lives. One of the most ubiquitous is the telephone directory. It is a collection of data organized according to a clear structure. In order to derive useful information from it, we must understand its structure. It is a collection of facts organized by an individual's, a family's, or an establishment's name, residence, and phone number. The phone number is a unique identifier. Only one person, one family, one institution or business can have that phone number. When you search the phone book, you are normally looking for someone's phone number. The phone book allows you to find this information because the names are alphabetized. Searching through the alphabetical listing of names as the key, you find the name and corresponding phone number as part of the individual record. The record is composed of all of the data related to that individual entry (i.e., name, address, and phone number). Knowing only the address but not the name, it would be an extremely difficult task to find the phone number. Although the purpose of the phone directory is the listing of the telephone numbers, the name is the key to its successful use. Reverse directories organized as a numerical listing of phone numbers exist for the purpose of providing names and addresses once the phone number is known. We see that the structure or organization of the database is the key to its usefulness.

We have defined the concept of *tool* as something used to facilitate the performance of a task. Chapter 5 dealt with the selection of the proper tool. A database manager is an appropriate tool in the management of information if it meets one or more of the following rubrics:

- It increases the speed of information acquisition
- It increases the ease with which information is acquired
- It increases the quality of the information acquired in terms of both accuracy and completeness
- It improves the dissemination of information

If I had an electronic version of a phone book on my computer and I were looking for Peggy Cummings's phone number, I could enter a find request by typing her name in the name field. Within moments I would see the complete record including her name, address, and phone number displayed on the screen instead of having to browse through pages looking for first "C," then "Cum," reading down a column to find "Cummings," and then finally isolating the record for Peggy Cummings. This could be considered an example of effective tool use in that it meets criteria specified in the first and second rubrics.

This chapter will deal with concepts related to understanding, creating, and using a data file. It will examine a database manager and its component parts. It will discuss Boolean logic and the searching and sorting of data to develop search strategies. Some concepts associated with database management are fairly abstract. In an effort to bring them to a more concrete level we will use examples created with FileMaker Pro published by Claris for both the Macintosh and Windows platforms.

## Advanced Organizers

1. What is a database?
2. What are its component parts?
3. How do you find information in a database?
4. What is a database manager and how does it work?
5. What are the important concepts related to data storage and retrieval?
6. How can you create and use files with a database manager?
7. How could the problem-solving strategies discussed in Chapter 5 be applied to designing databases?
8. Following a linear problem-solving approach, how can a community resource file be developed in a database?
9. How might you and your students use a database as a productivity tool to store, retrieve, and analyze information?

## FILE/DATABASE MANAGERS

What is a **database?** A database is an organized, structured collection of facts about a particular topic. At times these facts are grouped together in subsets called **files.** Examine the organization of data presented in Figure 7–1. Notice that true databases and files are not the same. An address file and a health file are both part of the student database in this example. A database may consist of a single file or a number of related files. Systems for file management are often called **database managers.** The term implies the capability of managing a number of files of data simultaneously or at least in a

**FIGURE 7–1**
*Data organization*

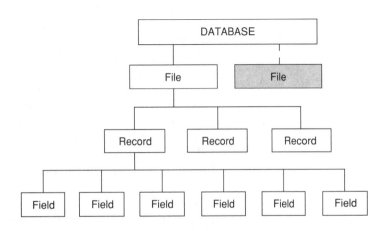

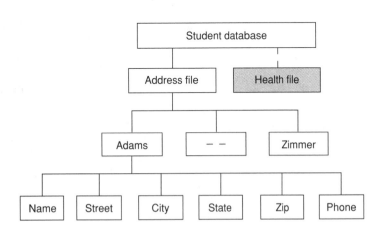

closely related manner. Programs with this capability are properly called **re-lational database** managers. Other software designed to manage a single file is properly referred to as a file manager. Through popular usage, however, distinctions have blurred and the terms have come to be used interchangeably, with file managers now being called database managers or simply databases. Many types of software commonly used in schools are truly file managers but have come to be known as database managers. We will accede to this change of terminology so that when reference is made to *database* we will treat it synonymously with *file*.

## Database Operation

What is a database manager and how does it actually work? Figure 7–2 presents the seven major functions of a database manager and indicates that database management software is designed to allow the user to create a structure for the storage, manipulation, and retrieval of data. Once data are entered into the file, the software also allows the user to act on those data in a variety of ways. New data can be created through calculations based on existing data entered into the file. A good **file management** system lets you do three basic things: gather related data into a central collection, reorder those data in various ways depending on need, and retrieve the product of that reordering in a useful form. The products of file managers fall into two main categories: the real-time, "on-line" search for specific information and the ability to print reports organized in a particular fashion.

**FIGURE 7–2**

*Functions performed by a database manager*

- **File design:** Establish structure of file by creating data fields of appropriate type
- **Form design:** Create a layout of fields and where they will appear displayed on the screen or printed on paper
- **Record editing:** Allow data to be entered, altered, and deleted
- **Record finding:** Facilitate the selection of certain records while ignoring others
- **Record sorting:** Organize records according to some field order
- **Report creation:** Find specific records, sort them, and arrange them on a selected form
- **Report printing:** Display the information on paper or on the screen

## File Design

The individual data item is the most discrete element of a database and is called a data field or simply a **field.** In the case of the telephone directory, a phone number is an individual field, as are address and name. Fields can contain text, numeric values, dates, and even pictures or sounds. Fields can contain calculations that perform mathematical operations on other numeric fields within the record and store the resulting values (e.g., multiplying the contents of two other fields). Fields can also contain summaries of data across a number of records and display the result (calculate the total or the average of specific field values for a group of records). In order to assist recognition of fields on the screen or in reports, field **labels** are created. Figure 7–3 illustrates fields and their labels. Keep in mind that labels simply identify or describe the fields where the data are actually stored.

The data record, or simply **record,** is the building block of the file. A record is composed of all of the related fields. An individual record in the phone book contains all the data related to that entry (i.e., name, address, phone number). A **file** is the aggregation of all of the records. The phone book file is the collection of all the records for that city, town, or region. A file, then, is composed of individual records that are themselves composed of individual fields. Review Figure 7–1 and notice that a *field* is the most specific and discrete piece of information. A *record* is composed of a group of related fields. Records accumulate into a *file.* A *database* may be made up of several files.

**FIGURE 7–3**
*A record showing fields and their labels*

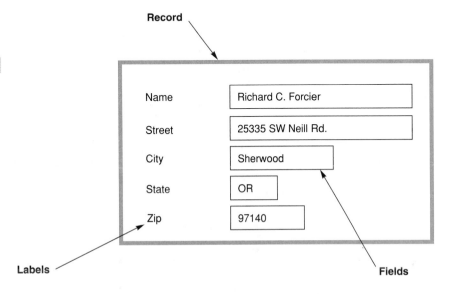

### Form Design

As fields are defined, labels are created and grouped together creating a **form** or **layout,** which appears on the screen with blank spaces where data are to be entered. It is common to create several layouts for a file. Once data are entered, the layout that is selected or created can be thought of as a window through which to examine data in selected fields. Some file managers allow you a good deal of freedom in custom designing a layout while others are much more limited. Figure 7–4 shows a layout on the left where fields and their labels are included to facilitate data entry, for example, and a second layout on the right containing only the fields, perhaps to be used as a mailing label. Layouts are created based on the information required by the user. Fields are individually chosen to appear in a layout and their most appropriate position determined.

### Data Entry and Editing in a Record

After each field has been defined, this information will be saved as the file structure (how the data in each record are to be stored). During data entry, the file manager displays the field labels on the screen, places the cursor at the first position in the first field, and facilitates the entry of data (e.g., letters, numbers, pictures, or sounds). The user is free to alter or change the data in any field in any of the records at any time. To edit records, you would place the cursor in the appropriate field and type the change.

### Record Finding and Sorting

The software allows the user to perform a **logical search,** sometimes called a query, to select records based on a wide range of criteria. An exact match of a value in a field can be requested (find field value equaling "Francis" = **Francis**). A match containing a value in a field can be

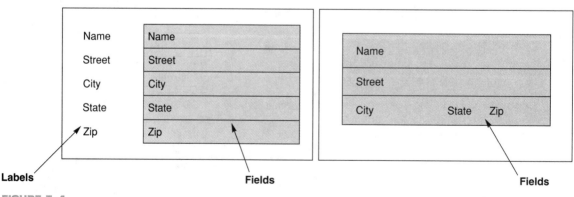

**FIGURE 7–4**
*Two different layouts of the same data*

**FIGURE 7-5**
*Boolean connectors*

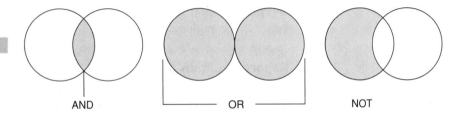

AND                OR              NOT

requested (find field value containing "Francis" = **Francis,** San **Francis**co, etc.). Many other searches can be performed including those greater than, less than, or not equal to a value. Searches can be performed on ranges of data by specifying the extremes of the range (e.g., minimum and maximum values). Searches can find all the records except those indicated to be omitted. Compound searches can be constructed to examine data in multiple fields using the Boolean connectors illustrated in Figure 7–5. The use of the AND connector restricts the search and makes it more specific. The use of the OR connector expands the search, making it less specific. The NOT connector removes those records having the second search criterion from the set of records otherwise found.

For example, as illustrated in Figure 7–6, one could search a student file by gender and address for all records of girls who lived in Springfield, a specific town in the attendance area. The search would be "girls" AND "Springfield." Both criteria would have to be present in the same record in order to select that record. On the other hand, one could search the file for records of girls or records of all students (boys or girls) who lived in Springfield. The search would be "girls" OR "Springfield." Either criterion would have to be present in a record in order to select that record. All records of girls plus all records of the specified town (both boys and girls) would be selected. A popular way of distinguishing between the two selection connectors is to remember that "OR is more." The NOT connector would be used to find all girls who were not living in Springfield.

Data can be sorted or arranged in a prescribed alphabetic, numeric, or chronological order in either ascending (e.g., A–Z, 1–99, 1941–1996) or descending (e.g., Z–A, 99–1, 1996–1941) fashion. This organization of records within the file can be based on any individual field. Most software also allows nested or multilevel sorts. For example, one could sort a grade book in ascending alphabetical order by last name and then as a second level, by first name. This would create an alphabetic list of students by last name

**FIGURE 7-6**
*Selection results using Boolean connectors*

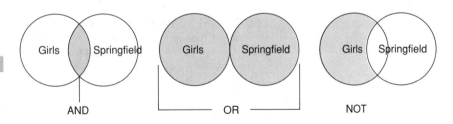

AND                OR              NOT

and then if any students shared the same last name, the sort would alphabetize those students by first name.

## Report Creation and Printing

To develop a report for printing information from the file, the user first selects the appropriate layout, then selects the records to be included in the report (*search* for or *find* the records), and finally, designates their order (*sort* the records found). For example, to print a report consisting of student's first name, last name, and birth date, the user would:

- Designate the size of the printed page and create column titles that would serve as labels:
  *First Name, Last Name, Birth Date*
- Choose the records to be printed:
  All records?
  Only those after a certain birth date?
- Define the order:
  Alphabetic by last name?
  Birth date order?

In this example, the report might be sorted by birth date, and if two or more students had the same birth date, these names would be sorted alphabetically, by last name. This technique is referred to as a **nested sort** or a **multilevel sort**.

Many different reports can be produced from the same file. In our example, another useful report would print mailing labels on continuous-form label stock. Both the mailing labels and the student lists constitute reports. By adding fields for grade level and teacher's name, reports could be generated presenting a list of students by grade or teacher, thereby increasing the usefulness of the file.

The power of database managers is that the information can be entered once and many reports can be generated simply by instructing the computer program how to organize the data. You do not have to rework the collected information by hand. All of your time and energy goes into the data entry and maintenance. Very little time is spent generating reports.

## Using a Database Manager

To make the best use of a file management system, the user must be able to meet the following four requirements:

1. *Understand your information needs.* Know the information you want your system to manage. Analyze what you are doing, what information is used, and how it is being used. How could the processing of that information be improved?
2. *Specify your output needs.* Although you cannot predict everything you will need from your file, you know the reports that are commonly

needed and the information that is frequently accessed. Design those report formats.

3. *Specify your input needs.* Once you have determined output needs, input needs become obvious. Take advantage of the features of your file manager that will simplify and expedite data entry.

4. *Determine the file organization.* Consider the file input and output requirements in completing the record design.

When contemplating the use of a file manager, analyze what you are doing and determine what you would like to do. If you cannot design a way to perform a task by paper and pencil, a file manager probably can't help you.

## PROBLEM SOLVING WITH DATABASES

Consider the process of problem solving discussed in Chapter 5 that might be approached by an individual with a sequential learning style. Let us review the linear method and the illustration that was presented. Figure 7–7 illustrates the two phases, the *analysis* phase and the *synthesis* phase. In the analysis phase we are developing a clear definition and understanding of the problem and of the component tasks that relate to the problem. In the synthesis phase we plan our strategy and carry out the solution to the problem. Evaluation provides feedback that could modify decisions made in both the analysis and synthesis phases.

### Analysis

Remember that analysis is defined as the separation of a whole into its component parts for the purpose of examination and interpretation. The need is to clearly define the problem and clearly identify the specific tasks that must be accomplished. In defining the problem you will establish a need.

**Problem Statement**

A teacher wishes to make the best use of the local resources in the community.

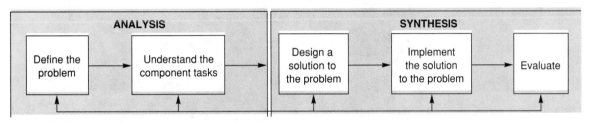

**FIGURE 7–7**
*A sequential approach to problem solving*

In an effort to bring the problem-solving process into sharper focus and to understand component tasks, let's consider the management of some resources external to the classroom. Apply the problem-solving process just reviewed and illustrated in Figure 7–7 to accomplish the task stated. Begin by analyzing the output required and formulating questions, such as those that follow, to help determine what is necessary to produce this result.

**Understanding Components**

What are the resources?
How do they align with the curriculum?
How might they be accessed by teachers and students?

These items could certainly be further expanded, refined, and organized in an outline fashion. Chapter 5 presented the written algorithm and the flowchart as effective outlining tools particularly adaptable to sequential operations. An outlining strategy is often helpful in reaching a better understanding of the components. The top-down outlining approach illustrated in Figure 7–8 is one that proceeds from global to specific concerns and facilitates systematic analysis.

As you attack the problem of managing external resources, you must make sure that you understand what is required of the software *before* you attempt to solve the problem. You may otherwise select the wrong software or spend a lot of time and effort producing something that will not meet your expectations.

The outline presented in Figure 7–8 identifies Type, Curriculum Areas, and Access as the major headings in response to the questions above. It refines each heading by more specific subheadings and in some instances even more specific third- and fourth-level subheadings.

*These fifth graders are collaborating on a project. They are discussing how to design a database so that the resulting information is useful to their report on weather patterns.*

**FIGURE 7–8**
*Outlining components*

Resources
   Type
      Industrial corporations
      Retail commercial ventures
         Goods
         Services
      Government agencies
      Nonprofit corporations
      Individuals
   Curriculum Areas
      Occupations
      Social studies/language arts
      Science/mathematics
      Performing arts
      Health/physical education
   Access
      Contact
         Name, address, phone number
      When available
      Come to the school
         To the classroom
            Speakers/demonstrations
            Film/video
         To an assembly
      Host on their site
         Group size
         Safety issues

## Synthesis

*Synthesis* is defined as combining elements to form a coherent whole. The primary purpose of the synthesis phase of problem solving is to help ensure that solutions designed to address the identified tasks are carried out in an effective and efficient manner and that the results are evaluated.

### Field Definition

The solution to the information management problem just outlined involves designing a database to store relevant data and to allow easy retrieval of useful information. Referring to the outline developed in Figure 7–8, a Resources file can be developed by defining appropriate fields.

Figure 7–9 presents the fields derived from the outline presented in Figure 7–8. Notice that a field to store the record entry date is also included so that the information can be examined on a periodic basis to determine its validity or usefulness.

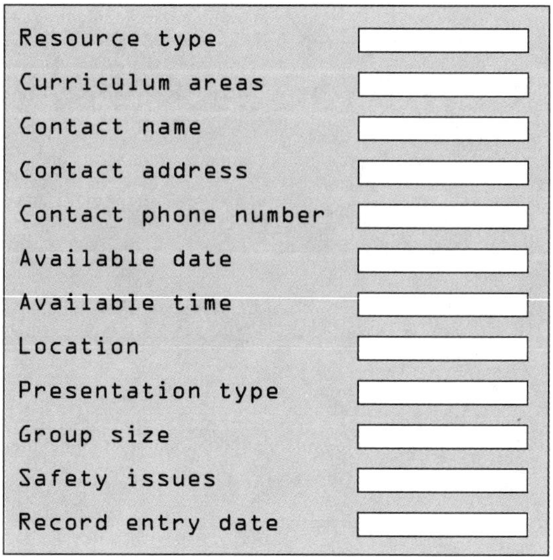

**FIGURE 7–9**

*Fields defined for the*
*Resources file*

| Resource type | |
|---|---|
| Curriculum areas | |
| Contact name | |
| Contact address | |
| Contact phone number | |
| Available date | |
| Available time | |
| Location | |
| Presentation type | |
| Group size | |
| Safety issues | |
| Record entry date | |

## Error Trapping

There is an old saying in computer circles, *Garbage In, Garbage Out* (GIGO). Accurate data entry is essential to the production of meaningful information from a database. Error trapping is a process of designing safeguards into your solution. In error trapping, a designer makes sure that entry of incorrect data is not accepted by the program. If certain values must be excluded when entering data into the file, then a technique must be employed to ensure that the unwanted data cannot be entered, thereby preventing potential errors that could cause the program to yield faulty information. Depending on the capability and sophistication of the software being used, the *Resource type* field in the Resources file example could present checkboxes on the screen, as shown in Figure 7–10, representing the available entries rather than depend on input typed from the keyboard. The *Curriculum areas* field might present the user a list from which to select. The *Available date* field, shown in Figure 7–9, might be restricted to accept values that fall between 9/1/96 and 6/5/97, for example, to make sure that the date falls in the correct school year.

An example of error trapping data entry in a student records database would be to designate a range of values from 0 to 4.0 in a field designed to store a numerical equivalent of an F to A course grade. Limiting data entry to this range would catch typing errors such as a double key press that might attempt to enter a nonsensical value of 33, for example.

## Debugging

Debugging is the process of correcting logic and construction errors. In designing a database, it is especially important to verify calculation and summary fields. An often used debugging procedure is to give the program some test data that will produce known output. If the results are other than expected, debugging allows you to verify the correctness of your data entry and calculations, the appropriateness of the functions you employed, and the logic of your design.

### Documenting the Application

Documentation should clearly point out the intent of the database. Detailed written instructions about how to use the program can better ensure that the program is used effectively. The use of screen shots, such as those commonly found in software manuals, replicating what the user sees at any given point of using the program is often helpful in illustrating the instructions. The instructions must clearly tell the user where data are to be entered in appropriate layouts, how to find and sort information, and how to print resulting reports.

## Database Applications

Teachers want help in alleviating the paperwork demands made on them. They want help in accomplishing activities that do not involve students directly and are quite often done outside of actual class time. If the time required to perform these tasks could be decreased, the teacher would have more time to devote to working with students.

Students need access to increasing amounts of information if they are to construct their own knowledge. The teaching of information organization and retrieval skills can be taught through the use of databases. The database is an ideal tool for students to gather and arrange data, examine trends and relationships, and test theories.

Following are a number of activities to illustrate how a database might be used as a tool by the student or the teacher. These examples can be modified to serve in a variety of subject areas and grade levels. If students are to capitalize on the power of the database manager as a tool and employ it with confidence, they must develop an understanding of its application and a reasonably high level of skill in its use.

**FIGURE 7-10**

*Checkboxes for data entry*

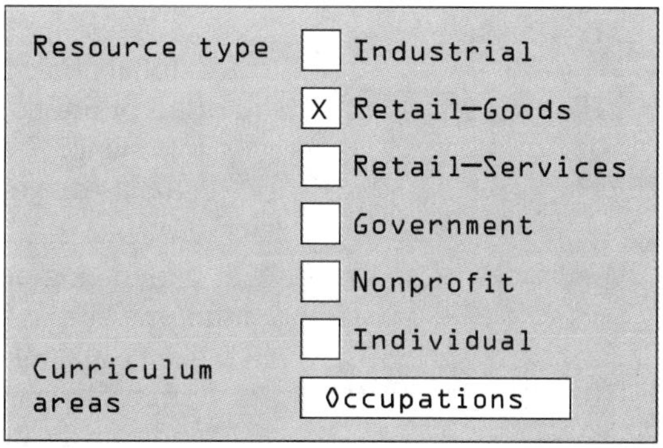

Resource type
☐ Industrial
☒ Retail—Goods
☐ Retail—Services
☐ Government
☐ Nonprofit
☐ Individual

Curriculum areas    Occupations

> *"Information skills are taught using the computer to access research tools. Kids who might neglect or not get too excited about using hardbound reference books will stand in line to use those on CD-ROM. The color, graphics, movement, and sound are very attractive to them."*
>
> Lisa Hearn, Library Media Specialist
> Canongate Elementary Shool, Sharpsburg, GA

## U.S. Presidents File

1. The process of entering data into the fields defined in Figure 7–11 will require the students to conduct some research to gather the relevant facts.
2. Students can print out the following informational tables:
   a. Chronological list of presidents containing the following:

   ```
   RANK   TERM DATES   FIRST/LAST NAME   PARTY   VICE PRESIDENT

   ____   ____ _ ____     ____ , ____     ____   _____
   ```

   b. Alphabetical list by last name of presidents to find information pertinent to a specific president and containing the following:

   ```
   LAST/FIRST NAME   RANK   TERM DATES   PARTY   VICE PRESIDENT

   ____ , ____       ____   ____ _ ____  ____   _____
   ```

   c. List of presidents sorted by party to examine voting patterns and containing the following:

   ```
   PARTY        FIRST/LAST NAME        RANK        TERM DATES

   _____       ____ , ____            ____        ____ _ ____
   ```

   d. List of presidents sorted by home state to examine any geographical patterns and containing the following:

   ```
   HOME STATE            FIRST/LAST NAME        TERM DATES

   _____           ____ , ____            ____ _ ____
   ```

   e. Chronological list of presidents and events to examine events as possible expressions of party philosophy at the time and containing the following:

   ```
   LAST NAME    PARTY    EVENT 1_____
                         EVENT 2_____
                         EVENT 3_____
   ```

   f. Alphabetical list of the prior employment of presidents (or a selection of only one employment such as attorney) and containing the following:

   ```
   PRIOR EMPLOYMENT            PRESIDENT            TERM DATES

   _____           ____ ____            ____ _ ____
   ```

3. The following printouts could serve as games, as contests, and for drill and practice.
   a. Leave a blank column for the president's Last Name and print a column of Events for a selected date range based on the *Term of Office* field. Indicate the president who was in office when each event occurred.

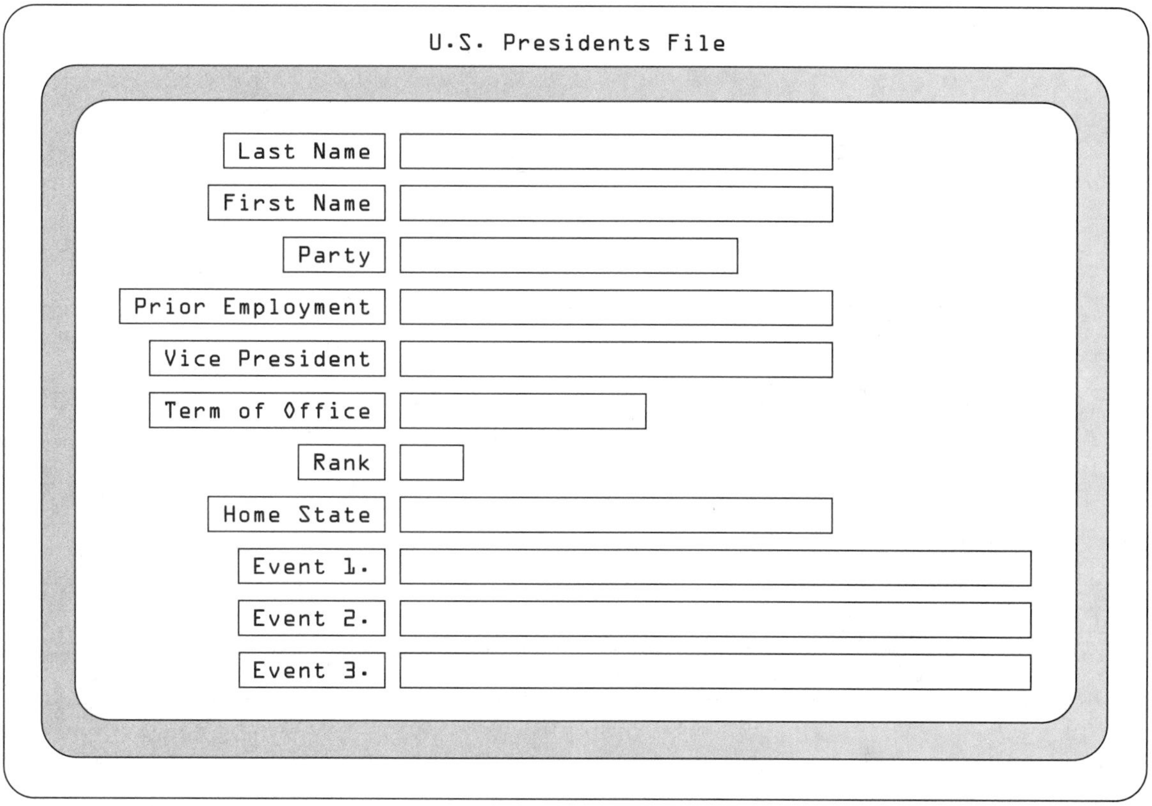

```
                        U·S· Presidents File

            Last Name  [                                        ]
           First Name  [                                        ]
                Party  [                            ]
     Prior Employment  [                                        ]
       Vice President  [                                        ]
       Term of Office  [                        ]
                 Rank  [    ]
           Home State  [                                        ]
            Event 1.   [                                            ]
            Event 2.   [                                            ]
            Event 3.   [                                            ]
```

**FIGURE 7–11**
*Presidents file*

b. Print two lists in alphabetical order, one of the presidents and the other of events, with the objective being to match presidents and events.
c. Print any of the tables suggested above with a blank column requiring information to be entered.

### Geography File

1. The database suggested in Figure 7–12 might be set up for all countries of the world or only for countries in a specific geographic region. The process of entering data will require the students to conduct some research to gather the relevant facts. As information about the countries is studied, students could be encouraged to suggest additional fields for the database. The database as illustrated in Figure 7–12 contains three calculation fields. The *Area/U.S.* field takes the value from the *Area* field, divides it by the area of the United States, and expresses the ratio. The *Population Density* field takes the value

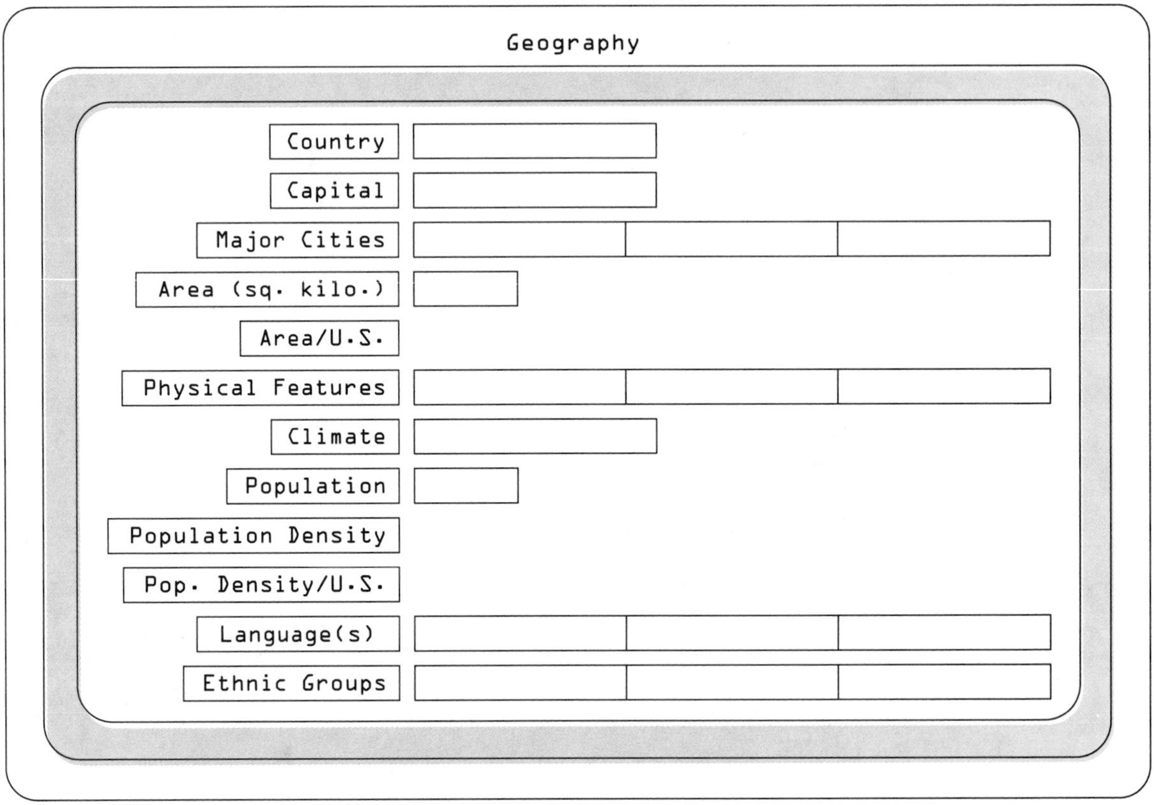

**FIGURE 7–12**
*World or regional geography file*

from the *Population* field, divides it by the value in the *Area* field, and expresses the ratio. The *Pop. Density/U.S.* field takes the value calculated in the *Population Density* field, divides it by the population density of the United States, and expresses the ratio. Four fields (*Major Cities, Physical Features, Language(s),* and *Ethnic Groups*) are defined to be able to store up to three different values.

2. Students can print out the following informational tables:

a. Alphabetical list by name of country to find information pertinent to cities in a specific country.

| COUNTRY | CAPITAL | MAJOR CITIES | | |
|---------|---------|--------------|---|---|
| ——— | ——— | ——— | ——— | ——— |

b. Alphabetical list by name of country to find information pertinent to land mass, population in a specific country, and comparison to United States.

| COUNTRY | AREA | AREA/US | POP | POP DENS | POP DENS/US |
|---------|------|---------|-----|----------|-------------|
| ——— | —— | — . — | —— | ——— | — . — |

The same data could be printed as a list in order of area, population, or population density to examine relationships based on the particular criteria.

c.  Alphabetical list by name of country to find information pertinent to climate and physical features in a specific country.

COUNTRY      CLIMATE      PHYSICAL FEATURES

_____      _____      _____      _____      _____

d.  Alphabetical list by name of country to find information pertinent to ethnic groups and languages in a specific country.

COUNTRY      ETHNIC GROUPS_____

_____      LANGUAGE(S)_____

3.  Specific inquiries might be made such as, "Which country has the largest land mass? Which country has the highest population density? What countries have significant rivers and/or mountains? Which countries are Spanish speaking? What countries have the same ethnic groups?" Once information is generated, relationships can be explored. Does the area of the country relate directly to its population density? Is climate related to population density? Referring to a map of the region, do any of the physical features (rivers, mountains, etc.) form political boundaries? Examining countries that speak the same language, do they share something else in common? Were they part of a political union? An empire? A number of other relationships can be explored based on the students' interest, need for information, and the teacher's direction.

4.  A travel agency classroom simulation could be designed to explore existing countries in the database and to determine interests of students. Students could ask to go mountain climbing, to spend time in the sun, to go somewhere where they could practice a foreign language they were learning. As students revealed a variety of interests, additional fields could be added to the database on that basis.

5.  As a departure from the example illustrated in Figure 7–12, a database could be designed and data entered by students who using the program *Where in the World is Carmen Sandiego?* The following fields could be defined: *Country, City, Currency, Language, Chief Products, Points of Interest, Bodies of Water, Mountains, Deserts,* and *Miscellaneous*. As students encounter clues they could search the database and if results were not achieved, they could research the relevant information and create a new record in the database. The database would grow more powerful as more clues are encountered and students would be refining their information-gathering skills.

## Recommended Books File

1.  The database suggested in Figure 7–13 would be created by and for students. Unlike the previous examples, it would be used mainly for on-line searching. It is not intended to replace a library automation system's public access catalog but rather to be a file of student opinion regarding books in the school library.

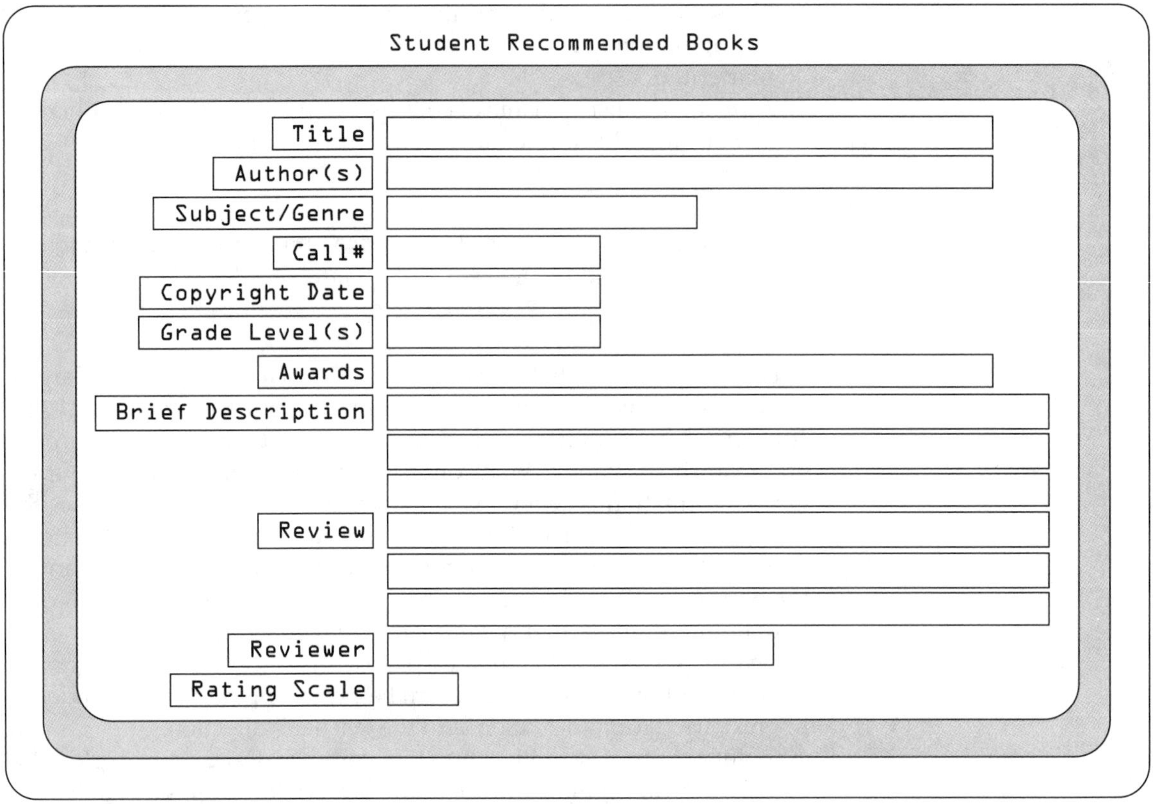

**FIGURE 7-13**
*A file of student-recommended books*

2. Data would be gathered by students and might serve as a motivation to read for some. It could be gathered as part of a school library's reading promotion effort. The data entry itself might be restricted to a few students in order to control the integrity of the file. An **authority list** (approved headings) might be used for the *Subject/Genre* field to facilitate accurate retrieval of information. A high to low numeric rating scale would be devised (e.g., 4–1). The file could be designed to hold multiple reviews and reviewers' names.

3. Students might query the database by a specific *Subject/Genre*, asking for a list of titles at a particular *Grade Level*, and then sorted in descending order by *Rating Scale*. They would then be able to find the most popular books in their area of interest.

SUBJECT/GENRE    TITLE                GRADE    RATING
_____    _____        ____     _____

4. Once having selected a group of records to examine, students could change to a layout that would let them read the *Brief Description, Review,* and *Reviewer*

name in order to choose a book that appealed to them. The addition of the *Call #* in the layout would let students find the book on the library shelf.

```
CALL #   TITLE            REVIEWER

_____   _____   _____

DESCRIPTION
_____
```

5. A student could search for a favorite *Author* and get a list by *Title, Copyright Date,* and *Rating Scale* to find the most recent and popular work by that author.

```
AUTHOR   TITLE        COPYRIGHT   RATING

_____   _____   _____   _____
```

6. A layout that listed the *Awards* (e.g., Caldecott, Newbery, Young Reader's Choice), the *Rating Scale,* and the *Reviewer* name for each *Title* would allow students to form their own opinion of a reviewer's judgment when compared against a broader measure.

```
TITLE            AWARD           RATING   REVIEWER

_____   _____   ____     _____
```

7. A paper index could be printed and made available in the library that would sort the file by *Subject/Genre* and would list books in alphabetic *Title* order and display the *Rating Scale* and the *Call #* for each.

```
SUBJ/GENRE   CALL #   TITLE            RATING REVIEWER

_____   _____   _____   ____   _____
```

## Test Items File

1. Exams have been prepared by typewriter for many years and, more recently, by word processor. The database suggested in Figure 7–14 would allow a teacher the highest degree of flexibility in test construction for a paper and pencil objective exam. Though the example shows only true/false and multiple choice questions, other forms such as matching, fill-in, and short answer are also feasible in a database format.

2. A data entry layout would include a *Question* field, an *Answer Key* field to store the correct response, a *Topic* field or for concept identification, a *Chapter* field correlated to a text, and an *Exam* field that could be used to note different exams or different forms of the same test. The layout might resemble the following:

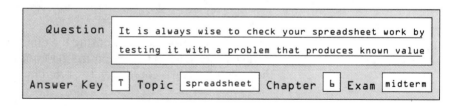

```
                          Test Item Database

  CSE 410 Computers in Education                  Midterm Exam
  True-False

  Please respond on the answer sheet provided.  Mark the first column (a) if the
  answer is TRUE or the second column (b) if the answer is FALSE.
  - - - - - - - - - - - - - - - - - - - - - - - - - - - - - - - - - - - - - - - -
  7.  It is always wise to check your spreadsheet work by testing it with a
      problem that produces known values.


  CSE 410 Computers in Education                  Midterm Exam
  Multiple Choice

  Please respond on the answer sheet provided.  Select the best answer for each
  question.
  - - - - - - - - - - - - - - - - - - - - - - - - - - - - - - - - - - - - - - - -
  17. The process of correcting application program design errors is
      referred to as
      a.  error trapping
      b.  programming
      c.  documenting
      d.  debugging
```

**FIGURE 7-14**
*A file of test items*

3. A layout could be designed for the purpose of selecting questions to include in the exam. This layout might closely resemble the previous one with the addition of a *Select? (Y/N)* field.

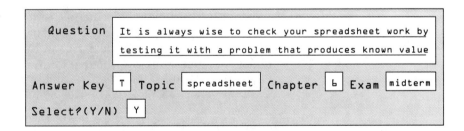

The exam is composed by choosing the questions marked for selection. If the teacher wishes to randomize the topics or the correct responses, the selected records could then be sorted by question. When preparing a final exam at a later date, observing whether or not a question was used in the midterm might influence its selection.

4. A layout in a multiple choice format might resemble the following:

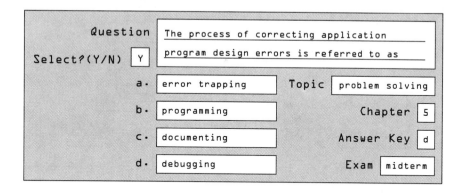

5. After carefully choosing the questions and sorting them, by selecting the proper layouts, a teacher could print a master copy of the exam for duplication and a copy to serve as the answer key.
6. A **template,** or empty copy of the file with all the fields defined and all the layouts built, could be shared among a group of teachers. They could tailor it to their own needs and then share the modified version.

## Menu Planning and Nutritional Analysis Files

This last example is more complex than the previous ones. It is composed of two related files and could be designed on any relational database. It can also be built on FileMaker Pro, a flat file manager that has a lookup capability from one file to another. The main file, named Menu Planner, as shown in Figure 7–15, is designed to allow the user to create a menu for a number of meals in a given week by choosing items from the four main food groups. The secondary or lookup file named Nutritional Values (Figure 7–16) contains nutritional information on a large number of food items. A record in this file would contain the name of a meat, dairy, vegetable/fruit, or cereal/bread item and its corresponding values of calories, fat, cholesterol, and the percentage of average daily requirements in vitamins.

As a user enters food items in the Menu Planner file, corresponding nutritional data are entered from the lookup file. An entire week's menus could be planned and using the summary capability of the database software, the total nutritional value of the week's menus could be analyzed as shown in Figure 7–17. By changing various food items a healthier menu might be achieved.

## Menu Planner

| | |
|---|---|
| Day | ○ Sun ○ Mon ○ Tue ○ Wed ○ Thu ○ Fri ○ Sat |
| Meal | ○ Breakfast ○ Lunch ○ Dinner |
| Meat | |
| Dairy | |
| Vegetable/Fruit | |
| Cereal/Bread | |

**FIGURE 7–15**
*A menu planning file*

## Nutritional Values

| | |
|---|---|
| Meat | |
| Dairy | |
| Vegetable/Fruit | |
| Cereal/Bread | |
| Calories | |
| Grams of Fat | |
| Cholesterol | |

% ADR Vitamins:

| | |
|---|---|
| A | |
| B | |
| C | |
| D | |
| E | |

**FIGURE 7–16**
*A nutritional analysis file*

**FIGURE 7–17**
*Nutritional analysis of a week's menus*

| Day | Meal | Food | Cal | Fat | Cholest | VitA | VitB | VitC | VitD | VitE |
|---|---|---|---|---|---|---|---|---|---|---|
| —— | ——— | "meat" | —— | —— | —— | —— | —— | —— | —— | —— |
| | | "dairy" | —— | —— | —— | —— | —— | —— | —— | —— |
| | | "veg/frt" | —— | —— | —— | —— | —— | —— | —— | —— |
| | | "cer/brd" | —— | —— | —— | —— | —— | —— | —— | —— |
| —— | ——— | "meat" | —— | —— | —— | —— | —— | —— | —— | —— |
| | | "dairy" | —— | —— | —— | —— | —— | —— | —— | —— |
| | | "veg/frt" | —— | —— | —— | —— | —— | —— | —— | —— |
| | | "cer/brd" | —— | —— | —— | —— | —— | —— | —— | —— |
| | | **TOTAL:** | —— | —— | —— | —— | —— | —— | —— | —— |

## COMMERCIALLY AVAILABLE DATABASES RELATED TO CURRICULUM

A number of commercial databases are being marketed to address specific content areas. Databases of scientific facts (e.g., periodic table, scientists, inventions), historical facts (e.g., famous people, events, time-lines), and geographic facts (e.g., map locations, climates, migration) are becoming readily available from various publishers of educational software.

The examples that follow as Figures 7–18 through 7–20 are taken from an award-winning program called *MacGlobe* (also available as *PC Globe* for DOS machines), a rich database of geographical facts covering every country in the world. It begins with a world map and lets the user choose from regional maps (e.g., continents, political and economic alliances), country maps (e.g., political and elevation), and thematic maps (e.g., population, natural resources, agricultural production, education). The user can paint selected countries or regions in a chosen pattern and return to the world map to observe the results. The program can also display the flag of any country and can display distances, currency conversions, and a number of charts revealing information about each country.

Programs such as this one present the student with a valuable resource of information with which to make comparisons, draw inferences, and construct knowledge. After examining the following figures, what would you say in describing Malawi to another student? How is it similar and how is it different from the U.S.? What else do you want to know about that country?

The top screen in Figure 7–18 shows the location and population of the major cities of the African country of Malawi. The bottom screen shows the elevation of the different regions in the country.

Figure 7–19 explores differences. The top screen gives the user a sense of the distance from the west coast of the United States to the African country of Malawi (distance can be calculated between any two points on the

**FIGURE 7–18**
*Map screens from*
MacGlobe
(Courtesy of Broderbund
Software, Inc.)

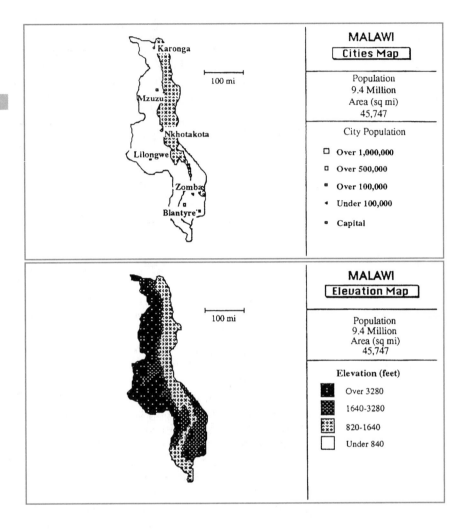

globe). The middle screen reveals time differences between the local point and the distant country. The bottom screen converts currency between the two countries. The three screens in Figure 7–20 reveal statistics about the health and education of the Malawi population.

## Advantages in Developing and Using Databases

In developing a database, students are engaged in activities that contribute to the development of organizational skills and higher order thinking skills. They refine a specific vocabulary. They research information on a given topic. They verify the accuracy of data, note the similarities and differences among data examined, and explore relationships. They classify

**FIGURE 7–19**
*Screens from* MacGlobe
(Courtesy of Broderbund
Software, Inc.)

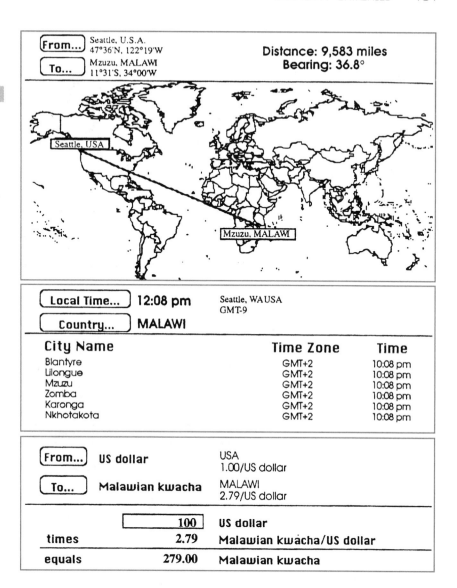

information discovered. They consider how information might be communicated effectively to others.

In searching for information in a database, students develop and refine information retrieval skills. They improve their ability to recognize patterns, trends, and other relationships. They are encouraged to think critically by interpreting data and testing hypotheses. All of these skills have real-world applications and contribute to preparing students to take their place as productive members of society.

FIGURE 7–20
*Screens from MacGlobe*
(Courtesy of Broderbund
Software, Inc.

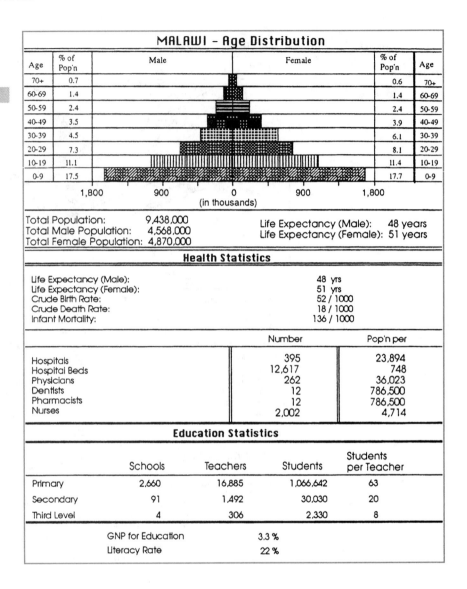

| | | MALAWI – Age Distribution | | | |
|---|---|---|---|---|---|
| Age | % of Pop'n | Male | Female | % of Pop'n | Age |
| 70+ | 0.7 | | | 0.6 | 70+ |
| 60-69 | 1.4 | | | 1.4 | 60-69 |
| 50-59 | 2.4 | | | 2.4 | 50-59 |
| 40-49 | 3.5 | | | 3.9 | 40-49 |
| 30-39 | 4.5 | | | 6.1 | 30-39 |
| 20-29 | 7.3 | | | 8.1 | 20-29 |
| 10-19 | 11.1 | | | 11.4 | 10-19 |
| 0-9 | 17.5 | | | 17.7 | 0-9 |

1,800        900        0        900        1,800
(in thousands)

Total Population:        9,438,000
Total Male Population:   4,568,000          Life Expectancy (Male):    48 years
Total Female Population: 4,870,000          Life Expectancy (Female): 51 years

**Health Statistics**

| | |
|---|---|
| Life Expectancy (Male): | 48 yrs |
| Life Expectancy (Female): | 51 yrs |
| Crude Birth Rate: | 52 / 1000 |
| Crude Death Rate: | 18 / 1000 |
| Infant Mortality: | 136 / 1000 |

| | Number | Pop'n per |
|---|---|---|
| Hospitals | 395 | 23,894 |
| Hospital Beds | 12,617 | 748 |
| Physicians | 262 | 36,023 |
| Dentists | 12 | 786,500 |
| Pharmacists | 12 | 786,500 |
| Nurses | 2,002 | 4,714 |

**Education Statistics**

| | Schools | Teachers | Students | Students per Teacher |
|---|---|---|---|---|
| Primary | 2,660 | 16,885 | 1,066,642 | 63 |
| Secondary | 91 | 1,492 | 30,030 | 20 |
| Third Level | 4 | 306 | 2,330 | 8 |

| | |
|---|---|
| GNP for Education | 3.3 % |
| Literacy Rate | 22 % |

## Summary

Information is purposefully structured and organized data to which we give meaning. A database manager is software designed to structure data to produce information. It is an information management tool with the potential to increase the speed of information acquisition, the ease with which information is acquired, and the quality of the information acquired in terms of both accuracy and completeness.

A database is an organized structured collection of facts about a particular topic. A database may consist of a single file or a number of related files. Database management software is designed to allow the user to create a structure for the storage, manipulation, and retrieval of data. The products of file managers fall into two main categories: the real-time, "on-line" searching for specific information and the ability to print reports organized in a particular fashion.

The individual data item is the most discrete element of a database and is called a field. Fields can contain text, numeric values, dates, pictures, sounds, and calculations that perform mathematical operations on other numeric fields within the record and store the resulting values. Fields can also contain summaries of data across a number of records and display the result. Field labels are created that identify or describe the fields where the data are actually stored.

The record is the building block of the file and is composed of all the related fields. A file is the aggregation of all the records. As fields are defined, labels are created and grouped together, creating a layout that appears on the screen. Once data are entered, the layout that is selected or created can be thought of as a window through which to examine data in selected fields.

The database manager software allows the user to search for and select records based on a wide range of criteria. Compound searches can be constructed to examine data in multiple fields using the Boolean connectors AND, OR, and NOT. Data can then be sorted or arranged in a prescribed alphabetic, numeric, or chronological order in either ascending or descending fashion based on any individual field. Most software also allows nested or multilevel sorts.

To develop a report for printing information from the file, the user first selects the appropriate layout, then selects the records to be included in the report, and finally, designates their order. Information can be entered once and many reports can be generated simply by instructing the computer program how to organize the data.

To make the best use of a file management system, the user must be able to meet the following four requirements: (1) understand your information needs, (2) specify your output needs, (3) specify your input needs, (4) determine the file organization.

Teachers want help in alleviating the paperwork demands made on them. They want help in accomplishing activities that do not involve students directly and are often done outside of actual class time. Students need access to increasing amounts of information if they are to construct their own knowledge. The teaching of information organization and retrieval skills can be taught through the use of databases.

# Chapter Exercises

1. List at least three database management applications for each of the following and explain how the database addresses a particular need.
   a. Classroom teacher
   b. Library/media specialist
   c. Student
2. Look at your personal records. To what areas might you apply a file manager? Do you have records in a paper format that could be stored and manipulated electronically? What would be the advantages and disadvantages of doing this?
3. Develop the field definition for a file that would include all the information you would need on the students in a given class.
4. Determine the kinds of reports you would need if the entire student population of your school was put on a database. What kind of information would have to be placed in the database and how often would this information have to be updated?
5. Select one of the database examples illustrated in Figures 7–11 through 7–15 and create it using the database software available to you. Add, delete, or change the fields suggested in order to modify the database to suit your particular needs. Enter sample data and prepare a user's guide so that a classmate can run some reports.
6. After examining Figures 7–18, 7–19, and 7–20 as products of the software *MacGlobe*, write a brief description of Malawi. Be sure to point out similarities to and differences from the United States. Indicate what else you would like to know about Malawi.

# Glossary

**authority list**   A list of approved headings, names, terms, etc., designed to control what is entered into a field.

**database**   The collection of related data records stored and accessed electronically by computer. By popular use, now used interchangeably with the term *file*.

**database manager**   Software that is designed to manage electronic files.

**field**   The group of related characters treated as a unit within a record; for example, the last name of a student. The smallest, most discrete element of a file. A group of fields constitutes a record.

**file**   A collection of related records treated as a unit.

**file management**   A systematic approach to the storage, manipulation, and retrieval of information stored as data items in the form of records in a file.

**form**   See *layout*.

**label**   The descriptor related to a data field.

**layout**   The selection and positioning of fields and their labels for screen or printed use.

**logical search**   The ability to apply logical operators to a search, for example, "Find all words that contain 'th' " or "Find all values greater than 100."

**multilevel sort**   A series of second, third, etc. levels of sorts performed after a primary one was performed. For example, sorting a group of students by first name after they were first sorted by last name.

**nested sort**   See *multilevel sort.*

**record**   A group of related fields treated as a unit. For example, in a student file, a record might be all the information stored related to a given student. A group of records constitutes a file.

**relational database**   A collection of related data files stored and accessed electronically.

**template**   A blank form in a file manager containing labels and perhaps report formats but no data.

## Notes & Suggested Readings

Beare, R. (1992, December). Software tools in science classrooms. *Journal of Computer Assisted Learning, 8*(4), 221–230.

Benjamin, L. (1993, April). Motivational meteorology. *Science Teacher, 60*(4), 20–25.

Browning, C. A. (1992, December). A 'handy' database activity for the middle school classroom. *Arithmetic Teacher, 40*(4), 235–238.

Cox, A. C. (1991, July–August). Western Europe—A trading game. *Journal of Geography, 90*(4), 168–173.

Davey, C., & Jarvis, A. (1990). Microcomputers for microhistory: A database approach to the reconstitution of small English populations. *History and Computing, 2*(3), 187.

Dean, B. R. (1992, May–June). Curriculum connection: Take technology outdoors. *Instructor, 101*(9), 66–68.

Ennis, D. L. (1993). A transfer of database skills from the classroom to the real world. *Computers in the Schools, 9*(2–3), 55–63.

Gettys, D. (1994, October). Journaling with a database. *The Computing Teacher, 22*(2), 37–40, 48.

Hauserman, C. (1992, November). Discipline tracking with databases. *The Computing Teacher, 20*(3), 20.

Hollis, R. (1990, March). Database yearbooks in the second grade. *The Computing Teacher, 17*(6), 14–15.

Jankowski, L. (1993–94, December/January). Getting started with databases. *The Computing Teacher, 21*(4), 8–9.

Kawasaki, G. (1991). *Database 101: A database primer for the rest of us.* Berkeley, CA: Peachpit Press.

Mernit, S. (1991, February). Black history month—Let your database set the stage. *Instructor, 100*(6), 109–110.

North Carolina State Department of Public Instruction. (1992). *Voteline: A project for integrating computer databases, spreadsheets, and telecomputing into high school social studies instruction* (ED350243). Raleigh.

Rae, J. (1990). Getting to grips with database design: A step by step approach. *Computers and Education, 14*(6), 281.

Salant, A. (1990, April). A fully integrated instructional database: Promoting student research skills. *Educational Technology, 30*(4), 55–58.

Smith, C. B. (1991, February). The role of different literary genres. *Reading Teacher, 44*(6), 440–441.

Thomas, R. (1993, March). Envisioning data: Tables, scatter plots, choropleth maps, and correlation. *The Computing Teacher, 20*(6), 37–40.

# 8

# NETWORKING AND TELECOMMUNICATIONS

**Telecommunications** is defined as the sharing of information over distance. In its simplest form, one computer connected to another could be thought of as sharing information over distance. In simple terms, telecommunications allows users to exchange messages, view files on remote computers, and transfer files. A cluster of interconnected computers in the same room are sharing information in a fashion that we have come to call a **network.** It seems appropriate, therefore, to discuss physical networks and the virtual networks of long-distance telecommunications together.

Networks are constructed in order to maximize the use of software and the exchange of information. Software made available on a network can be accessed by a number of different machines providing that the appropriate license fee has been paid to the software publisher. **Electronic mail,** commonly referred to as **e-mail,** allows messages to be exchanged between users. Electronic bulletin boards allow documents to be read simultaneously by a number of networked users.

Networks, though they are sometimes thought of as local facilities, in reality span the globe. Effective long-distance communications are in fact moving us toward the promised *global village.* Over a decade ago, Naisbitt (1984) identified the trend toward the shrinking information float, that is to say, the time lag between the occurrence of an event and widespread knowledge of its occurrence. For all practical purposes, the information float no longer exists.

As teachers are becoming comfortable with telecommunications, they are exploring the concept of *global classrooms.* These are composed of computers in classrooms around the world interconnected for the purpose of sharing information, ideas, interests, collaborative projects, and questions. Children and young adults in global classrooms are indeed in the process of becoming citizens of the world.

## Advanced Organizers

1. Why are computers interconnected into networks?
2. How are physical connections accomplished?
3. How are networks configured?
4. How should computer labs be designed?
5. How do digital and analog signals differ?
6. How does hardware serve as a communication tool?
7. What software is necessary to use a computer as a communication tool?
8. What are the most common applications of telecommunications?
9. What is the Internet?
10. What are some resources on the Internet?
11. What are some tools to use on the Internet?

## NETWORKING

Networking is the interconnecting of computer stations with each other as well as with selected input and output peripheral devices. It offers several important advantages to schools. A network permits resource sharing, that is, the sharing of software and peripheral equipment. Network licenses are considerably less expensive than purchasing multiple copies of individual software packages. Without a network one peripheral device such as a printer can serve only one computer. A network allows many computers to access connected peripheral devices no matter where they are physically located.

A network promotes resource management. Individual users do not have to have every program or file on a disk since those resources can reside on a central network server. Many school networks employ student data management software that provides security and record-keeping functions. Finally, and most importantly, a network facilitates information exchange and student collaboration. Students can read files created by a teacher, exchange files among themselves, communicate with others by e-mail, or, with the proper software, work simultaneously and interactively on a project.

When the network is composed of devices that are housed in close proximity to one another such as in one building or on a campus the network is referred to as a **local area network** or **LAN.** A network that spans great distances or covers a wide geographical area is called a **wide area network** or **WAN.** LANs may be classified by the type of interconnection and by the topology or configuration that facilitates either a peer-to-peer relationship in which computer stations can exchange files between each other, or a client/server relationship in which computer stations exchange files between themselves and a central computer.

## Network Cabling

Cabling, as illustrated in Figure 8–1, is most often twisted pair wiring such as has been used in the telephone system and is now being gradually replaced by optical fiber or coaxial cable such as that used in a closed-circuit television system. The most recent mode of interconnection is *wireless*, which employs either infrared or radio wave transmission and reception. Infrared communication, such as that employed by a TV remote control, is limited since it cannot penetrate solid objects and is, therefore, restricted to close ranges, usually within a room. Radio wave communication does not have these restrictions and exhibits properties similar to cable networks without the limitations of being hard wired. In July 1992, the FCC designated a band of radio waves for User-PC products. Melanie McMullen, a specialist in mobile computing and networking, predicts that "By the year 2000, wireless LANs will account for 10 percent of all nodes" (McMullen, 1993).

**Twisted pair** is the least expensive copper cabling, often used for wiring phone systems, and is suitable for short distances. Pairs of wires are used in a circuit but many pairs are often wrapped in a bundle surrounded by an outer sheath. An unused pair of wires in a building's existing phone system can often be used to network computers. If unshielded twisted pair wiring is used, the network may be susceptible to electromagnetic or radio frequency interference. **Coaxial cable,** composed of a central core conductor

**FIGURE 8–1**

*Types of cabling*

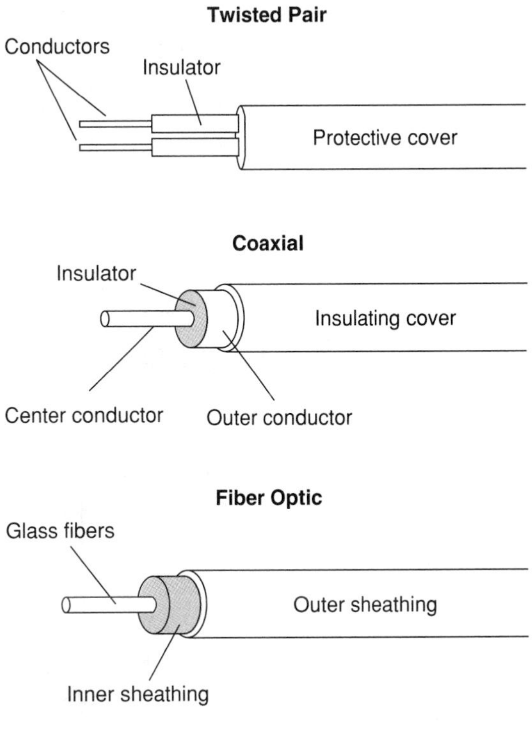

**Twisted Pair**

Conductors

Insulator

Protective cover

**Coaxial**

Insulator

Insulating cover

Center conductor    Outer conductor

**Fiber Optic**

Glass fibers

Outer sheathing

Inner sheathing

surrounded by insulation and then by a second conductor, is more expensive and more difficult to install. It has the advantage, however, of transmitting a much greater quantity of data at a much higher speed. It is also resistant to most interference. The 75 ohm or broad-band cable capable of supporting up to 32 simultaneous channels is usually used. In new or remodeled construction, **optical fiber** is often installed. Although it is the most expensive cabling, it has the greatest bandwidth, allowing up to 600 voice-grade channels to be used simultaneously. It is capable of the highest speed transmission and is virtually impervious to unauthorized access or tapping.

## Network Protocols and Topologies

Network software **protocols** or standardized rules allow many devices to share the network cabling without interfering with one another. Two popular ones are Ethernet and Appletalk. The latter has been built into every Macintosh. Ethernet can be added to a computer by purchasing an interface card and connecting cable. The newer Macintosh and Power PC computers come ready to connect to Ethernet. The various topologies or physical configurations may support either software protocol.

The linear **bus topology** shown in Figure 8–2 is the most common configuration for small networks designed primarily to share peripherals or where each computer may house information in its hard drive to share with others on the network. In a peer-to-peer function, the failure of one computer does not disable the rest of the network. It is also possible to dedicate one computer in this configuration as a **network server** or **host,** that is, a device that all other client computers access for programs and files.

The main wiring sometimes referred to in this configuration as the "backbone," may be twisted pair, coaxial cable, or optical fiber with connectors for each node. An advantage of this topology is the ease of network expansion. This also leads to one of its drawbacks. As the network expands

**FIGURE 8–2**
*Bus network configuration*

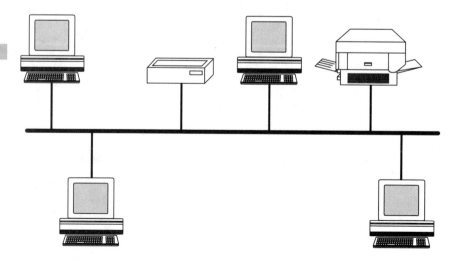

in length and in number of nodes, the system slows down because messages collide more frequently and must be resent. The user notices the degradation of performance as operations such as accessing a remote computer, opening files, and saving files become slower.

The **star topology** shown in Figure 8–3 is also a popular one. One computer is dedicated as a network server. If it fails, however, the entire network ceases to operate. The other computers connected on this network are considered clients to the host network server. Communication between any two client computers must go through the host. A common application is the storage of a database meant to be accessed by several computers. An electronic mail service is easy to implement. Each client computer has a mailbox on the network server and messages are easily routed and stored and responses sent. Network operating system software such as Novell Netware or AppleShare is located on the server and controls access and security on the network.

The **ring topology** illustrated in Figure 8–4 is the one used least often. Although a ring network may provide multiple access, it usually employs a special coded message called a token that the operating software passes in sequence to each computer on the network. This type of configuration, as implemented by IBM, is referred to as a token ring network. The ring topology has advantages and drawbacks similar to the bus configuration.

Once again, there are several advantages to local area networks. Costly peripherals are shared instead of duplicated; programs and files also can be shared between computers on the network; electronic mail can travel over the network, facilitating a rapid and timely exchange of information; a network can facilitate computer use by minimizing the number of floppy disks needed.

**FIGURE 8–3**
*Star network configuration*

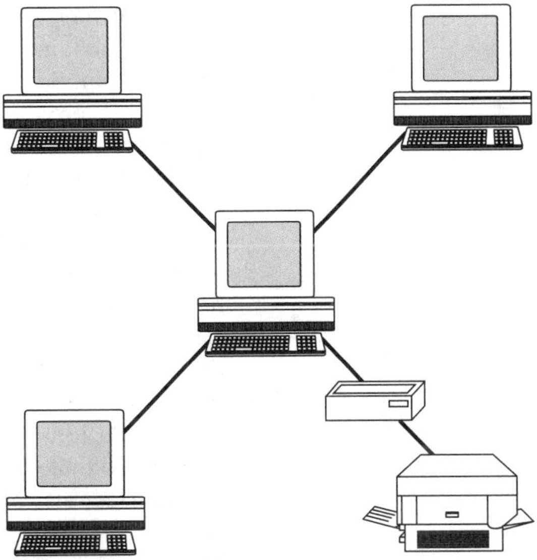

**FIGURE 8-4**
*Ring network configuration*

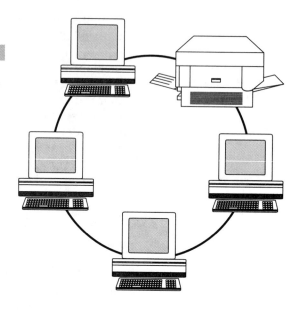

## Computer Labs

Although networks can exist throughout a school building, the most obvious place is in a networked computer lab. There, computers are interconnected to a file server (often located in another room) and to one or more printers. They may even be connected in an interactive manner to each other. The file server may store programs as well as files meant to be accessed by all the computer stations.

The design of the physical space of the computer lab will be affected by the number of computer stations; the number of peripheral devices such as printers, scanners, **MIDI** keyboards (musical synthesizers), and so on; and, most importantly, by the style of teaching that will predominate in that room. Figures 8–5 through 8–7 suggest designs to accommodate a teacher-centered lecture style and a student-centered collaborative learning environment.

Figure 8–5 illustrates a design of one student per computer station. All student stations face toward the front of the room to attend to the instructor as a lecture/demonstration is conducted. This configuration is really a teacher-centered classroom design rather than a laboratory. All stations have an unobstructed view of the projection screen since the video projector is suspended from the ceiling. Students can easily replicate at their stations whatever is being projected on the screen and instruction can progress in somewhat of a lock-step manner.

The design illustrated in Figure 8–6 has stations with large desktop surfaces so that students can gather around a computer and monitor. The large surface also allows room for students to work in pairs at one station. All stations face outward to facilitate students' moving around and viewing other stations' monitors. Software also exists to allow the image from

**FIGURE 8-5**

*A 24-station instructor-centered lab design*

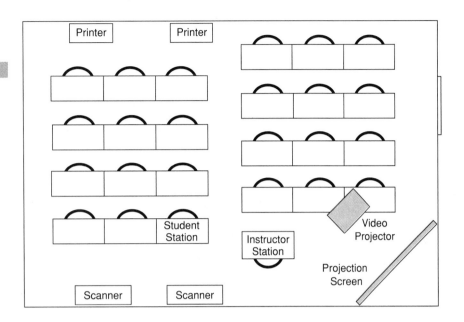

**FIGURE 8-6**

*An 18-station student-centered lab design*

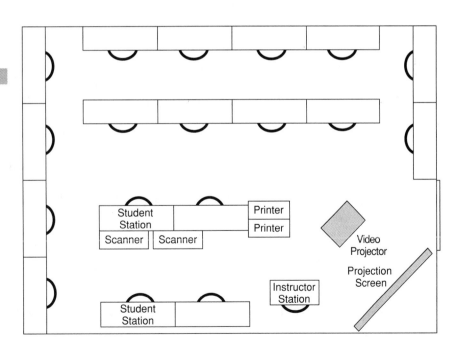

**FIGURE 8–7**
*A 24-station student-centered lab design with worktables*

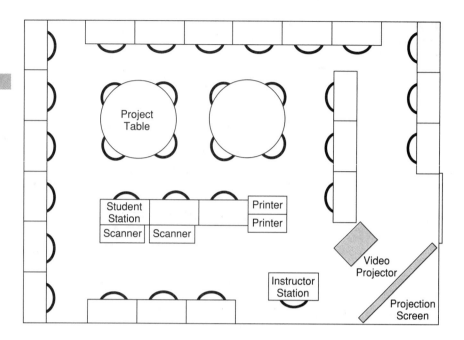

one monitor to be displayed on all others simultaneously. Some movement would be required when students are called on to view an image projected on the screen.

The design illustrated in Figure 8–7 has smaller desktop surfaces in order to accommodate more stations in a restricted space. Once again, all stations are facing outward to facilitate students' moving around and viewing other stations' monitors. Worktables are provided to encourage off-computer work by individual students and collaborative groups. Some movement would also be required when students are called on to view an image on the projection screen. Scanners and printers are provided as necessary peripheral devices to many activities conducted in a computer lab.

A lab should accommodate large groups, small groups, or individual work. In planning a computer lab, the question must be answered, "Will this room truly function as a laboratory where students will employ the computers as tools in their exploration of concepts, or is this room primarily intended to be a demonstration classroom?" It is difficult for one room to optimally serve both functions.

## TELECOM-MUNICATIONS

Telecommunications involves taking the concepts present in a local network and extending them to buildings within a school district, to the community at large, to the state, to the nation, and even to the entire world. Through advances in technology and with federal and state government support,

**FIGURE 8–8**
*Digital and analog signals*

telecommunications is becoming far easier, less costly, and much more prevalent as teachers and students receive a modest amount of training.

## Fundamental Concepts

As was discussed in Chapter 2, computers are composed mainly of digital circuits. They process information as voltage in a digital or **binary** code of 1s and 0s.

Consider the illustration in Figure 8–8. **Digital** signals are high or low with no smooth, gradual transition. **Analog** signals, on the other hand, are continuous signals varying in amplitude and frequency that flow from high to low with varying intervals between peaks. One way of understanding the difference might be to think of a clock. Its ticking is a digital signal. It makes a ticking sound and then there is silence; in other words, a binary state exists—a tick or silence. Most clock faces, however, are analog in the sense that hands sweep through a continuous unbroken circle.

Until very recently telephone lines were designed to carry only analog signals. A hardware device called a **modem** (*MO*dulator-*dem*odulator) was created to translate digital and analog signals. Figure 8–9 illustrates the connection of computers by phone lines. Notice that a modem connected to a computer must be present at both sites.

## Communications Hardware

A connector or port on a computer allows data to flow between the computer and the outside world. These interface ports allow the user to connect a cable linking the computer and a peripheral device. Most ports supply data in a serial fashion. The RS-232 is the most common serial port. It is so named for Recommended Standard No. 232 of the Electrical Institute of America.

A modem is connected to the serial port in order to convert the digital data into analog form to transmit over the phone lines. A modem connected

**FIGURE 8–9**
*Communication by modem*

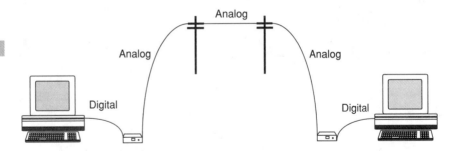

to the serial port of a receiving computer translates the analog data back to digital form. Modems were identified by the term **baud rate,** a measure of signaling speed. The higher the baud rate, the faster the modem could transmit data. Common rates in the early days of telecommunications were 300 and 1200 baud. The advent of the 2400 baud modem created quite a bit of excitement. It was deemed so efficient that commercial information services increased the connection charges to users of 2400 baud and faster modems.

The measure *bits per second* **(bps)** has gradually replaced baud rate as the indicator of data transfer rate. Remember that a bit (a contraction of *binary digit*) is the smallest data unit in a digital system. Bps is a more accurate unit of measure at higher speeds since modems are now designed to encode more than one bit in a signal element; 9600 bps and 14,400 bps modems are now common with 28,800 bps modems becoming a significant factor in the marketplace. Faster modems mean lower long-distance phone charges and perhaps lower connection fees from services that assess time charges. Telephone line quality is now placing a practical limit, however, on the transfer rate.

A modem contains instructions that interpret and respond to commands typed at the computer keyboard. The command mode illustrated in Figure 8–10 controls the action of the modem. In addition to the *dial-a-number* and *disconnect-the-call* commands, a user can directly address the modem in command mode to set the baud rate, number of bits per character, and error checking conventions. Most of these commands, however, are taken over and simplified by the communications software.

The industry standard command set is the AT set developed by the Hayes Corporation. Employing this set, a user could type AT DT followed by a phone number. The Hayes-compatible modem would recognize that AT signified a modem command and the following DT would signal that it was to dial a touch-tone call. (DP would signify the older pulse dialing convention.) Once an answering signal is heard, the modems maintain this carrier signal and switch to data transfer mode.

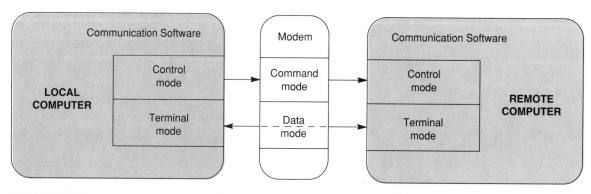

**FIGURE 8–10**
*Modems communicate through a command and a data mode*

## Communications Software

As illustrated in Figure 8–11, telecommunications software has both a control mode and a terminal emulation mode. The control mode regulates the performance of the modem to match the remote computer and modem. In control mode, the user sets the speed of the data transfer and determines the number of bits per character and parity. The number of bits per character is usually set at eight bits to allow for the transmission of text and graphics symbols. Eight bits also closely matches the format used by computer programs and is, therefore, commonly used in personal computer communications. **Parity** is a simple form of error checking that the user usually sets to even, odd, or none. Even parity would turn a bit on or off to ascertain that the number of binary 1s in a character is always an even number. Odd parity would turn a bit on or off to ascertain that the number of binary 1s in a character is always an odd number. None is the most common setting today. The control mode also governs file access and storage as well as printer operation.

Terminal emulation mode primarily governs screen display format. The VT-100 is the name of a computer terminal developed by Digital Equipment Corporation and the VT-100 terminal emulation mode has become an industry standard. When the user selects VT-100 emulation, the computer screen display (line length and spacing, carriage returns, line feeds, and cursor movement) resembles that of a VT-100 terminal.

## Applications of Telecommunications

In 1992, Margaret Honey and Andrés Henríquez surveyed teachers who use telecommunications in their classrooms (1993). The respondents were highly self-motivated and generally self-taught—the pioneers of an emerging movement. Fred D'Ignazio (1990) describes the paradigm shift teachers will need to make before networking and telecommunications become widespread in the classroom:

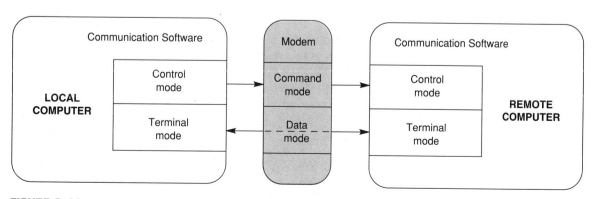

**FIGURE 8–11**
*Computers communicate through a control and a terminal mode*

Most teachers see the computer as a kind of electronic Cuisinart. You pour information into the computer and—it slices. It dices. It blends. It whips. It purees. And then it disgorges—. . .

A new paradigm for "computer" is suddenly emerging. Associated with this paradigm are the concepts: *network, communication, connectivity, multimedia,* and *vehicle.*

We are overnight crossing the threshold from personal computing to *interpersonal computing.* In tomorrow's workplace, we will all be using *workstations* instead of mere computers. The word "workstation" implies communication. The workstation must talk with the other people and the other machines. . . .

If we couple this concept of a communicating workstation with multimedia, we can see how the computer is no longer a stationary device, but a *vehicle.* . . . Students and teachers can ride that vehicle to the furthest reaches of human knowledge and imagination.

Among the applications of telecommunications that allow the computer to become a vehicle to transport students and teachers along the information highways are e-mail, electronic conferencing, commercial information services, and educational networks.

## E-Mail

E-mail allows users to exchange messages within a local area network or with users in faraway places. E-mail has phenomenal holding power. Students eagerly spend time each day reading and writing at the computer. What an opportunity to develop language arts skills! Once the novelty and electronic pen-pal syndrome wear off, students might see e-mail as a means of accessing information on specific topics and learning about different cultures.

E-mail is a great equalizer. Recently a librarian at the Seattle Public Library was discussing e-mail with a homeless person who was sitting at one of the library terminals connected to the Internet. The person indicated that he was contacting other users hoping to find a job or perhaps job training. He commented that it didn't matter if he were black, Hispanic, or physically impaired; the other users simply reacted to him as an electronic contact. It strikes me that students building relationships with each other on e-mail might look at old prejudices in a new light.

A simple, cost-effective way of preparing your students to use e-mail is to place two computers back-to-back and switch their monitor cables so that computer A connects to monitor B. Students sitting at the computers cannot see the monitor on which the message they type appears. Unable to use body language, students would have to be precise and succinct in their communication. This process would teach students to repeat the important elements of the incoming message to which they were responding. This exercise also simulates the ability to "chat" on some bulletin boards.

## Bulletin Board Systems

As their name suggests, electronic **bulletin board systems (BBS)** organize groups of messages by topic. They are the telecommunications equivalent of the multicolored notices tacked up in a college's Student Union to announce meetings, roommates wanted, or items for sale. Subject areas may be referred to as conferences, forums, or echoes; they span the broad range of human interests from astrology to zoology. Whereas e-mail allows an individual to correspond with another individual, an electronic bulletin board permits an individual to publish his or her views to a multitude of readers who may be located anywhere in the world.

Using skills and techniques acquired in the design and creation of databases, you can develop a simple, cost-effective way of preparing your students to use bulletin boards. A computer could be set up in a common area such as the school library or a computer lab to resemble a message area of a bulletin board. Figure 8–12 suggests some fields that might be used.

A series of topics ranging from local, statewide, or national issues could be chosen and students would be encouraged to leave specific messages on one or more of the topics. They would also be encouraged to search for responses to questions they might have on any of the topics.

Once this has proven to be successful, a follow-up to the simulation might be to establish your own in-school bulletin board. Software to establish a local bulletin board system is freely available on many existing BBSs.

## Commercial Information Services

A number of companies market services such as e-mail, conferencing, and database access for a fee. There is usually a monthly membership fee and there may also be connect-time charges. Appendix L list names, addresses, and phone numbers for the five most popular vendors. Three commercial vendors are discussed as examples in the following section.

America Online.    America Online (AOL) is a commercial service that provides live interactive conferencing; databases of games, graphics, and computer applications; electronic versions of popular magazines; e-mail; and a gateway to the Internet—all this for a modest monthly subscription fee. Over 250 hardware and software producers maintain bulletin boards

**FIGURE 8–12**
*Message database*

| NAME | Text |
|------|------|
| DATE | Auto enter today |
| SUBJECT | Text |
| TO | Text |
| FROM | Text |
| MESSAGE | Text |

to offer assistance with their products. The latest news, weather, sports, and stock market information is available. Thousands of public domain software programs are available. The EAASY SABRE reservation system allows the user to make airline and major hotel reservations.

CompuServe.   CompuServe is another commercial service that provides electronic conferencing; games, graphics, and computer applications; electronic versions of popular magazines; e-mail; and a gateway to the Internet. The basic monthly subscription is quite modest with surcharges applied for access to some areas. Check the latest news on the *Associated Press Online* hourly summaries, read the current issue of *U.S. News and World Report,* search for the treasure in *CastleQuest,* or "shop 'til you drop" in the *Electronic Mall*®.

Prodigy.   Prodigy is yet another commercial service that provides e-mail, a number of USENET groups and bulletin boards of interest to educators, and a gateway to the Internet. It was formed in the fall of 1988 as a joint venture between Sears and IBM. It carries news on *Associated Press Online,* sports on *ESPN Online,* and a good deal of business and investment information including fifteen-minute-delayed stock quotes. Subscription kits are available from Sears and computer retailers.

### Educational Networks

A number of networks aimed primarily at K-12 education have developed during the last few years. The names, addresses, and phone numbers of the five major educational networks are listed in Appendix L.

AT&T Learning Network.   This network is designed to connect students and teachers in seven to nine classrooms in different locations into a Learning Circle. The Learning Circles form according to specific themes and for a specific duration. Students investigate a topic, share ideas, and collaborate in producing a final publication.

FrEdMail.   Free Educational Electronic Mail Network (FrEdMail) is a loosely organized international network of over 150 school-based electronic bulletin boards. Messages are exchanged between sites during off-peak hours. Users issue calls for collaboration on specific project ideas. FrEdMail also publishes a newsletter including project ideas, most of which are designed to promote writing activities.

In 1991, over 5,000 classrooms around the country participated in such projects as "Acid Rain," in which students collected rain samples, plotted the resulting data, and shared conclusions on the causes and effects of acid rain.

Since a single individual is not in charge of a project and has no authority to require participation, some projects are never completed. This can lead to some frustration among participants.

### K12 Net.

K12 Net is a collection of **electronic conferences** specifically designed for use in schools. There are more than three dozen of these forums devoted to curriculum (e.g., art, music, science, and math); language exchanges with native speakers in French, German, Japanese, Russian, and Spanish; and classroom-to-classroom projects designed by teachers and listed each week in the "projects" conference. There are also four informal chat areas for elementary, middle, and high school students as well as teachers. The conferences are privately distributed as a group to more than 600 participating FidoNet-compatible bulletin board systems on six continents *and* to the Internet as Usenet newsgroups in the k12.* hierarchy. Participants are located all over the world; every message in every conference can be read by students and teachers on every system, so any inquiry may receive a reply from Taiwan or South Africa as well as from the U.S. and Canada.

K12 Net is supported by the system operators of the bulletin boards that participate, so it is *free* to users who can connect with a local phone call. The messages are compressed and exchanged late at night when phone rates are cheapest. K-12 educators and students who do not have access to the Internet have found K12 Net to be an exciting "network with training wheels" to learn and teach about telecommunications.

### National Geographic Kids Network.

This is a highly structured international network that allows middle grade students to participate in science and geography projects developed by curriculum specialists under the joint funding of the National Geographic Society and the National Science Foundation. Activities on the network are based on the belief that children learn by doing. Students use instruments in hands-on experiments and record changes over time. They conduct surveys, read maps, and create graphs. Students analyze data they collect locally and share with others on the network. They form and test hypotheses, make comparisons and look for patterns, and they draw conclusions and discuss the implications. The information is also analyzed by experts and summaries of their findings are sent back to the students. In the past, topics have included acid rain, water pollution, weather, recycling, solar energy, and nutrition. In this *top-down* curriculum model, participants receive a teacher's guide, handbooks, and activity sheets.

### SpecialNet® (GTE Education NetServices).

SpecialNet® is a commercial network in operation since 1981 aimed specifically at education and serving the United States and Canada. It provides e-mail, databases, and a variety of conferences on education-related topics. These include federal legislation, employment opportunities, promising practices, new products and publications, computer applications and software, and a wide variety of special education topics.

## The Internet

The **Internet** is without a doubt the best known network today. In reality, though, it is a network of networks. How did this supernetwork begin? In the early 1970s, the Advanced Research Projects Agency (ARPA) of the Department of Defense created a packet-switched computer network linking four different sites. They called this the ARPANET. By the mid-1970s this network grew significantly and evolved into a network serving the entire Department of Defense. A set of standards called **Transmission Control Protocol/Internet Protocol (TCP/IP)** was developed to allow different networks to interconnect. Following on the heels of this success, the National Science Foundation (NSF) created CSNET in 1981. An agreement between ARPA and NSF allowed the interconnection of the two networks. By 1984, CSNET had evolved into the much more significant NSFNET. Campuswide networks at the major U.S. universities as well as large regional networks interconnected with ARPANET/NSFNET. In 1990, the Department of Defense discontinued support for the ARPANET, leaving

**FIGURE 8–13**
*OSSHE Net connected to Northwest Net*

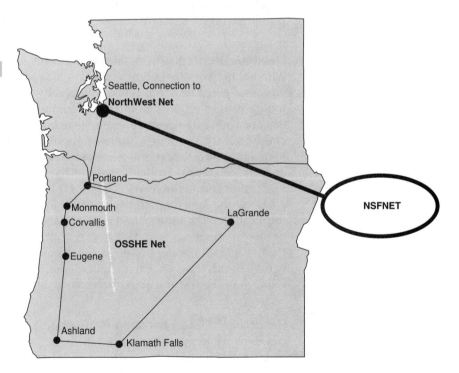

NSFNET as the major backbone in the United States in what is now known as the Internet, an interconnection of thousands of networks that spans the globe and serves millions of users.

Figure 8–13 illustrates the Oregon State System of Higher Education (OSSHE) OSSHE Net, a statewide network connecting the public institutions of higher education in the state of Oregon linked to Northwest Net, a regional network service provider headquartered in Seattle, Washington, and through that network to the Internet.

### Resources on the Internet

As one would expect in this interconnection of networks, various resources are available. The primary ones are e-mail, electronic conferencing, databases, and LISTSERVs. As software has become increasingly user-friendly, it is less likely that one will need to learn the arcane UNIX commands that typified early Internet connections.

E-Mail.   Any user connected to an e-mail system with an Internet connection can exchange messages with any other user on a connected e-mail system providing the e-mail address is known. The author's e-mail address is *forcier@fsa.wosc.osshe.edu*. It is composed of several parts called a domain and subdomains.

Figure 8–14 identifies the parts of an Internet e-mail address. Reading from right to left, *edu* represents one of the major domains on the Internet and identifies my site as an educational institution. (Some other domains are commercial <.com>, government agencies <.gov>, networks <.net>, and organizations <.org>. International sites are frequently identified geographically by two characters representing the country in which they are located, e.g., Canada <.ca>, United Kingdom <.uk>, Australia <.au>. Because of the phenomenal volume of new users joining the Internet, a new convention of using  geographic identifiers within the United States is replacing the use of <.edu> , and similar domain names.) Each part of an address is separated by a dot (period). The next part of my address, *osshe,* identifies the subdomain of the Oregon State System of Higher Education. The next part, *wosc,* identifies the subdomain that is my campus, Western Oregon State College. The next part, *fsa,* identifies the name of the computer to which I'm connected (File Server A) on our campus LAN. The symbol @ separates the leftmost part of my address that is my user ID, *forcier.* User IDs

**FIGURE 8–14**
*Parts of an Internet e-mail address*

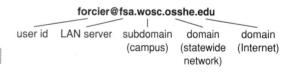

on our campus are composed of the first six letters of our last name and the first letter of our first name. In my case, it spells out my last name exactly. Now that you know my address, I expect to hear from you.

Electronic Conferencing.    Electronic conferencing allows users with similar interests to exchange information and opinions. Usenet newsgroups are the most widely used topic-oriented conferences on the Internet. Newsgroups are organized hierarchically into groups with identifiers such as news, info (information), comp (computers), alt (alternative), misc (miscellaneous), soc (social), and k12 (K-12 education).

Messages posted to newsgroups may be seen by thousands of readers all over the world. Messages should be kept brief and purposeful. When responding to a message, a user should consider sending e-mail to the individual if the message would not be appropriate to the broader readership. Users should quote enough of the message in the reply to give a clear context to the response.

Teachers should educate their students in appropriate use of the network (netiquette) and monitor their usage because some newsgroups contain material not suitable to minors. A table of netiquette rules is included at the end of this chapter. Many school districts and statewide networks have developed acceptable use policies and require parental permission forms before allowing students access to the Internet (Appendix K).

Databases.    The Internet provides access to many types of databases, some accessible at no charge and others that charge an access fee. Some no-fee databases are campus directories; others are lists of people with Internet accounts and their addresses; others are library public access catalogs; and still others are government databases.

It's fascinating to search the library catalogs at Harvard, UCLA, and Oxford. Once a resource is identified, even in a faraway library, it may be possible to borrow it with the assistance of the interlibrary loan department of your local library. One may even be surprised to discover that the same resource is available closer to home!

The Eisenhower National Clearinghouse (ENC) for Mathematics and Science located at Ohio State University is funded by the U.S. Department of Education. Its purpose is to improve access to the most current materials in math and science resources in the nation. Descriptions and evaluations are available. ENC can be reached electronically at galileo.enc.org.

The Educational Resources Information Center (ERIC) provides access to its extensive collection of education-related literature, archives of LISTSERVs, and electronic library listings through a gopher server and e-mail inquiries directed to AskERIC@ericir.syr.edu.

Another government database, the Science and Technology Information System (STIS), contains announcements and reports of National Science

Foundation activities including grant-related information. Information for accessing many of these databases is provided in Appendix M.

LISTSERVs.  **LISTSERVs** may be thought of as e-mail by subscription. Groups of users develop around common topics or interests. Once a user joins or subscribes to a LISTSERV any message sent by that user will be distributed to all participants of the LISTSERV. That user will also receive all messages. It becomes important to delete read or unwanted messages in order to effectively manage your mailbox.

Information for accessing a number of LISTSERVs is provided in Appendix M of this text. A word of caution! LISTSERVs can easily generate 40 or 50 messages a day that have to be read, saved to disk, or deleted. You can imagine how many messages might be waiting for you after spring break if you don't know how to turn off a LISTSERV before vacation. Don't oversubscribe to LISTSERVs. You will find that they require considerable time every day to deal with messages.

### Internet Tools

As you contemplated 15,000+ networks serving over 8 million users around the world, you may have thought, "How can I possibly find my way through this maze?" There are a multitude of recently published books promising to guide new users' explorations of the Internet available at your local computer store or bookstore. Evaluate their usefulness by realistically assessing your own level of expertise and skimming several sections to find one with a writing style and level of technical detail appropriate for you.

Because the Internet is a volatile, rapidly changing environment, the best and most current resources are always online rather than in print. This places the new user in the uncomfortable position of needing to be online in order to maximize online effectiveness. There are some navigation tools that can be of great help.

FTP.  **File Transfer Protocol (FTP)** is used to transfer files between two remote computers. A user can **download** (copy) a file by using software designed for that purpose, providing the address for the remote site is known as well as a valid user ID and sometimes a password. Many FTP sites allow the use of *anonymous* as a log-in or user ID and your e-mail address as the password. The same software and three pieces of information will be required on the rare occurrence when a user wishes to **upload** (send) a file to an FTP site.

Gopher.  The easiest way to understand a **gopher** is to think of it as a local menu of available files. It was originally created at the University of Minnesota and named after their athletic teams' mascot (the Golden Gophers). It has since spread to Internet sites around the world. Client software in Macintosh or PC format on the user machine interfaces with server software on the remote site's computer.

Archie.   **Archie** is a service provided by McGill University in Montreal, Canada. It is an updated integrated list of directories from participating anonymous FTP sites of the more than one million host computers connected to the Internet. Employing Archie greatly facilitates the user's search for information.

Veronica.   Examining the names of the Internet tools mentioned so far, you've discovered that Internetters have a sense of humor. A burrowing rodent and names from comic strip characters of the past! There is a suspicion that the name **Veronica** was chosen to accompany Archie and then an acronym was fabricated (*Very Easy Rodent-Oriented Netwide Index to Computerized Archives*). A user must go through a gopher in order to reach Veronica. It is a collection of Gopher menus. In other words, Veronica is to Archie as Archie is to gophers.

It is evident that Veronica, Archie, and Gopher are tools designed to support broadcast rather than serial searches for information. Rather than the user being required to search a multitude of individual directories, those tools provide an umbrella that can be searched with the result ending up in one particular directory or file. The relationship between Veronica, Archie, and Gopher menus is illustrated in Figure 8–15.

World Wide Web.   **World Wide Web (WWW)** is an Internet navigation system developed at the European Centre of Particle Physics in Switzerland. Information is stored in a format that has addresses of other sites with similar information embedded in it. Client software on the user's machine interfaces with server software on the remote site's computer and is needed to access the World Wide Web (Descy, 1994). **Mosaic** for the Macintosh, Windows, and other platforms is a popular graphical user interface client software for information searching and retrieval. It is currently available free for school use from the National Center for Supercomputing and can be downloaded by FTP from FTP.NCSA.UIUC.EDU. Commercial versions of Mosaic with some enhanced features are also being marketed. Using Mosaic

**FIGURE 8–15**
*Relationship of some Internet tools*

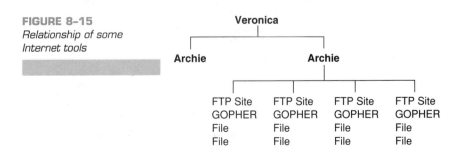

*Netscape is a user-friendly graphical interface to the World Wide Web.*

to navigate the World Wide Web's hypertext-like system, each screen element can be linked to another document, graphic, database, sound, or video clip and all the user has to do is point and click (Goodrich, 1994).

**Netscape Navigator** is another powerful graphical navigation tool for the World Wide Web. Some find it the easiest tool to use since it has all of the linking and graphics capability of Mosaic and it also facilitates leaving a trail of sites browsed in order to determine your current location on the Internet. Netscape allows you to create bookmarks to identify sites so you can return to them easily. Your bookmarks, in fact, become your personalized directory of your favorite Web pages.

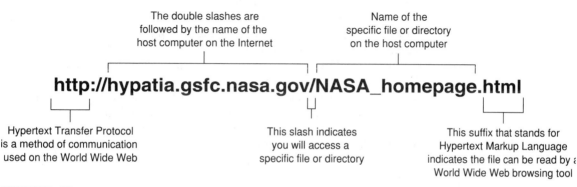

The double slashes are followed by the name of the host computer on the Internet

Name of the specific file or directory on the host computer

**http://hypatia.gsfc.nasa.gov/NASA_homepage.html**

Hypertext Transfer Protocol is a method of communication used on the World Wide Web

This slash indicates you will access a specific file or directory

This suffix that stands for Hypertext Markup Language indicates the file can be read by a World Wide Web browsing tool

**FIGURE 8-16**
*The components of a URL*

**FIGURE 8–17**
*Netiquette: Network com-*
*munication etiquette*
(Bennett, 1994)

- Compose all but brief messages off-line to minimize network traffic.
- Limit each message to one topic and keep it succinct.
- Use subject headings that are very descriptive.
- Reply promptly to messages received.
- When replying, restate enough of the message to clearly identify context.
- Delete messages once you have read them.
- Don't be vulgar or offensive.
- Don't criticize ("flame") others on the network.
- Supply clues if you are intending to write using humor, irony, sarcasm, or emotion. Your intent may not be obvious to the reader. Using all uppercase in a word or phrase SHOUTS. Try :-) for a sideways smile or ;-) for a wink.
- Use a signature footer that includes you name, school, and e-mail address.
- Practice safe communications. Don't spread viruses! Check downloaded executable files.
- Consider yourself a guest on the system and behave accordingly.

The World Wide Web is described as a system but some may prefer to think of it as an index. Each site accessible by a browsing tool such as Mosaic or Netscape has what is referred to as a Web page. Each site also has its own Uniform Resource Locator (URL) or address. Typing a URL in the browsing tool connects the user with a computer at that particular location. The parts of a URL are explained in Figure 8–16.

Figure 8–17 lists some pointers on courteous navigation through the Internet.

## Importance of Telecommunications to Education

Telecommunications offers significant advantages to classroom teachers and other educators because it allows them to transcend the isolation that typifies their profession. Library media specialists and teachers of art, music, and other subjects, who are frequently one of a kind in their buildings, can share teaching strategies and curriculum ideas with their peers in a daily electronic "convention."

Information is broadcast across electronic networks sooner and in greater quantity than in any other publication medium. Many newspapers, government documents, and periodical indexes are published electronically as well as in print. For teachers of health and social studies, timely access to current resources is a major incentive to use telecommunications in their curriculum.

Social studies and foreign language teachers are also enthusiastic about wide-area computer networking because it facilitates significant cultural exchanges. Since personal appearance, physical handicaps and special needs are invisible on the network, students who are set apart from their classmates can participate as equals. Many who are reluctant participants in the classroom become eager contributors when they can compose their inquiries and responses on their own time.

Telecommunications supports the reform movement in education by facilitating cooperative and interactive learning. Science teachers can expand the scope of their data collection far beyond their local environment by collaborating with classrooms across the country or, indeed, the world. Finally, because students are evaluated by the clarity of their written expression with immediate feedback from their peers, they are highly motivated to improve their writing skills.

Telecommunications allows educators to create a virtual classroom without walls, bringing global resources and experiences to their students.

## Summary

Networking is the interconnecting of computer stations with input and output devices to facilitate sharing of information and equipment and to reduce the number and cost of peripherals. When the network is composed of devices that are housed in close proximity to one another the network is referred to as a local area network or LAN. Network cabling is most often inexpensive twisted pair wiring such as that used in the telephone system or high-speed, broad-band coaxial cable such as that used in a closed-circuit television system. Optical fiber has the greatest bandwidth, thereby allowing the greatest number of channels to be used simultaneously.

Network software protocols allow many devices to share networked resources without interfering with one another. The bus topology is the most common configuration for small networks mainly designed to share peripherals. The star topology is a popular one with one computer dedicated as a network server. The ring topology usually employs a special coded message called a token that is passed in sequence to each computer on the network. Local area networks allow costly peripherals, programs, and files to be shared. Electronic mail can travel over the network facilitating a rapid and timely exchange of information.

The design of the physical space of the computer lab will be affected by the number of computer stations, the number of peripheral devices such as printers, scanners, MIDI-keyboards, and so forth, and, most importantly, by the style of teaching that will predominate in that room. It is difficult for one room to truly function as a laboratory for students and as teaching station or demonstration classroom.

Telecommunications involves taking the concepts present in a local network and extending them to buildings within a school district, to the community at large, to the state, to the nation, and even to the entire world.

The computer processes digital signals as voltages in a binary code of 1s and 0s. Digital signals are high or low with no smooth, gradual transition. Analog signals are continuous signals varying in amplitude and frequency that flow from high to low with varying intervals between peaks. A modem is connected to the computer's serial port to convert the digital data into analog form to transmit over the phone lines. A modem connected to the serial port of a receiving computer will translate the analog data back to digital form. The measure *bits per second* (bps) has gradually replaced baud rate as the indicator of data transfer rate; 14,000 bps modems are often used and faster 28,800 bps modems are becoming common as well.

Telecommunications software has both a control mode and a terminal emulation mode. The control mode regulates the performance of the modem to match the remote computer and modem. Terminal emulation mode primarily governs screen display format.

In order to take advantage of telecommunications, teachers must move from seeing the computer as a static piece of equipment they use to process data to seeing the computer as a vehicle capable of transporting them and their students along a myriad of information highways. Among the applications of telecommunications that allow the computer to become this vehicle are e-mail, electronic conferencing, commercial information services, and educational networks.

The Internet is a network of networks that span the globe serving millions of users. The primary resources available are e-mail, electronic bulletin boards, databases, and LISTSERVs. Tools such as Gopher, Archie, Veronica, and FTP are available to navigate this labyrinthine network.

Telecommunications offers significant advantages to the educator who wishes to collaborate with colleagues, access current information, and expose students to a broad range of cultures and curricular resources. Electronic networks overcome traditional barriers of social and geographic isolation, facilitate interactive and cooperative learning, and serve as highly effective motivators to reluctant writers.

## Chapter Exercises

1. Using an electronic encyclopedia on CD-ROM to find the necessary information, explain the basic difference between analog and digital circuits.
2. Locate a modem. Write down its manufacturer's name, the model, and its data transmission rate.
3. Locate the communications software and manual intended for use on the modem located in exercise 2. Determine how to set up the software for that modem. Set the terminal emulation mode.

4. Call a local computer store or your public library and get the phone number of the local node of K12 Net or FidoNet. Using a modem connected to your computer, dial that number and follow instructions presented to you. Describe the process and the result.
5. Using the fields suggested in Figure 8–12, develop a database to resemble a message area of a bulletin board. Select topics dealing with national issues and encourage your colleagues to leave specific messages on one or more of the topics. Encourage them to search for responses to questions they might have on any of the topics.
6. Referring to Appendix L, contact two commercial vendors requesting materials describing their services.
7. Referring again to Appendix L, contact educational network providers requesting materials describing their services.
8. Determine if your college library has an on-line public access catalog. If so, does it provide a gateway to other academic library catalogs? If it does, spend a few minutes exploring other libraries.
9. Interview the director of your library or the director of academic computing on your campus and determine whether or not students are permitted to establish Internet accounts. If so, ask for an account. Inquire about available training.
10. Look up the author's e-mail address in the text. Send a brief message stating your opinion of this textbook. You might suggest improvements you would like to see or ask questions about some of the newer technology. Share some ideas. How are you using the computer as a productivity tool?

## Glossary

**analog** Signals of continuous nature that vary in frequency and amplitude. Analog signals can be transmitted over telephone lines.

**Archie** An updated integrated list of directories from participating anonymous FTP sites of the one million-plus host computers connected to the Internet.

**baud rate** A rate of data transmission term that has been replaced by BPS.

**binary** Consisting of two parts; limited to two conditions or states of being. Computer memory is designed to store binary digits symbolized by 0s and 1s in a code. The computer circuitry is designed to manipulate information in an on/off state.

**bps** A measure of a modem's data transmission speed between computers in bits per second. Common rates are 9,600 and 14,400 bps.

**bulletin board systems (bbs)** Dial-up accessible telecommunications systems that usually feature e-mail, topic-oriented electronic conferences, and files available to download.

**bus topology** A network configuration consisting of a major wiring circuit to which nodes are connected.

**coaxial cable**   A cable composed of a central conductor surrounded by insulation and then by a second conductor; used for television distribution and for high-speed computer networks.

**digital**   Signals of a discrete high or low state represented by the digits 0 or 1.

**download**   To transfer a file from a remote computer to a local one.

**electronic conferencing**   Electronic forums usually organized around specific topics designed to allow the exchange of information by a number of simultaneous users.

**electronic mail**   Software that allows messages to be exchanged between users.

**e-mail**   See *electronic mail.*

**FTP (file transfer protocol)**   A set of standards facilitating the transfer of files between two computers over a network.

**gopher**   A local menu of files available to users at remote sites on the Internet. Client software on the user machine interfaces with server software on the remote site's computer.

**host**   See *network server.*

**internet**   The Internet is a worldwide network of networks based on the TCP/IP protocol.

**LAN**   See *local area network.*

**LISTSERV**   E-mail available by subscription to user groups that develop around common topics or interests. A message sent by a subscriber will be distributed to all participants of the LISTSERV. That subscriber will also receive all messages.

**local area network (LAN)**   A network composed of devices located in close proximity.

**MIDI**   Musical Instrument Digital Interface is a standard agreed upon by manufacturers of musical synthesizers that allows the communications of musical signals. MIDI interface and software allow the computer to control musical instruments.

**modem (modulator-demodulator)**   A device that translates digital computer information into analog signals that can be transmitted over telephone lines and analog signals into a digital form that can be processed by a computer.

**Mosaic**   A popular graphical user interface client software for information searching and retrieval on the Internet. It is available for the Macintosh, Windows, and other platforms.

**netscape navigator**   A graphical browsing tool for the World Wide Web.

**network**   The interconnection of computers to allow multiple users to access software and to exchange information.

**network server**   A computer dedicated to the operation of a network and providing file storage.

**optical fiber**   The most expensive cabling with the greatest bandwidth allowing up to 600 voice grade channels to be used simultaneously. It is capable of the highest speed transmission and is virtually impervious to unauthorized access or tapping.

**parity**   A simple form of error checking that the user usually sets to even, odd, or none. Even parity would turn a bit on or off to ascertain that the number of binary 1s in a character is always an even number. Odd parity would turn a bit on or off to ascertain that the number of binary 1s in a character is always an odd number.

**protocol**    Software standards governing information exchange between computers.

**ring topology**    A network configuration in which all data flow in a single direction from one device to the next one  in the circuit.

**star topology**    A network configuration that employs a computer dedicated as a network server through which all communications pass.

**TCP/IP (Transmission Control Protocol/Internet Protocol**    A set of standards developed to allow different networks to interconnect.

**telecommunications**    The sharing of information over distance.

**twisted pair**    The least expensive copper cabling often used for wiring phone systems and suitable for short distances. Pairs of wires are used in a circuit but many pairs are often wrapped in a bundle surrounded by an outer sheath.

**upload**    To transfer a file from a local computer to a remote one.

**Veronica**    A collection of Gopher menus that must be accessed through a gopher.

**wide area network (WAN)**    A network that spans great distances or covers a wide geographic area. Wide area networks often interconnect LANs. The Internet is an example of a wide area network.

**World Wide Web**    An Internet navigation system that allows users to access information organized by hypertext-linked screens called pages.

## Notes & Suggested Readings

Apple Computer, Inc., *Teaching, learning, and technology kit.* Santa Barbara, CA: Intellimation.

Barron, D. D., (1991, February). EMail: Linking schools in the Net. *Information Searcher, 3*(2), 1–3.

Bennett, R. (1994, May). *Accessing the Internet.* An inservice presentation given to the Western Oregon State College faculty.

Bingham, M. H. (1992, November). Results of two studies on the benefits and pitfalls of technology-based information accessing. *T.H.E. Journal, 20*(4), 88–92.

Cahall, L. (1994, February). The urban child and the AT&T Learning Network. *The Computing Teacher, 21*(5), 19–20.

Daly, K. (1994, September). A planning guide for instructional networks. *The Computing Teacher, 22*(1), 11–15.

Descy, D. E. (1994, September). World Wide Web: Adding multimedia to cyberspace. *Tech Trends, 39*(4), 15–16.

D'Ignazio, F. (1990, May). Electronic highways and the classroom of the future. *The Computing Teacher, 17*(8), 20–24.

Goodrich, T. (1994, November/December). Mining the Internet: Tools for access and navigation. *Syllabus, 8*(3), 16–22.

Harris, J. (1994, February). People-to-people projects on the Internet. *The Computing Teacher, 21*(5), 48–52.

Honey, M., & Henríquez, A. (1993, June). *Telecommunications and K-12 educators: Findings from a national study.* New York: Center for Technology in Education.

Kinnaman, D. E. (1991, November/December). Networking—The missing piece? *Technology & Learning, 12*(3), 28–38.

McKeon, J. (1993, October). Building vehicles for the information highway. *Communications Industry Report*, 1, 6.

McMullen, M. (1993, December). Toys of the Trade. *LAN, 8*(13), 40–48.

Mintz, D. (1993–94, December/January). Networks in classrooms. *The Computing Teacher, 21*(4), 27–29.

Murray, J. (1992, Fall). Dreaming . . . of a truly global village. *Interchange*, 19–21.

Murray, J. (1993, August). K12 Network: Global education through telecommunications. *Communications of the ACM*, 36–41.

Naisbitt, J. (1984). *Megatrends: Ten new directions transforming our lives.* New York: Warner Books.

Northwest Regional Educational Laboratory. (1994, February). *Northwest report.*

Rogers, A., Andres, Y., Jacks, M. & Clausen, T. (1990, May). Keys to successful telecomputing. *The Computing Teacher, 17*(8), 25–28.

Sellers, J. (1994, February). Answers to commonly asked 'primary and secondary school Internet user' questions. IETF School Networking Group, Internet FYI RFC1578.

# 9

# INSTRUCTION AND LEARNING

Instruction and learning, though closely related, are not the same thing. This chapter will establish the groundwork for looking at the computer's role in teacher-centered instruction and will examine its role in student learning. Recognizing that there are several theories of instruction, that classroom practice is often based on one or more of these theories in combination, and that this text does not purport to be an instructional theory textbook, we will review Robert Gagné's work and allude to other theories covered in greater depth in courses dealing with pedagogy. The intent here is to demonstrate that the computer can be a practical tool used in concert with teaching strategies that have a solid theoretical basis.

Acknowledging that there is a growing interest in constructivist theories of learning, this chapter will present an overview of a moderate constructivist perspective so that the use of the computer as a productivity tool can be better understood. The thoughtful application of the computer can make students more productive in the construction of their knowledge.

In support of both the objectivist and constructivist perspectives, the acquisition of perceptions will be examined and aspects of motivation will be considered as they relate to teaching and learning. This chapter will define instructional communications and examine appropriate communications models, deriving a basis for sound software development and use.

## Advanced Organizers

1. What are the basic tenets of behaviorism?
2. What are the basic tenets of constructivism?
3. How can the computer support each perspective?
4. How is information acquired?

5. What is the relationship between concrete and abstract experiences?
6. How does motivation relate to instruction and learning?
7. What constitutes instructional communications?
8. What is virtual reality?
9. How does communication differ in virtual reality from other modes of learning?
10. What promise does virtual reality hold for education?
11. How can the presentation of the message be enhanced in computer software?

## PERSPECTIVES ON TEACHING AND LEARNING

Every learning environment has an implied method of information presentation. Learning activities are based on a belief of how students best learn. Of the many philosophical doctrines, two stand out rather clearly as examples related to software development, selection, and use.

*Behaviorists* view the teacher as the manipulator of the environment that is experienced by the learner. B. F. Skinner, well known for his work in behavior modification through operant conditioning, has long been a proponent of programmed instruction. Skinnerian-style lessons use carefully planned steps of stimulus-response pairing and reinforcement to reach a goal. The lessons and their accompanying drills are administered in small incremental steps to minimize the likelihood of incorrect responses. The techniques employed reflect a belief that by tightly structuring the environment, the behavior of the organism (the student) can be shaped to achieve desired changes (learning). Linear programmed instruction is an example of this concept of education, where the accumulation of knowledge is preparing the student for predicted future needs. Traditional classroom instruction has included strong components of this theory. The teacher, with the prescribed textbook, is the source of information. Behavioral objectives are identified, lessons are planned, instruction is delivered, guided practice is provided, retention and transfer of learning activities are encouraged, and testing the information taught is the standard means of assessment.

In direct contrast is the perspective espoused by *constructivists,* who view education as inseparable from ordinary life. Through developmental exploration and play, students assume control of educational activities by making choices related to individual interests. The students discover rules and concepts during the course of interactions in an environment that encourages the use of problem-solving strategies, which in turn are developed while learning how to think. The teacher learns along with the students and becomes a guide, a facilitator, and a supportive partner in this educational process. Education is considered to be a guided tour of preparatory experiences in which students practice making decisions by simulating real-world situations. The teacher becomes the facilitator of education by selecting the experiences that offer the appropriate practice to the students. In this way students construct their own knowledge and gain skills that will be needed in a future environment, which may be quite different from the present one.

Software may reflect one or both of these approaches and may make assumptions about the teaching/learning style that will be employed in the classroom when it is actually used. Different techniques are selected to achieve educational goals in relation to different philosophical perspectives. For example, drill and practice or tutorials can help accomplish mastery of basic skills and concepts while simulations offer interaction with real-world experiences. Teachers must learn to identify the instructional approaches embodied in particular software, if they are to effectively harness the power of the computer in their classrooms.

## THE BEHAVIORIST PERSPECTIVE ON INSTRUCTION

Robert Gagné (Gagné, Briggs, & Wager, 1992, pp. 54–66) lists five types of intellectual skills in a **linear** scheme ranging from simple discriminations to the complex problem-solving process. This approach is predicated on the belief that the acquisition of knowledge at any stage depends on what has been learned at an earlier one. Thus, a learner must master the lower-level abilities before tackling the higher orders.

### Split Brain Theory

Not only do students learn in stages, but learning activities should involve all of the student's senses and should engage the entire brain. Many believe that linear, sequential activities, such as learning facts and rules, are processed by the left hemisphere of the brain, whereas more holistic and random activities, such as concept learning and problem solving, are addressed by the right hemisphere.

### Elements of a Good Lesson

A great deal of research has gone into identifying the components of a good learning situation. Gagné views learning theory as technology—that is, there is a set of rules that can be followed in the design of instructional events. His point of view draws on many theories of outstanding psychologists and resulted in the formulation of the following instructional events as elements in a good lesson (Gagné, Briggs, & Wager, 1992, p. 190):

1. Gaining attention
   *Stimulation to gain attention to ensure the reception of stimuli*

2. Informing learner of the objective
   *Informing learners of the learning objective to establish appropriate expectancies*
3. Stimulating recall of prerequisite learning
   *Reminding learners of previously learned content for retrieval from long-term memory*
4. Presenting the stimulus material
   *Clear and distinctive presentation of material to ensure selective perception*
5. Providing learning guidance
   *Guidance of learning by suitable semantic encoding*
6. Eliciting the performance
   *Eliciting performance involving response generation*
7. Providing feedback about performance correctness
   *Informing students about correctness of responses*
8. Assessing the performance
   *Following the opportunity for additional responses, inform the learner of mastery and give further directions*
9. Enhancing retention and transfer
   *Arranging variety of practice to aid future retrieval and transfer of learning*

Wedman (1986) found it quite revealing to examine the elements of a good lesson related to the instructional functions provided by CAI software. By describing common ways in which software provides each of the instructional events he offers a method of software analysis of a program's strengths and weaknesses relative to the elements in a good lesson as described by Gagné, Briggs, and Wager. Wedman then examines the teacher's role in complementing the instruction provided by the software to provide a complete instructional unit. The chart presented in Figure 9–1 displays the CAI software and teacher techniques related to each instructional event.

A diagram of these events as they might occur in a computerized lesson using the program *O'Dell Lake* (MECC) is provided in Figure 9–2. This example uses all the instructional events described by Gagné, Briggs, and Wager. Some software, of course, uses only some of the instructional events. In such cases the teacher must provide the missing events for the lesson.

Figure 9–3 presents a schematic view of the steps involved in the process of structuring the sample *O'Dell Lake* lesson following the steps outlined by Gagné and Briggs (1974).

## Human Factors

A great deal of attention has been given to individual responses to interaction with computers. These effects are critical to a program's effectiveness because they influence the learning events of a good lesson. Early writings by Gagné and Briggs (1974, p. 11) recognized six human factors affecting the learning event. These factors, identified as external stimulus factors and internal cognitive factors, are listed in Figure 9–4. The three external stimulus factors are contiguity (time relationship between stimulus

| Events of Instruction | CAI Techniques | Teacher Techniques |
|---|---|---|
| 1. Gaining Attention | Graphics<br>Sound<br>Games | Demonstrate relevance of content<br>Present high-involvement problems<br>Use related, highly attractive media<br>Assign groups to use software |
| 2. Informing Learner of Objectives | Pretest<br>Textual statement of objectives<br>Graphic illustration of objectives<br>Brief interactive demonstration | Pretest<br>Tell the learner what is expected<br>Demonstrate use of the content |
| 3. Stimulating Recall of Prerequisites | Pretest for prerequisites<br>Textual review of prerequisites<br>Graphic display of prerequisites | Test prerequisite content<br>Review prerequisite content and vocabulary |
| 4. Presenting Stimuli | Textual display of new content<br>Graphic display of new content<br>Learner control over presentation sequence and display rate<br>Reference to non-CAI material | Use other media to present new content |
| 5. Providing Guidance | Attention-focusing devices (e.g., animation, sound, pointers)<br>Help screens<br>Examples and illustrations | Organize peer tutoring<br>Cross-reference difficult content to examples and remediation in other materials |
| 6. Eliciting Performance | Questions on new content<br>Applications of new content to solve problems or control situation (e.g., flight simulator) | Ask questions<br>Create performance tasks to let the learner apply the new content (e.g., lab experiment) |
| 7. Providing Feedback | Display score and/or correct answer<br>Help screens for incorrect answers<br>Additional information or examples | Provide answer keys<br>Provide reference materials coordinated with correct answers<br>Provide outcome guides coordinated with performance tasks (e.g., lab experiment check sheet) |
| 8. Assessing Performance | Test questions<br>Limited response time (for memory-level questions)<br>Record keeping | Give paper and pencil tests<br>Conduct performance tests<br>Use computers for context rich testing |
| 9. Enhancing Retention and Transfer | Repeating content not mastered<br>Applying new content to a different but related situation | Provide alternative instructional materials for content not mastered<br>Create situations (not involving a computer) to let students apply new content |

**FIGURE 9–1**
*CAI and teacher techniques related to events of instruction*
(Wedman, 1986. Courtesy of *The Computing Teacher*)

**FIGURE 9–2**

*Elements of a good science lesson demonstrated in O'Dell Lake:* Simulation of a predator/prey model

*Gaining attention*
   A lake is shown with fish swimming around.

*Stating the objective*
   Picture fades when a student presses the spacebar and student is informed that the object is to discover the relationships between the listed fish. Student is asked to pick a fish and state how the fish is to behave in a given situation.

*Stimulating recall of prerequisite learnings*
   Student is reminded to use all of the information presented in the picture and to make choices based on what different fish might eat and which animals may prey on the chosen fish.

*Presenting the stimulus material*
   When the student has chosen a fish and read the given information, the computer generates a picture of the lake with the chosen fish shown in some situation.

*Eliciting the performance*
   The student is asked to make a choice about the fish's behavior.

*Assessing the performance*
   The computer states whether the chosen behavior was correct, incorrect, or indifferent.

*Providing feedback about the performance*
   The action in the given lake situation is carried out demonstrating the behavior chosen by the student.

*Enhancing retention and transfer*
   Another situation is presented to the student based on past performance. The new situation may involve another animal or may involve choosing a different fish to observe.

and response), repetition (frequency and rate of exposure to a stimulus), and reinforcement (follow-up to the reception of a stimulus). The three internal cognitive factors are factual information (from memory or external sources), intellectual skills (ability to manipulate information), and cognitive strategies (ability to process or interpret into meaningful information). Added to these are the internal affective factors of inhibition (reluctance to react to a stimulus) and anxiety (a tension often stemming from a lack of confidence).

These factors relate to a theory of how information is stored in and retrieved from short-term and long-term memory. Gagné and Briggs believe that information that is sensed is held in the auditory, visual, or tactile register for only a second before it is disregarded or sent to short-term memory. There it is encoded for about thirty seconds before storage in long-term memory. Because of the short time periods involved, a *stimulus* must be limited to one idea, and there must be enough time to process and store the information without interference or overload. Meaningful repetition is

**FIGURE 9–3**
*Flowchart of events in the*
O'Dell Lake *lesson*

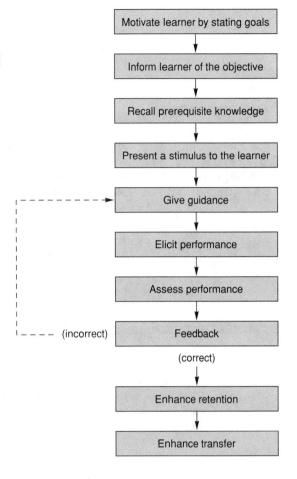

**FIGURE 9–4**
*Eight human factors affect-
ing the learning event*

**External Stimulus Factors**

- contiguity
- repetition
- reinforcement

**Internal Cognitive Factors**

- factual information
- intellectual skills
- cognitive strategies

**Internal Affective Factors**

- inhibitions
- anxieties

believed to contribute to control of the processes and in turn to learning. The effectiveness of a lesson depends on the internal responses to a stimulus, the senses used, and the ease of use to minimize distractions during computer-assisted learning.

# THE CONSTRUCTIVIST PERSPECTIVE ON LEARNING

Cognitive psychologists as early as Whitehead (1929) have insisted that learning is an active and highly individualized process. They clearly point out that learners must actively construct new knowledge based on their own individual experiences and understandings. This constructivist model of learning is based on the concept that knowledge is produced by the individual learner rather than processed from information received from an external source. The student becomes the producer rather than the consumer of information. The teacher becomes the guide and facilitator of learning rather than the director of instruction. Goals are still set, but the learner is given significant freedom in how to attain them. Assessment is still performed, but benchmarks are established and the teacher employs authentic measures such as evaluating a product or examining a portfolio.

## Stages of Development

A foundation for some of the current constructivists beliefs can be found in the work of Jean Piaget. He is best known for proposing four stages of development in a child's cognitive abilities: (1) from birth to about age 2, the *sensorimotor stage* (when children begin to explore their environment and to differentiate themselves from the world around them); (2) from age 2 to about 7, the *preoperational stage* (when language and intuitive thought develops); (3) from age 7 to about 12, the *concrete operational stage* (when classifying and ordering of items and inductive reasoning develop); and (4) from about age 12 on, the *stage of formal operations* (when more abstract and formal thought, control of variables, and proportionality can be managed). Piaget attributed these stages to a naturally occurring process of maturation and the appropriate exposure to experiences that encourage development.

The idea that children learn without being taught is central to this learning theory. Long before children enter school they have mastered the complexities of language and speech enough to understand and communicate with those around them. They have gained a sense of intuitive body geometry that enables them to get around in space, and they have learned enough logic and rhetoric to convey their desires to parents and peers. Children learn all these things effectively without formal teachers and curriculum, and without explicit external rewards or punishments. They learn by simply interacting with their environment, relating what is new to what they know from past experience.

For example, a very young child can build a cognitive structure or a concept of "dogness": dogs look, feel, sound, and smell a certain way. Whenever a dog is encountered, the child attempts to make sense of the experience by calling on a previously formed cognitive structure of "dog." Piaget calls this *assimilation*. But a new dog may be different from the one met before. As new elements are encountered (a curly tail instead of a straight one; long, shaggy hair instead of short hair, and so on), the cognitive structure for "dog" must be modified and enlarged to encompass the new information, a process Piaget called *accommodation*.

If we think of learners in Piagetian terms, as the active builders of their own cognitive structures, we should consider the kinds of experiences and material our culture provides for use in this building process and examine the potential contribution of the computer.

### Constructivist Implications

Saunders (1992) illustrated the constructivist perspective with the model shown in Figure 9–5. He states: "Constructivism can be defined as that philosophical position which holds that any so-called reality is, in the most immediate and concrete sense, the mental construction of those who believe they have discovered and investigated it." Learners, therefore, must be provided a rich environment of sensory experiences to which they will respond in order to build understandings. The computer, through its use of text, sound, graphics, animation, and multimedia control, is ideally suited to present such a rich environment.

## PERCEPTION

What we know about the world, we have experienced through our senses. Free of any physical impairments, we normally gain information through all five senses. Infants are intrigued by the wondrous variety of sounds and sights and smells to which they are exposed and they seek to explore every sensory stimulus. As we mature, our visual and aural senses assume an overwhelming importance in the acquisition of knowledge. Indeed, a great deal of the information we possess as adults has been acquired through the sense of sight.

Sensory stimuli are accepted by the learner and given meaning based primarily on past experiences. Thus sensory experiences result in **perceptions.** Since perceptions, in turn, are organized into understandings, the quality of the visual and aural stimuli embodied in software assumes great importance.

As an infant, the concept of "fiveness" might be acquired by handling five items (units); gradually seeing them represented by five fingers (digits); and then processing the meaning as the numeral 5 (symbol). Once a child has been exposed to a variety of **concrete** experiences, pictorial and then verbal experiences are an effective and much more efficient way of

**FIGURE 9–5**
*A constructivist learning model*
(Reprinted with permission from *School Science and Mathematics*)

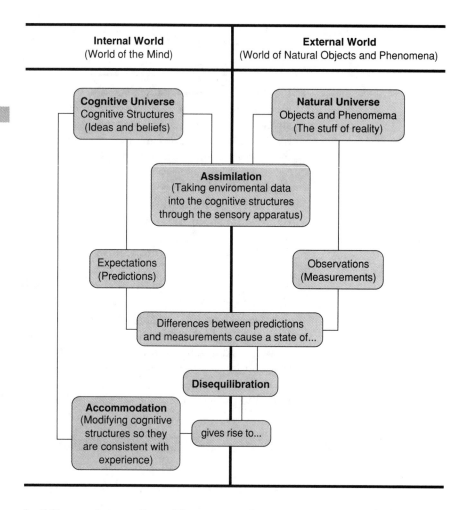

building understandings. These more **abstract** expressions of ideas must have a concrete basis. Examining well-designed software, we find that computer graphics, visuals, and certainly multimedia serve as a more concrete referent to meaning than the written word. Since visuals resemble the item they represent, they offer the viewer concrete clues to meaning. To enhance the perception of visual information in software, research by Guba et al. (1964) and others has shown that in good graphic design, distracting elements must be kept to a minimum.

## MOTIVATION

**Motivation** is an essential element in instruction and in learning. The continuous attention focused on well-designed software is due in large measure to the continuity of thought promoted when text is coupled with graphics and at times with sound. Motivation is further heightened when the learner is asked to respond to the program in an overt fashion. Even a response as simple as clicking a mouse button or pressing a key may contribute to the learner's involvement in the act of learning, hence becoming a significant factor when software presents learning sequences of longer duration, when the learner must control the **rate of presentation.**

One of the challenges we face as teachers is to understand learners and to elicit maximum responses from them. As Jack Frymier (1968), a former director of the Institute for Motivational Research at Ohio State University, has pointed out:

> Motivation to learn in school is in part a function of what resides within the individual and in part a function of the external world he encounters. Some positively motivated youngsters seem to draw most heavily upon forces located within themselves to enhance their learning. They believe in learning and knowledge, for example, and the new and novel excite them. Ambiguity and uncertainty intrigue them. Other students, equally well motivated, seem to be most positively affected by the quality and quantity of stimuli which they experience in school. Exciting lectures, fascinating movies, vivid illustrations, and intense discussions are likely to spark these students' efforts.

If we understand that students may be motivated differently, we accept that some will be enthusiastic consumers of information. They are the avid readers, the television watchers, the students who sit at the computer and patiently construct elaborate searches of electronic encyclopedias, who use the computer to search remote databases and browse through online news services. They are often the students who don't like to call attention to themselves. They may capture stunning images and create marvelous designs on the computer but are reluctant to show them to others, especially to large groups. Other students will be producers of information. They are the students who engage in music and drama performances, who write lengthy reports on the word processor, who construct elaborate multimedia products and love to stand at the overhead display panel in the front of the room and project their work for the whole class to view.

## COMMUNICATION

The opening quote of Chapter 1 is attributed to Marshall McLuhan, a professor of English and a popular philosopher of the 1950s and '60s. He devoted many years to the exploration of how a chosen medium affected the **message** or structured content being communicated. The media he studied most closely were the mass media of radio, television, newspapers, and magazines. We have defined media as tools between the user and information to be created, received, stored, manipulated, or disseminated. Tools are what McLuhan was referring to when he said media are extensions of our human capability. When we consider the computer as a multifaceted tool, we accept the fact that most of the communication occurs through the software. To select software that will provide appropriate vicarious experiences, we must understand the process of communication.

**Communication** is often defined as the transmission or sharing of ideas based on common understandings in one of three major modes: oral, visual, or written. Direct, face-to-face communication usually is oral. The visual mode often spans greater distances. This is also true of the written mode, the most abstract of the three. It is often suggested that communication implies an interaction, give-and-take, or feedback.

Since a learner cannot experience everything on a direct, purposeful, firsthand basis, a great deal of knowledge is gained through vicarious experiences. Meaning resides in the individual, not in the message—the structure of contextual clues and stimuli designed to evoke a desired response. **Instructional communication** can be seen as the transmission of this structured information organized to produce learning. The source of such a transmission might be a person speaking or demonstrating a skill or procedure. It might also be printed, projected, or electronic materials, such as textbooks, films, videos, or computer software. The computer software might take the form of drill and practice, tutorial, simulation, or interactive multimedia software that combines text, graphics, sound and animation and controls live-action video sequences.

## Communication Models

We will examine three communication models in order to better understand the process of instructional communications and the role of computer software. The first model, Figure 9–6, was proposed by Claude Shannon and Warren Weaver (1949), two mathematicians employed by Bell Telephone Laboratories. This linear, technical model is quite appropriate for understanding telephone or radio communication. A popular song, for example, might be selected by a disc jockey (information source), encoded by equipment (transmitter) into radio waves, received by a radio (receiver), and heard as music reaching your ear (destination). **"Noise"** might be static in the atmosphere or, as the authors defined it, anything that deteriorates the quality of the signal. It might even be visual distractions.

**FIGURE 9–6**
*Shannon-Weaver model*
(Copyright 1949 by the Board of Trustees of the University of Illinois. Used with permission of the University of Illinois Press)

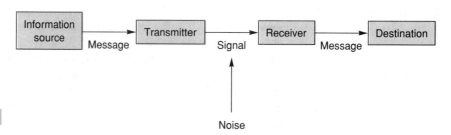

We might apply this linear model, well suited to examining the one-way transmittal of stored information, in the following manner. A message is stored as a file (information source) on a floppy disk, loaded into a computer (transmitter), displayed on a monitor screen (receiver), and examined by the user (destination). Noise that affects the message might be inadequate brightness and contrast levels on the monitor, restrictive screen size, glare on the monitor screen, or a flickering, unstable image. Noise affects the quality of the message being received. The user is placed in a passive mode.

Wilbur Schramm (1954), concerned with the instructional communication potential of educational television, adapted the Shannon-Weaver model to reflect the interpretation of meaningful symbols, as shown in Figure 9–7. For communication to take place, the fields of experience of the sender and of the receiver must overlap. The signal that is shared is subject to each party's perceptions. The sender encodes the message according to skills possessed, biases, cultural influences, attitudes, and so on. The receiver calls on like factors to decode (understand) the message.

A further adaptation of this model, as suggested in Figure 9–8, examines the role of computer software in instructional communications. Since meanings cannot be transmitted, the model illustrates that the message designed under the influence of meanings, which reside in the sender (the program design team), must elicit accurate and appropriate meanings in the receiver (the computer user). In turn, the message being communicated is embodied in the software. Meanings that reside in the field of experience of the program design team have a direct influence on the coding of the message. The decoding (understanding) of the message depends on meanings that reside in the field of experience of the computer user. The software carries the message, serving as a channel or bridge between fields of experience. The more truly the software expresses meanings in each field, the better the communication. The quality of the software, as the vehicle carrying the message, depends on the content and its treatment, instructional design, and manner of presentation.

The message will be degraded or distorted if the content is perceived by the user as incorrect, biased, or incomplete. It will suffer if the

**FIGURE 9–7**

*The Schramm revision of the Shannon-Weaver model*

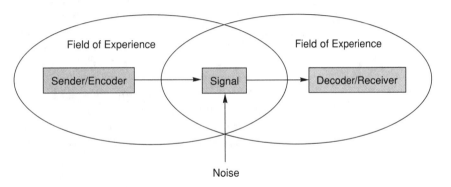

**FIGURE 9-8**
*A software-specific commu-*
*nications model adapted*
*from Figure 9–7*

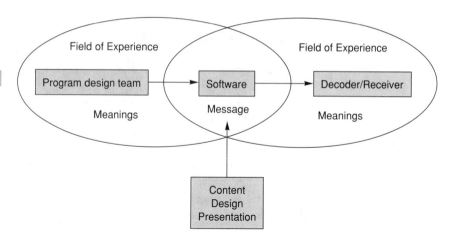

| Program Design Team | Software | Computer User |
|---|---|---|
| Drawing on knowledge of content and on learning theory, the design team prepares the software for an intended audience. | The content of the message must be authentic and accurate. Its design must be pedagogically sound and its presentation must stimulate and tie to the learner's "reality." | Drawing on a concrete base of experience, the computer user extracts meaning transmitted by the software. |

sequencing is wrong, if it is too fragmented, or if too much information is presented to be absorbed by the user. The message will be lost if the presentation is boring. Distractions will enter as "noise" in the communication process if the predetermined pacing is wrong (too slow or too fast) for the user, or if the presentation employs verbal or visual techniques that are foreign to the user.

### Virtual Reality

**Virtual reality (VR),** although still in its infancy, is being defined as a computer-generated simulated environment delivered to the user by a head-mounted display consisting of a helmet or goggles with integrated sensors and additional sensors attached to gloves and other clothing worn by the user. The sensors provide feedback to the computer in order to modify the simulated environment.

Virtual reality is a computer-based technology that creates an illusion of reality in which the participants interact with, and in fact are immersed in, an artificial environment to the degree that it appears real; it is highly interactive, multisensorial, and vivid enough for the participants almost to think it is reality.

### Virtual Reality in the Round

Novak (cited in Schmitt, 1993, p. 86) states that one of the most characteristic differences between virtual reality and other forms of representation is that information "surrounds" the participant. The notion of being inside the communication medium, or channel, is prevalent in the virtual reality literature.

Three characteristics of communication in virtual reality stand out as being very different from traditional models of communication. First, participants in virtual reality are perceived to be in the center of the communication medium or channel instead of sending information through a communication medium or channel. Second, virtual reality participants not only communicate with other participants simultaneously, but also communicate with themselves. Third, sources of noise in traditional communication may also be noise in virtual reality or may be sensual links to the real world that make virtual reality seem more real. Clearly, traditional models of communication do not capture these differences.

Figure 9–9 depicts a new model of communication created by Sylvia Sandoz (1994) that does describe these differences of communication in virtual reality. It portrays the participant or participants inside the communication medium, inside virtual reality. The white outside the communication medium depicts reality. The more immersed the senses are, the more virtual reality appears to be real. Making the virtual world "look real, act real, sound real, feel real" is what Sutherland (1965, p. 507) calls the point of perfect presence. The center of the model is also white, depicting that if virtual reality achieves perfection, participants will not recognize the difference between reality and virtual reality. Virtual reality, according

**FIGURE 9–9**
*Sandoz model of communi-cation in virtual reality*

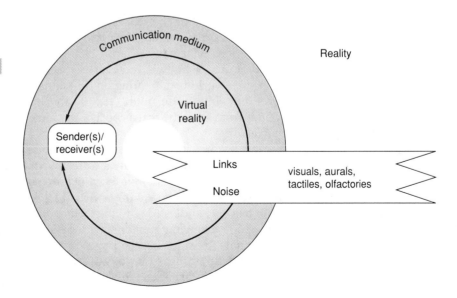

to Furness (Miller, 1992, p. 14), is "just like you're walking into another world, and you're perceiving it as if it becomes reality itself."

## Who's Communicating with Whom?

The second difference between traditional communication and communication in virtual reality is that virtual reality participants communicate with themselves as well as others. In virtual reality the communication medium, for example, a computer, is no longer just a means of connecting sender and receiver. The focus of attention, according to Steuer (1992, p. 78), is the relationship "between an individual who is both a sender and a receiver, and on the mediated environment with which he or she interacts. Information is not transmitted from sender to receiver; rather, mediated environments are created and then experienced." In other words, participants in immersive virtual reality are in constant communication with the medium itself, the computer, and with themselves as the object of their communication.

## Our Senses: Noise or Links?

The third difference between traditional communication and communication in virtual reality is that virtual reality participants may experience the connection to reality through the senses as noise that distracts from the sense of reality or as a link that adds to a sense of reality. How real are the sounds in virtual reality? How real are the visuals? Can the participants become so engaged that they forget they are not experiencing something real? When move their heads, does the environment change? Tactile feelings have a sense of reality as well. When a participant picks up an object, does she feel the proper amount of resistance or weight in the object?

"Noise need not be senseless; perfectly good information, even an organized message, can act like noise when it interferes with or disturbs reception of some signal" (Klapp, 1986, p. 84). To a participant in a virtual world of the 1804 Lewis and Clark expedition, noise might be a passerby in the real world commenting on the status of Social Security or the latest space mission. Noise might also be the literal noise of airplane traffic sounds from a nearby real airport or the fumes of diesel fuel from a nearby real factory.

Just as our senses can be sources of noise in virtual reality communication, so too can they be links to reality that make virtual reality seem more real. Real-time sounds from nearby co-participants can add to the sense of reality when playing a virtual game. Grabbing a physically real set of bicycle handles adds to the feeling of a virtual bike ride through the Swiss Alps. Chewing gum or smelling hot dogs adds to the sense of playing virtual big league baseball.

The sixth sense, psychology, is another consideration. Theater patrons agree to ignore the backstage, risers, and stagehands. With a computerized virtual world, according to Pimentel and Teixeira (1993, p. 157), participants enter into the same "conspiracy" and agree to forget the computer, the software, the head tracker, the glove and goggles. According to Pimentel and Teixeira (1993, p. 154), "full sensory stimulation isn't always useful or effective."

In virtual reality, we communicate through all our own senses and our own senses determine the amount of noise or how linked we are to reality. "It is an irony of the information society that information gets in its own way—or, as one might put it, communication becomes noise to its own signal" (Klapp, 1986, p. 85). In Figure 9–9, the connection between reality and virtual reality is the senses. Inside the connector, the horizontal dark gray area depicts noise and the horizontal white area depicts links between reality and virtual reality. Whether what we sense is noise that detracts from the sense of reality or links that add to the sense of reality depends on the specific application of virtual reality.

## How Does One Experience Virtual Reality?

At present, VR experiences are achieved most often by using equipment that controls all visual and auditory input. The head-mounted display takes the form of a helmet with earphones and miniature video screens positioned directly in front of the user's eyes. Slightly different scenes are sent to each eye screen, thus producing 3-D images. The "surround sound" effect is similar to that used in movie theaters or home entertainment centers. The helmet blocks out all other surrounding visual and auditory input, thus heightening the illusions resulting from the data sent directly by the computer. More sophisticated VR equipment also includes gloves to wear. At times, even full body suits are employed. These interpret the movements of the wearer (as does the helmet) and cause the computer to create scenes that change in response to the movement of the user.

As you might guess, virtual reality requires a great deal of computing power and a phenomenal amount of programming. The remarkable increase in the power of affordable computers is one factor contributing to the rapid advances made by VR during the last few years.

It is difficult to imagine how extremely exciting VR is until one has had the opportunity to experience it. Imagine being able to fly through the air, or to walk around on the ocean floor, without ever leaving home! The experience seems so real that it *could* be real. This certainly has the potential to be very powerful technology!

Virtual reality offers us the opportunity to explore reality in a new way. We can generate a model and then manipulate it in ways that were not previously possible. For example, we can travel through our model and view it from angles that would be impossible in our physical reality. We can also put abstract ideas into a form that can be perceived and manipulated. Theoretically, anything represented by a computer can be placed within a virtual framework for interaction within a virtual reality context.

### Applications of Virtual Reality in Education

At present there are mixed opinions about the future of VR in the classroom. Some seem excited about the possible educational applications while others appear more concerned with what seem like the insurmountable technical and financial challenges. Clearly virtual worlds could be used in many different ways in schools if the challenges can be overcome.

Educational applications, though mainly in the future, might be found in a number of disciplines, or better yet, they may exist in a cross-disciplinary framework. The phenomena of physics might be explored as virtual objects to manipulate. Virtual molecules might be examined in chemistry. Imagine the pleasure of dissecting a virtual frog! (Hopefully without the virtual smell of formaldehyde.) Current and historical cultures experienced in a virtual environment might lead to a better understanding and acceptance.

Students might also work collaboratively to build virtual worlds with their classmates. Portfolio assessments in the future might include virtual worlds created by students. "Over their years in school, students could create a universe of learning worlds that reflected the evolution of their skills and the pattern of their conceptual growth. Evaluating comprehension and competence would become experiential as well as analytical, as teachers explored the worlds of thought constructed by their students" (Bricken & Byrne, 1992, p. 11).

Designing virtual worlds for education may become a whole new field of specialization. "It is one thing to present a richly textured world for immersion and exploration, it is entirely another matter for educators to properly structure this kind of a setting for profitable learning" (Woodward, 1992, p. 4). Woodward (1992, p. 5) goes on to state that unless we "do a better job of directing the learner toward explicit, measurable outcomes—it is likely that the value of simulations as educational techniques will remain modest." Woodward also feels that the same may be true for the highly promising virtual reality systems.

The promise of a technology such as virtual reality can be both exciting and frustrating—exciting to reflect on the potential, frustrating to contemplate the inherent funding problems. Realizing that most teachers don't even have a telephone in their classroom, expensive technologies always seem to be in the distant future. Someone once said that take away the television set, the VCR, the stereo system, the computer and printer from my home and you will have made it a much more sterile and information-poor environment. Attempt to do the same to my classroom, and you will have little effect on it since those items are not there to begin with.

---

**FROM THEORY TO APPLICATION**

Hopefully, good practice is based on an understanding of sound theory. As we study theories of learning, reflect on our experiences, and examine our own beliefs and values, we should seek to develop a knowledge base and a skill level that will enhance our application of computers to the classroom. This knowledge and skill will guide us through many decisions related to curriculum, teaching and learning strategies with the computer, equipment purchases, and computer software selection.

## Appropriateness of Software

Since the learning theory on which software design is based dictates the role of the computer, the role of the teacher, and the role of the student, recognizing these elements is an important first step toward making good use of the computer in the classroom. Instructional objectives will only be met if the software and the intent of the lesson are closely related.

To understand why the computer lesson must be consistent with the kinds of learning students have come to expect, consider the following example. Imagine that you prepared a lesson plan calling for practice on the subtraction of whole numbers less than one hundred. Surveying a curriculum resource guide for software to use, you find a program that presents a subtraction algorithm. This software on subtraction is designed for discovery learning. That is, when a student misses the answer, the software **branches** back to work that should have been mastered earlier and presents a different problem. However, if your classroom method prior to this lesson has been directive, replete with examples, some students would be frustrated by the computer lesson because it failed to give them the information they expected. Clearly your students would be better served by software built around a more linear approach.

## Effectiveness of Software

In assessing the effectiveness of software, keep in mind that the internal responses to a stimulus correspond very closely with the events of a good lesson. The student is alerted or motivated, perhaps by curiosity, to interact with the program. The objective of the program sets an expectancy for performance that interests the student. The student must be able to retrieve or recall prerequisite information that provides meaning to the activity. The stimulus of new information must be perceived selectively over time, or through repetition, for processing to memory. Feedback in the form of favorable reinforcement should bolster self-worth. The information should have relevance to the student's environment for generalization and transfer of learning to occur. If the progression of these responses is not smooth, the chain of events is interrupted and the lesson becomes less effective.

Multiple senses can be utilized to appeal to students' interest and gain their attention. As with other classroom activities, a variety of events is more effective than one or two continuously repeated actions. Variety can be achieved by offering, for example, interaction through the tactile response of typing on the keyboard, different sounds, bright colors, interesting graphics, and new topics to challenge reasoning. In addition, students should be able to perform at the appropriate level to avoid frustration or boredom.

When evaluating software, remember that the process of interacting with the computer must be simple, so students can concentrate on the content of the program. Elements that contribute to easy use are centralized around simple means of input and simple presentations of output. To simplify input, a simple *mouse click, single-key command* and *single-key selection* of activities from a menu of options limit typing errors and speed up program execution. Error-free programs (no bugs) and error-trapped designs (mistakes are correctable or not accepted at all) avoid the frustration of stalled or prematurely terminated lessons.

Clarity in eliciting responses from the student also avoids confusion when interpreting what to respond or how. Output can be simplified by, for example, *limiting the field* of perception by presenting simple, *uncluttered displays* one page at a time; *double-spacing text* for readability; *grouping ideas* for easy understanding; *formatting the screen* to focus on one point; and *highlighting major points* by effectively using color, animation, and sound. Most of these same features are frequently encountered in films, slides, textbooks, and other instructional materials.

Based on an understanding of learning theories and an awareness of factors dealing with perception, motivation, and communication, it is possible to postulate the following guidelines for effective software:

1. Software must stimulate a high degree of interest in the learner.
2. Software must contribute to developmental learning and thereby increase its permanence.
3. Software must be based in concrete experience to enhance understanding.
4. Software must make optimum use of the visual and, where appropriate, the aural sensory channels to strengthen the reality of the experience.

## Summary

Behaviorism views the teacher as the manipulator of the environment that is experienced by the learner. The techniques employed reflect a belief that by tightly structuring the environment, the behavior of the student can be shaped to achieve learning. Constructivism views education as inseparable from ordinary life. Learning is seen as an active and highly individualized process in which learners must construct new knowledge based on their own individual experiences and understandings. Knowledge is produced by the individual learner rather than processed from information received from an external source.

Sensory experiences result in perceptions. Sensory stimuli are accepted by the learner and given meaning based primarily on past experiences. As perceptions are organized into understandings, it becomes evident that the quality of the concrete visual and aural stimuli embodied in the software assumes significant importance. The more abstract expressions of ideas must have a concrete basis. Examining well-designed software, we find that computer graphics, visuals, and certainly multimedia serve as a concrete referent to meaning. Continuous attention focused on well-designed software is due in large measure to the continuity of thought promoted when text is coupled with graphics and at times with sound. Motivation is further heightened when the learner is asked to respond to the program in an overt fashion.

We have defined media as extensions of our human capability, tools between the user and information to be created, received, stored, manipulated, or disseminated. When we consider the computer as a multifaceted tool, we accept the fact that most of the communication occurs through the software. To select software that will provide appropriate vicarious experiences, we must understand the process of instructional communication, which may be defined as the structured transmission or sharing of ideas based on common understandings in order to produce learning.

Virtual reality (VR), in its immersive mode, is a computer-generated simulated environment delivered to the user by a head-mounted display with integrated sensors and additional ones attached to items of clothing worn by the user. This computer-based technology creates an illusion of reality in which the participants interact with, and in fact are immersed in, an artificial environment to a degree that appears real; it is highly interactive, multisensorial, and vivid enough for it to seem to the participants almost as if it were reality.

As we study theories of learning, reflect on our experiences, and examine our own beliefs and values, we should seek to develop a knowledge base and a skill level that will enhance our application of computers to the classroom. This knowledge and skill will guide us through many decisions related to curriculum, teaching and learning strategies with the computer, equipment purchases, and computer software selection. Based on this understanding, we can postulate some guidelines for effective software.

## Chapter Exercises

1. Select one piece of software in a curriculum area that is of special interest to you and analyze it in light of Gagné's events of instruction as elements of a good lesson.
2. Analyze the same piece of software from the constructivist viewpoint as described in the section "The Constructivist Perspective on Learning."
3. What attributes of that piece of software enhance the concreteness of the learning experience for students?
4. What constitutes instructional communications? Describe an example that would be applicable to software use.
5. What are the design elements of software that can increase the student's motivation to learn?

6. Do a library search for the five most recent articles on virtual reality. What do the authors believe is the apparent impact on education? When are they predicting this impact will be felt in any meaningful way?

## Glossary

**abstract**    Describing symbolic representations of the actual object, event, or occurrence, which can be observed by the learner.

**branching**    A design that allows for multiple paths or options.

**communication**    The transmission or sharing of ideas based on common understandings in one of three major modes: oral, visual, and written.

**concrete**    Describing actual, direct, purposeful happenings involving the learner as a participant.

**instructional communication**    The encoding, transmission, and decoding of structured information organized to produce learning.

**linear**    Proceeding in a step-by-step, sequential manner.

**message**    A structure of contextual clues and stimuli designed to evoke a desired response (meaning).

**motivation**    The incitement of a desire that causes a learner to act and the continued fostering of that desire.

**noise**    In the context of a communication model, any distraction or condition that may disrupt the transmission or reception of a message.

**perception**    The acceptance of sensory stimuli by the learner, given meaning based primarily on past experiences.

**rate of presentation**    The pace at which informational material is introduced to the learner.

**virtual reality**    A computer-generated simulated environment delivered by a head-mounted display with integrated sensors attached to items of clothing worn by the user.

## Notes & Suggested Readings

Biocca, F. (1992). Virtual reality technology: A tutorial. *Journal of Communication, 42* (4), 23–72.

Bricken, M., & Byrne, C. M. (1992). *Summer students in virtual reality: A pilot study on educational applications of virtual reality technology.* Seattle: Washington University Technology Center.

Frymier, J. R. (1968, February). Motivating students to learn. *National Education Association Journal,* 37–39.

Gagné, R. (1982, June). Developments in learning psychology: Implications for instructional design, and effects of computer technology on instructional design and development (interview). *Educational Technology,* 11–15.

Gagné, R., & Briggs, L. (1974). *Principles of instructional design.* New York: Holt, Rinehart and Winston.

Gagné, R., Briggs, L., & Wager, W. (1992). *Principles of instructional design.* Fort Worth: Harcourt Brace Jovanovich.

Griest, G. (1993, April). You say you want a revolution: Constructivism, technology, and language arts. *The Computing Teacher, 20*(7), 8–11.

Guba, E., Wolf, W., DeGroot, S., Kneneyer, M., VanAtta, R., & Light, L. (Winter 1964). Eye movements and TV-viewing in children. *AV Communications Review, 12,* 386–401.

Klapp, O. E., (1986). *Overload and boredom: Essays on the quality of life in the information society.* Westport, CT: Greenwood Press.

Lanier, J., & Biocca, F. (1992, Autumn). An insider's view of the future of virtual reality. *Journal of Communication, 42*(4), 150–172.

Maley, D. (1993, Summer). Technology education: A natural for middle level students. *Schools in the Middle, 2*(4), 10–14.

Miller, C. (1992, November). Online interviews: Dr. Thomas A. Furness, III, virtual reality pioneer. *Online, 16*(6), 14–27.

Norton, P. (1992). When technology meets the subject-matter disciplines. *Educational Technology, 32*(3–5).

Nugent, W. R. (1991). Virtual reality: Advanced imaging special effects let you roam in cyberspace. *Journal of the American Society for Information Science, 42*(8), 609–617.

Pimentel, K., & Teixeira, K. (1993). *Virtual reality: Through the new looking glass.* New York: Intel/Windcrest/McGraw-Hill.

Sandoz, S. (1994). *Innovation in virtual reality is about the power of the mind.* Unpublished manuscript, Western Oregon State College.

Saunders, W. L. (1992, March). Constructivist perspective: Implications and teaching strategies for science. *School Science and Mathematics, 92*(3), 136–141.

Schmitt, G. N. (1993). Virtual reality in architecture. In N. M. Thalmann & D. Thalmann (Eds.), *Virtual worlds and multimedia* (pp. 85–97). Chichester, England: John Wiley & Sons.

Schramm, W. (1954). Procedures and effects of mass communication. In N. B. Henry (Ed.), *Mass media and education,* Fifty-Third Yearbook of the National Society for the Study of Education, Part II (p. 116). University of Chicago Press.

Shannon, C. E., & Weaver, W. (1949). *The mathematical theory of communication.* Champaign: University of Illinois Press, 7.

Steuer, J. (1992, Autumn). Defining virtual reality: Dimensions determining telepresence. *Journal of Communication, 42*(4), 73–93.

Sutherland, I. (1965). The ultimate display. *Proceedings of the International Federation of Information Processing Congress, 2,* 506–508.

Wedman, J. F. (1986, November). Making software more useful. *The Computing Teacher,* 11–14.

Whitehead, A. N. (1929). *The aims of education,* New York: Macmillan.

Woodward, J. (1992). *Virtual reality and its potential use in special education: Identifying emerging issues and trends in technology for special education.* Washington, D.C.: Cosmos Corp.

# 10

# STRATEGIES FOR COMPUTER USE

The title of this book is *The Computer as a Productivity Tool in Education*. All too often the term *productivity tool* has been used with a limited vision. The term has been easily understood and readily applied to word processors, graphics, spreadsheets, and database use. A deeper understanding would also apply it to computer-assisted instruction and to computer-enhanced learning.

Dave Moursund (1989), in an editorial written for *The Computing Teacher*, builds a case for a broader understanding and further states that,

> For all practical purposes, the computer industry has been driven by the productivity gains accruing to computer users. IBM has yearly sales of nearly $60 billion because over a wide range of job categories the people who use computers effectively are more productive than those who lack computer access. This has led to huge changes in business and industry, where productivity gains lead to increased profits, or at least to remaining competitive and staying in business. (p. 5)

Changes are also occurring in education. School restructuring is suggesting a different look at teacher effectiveness. Pupil learning gains are being included in a discussion of productivity. Drill and practice, tutorial instruction, and simulation are time-tested teaching strategies. If computer software implements these strategies in an effective and efficient manner, should not this software be seen as a teacher productivity tool? Teaching and learning, though closely related, are not the same thing. If we believe that education is in the business of fostering student learning, computer applications that help students to learn more easily should be seen as productivity tools.

Logo is briefly examined as a tool that is learned through a process of active, creative exploration. Employing Logo's turtle graphics, a student may issue commands and use the computer to control the "turtle" as an electronic pencil and draw lines on the screen. Knowledge that was formerly accessible only through abstract, formal thinking can be approached concretely with the turtle, a cybernetic animal existing in the Logo environment.

Multimedia is explored as a multisensory teaching and learning tool. Authoring programs are mentioned and related equipment is discussed in detail. The concept of optical storage is explained and various optical media are compared. The discussion of multimedia leads to the chapter conclusion, a plea to recognize the importance of multidisciplinary curriculum integration.

## Advanced Organizers

1. What is a typical drill and practice lesson format?
2. How can the computer be used in a drill and practice strategy?
3. What is a typical tutorial lesson format?
4. How can the computer be used in a tutorial strategy?
5. What is a typical simulation lesson format?
6. How can the computer be used in a simulation strategy?
7. What are the roles of the student and of the teacher in those three strategies?
8. What does Logo offer in a problem-solving strategy?
9. What constitutes multimedia and what does it have to offer the learner?
10. Why strive toward curriculum integration?

## STRATEGIES TO CONSIDER WHEN USING THE COMPUTER

Regardless of the underlying philosophy in the classroom, drill and practice, tutorial instruction, and simulation are indeed time-tested instructional strategies. They are strategies that behaviorists can apply in a teacher-centered instructional situation and that constructivists can apply in a student-centered learning environment. Depending on how they are employed, they are strategies that can gain attention, stimulate recall of prior learning, and present new information in ways that approximate real-life situations at a more concrete level than most media used in the classroom.

They are strategies that address the right or the left hemisphere of the brain. They can be tailored to support activities favored by students with concrete-sequential, concrete-random, abstract-sequential, or abstract-random preferred learning styles. Teachers who understand the individual needs of their students will tailor their strategies and the computer applications to meet those needs.

### Drill and Practice

A time-honored technique, **drill and practice,** is used by teachers to reinforce instruction by providing the repetition necessary to move acquired skills and concepts into long-term memory. In the past, teachers have used flash cards, worksheets, board games, and verbal drills to achieve results. Computer programs now present an additional alternative.

Criticism leveled in the past at drill and practice software was really aimed at examples of poorly designed software that was boring, treated all users the same regardless of ability, and often employed undesirable feedback. Teachers tell of students deliberately giving incorrect responses in order to see flashy animated graphics on the screen. The reward offered by that software for making correct responses was the presentation of another boring problem. A typical format used in drill and practice programs is illustrated by the diagram in Figure 10–1. Whenever this technique is used, the assumption is made that the topic has already been introduced to the student and that some prior instruction has taken place. In a behaviorist model, the teacher's role, in addition to determining the appropriate lesson objective and to delivering the initial instruction, is to select the appropriate software, monitor the student's progress through the material, and assess the student's performance. In a constructivist model, drill and practice software may be suggested by the teacher as a way for the student to refine a particular skill or concept once its value is recognized. The teacher's role, in addition to determining that the student understands and accepts an agreed-upon goal, is to ascertain that initial information has been acted upon by the student, to select the appropriate software, and to assess the student's performance as the skill or concept is applied to a meaningful task.

The student must interact with the computer by responding to screen prompts and by providing appropriate keyboard or other input. The student should request teacher or peer assistance if necessary and examine the results of the activity. The computer presents material for student interaction, provides appropriate feedback to student responses, and usually records the rate of success, often displayed as a score or percentage. Effective software requires the student to respond based on deductions and inferences as well as recall.

Figure 10–2 illustrates screens from a popular drill and practice program from MECC called *Number Munchers.* In the top half of the illustration, the number muncher is seen in the fourth row of the third column. The user guides the character to those boxes that contain numbers that are

> *"Many students choose to spend considerable time on the computer performing drill and practice writing lessons in a game format. They get immediate feedback on anything they do. It makes learning exciting for them."*
>
> Becky Benjamin, 7th Grade Language Arts Teacher Carrollton Junior High, Carrollton, GA

**FIGURE 10–1**
*A typical drill and practice format*

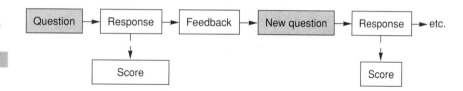

factors of 36. Beware of the Troggle, though, that eats number munchers. The entertaining video game format encourages users to spend extended time at the keyboard practicing skills they have acquired.

A number of factors influence the effectiveness of drill and practice software. The teacher must know the program well enough to determine the accuracy of the content and the match between the presentation of the material and an individual student's learning style. If the software is to be used in a group setting, are intrinsic **gaming** strategies employed or can external

**FIGURE 10–2**
*Number Munchers*
(Courtesy of MECC)

gaming strategies be used by the teacher? Gaming, though often found in drill and practice programs, can be found in all computer-assisted instruction (CAI) categories. The technique includes a set of rules and a clear contest. Students or groups of students may compete against each other or against the computer or other fixed standard. Students must find the material and its presentation interesting enough to be willing to become mentally and emotionally involved. The program's use of basic graphic design as well as a variety of stimuli such as color, sound, and animation in both its presentation and feedback screens greatly enhances its effectiveness.

The drill and practice program called *Math Blaster* provides practice of higher level thinking skills. See the word problem presented in Figure 10–3. Each screen guides the learner through a problem-solving strategy.

**FIGURE 10–3**
*Math Blaster Mystery*
(Courtesy of Davidson &
Associates, Inc.)

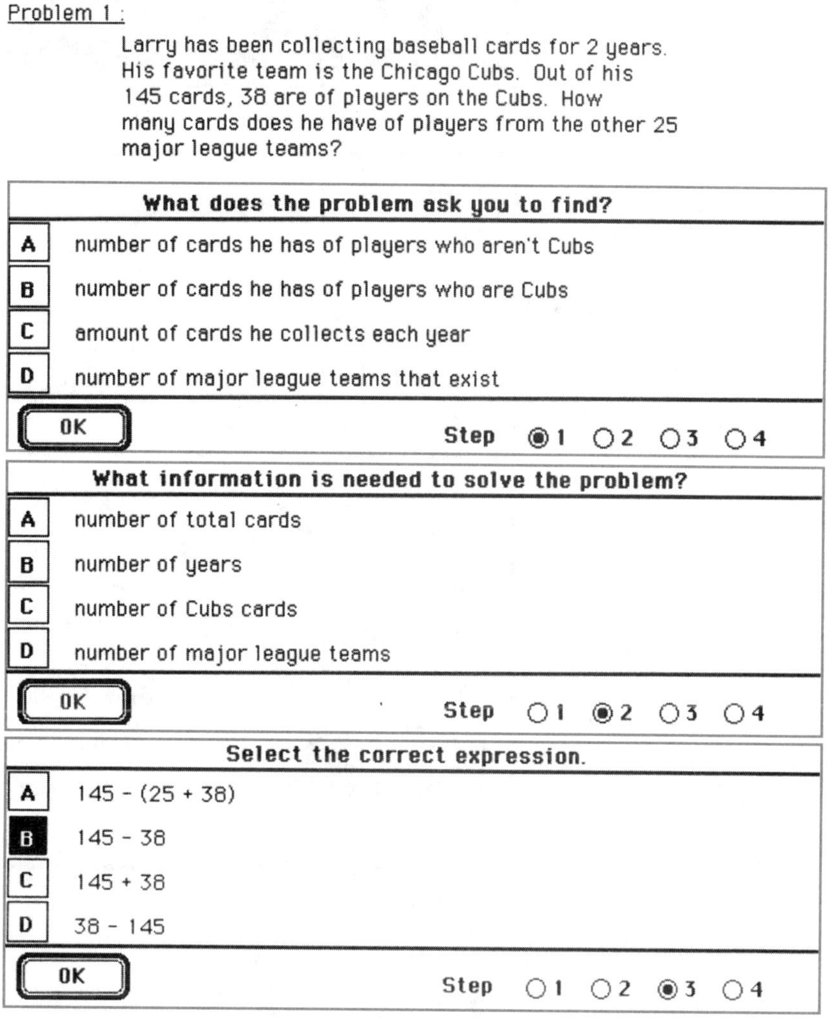

Problem 1 :

Larry has been collecting baseball cards for 2 years. His favorite team is the Chicago Cubs. Out of his 145 cards, 38 are of players on the Cubs. How many cards does he have of players from the other 25 major league teams?

| **What does the problem ask you to find?** |
|---|
| **A** number of cards he has of players who aren't Cubs |
| **B** number of cards he has of players who are Cubs |
| **C** amount of cards he collects each year |
| **D** number of major league teams that exist |

OK        Step   ● 1   ○ 2   ○ 3   ○ 4

| **What information is needed to solve the problem?** |
|---|
| **A** number of total cards |
| **B** number of years |
| **C** number of Cubs cards |
| **D** number of major league teams |

OK        Step   ○ 1   ● 2   ○ 3   ○ 4

| **Select the correct expression.** |
|---|
| **A** 145 – (25 + 38) |
| **B** 145 – 38 |
| **C** 145 + 38 |
| **D** 38 – 145 |

OK        Step   ○ 1   ○ 2   ● 3   ○ 4

The three screens shown in Figure 10–4 reward the student by presenting a graphic, by listing the student's performance, and by printing a certificate of accomplishment.

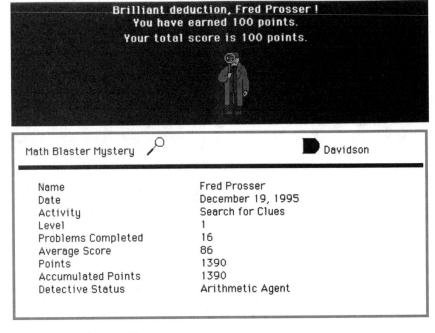

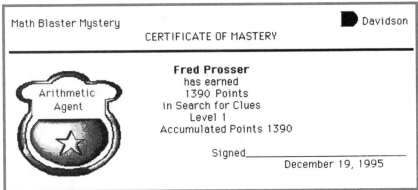

**FIGURE 10–4**
Math Blaster Mystery *reward screens*
(Courtesy of Davidson & Associates, Inc.)

## Tutorial

A **tutorial** program is designed to introduce new information to the student and can be in a **linear** or **branching** format. Both formats present information and questions that lead toward an identified goal. Linear programs (Figure 10–5) present information in a sequential manner and do not attempt to remediate errors made. Tutorial instruction often includes a placement test to ensure student readiness and sometimes a pretest on specific objectives to validate the placement test. It presents new information to students and questions them on that information. Tutorials often include initial guidance

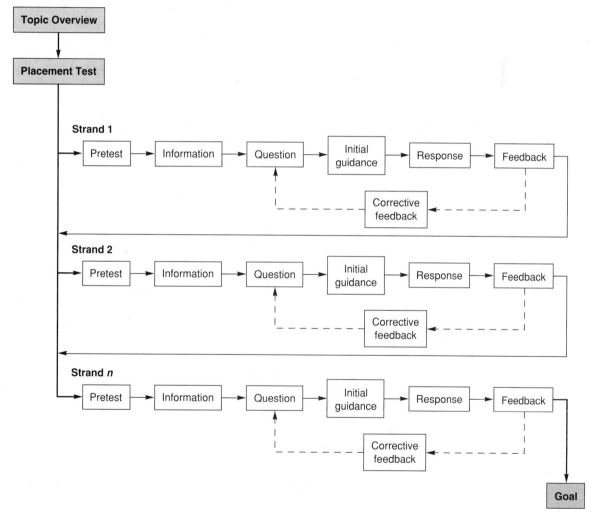

**FIGURE 10–5**
*A typical tutorial format*

in the form of prompts to encourage the student to answer correctly, especially at the outset of the lesson.

The diagram in Figure 10–5 illustrates a representation of a linear format often used in tutorial programs. This technique exposes the student to material that is believed not to have been learned. In a behaviorist model, the teacher identifies the proper lesson objectives, selects the appropriate computer program, maintains a reasonably comfortable environment free from unnecessary distractions, and where needed, provides additional resources and encouragement to the student. The teacher must also monitor the progress made by the student by interpreting data collected by the computer program and be prepared to intervene if necessary. In a constructivist model, tutorial software may be suggested by the teacher as a way for the student to acquire a particular skill or concept once its value is recognized. The teacher's role is to ascertain readiness on the part of the student, to select the appropriate software, assess the student's performance as the newly acquired skill or concept is applied to a meaningful task, and determine if further practice is required.

The computer usually assesses a student's prior learning, determines readiness for the material, and presents material for student observation, note taking, and other interaction. New material is commonly provided in small increments replete with instructional guidance and appropriate feedback to encourage correct student response. Some programs employ modest branching techniques to provide alternative paths or *branches* for remediation or acceleration. Tutorials must record student responses and allow for teacher analysis of the student's progress to determine if the goal has been met.

Tutorial programs, such as the example in Figure 10–6, are often used to help students who have been absent from class. They may also be effective when assigned as independent study to students exhibiting difficulty with specific skills and concepts. Working directly at a computer on a tutorial program can provide interest and motivation, if the teacher keeps in mind that it is only one alternative among various strategies to teach specific skills or concepts. The educational quality of the program must be ascertained and to maintain its effectiveness, the strategy should not be overused.

## Simulation

**Simulation** is another time-honored teaching strategy used to reinforce instruction by providing an environment for discovery learning to take place or for newly acquired skills and concepts to be tested. In the past, teachers have used board games, drama, and role playing to implement the simulation technique. The computer is a useful tool to manage this technique. It can present the facts and rules of a situation and adjust to any interaction by the student.

**FIGURE 10–6**
*Calculus*
(Courtesy of Broderbund
Software Inc.)

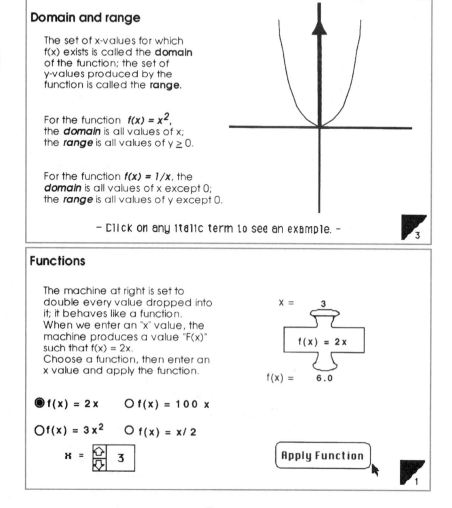

Simulations can present a sample of a real situation and can offer genuine practice at solving real problems unhampered by danger, distance, time, or cost factors. High levels of cognitive skill are involved in the synthesis of facts, rules, and concepts in solving problems. Simulation permits this synthesis to take place within the classroom.

Consider, for example, the teacher who wants to teach the concept of free elections in a representative democracy. Figure 10–7 suggests a common flow of events in a typical simulation. A classroom simulation might call for the creation of class offices including development of a nomination process, establishment of platforms, identification of a polling place, preparation of secret and secure ballots, and agreement on term of office for the successful candidates. The simulation just described has been conducted for years without a computer. A computer program, however, can increase the

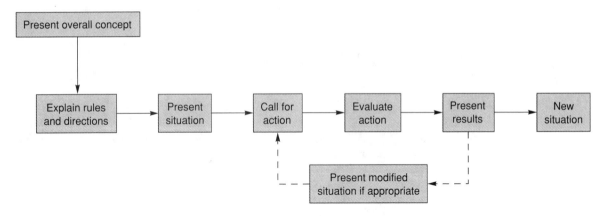

**FIGURE 10-7**
*A typical simulation format*

sophistication of the simulation and can extend it into a broader context. For instance, it could introduce a number of historical variables that might influence decisions made in the running of a presidential election campaign. In this case, the program could store a wealth of data that can be called upon as needed and cross-referenced to demonstrate cause and effect.

Simulation software can provide highly realistic practice at solving real problems in the classroom without many of the limiting factors often found in real life. As in any use of CAI, the role of the teacher is to identify the proper lesson objectives and to select the appropriate computer program. When using simulation software in a behaviorist model, the teacher often provides background information and may be called upon to teach related skills and concepts and to provide additional resources where needed. The teacher must also monitor the progress made by the student or by the group of students and assess their performance. Simulations, lending themselves to group use, promote social interaction and can often be used as an introductory activity for a unit. In a constructivist model, simulation software may be suggested by the teacher as a way for the student to develop a particular skill or concept in a manner that is close to a real-life situation. The teacher's role is to ascertain readiness on the part of the student, to select the appropriate software, discuss the student's performance in the simulation, and suggest a real-world application.

The top screen in Figure 10–8 is from a program called *Ballistic*. The user sets initial parameters of initial velocity, angle of projection, and drag medium. By turning on the Friction control but leaving the Decay control turned off, a medium of constant density is simulated. Turning on the Decay control simulates a medium whose density decreases with altitude. Once launched, the projectile leaves a trace in the display window. By varying the parameters of initial velocity, angle of projection, air friction as

"I use Sim Earth *on the one computer I have in my classroom along with an LCD panel on an overhead projector. The first team of students designs their environment to maximize population expansion; the second to maximize plant life; the third to maximize sustainable growth; and the fourth to factor in natural disasters. Each team presents to the whole class. Ensuing discussion examines consequences of each choice.*"

Jim Long, Marine and Environmental Science Teacher
North Salem High School, Salem, OR

**FIGURE 10–8**

*Physics simulation series*
(Developed by Blas Cabrera,
Stanford University, and pub-
lished by Intellimation, Santa
Barbara, CA)

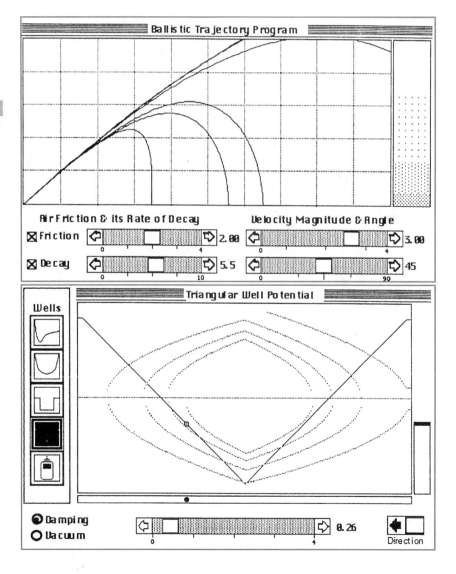

the drag medium, and altitude-related decay, the user can compare the results of these combined factors as traces in the display window.

The bottom screen in Figure 10–8 is from a program called *Potential*. Users choose from four one-dimension potential wells or create their own. The illustration represents a triangular well: A ball travels downward along the left slope, reaches bottom, and rolls a certain distance upward on the right slope, then reverses its direction. This is repeated with diminishing distances until all energy is spent. A damping effect can be employed to observe the effect of various dissipating conditions. Kinetic and potential energies are continually displayed in a column at the right of the screen. Velocity or acceleration can be plotted for each travel of the ball.

Both of these examples are intrinsic simulation models that create an artificial environment for the user to explore. In these microworlds elements of the environment operate according to a regular set of rules. The student manipulates things to learn what their characteristics are within the artificial environment.

As you examine Figure 10–9, note the richness of graphic details in this award-winning program from MECC. The user is placed in the position of

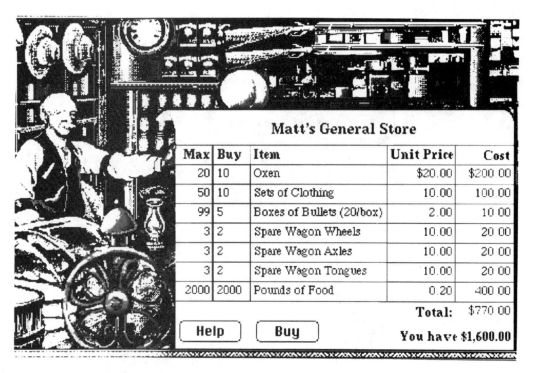

**FIGURE 10–9**
Oregon Trail *title page and general store*
(Courtesy of MECC)

traveling the 2,000-mile Oregon Trail from Independence, Missouri, to Oregon's Willamette Valley. Having declared an occupation and thereby receiving an allocation of available funds, the user begins preparing for the journey by carefully purchasing supplies as shown in Figure 10–9. The screen of Figure 10–10 is a typical one seen as the program progresses. An oxen-pulled wagon moves in animation across the top. A map tracing the user's progress appears below. A log or diary of the journey appears below the map. Five buttons are arranged in columns down each side of the screen, presenting the user with options. The Guide button reveals pertinent information about the geography of the region in the window usually occupied by the map. Status reveals the list of the user's current supplies. Rations, Buy, Trade, Rest, and Pace allow the control of applicable elements. Hunt calls forth an arcade-type game allowing the user to collect food. Talk often reveals clues or historical facts.

A Wagon Score is displayed only if the user successfully crosses the trail. (The author often perishes before crossing the Rockies.) A value is placed on the people and supplies that complete the journey. Some occupations receive a smaller allocation of funds than others, so have a more

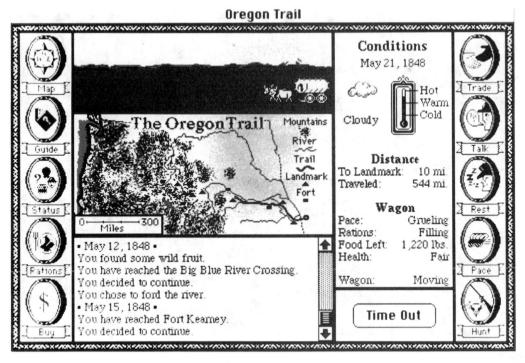

**FIGURE 10–10**
*Traveling the Oregon Trail and final score*
(Courtesy of MECC)

difficult time successfully completing the trip. A factor is, therefore, employed depending on the user's chosen occupation.

The program has a management option protected by a password that allows the teacher to clear the List of Legends, adjust the simulation speed and hunting time, and determine network use, if any. A new network version of the program allows a number of users to interact simultaneously with one another on their journey.

The award winning *Carmen Sandiego* series of programs (*Where in the U.S.A.....*, *Where in the World . . .*, *Where in Europe . . .*, etc.) is the all-time best-selling software in grades K-12. The premise of each program is that as a detective you must pick up the trail of one of Carmen's villainous gang and, following geographic (or historic) clues, deduce the identity of the villain, follow the trail, and ultimately apprehend the culprit (Figure 10–11). The program is so popular that it spawned a television program and there are *Carmen Sandiego* clubs all over the country. It simulates actions that might be taken in the real world and calls upon the user, often working cooperatively with others, to make decisions based on facts gathered. Each program provides an appropriate reference book such as *Fodor's USA*. The computer's role usually is

**FIGURE 10–11**
*Four screens from* Where in the U.S.A. is Carmen Sandiego?
(Courtesy of Broderbund Software Inc.)

to create a realistic environment and present material for student interaction, to provide appropriate feedback to student responses, and based on decisions made by students, to modify the environment and present new material allowing the students to witness the results of their decisions.

Students might be asked to trace their travels in the simulation on a map and list the countries through which they travel. Students could be named as "ambassadors" representing each country. They would research the country they represent and present brief reports or hold a mock United Nations meeting and discuss issues of importance to them.

In a simulation, students interact with the environment and perhaps with each other, make decisions based on the material presented by the computer, and make choices they deem appropriate. As part of the overall activity, they may discuss results of the simulation. Since the learning theory on which software design is based dictates the role of the computer, the role of the teacher, and the role of the student, recognizing these elements is an important first step toward making good use of the computer in the classroom.

A table summarizing the teacher, student, and computer roles in CAI is presented for your review as Figure 10–12.

## Software as an Information Resource

Some software does not easily fit the categories of drill and practice, tutorial, or simulation but relates in some manner to all categories depending on its use. This software, namely, word processors, spreadsheets, and databases, is often seen as an information utility. Previous chapters have dealt with this software in detail and have emphasized the access to information or the construction of knowledge.

## A Programming Language

**Logo** is the name assigned to the research group at M.I.T. headed by Seymour Papert, and it is the name of the computer programming language that was the result of that group's work. But more than that, Logo is an educational philosophy based on Piaget's learning theory and on ideas from the field of artificial intelligence. Logo was intended to be learned, but not taught. It is learned through a process of active, creative exploration, and in the process the child must think about thinking and learn about learning.

Logo is a structured programming language designed to help students of all ages develop an understanding of problem-solving strategies based on an individual's style of learning and concepts of meaningful problems as visual images. Employing Logo's powerful turtle graphics, the student explores spatial reasoning and uses the computer to control the "turtle" like an electronic pencil to create geometric shapes at any point on the screen.

| | Tutorial | Drill & Practice | Simulation |
|---|---|---|---|
| Teacher | Determines objectives | Determines objectives | Determines objectives |
| | Selects materials appropriate to students | Selects materials appropriate to students | Selects materials appropriate to students |
| | Monitors progress | Teaches original skills or concepts | Teaches related skills |
| | Assesses student performance | Monitors progress | Often prompts students to discover concepts |
| | | Assesses student performance | May take active role in a group |
| | | | Assesses student performance |
| Computer | Presents original material | Presents material in form of problems or questions | Presents a situation |
| | Assesses progress | Displays feedback | Elicits student response |
| | Displays feedback | May assess performance | Modifies situation |
| | Provides guidance | May record performance | May assess performance |
| | May assess performance | | Demonstrates result of student action |
| | Records performance | | |
| | Tests for objectives | | |
| Student | Interacts with computer | Interacts with computer | Reacts to situation |
| | Responds to feedback | Responds appropriately | Refers to external resources if needed |
| | Controls pace of presentation | Examines results | Confers with others as needed |
| | Examines results | | Makes choices based on information |

**FIGURE 10-12**
*Role comparison in CAI*

With Logo, knowledge that was formerly accessible only through abstract, formal thinking can be approached concretely by manipulating the turtle, a computer-controlled, cybernetic animal that exists in the Logo environment. There are floor turtles (physical objects that can be picked up like any mechanical toy), and there are screen turtles, which reside on the computer monitor screen. Both have the ability to draw lines as they move. The user communicates with the turtle and tells it what to do by speaking "turtle talk," the Logo computer language.

The screen turtle, or pointer, is moved by giving it commands through the keyboard. For example, by giving the series of simple instructions

**FIGURE 10–13**
*Drawing a box in Logo*

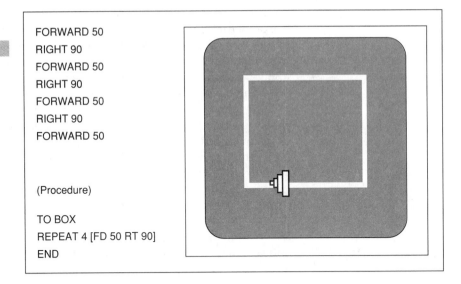

```
FORWARD 50
RIGHT 90
FORWARD 50
RIGHT 90
FORWARD 50
RIGHT 90
FORWARD 50


(Procedure)

TO BOX
REPEAT 4 [FD 50 RT 90]
END
```

found in the top left-hand corner of Figure 10–13, we can draw a box. We could, however write the *procedure* (program) found in the bottom left-hand corner of Figure 10–13 and BOX becomes a new command in the turtle's vocabulary. On the one hand, a child can learn by discovery, by approximation, through trial and error, and by intuition. On the other hand, a youngster who is comfortable with a more structured approach to learning can analyze a problem and develop a carefully planned approach to the solution. Mistakes are viewed as natural occurrences that must be corrected—"debugged"—to succeed.

Teachers often take advantage of the power of Logo by having young children "play turtle." After introducing some basic turtle talk commands such as FORWARD, BACK, LEFT, RIGHT, they provide many opportunities for children to walk out shapes and describe their actions in turtle talk. Children may practice by directing each other around the room or playground with turtle commands. In the process, they are taking the first step toward thinking about their thinking, because they must reflect on how they would do themselves what they would like the turtle to do. In addition, they are gaining a personal, visual, and kinesthetic sense of basic geometric principles.

## INTERACTIVE MULTIMEDIA

**Multimedia** is not a time-tested strategy such as drill and practice, tutorial, and simulation but rather a relatively recent development that allows the combination of a number of instructional resources to present information under the control of the computer. Its power lies in its ability to network information resources and to provide ready access to the learner. Multimedia employs more than one way of conveying information in a multisensory manner. As a teaching tool, for example, it might include the use of textual, graphic, audio, and video materials to convey information to the user, who would interact with it by reading, listening, and observing still and moving images. Multimedia is a logical extension of simulation with characteristics of drill and practice, tutorial, and problem-solving approaches. As suggested by Figure 10–14, multimedia computer programs are used to control the presentation of video information from external sources such as videotape or videodisc as well as graphic, audio, or textual information from CD-ROM. This audio and video information is presented to the viewer under the control of the computer and is usually accompanied by computer-generated text.

Multimedia also allows students to create their own visuals and incorporate them into their products or to create their own navigation through existing resources. It gives the student control of powerful tools in the exploration and creation of information. A camcorder, digital camera, optical scanner, CD-ROM drive, videodisc player, and video cassette recorder all become potential information-gathering tools. Multimedia tools allow a student to compose a complex statement that might include computer-generated sound, graphics, and animation along with sound and visual forms stored in another medium such as videodisc, videotape, or CD-ROM. Technological developments in laser disk optical storage have greatly facilitated the development of multimedia.

## Authoring Tools

No discussion of multimedia would be complete without a look at HyperCard, a program introduced by Apple Computer and said to have

**FIGURE 10–14**
*Equipment supporting multimedia*

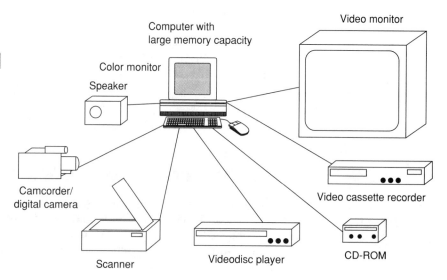

*"Students use HyperCard to draw maps of Alaska identifying geographical regions of the state, significant topographical features such as mountain ranges and bodies of water, animal distribution, population centers and cultural groups. Some students scan images and record sound into their HyperCard stack. I encourage them to then write adventure stories that provide multiple pathways and optional endings."*

Fred Ross, 6th Grade Teacher
Bering Strait School District, Unalakleet, AK

opened the door to multimedia as we know it today. The program has now been joined by a number of others, most prominent among them ToolBook and Linkway for the Windows operating system and Digital Chisel and HyperStudio for the Macintosh. These programs afford the novice user the satisfaction of creating a multimedia product. Other high-end, sophisticated, and expensive authoring programs such as Macromedia Director are more useful to multimedia programmers.

To understand HyperCard and similar multimedia programs, think of the analogy of a Rolodex. Each information screen is seen as a card. Cards can be arranged in any order and a user can navigate among the cards in a nonlinear manner. Cards are grouped into logical units called stacks and a user can navigate between stacks in a seamless fashion. Navigation, in most instances, is accomplished by clicking buttons. **Buttons** can be visible objects or invisible areas of the screen, often covering images or text. Buttons can be programmed using a scripting language to perform certain actions such as linking to another card or controlling another device. These programs come into their own as multimedia tools in their ability to contain text, graphics and sounds on their cards, and also to play short compressed video clips and, even more importantly, to fully control external devices such as CD-ROMs and videodiscs connected to the computer.

Imagine that you are using a geography stack and that you are looking at a card about a country. Buttons on that card may lead you to additional information about that country in the form of topographical or political maps, lists of products, population statistics, or climate conditions. A button could lead you to a digitized film clip recorded from yesterday's evening newscast of the country's president delivering a speech to the Unied Nations.

Interactive multimedia is not only a presentation tool for commercially prepared material, it is a tool with which the teacher can prepare information of a local or immediate nature. Most importantly, it is a tool for students to gather their own information, construct their own knowledge, and communicate their ideas effectively.

**FIGURE 10–15**
*Optical disk system*

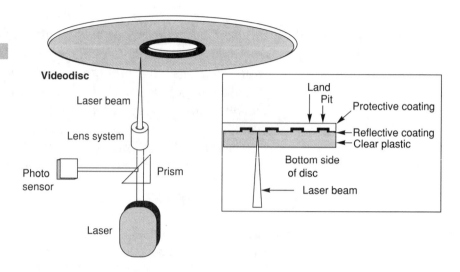

## How Optical Disk Media Work

As shown in Figure 10–15, a laser beam reads a precise series of tiny *pits* or depressions and smooth reflective areas called *lands* on the bottom surface of a optical disc. The lands reflect the laser beam to a photo sensor and the pits diffract the light beam. The recorded tracks composed of these pits are either spiral or concentric circles that can contain information in either analog or digital form. The length of each pit and distances between them determine the data in the videodisc format and translate them to analog video while reading an index code and audio in a digital manner. The data in a CD-ROM, however, are represented in terms of the transition between pit and land in a digital manner. Present systems are read-only memory (ROM), produced by a publisher; write once, read many (WORM), created by the user; or erasable systems. The optical disc reader or player employs a laser beam to detect the pits and then decodes the data into the original information to be displayed on a video screen or printed as hard copy.

Figure 10–16 shows a photograph taken by a scanning electron microscope of pits and lands on a CD-ROM surface. The photograph is a magnification of 2000x.

## Videodisc

The first of the optical technologies, **videodisc** was commercially introduced in 1978 and has been aimed primarily at the education/training, sales/promotion, and consumer recreation markets. A 12″ disc can contain up to 54,000 different images per side and two continuous audio tracks. (Imagine a carousel slide tray containing 54,000 color slides!) The information may be displayed as still pictures, drawings, or up to 120 minutes of live video and audio.

**FIGURE 10–16**
*A magnified view of pits and lands*
(Photograph courtesy of 3M)

Videodiscs are classified as either **CLV** (constant linear velocity), whose track is recorded as a spiral divided into data sectors of equal length, or **CAV** (constant angular velocity), whose tracks are recorded as concentric circles with radial data sectors. CLV discs allow for extended play time but are not frame-addressable. A search of a CLV disc is limited to playing time or to an arbitrary break called a chapter rather than to a specific frame. A CLV disc rotates at a variable rate of speed from 1800 rpm at the start (innermost point on the disc) and gradually slows to 600 rpm as the laser approaches the outer edge of the disc. Since each image frame occupies the same length of track, three times the amount of data is stored on the outer edge of the disc. CAV discs rotate at a constant 1800 rpm (30 revolutions per second, which corresponds to the rate of standard video imaging in the U.S.) Each revolution of a CAV videodisc corresponds to one frame of information, allowing each frame to be indexed and addressed individually. The maximum search time for any given frame on a CAV disc is 3 seconds. A new term, *interactive videodisc* (IVD), has evolved reflecting the primary use of CAV discs. Minimum predicted life expectancy of optical discs is in the vicinity of 25 years.

Videodisc players are classified into three levels according to how they can be controlled. **Level I** players are sometimes thought to be consumer models controlled by a remote control unit or bar code reader. These lend themselves to teacher-mediated presentations in large group instruction and are often accompanied by a bar-coded teacher guide with lesson plans. **Level II** players are industrial models with improved access time, programmable memory, and the ability to read a program track on the disc. Level II players are rarely used in education. **Level III** players are designed to interface with a computer and to operate under its control. Level III software packages contain both video discs and computer program discs. In addition to full searching capabilities, the software often allows the user to assemble information into a unique presentation. Students can experience truly interactive lessons and have their performance data stored in the computer.

Feature films, simulations, and visual databases containing still images including maps, sound, and motion sequences are found on videodiscs. Language arts teachers have used the CAV versions of some of the *Indiana Jones* series as a tool to examining screen writing. Simulations such as Tom Snyder Productions' *The Great Solar System Rescue* involve students in scientist and historian roles as they work together to solve problems. The *National Gallery of Art* by Videodisc Publishing is a visual database containing still images of works by the great masters as well as a guided tour of the gallery. It has been **repurposed,** that is, computer programs have been designed to use its content in ways different from its original intent in order to teach the basic concepts of visual design. *Communism and the Cold War,* and *Martin Luther King,* both by ABC News Interactive, are examples of multimedia visual databases. By using still images, recorded speeches, and video clips from its vast archives, ABC has compiled resources containing a wealth of information for teachers to present and students to examine and manipulate to construct their own understanding of complex issues.

## CD-Audio

The **CD-audio** (compact disc-audio) digital format, introduced in 1983, has achieved phenomenal success with millions of players installed all over the world. In only a few years it made record players obsolete. It has supplied the economy of scale and research and development funds that have contributed to the development of CD-ROM and other compact disc formats.

## Photo-CD

Eastman Kodak Company developed and marketed **photo-CD** technology to consumers. Anyone can walk in off the street at a location that handles the service, drop off up to 100 color slides or negatives, and have them scanned into a photo-CD at a reasonable cost. Played back in a photo-CD player or in most CD-ROM drives, the images can be viewed on a monitor or projected on a screen.

Libraries are creating large image databases by scanning fragile manuscripts and publications, maps, drawings, and photographs into what they regard as a stable, long-life medium. Universities, school districts, and individual schools with large slide collections are looking at this technology as an inexpensive and practical way to convert slides to an electronic form for archival and instructional purposes. Computer software by Kodak, Aldus, and other publishers makes it possible to index the images, view thumbnail representations in a slide sorter format, prescribe their subsequent viewing in a specific sequence, and create keyword searching capabilities.

## CD-ROM

This much-publicized medium, the **CD-ROM** (compact disk-read only memory), was introduced in 1985, two years after the introduction of the audio compact disk. It was initially seen primarily as a publishing or database medium aimed at users who needed relatively low-cost mass storage of information and rapid access and retrieval. *Grolier, Compton,* and *World Book* are electronic encyclopedias. The extended architecture version, CD-ROM XA, has added graphics and sound to the text data. The technology has since blossomed into a powerful interactive multimedia tool.

A direct comparison of the two most popular optical media presented in Figure 10–17 reveals that one developed in the entertainment field and grew into the education arena while the other has moved in the opposite direction. A CD-ROM is a digital format disc that measures only 4.75″ but can contain approximately 650 megabytes of data, the equivalent of approximately 300,000 typewritten pages of text. Text or graphic information can be displayed on a monitor screen by a CD-ROM drive attached as a peripheral device to a computer. Several popular computer models now include an internal CD-ROM drive. It is estimated that in 1995 approximately 70 percent of computers manufactured included one. Although the medium began as a read-only technology as its name implies, recorders are now entering the end-user marketplace. Technology breakthroughs in the CD-ROM medium may allow it to supplant videodisc.

**FIGURE 10–17**
*Comparison of videodisc and CD-ROM*

| Videodisc | CD-ROM |
|---|---|
| • Entertainment, training, and instruction | • Information storage, instruction and entertainment |
| • Analog | • Digital |
| • 2″ or 8″ | • 4.75″ |
| • 800 rpm | • 300–500 rpm |
| • Text, pictures, sound, and full-motion video | • Text, graphics, sound, and compressed video |
| • Up to 1 gigabyte, 108,000 image frames, or 120-minute video | • 650 megabytes |

## DVI

**DVI** (digital video interactive) is a hardware extension that adds value to the CD-ROM technology in compression/decompression algorithms (capable of a 100:1 compression ratio) stored on chips, which can efficiently store and play up to 72 minutes of high-quality full-motion video. Originally developed by General Electric's RCA division in 1987, it was subsequently bought and is currently owned by Intel Corporation and is actively supported by IBM. Intel manufactures and licenses plug-in cards that run under OS/2, DOS, and Windows to allow computers to take advantage of this technology. New Video Corporation markets a DVI board for the Macintosh computer.

## CD-I

**CD-I** (compact disc-interactive) is an outgrowth of CD-ROM technology designed to facilitate interactive performance between the user and the information on the disc. Sony and Phillips International jointly developed CD-I and aimed it at the consumer market when they released it in 1991. The stand-alone CD-I player incorporates a microchip and allows the display of text, graphics, sound, and animation but it is not viewed as a computer. Although keyboards and most computer peripherals can be attached, the remote control/joystick was initially the preferred controller.

| | System Platforms | Storage Medium | Image Storage | Video Storage | Audio Storage |
|---|---|---|---|---|---|
| Videodisc | Stand-alone with computer interface | 8″ and 12″ disks | 54,000 per side | 30 min./side (CAV) 60 min./side (CLV) | Same as video |
| CD-Audio | Stand-alone with computer interface | 4.75″ disk | NA | NA | Up to 74 min. (2 channel) |
| CD-ROM (XA) | SCSI interface | 4.75″ disk | NA | Limited | Up to 19 hrs. (2 channel) |
| CD-I | Proprietary hardware | 4.75″ disk integrated | 8,000 | 72 min. | Up to 19 hrs. (2 channel) |
| DVI | OS-2, DOS, Windows Macintosh | 4.75″ disk | 40,000 | 72 min. | Up to 40 hrs. (2 channel) |

**FIGURE 10–18**
*Optical media storage*

Early software titles released included *Time-Life Photography, Cartoon Jukebox, The Urban Gardener,* and *The Palm Springs Golf Open.* The technology has entered the school market with *Grolier's Encyclopedia* and other educational titles.

CD-I is a proprietary technology that is attempting to tap the lucrative multimedia market. The more generic CD-ROM, available for the Macintosh, OS/2, DOS, and Windows platforms, has gained far wider acceptance to date. Figure 10–18 compares videodisc, CD-audio, CD-ROM, CD-I, and DVI.

### Applications

The optical disk technologies have gained widespread acceptance as media for classroom instruction. Once a price/performance breakthrough occurs in large video screen, flat screen, and video projection, optical disk technologies will become universally accepted. The videodisc or CD-ROM player will replace the 16mm motion picture film projector and the filmstrip projector. The videocassette will continue in use for a time due to its local production characteristics until recordable disks become cost effective. The 35mm slide may become an endangered species as digital still camera technology is improved and becomes more affordable.

The CD-ROM medium is extremely accurate, compact, durable, and cost effective. Search time for any point on the disk is approximately one to three seconds. Low volume publishing, public access catalogs, and library archives are logical applications of write-once discs. Already, thousands of CD-ROM products, computer software, ready reference tools, encyclopedias, storybooks, indexes and abstracts have been published. As refinements improve the search and access times, the CD-ROM and its derivatives will become increasingly valuable information access tools in the library and in the classroom as electronic publishing media.

## CURRICULUM INTEGRATION

A danger in examining discrete elements and in categorizing software or computer applications is that we neglect the whole as we examine the separate parts. Much software available today spans more than one category. Tutorial software may well have drill and practice components. Simulation software may well introduce new concepts and repeat previously learned material. Classification schemes can become counterproductive if they interfere with an understanding of the potential application of software.

The somewhat arbitrary classification of curriculum over the past decades, especially at the secondary school level, into specific subject matter areas is now breaking down in favor of the integration of disciplines to foster richer learning environments. As we consider computer applications, then, we should keep the concept of integration in mind. The following discussion by David Thornburg (1991) in his book *Education, Technology, and Paradigms of Change for the 21st Century* is an excellent example of classroom application of the computer in an integrated curriculum:

---

. . . . suppose you are a teacher who is exploring California for social studies. One way to do this is to present the students with material right from the textbook. This familiar approach takes a fascinating topic and makes it boring. It causes some students to say, "Who cares?"

On the other hand, in the same period of time, a teacher who really cares about the subject may try a different approach. After exploring California's location on the planet and talking about the geologic upheavals that created some of the spectacular landscape, the students might be encouraged to imagine themselves as members of an ancient tribe of Indians, the Ohlones, for example. Student research on this tribe would allow them to think about the rich civilization these Indians had when the pyramids were being built in Egypt.

As the students learned more about these ancient people, they could learn how to identify animals from their tracks. For this task, students could use *Animal Trackers*, a program from Sunburst Communications that provides clues from which the students must identify a particular animal. Because this program supports databases for grasslands, desert and wooded areas, it can be used all over the country. Each clue provides information of a different sort—habitat, nesting, food, and footprints. After working with this program for a while, students will have learned a lot about native American animals, as well as honing their higher order thinking skills. This activity provides an opportunity for science to become integrated with social studies.

As the year proceeds, the students might see a new animal through Indian eyes—the strange creatures with two heads and four legs (the Spanish explorers on horseback). At this point some students might want to retain the Indian perspective and others might want to join forces with Portola or Father Junipero Serra as the colonization of California took place.

Later on in the course, the teacher might show the film *Dream West*, showing the life of Fremont as he explored the West and paved the way for the United States to expand its boundaries. At this point, students could use the *Oregon Trail* simulation from MECC to see how well they might fare on their own journey across the country (pp. 22–23)

---

## Summary

Computer software might take the form of drill and practice, tutorial, simulation, or interactive multimedia software that combines text, graphics, sound, and animation and controls live-action video sequences. Drill and practice is a technique used to reinforce previous instruction by providing the repetition necessary to move skills and concepts acquired into long-term memory. A tutorial program is designed to introduce new information to the student and often includes a placement test to ensure student readiness. Simulations provide an environment for discovery learning to take place or for newly acquired skills and concepts to be tested. Lending themselves to group use, they promote social interaction and can often be used as an introductory activity for a unit.

Logo, a computer programming language, is learned through a process of active, creative exploration, and in the process the child must think about thinking and learn about learning. Employing Logo's powerful turtle graphics, the student explores spatial reasoning and uses the computer to control the "turtle" like an electronic pencil to create geometric shapes at any point on the screen.

Multimedia employs more than one way of conveying information in a multisensory manner. Multimedia computer programs are used to control the presentation of video information from external sources such as videotape or videodisc as well as graphic, audio, or textual information from CD-ROM.

Multimedia tools allow a student to compose a complex statement that might include computer-generated sound, graphics, and animation along with sound and visual forms stored in another medium such as videodisc, videotape, or CD-ROM. Optical storage formats employ a laser beam that reads a precise series of pits and lands on the disc. Common formats include videodisc, CD-ROM, CD-audio, Photo-CD, and CD-I. A 12" videodisc can contain up 54,000 different images per side and two continuous audio tracks. The information may be displayed as still pictures, drawings, or up to 120 minutes of live video and audio. Videodiscs are classified as either extended-play CLV (constant linear velocity) or frame-addressable CAV (constant angular velocity).

Up to 100 color slides or negatives can be scanned into a photo-CD and played back in a photo-CD player or in most CD-ROM drives. Computer software makes it possible to index the images, view thumbnail representations in a slide sorter format, prescribe their subsequent viewing in a specific sequence, and create keyword searching capabilities.

The CD-ROM, a digital format disc that can contain approximately 650 megabytes of data, was initially seen as a publishing or database medium aimed at users who needed relatively low-cost mass storage of information. CD-ROM XA added graphics and sound to the text data, allowing the technology to blossom into a powerful interactive multimedia tool.

DVI is an extension that adds value to the CD-ROM technology with enhanced graphics and motion video. Its value is in the compression/decompression algorithms stored on chips that can efficiently store full-motion video.

CD-I is an outgrowth of CD-ROM technology aimed at the consumer market and designed to facilitate interactive performance between the user and the information on the disc. With a remote control/joystick as the preferred controller, the stand-alone CD-I player incorporates a microchip and allows the display of text, graphics, sound, and animation, but it is not viewed as a computer.

The somewhat arbitrary classification of curriculum over the past decades, especially at the secondary school level, into specific subject matter areas is now breaking down in favor of the integration of disciplines to foster richer learning environments. As we consider computer applications, then, we should keep the concept of integration in mind.

## Chapter Exercises

1. Describe a drill and practice format. Apply this description to a piece of software you have examined, being careful to identify the roles of the teacher, the student, and the computer.
2. Describe a tutorial format. Apply this description to a piece of software you have examined, being careful to identify the roles of the teacher, the student, and the computer.
3. Describe a simulation format. Apply this description to a piece of software you have examined, being careful to identify the roles of the teacher, the student, and the computer.
4. Describe how the use of gaming strategies might enhance or detract from drill and practice software. How might they affect a simulation?
5. Using an authoring program such as HyperCard, Digital Chisel, or Toolbook, create a family tree. Scan photographs into your project and record the sound of each member's name. Go back at least as far as your great-grandparents.
6. Evaluate a multimedia program from your school's software collection. Was it appropriate for the multimedia format? Did it take full advantage of the format? Did its complexity interfere with its effective use? Can you suggest a better way to convey the same information?
7. Choose a CD-ROM encyclopedia or another CD-ROM product and demonstrate it to a colleague.

## Glossary

**branching**    Some programs employ modest branching techniques to provide alternative paths or branches for remediation or acceleration.

**buttons**    Visible objects or invisible areas of the screen, often covering images or text that can be programmed using a scripting language to perform certain actions such as linking to additional information or controlling an external device.

**CAV (constant angular velocity)**    A frame-addressable videodisc format whose tracks are recorded as concentric circles with radial data sectors.

**CD-audio (compact disc-audio)**   A digital audio format introduced in 1983 that has achieved a phenomenal success with millions of players installed all over the world.

**CD-I (compact disc-interactive)**   An outgrowth of CD-ROM technology designed to facilitate interactive performance between the user and the information on the disc. The stand-alone CD-I player incorporates a microchip and allows the display of text, graphics, sound, and animation but it is not viewed as a computer.

**CD-ROM (compact disk-read only memory)**   The 4.75″ digital optical disc storage medium capable of containing approximately 650 megabytes of data was initially seen primarily as a publishing or database medium aimed at users who needed relatively low-cost mass storage of information and rapid access and retrieval. The extended architecture version, CD-ROM XA, has added graphics and sound to the text data and allowed the technology to blossom into a powerful interactive multimedia tool.

**CLV (constant linear velocity)**   An extended-play videodisc format whose track is recorded as a spiral divided into data sectors of equal length.

**drill and practice**   A category of computer software that employs the teaching strategy to reinforce instruction by providing repetition necessary to move acquired skills and concepts into long-term memory. Problems are presented and feedback provided to the student's response.

**DVI (digital video interactive)**   A compression/decompression technology for OS/2, DOS, and Windows that adds value to CD-ROM and boasts enhanced graphics and motion video.

**gaming**   A strategy that can be incorporated into all instructional software categories. Includes the elements of a set of rules and competition against others or against a standard.

**level I**   A videodisc classification that is thought to be consumer models providing still frame, chapter and frame addressability, and two-channel audio. The models lend themselves to teacher mediated presentations in large group instruction.

**level II**   Industrial models with improved access time, programmable memory, and the ability to read a program track on the disc. They allow students to independently interact with the instructional content on the disc through a keypad and bar code reader.

**level III**   Players designed to interface with a computer and to operate under its control. Students can experience truly interactive lessons and have their performance data stored in the computer.

**linear**   Linear programs present information in a sequential manner and do not attempt to remediate errors made. New material is commonly provided in small increments replete with instructional guidance and appropriate feedback to encourage correct student response.

**Logo**   A structured programming language embodying the philosophy of Jean Piaget, designed to help students of all ages develop an understanding of problem-solving strategies based on an individual's style of learning and concepts of meaningful problems as visual images.

**multimedia**　A technique that conveys information in a multisensory manner. It might include the use of textual, graphic, audio, and video materials to convey information to the user, who would interact with it by reading, listening, and observing still and moving images.

**photo-CD**　Eastman Kodak Company developed this technology that allows up to 100 color slides or negatives to be scanned onto an optical disc. Played back in a photo-CD player or in most CD-ROM drives, the images can be viewed on a monitor or projected on a screen.

**repurpose**　The use of computer programs to use content (usually stored on a videodisc) in ways different from the original intent.

**simulation**　A category of computer software that employs a teaching strategy based on role-playing within structured environments. It provides an environment for discovery learning to take place and for newly acquired skills and concepts to be tested.

**tutorial**　A category of computer software that employs the teaching strategy of determining the student's level of knowledge before introducing new information along with learning guidance. The computer usually assesses a student's prior learning, determines readiness for the material, and presents material for student observation, note taking, and other interaction.

**videodisc**　An optical storage technology composed of a 12″ disc capable of storing up to 54,000 different images per side and two continuous audio tracks. The information may be displayed as still pictures or up to 120-minute sequences of live video and audio.

# Notes & Suggested Readings

Balestri, D. P. (1991). Beyond the software manual: A library of perspectives on technology. *Change: The Magazine of Higher Learning, 23*(1), 54–58.

Barron, A. E. (1993, March). The marriage of computers and TV. *Media and Methods, 29*(3), 10.

Baumbach, D. J. (1990, Spring). CD-ROM: Information at your fingertips. *School Library Media Quarterly, 18*(3), 142–149.

Blanchard, J. S., & Rottenberg, C. J. (1990, May). Hypertext and hypermedia: Discovering and creating meaningful learning environments. *Reading Teacher, 43*(9), 656–661.

Bricken, M., & Byrne, C. M. (1992). *Summer students in virtual reality: A pilot study on educational applications of virtual reality technology.* Seattle: Pacific Science Center. (ERIC 358 853).

Brown, J. M. (1992, Spring). A computer-based cooperative learning project for preservice teachers. *Journal of Computing in Teacher Education, 8*(3), 11–16.

D'Ignazio, F. (1990, May). Electronic highways and the classroom of the future. *The Computing Teacher, 17*(8), 20–24.

Griest, G. (1993, April). You say you want a revolution: Constructivism, technology, and language arts. *The Computing Teacher, 20*(7), 8–11.

Hill, W. F. (1977). *Learning: A survey of psychological interpretations.* New York: Harper and Row, 214–16.

Maley, D. (1993, Summer). Technology education: A natural for middle level students. *Schools in the Middle, 2*(4), 10–14.

Moursund, D. (1989, May). Teacher productivity tools. *The Computing Teacher,* 5.

Norton, P. (1992, March). When technology meets the subject-matter disciplines. *Educational Technology,* 3–5.

Pantelidis, V. S. (1993, April). Virtual reality in the classroom. *Educational Technology,* 23–27.

Papert, S. (1980). *Mindstorms: Children, computers and powerful ideas.* New York: Basic Books.

Rickelman, R. J., Henk, W. A., & Melnick, S. A. (1991, February). Electronic encyclopedias on compact disk. *The Reading Teacher, 44*(6), 432–434.

Salpeter, J. (1992, April). Breakthroughs in digital video. *Technology & Learning, 12*(7), 66–74.

Saunders, W. L. (1992, March). Constructivist perspective: Implications and teaching strategies for science. *School Science and Mathematics, 92*(3), 136–141.

Sorge, D. H., Campbell, J. P., & Russell, J. D. (1993, April/May). Evaluating interactive video: Software and hardware. *Tech Trends,* 19–26.

Thornburg, D. D. (1991). *Education, technology, and paradigms of change for the 21st century.* San Carlos, CA: Starsong Publications.

Woodward, J. (1992, June). *Virtual reality and its potential use in special education.* Washington, D.C.: Cosmos Corp. (ERIC 350 766).

# MANAGING A SOFTWARE COLLECTION

**Collection management** is a term that describes the process by which libraries acquire a wide range of materials in a variety of formats to meet the information needs of teachers and students. The term is well suited to describe the responsibilities and activities related to the evaluation, selection, acquisition, maintenance, and promotion of computer software. This chapter will focus on examining the many factors that contribute to the process of selecting software that is compatible with a school's philosophy, goals, and objectives. A process of locating, evaluating, selecting, and managing software will be discussed. Evaluation guidelines and sample worksheets will be developed. A system will be discussed for the management of a software collection to ensure its currency and optimal access by teachers and students.

## Advanced Organizers

1. Where are the sources for locating software?
2. Why is it important to evaluate software?
3. What should be considered in rating software?
4. What should be considered in the selection of software?
5. How can the acquisition of software be facilitated?
6. How should a software collection be managed? That is, how might a software collection be treated in much the same way as a book collection with periodic assessment, weeding, and promotion of its use?

## SOFTWARE COLLECTION MANAGEMENT

Collection management, as described in the introduction to this chapter, is a series of processes and procedures, which together result in the evaluation, selection, acquisition, processing, organization, preservation, effective use, and even the eventual withdrawal of materials from a library's collection. These processes do not exist in isolation from each other or from other operations in a school; rather, they are a direct outgrowth of its mission and philosophy.

Figure 11–1 illustrates the interrelationship of these elements. Knowledge of the school's underlying mission and an awareness of the learning goals for its students is fundamental to developing the best possible software collection. Knowledge of the existing collection gained by a thorough assessment provides the base from which to work. Selection policies guide the development of the collection. Selection procedures include an awareness of selection tools such as journal reviews, selection sources such as educational vendors, and the evaluation of the software prior to selection. Acquisition policies and procedures guide the cataloging, classification, and processing of the software once it arrives in the school to ensure maximum accessibility. Maintenance policies and procedures include

**FIGURE 11–1**
*The components of collection management*

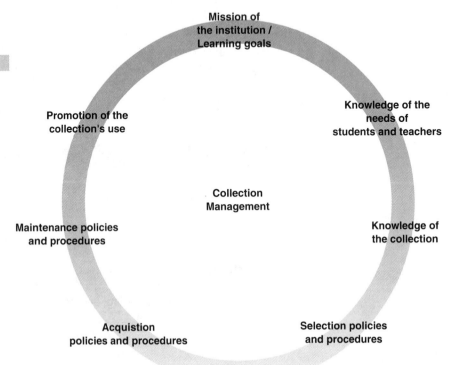

Mission of
the institution /
Learning goals

Knowledge of the
needs of
students and teachers

Promotion of the
collection's use

Collection
Management

Knowledge of
the collection

Maintenance policies
and procedures

Acquistion
policies and procedures

Selection policies
and procedures

**FIGURE 11-2**
*The process of building a collection*

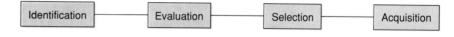

weeding of the software collection and discarding items that have outlived their usefulness. Promotion of the collection's use assumes that the collection exists for the benefit of all students and all teachers. It is an effort to assure that all are aware of new acquisitions as well as understand possible applications of current holdings. Promotion may take the form of notices of software arrivals but it may also entail some inservice work with teachers to demonstrate software and to discuss its potential applications.

Figure 11–2 illustrates four elements in the process of collection development: identifying sources along with product information and reviews, evaluating the product, selecting the product for adoption within a given setting, and acquiring the software. Once software is located, its evaluation and selection for instructional use requires the same professional skills that library media specialists and classroom teachers already perform so well when identifying needs, analyzing content, matching style, and constructing an environment for learning. Acquisition includes the usual value considerations of cost, timeliness of delivery, and after-sales support by the vendor.

## IDENTIFICATION OF SOFTWARE SOURCES

Earlier chapters have dealt with learning theories and with the need to understand, in general, software classifications. When searching for software, keep in mind what it is you wish to accomplish with the software. In order to have sufficient software to offer support to many subject areas at various grade levels, a school will make a sizable investment in time and money. The software selected must be intrinsically of good quality and able to be used effectively in the curriculum.

Gaining access to software for evaluation is no insignificant matter. The following are some likely places to look for information on software.

### Educational Software Vendors

Some companies that had been marketing general curriculum materials are now specializing in computer software. These vendors are familiar with schools and often employ strict selection policies of their own in order to present the best products from a number of publishers. They employ staff trained in teaching and in instructional materials. They exhibit at professional educational conferences and demonstrate software at inservice meetings. Some of these vendors print catalogs listing software by subject area and by computer make and model. The better ones offer "on approval" purchasing and a few even arrange for limited previewing of the software. They are prepared to offer support after the sale as well. Remember, however, that sales is their first objective and professional good judgment must be used in examining their promotional materials. These vendors are not the most objective source of information about the products they are selling.

### Software Publishers

Many companies (textbook publishers included) print catalogs listing their software by topic. Very few, however, offer a preview of their programs before purchase. Some of the companies may have sample disks which they will send to help you with your selection. Companies are reluctant to send out products for review because of the ease with which they can be copied. Books and other materials cost almost as much to duplicate (copy) as would purchasing another item from the company. Software, however, can be copied with very little investment of time or money. If a product is copied illegally, then the company has lost some of its investment in research and production. According to the Software Publishers Association (SPA), one-quarter to one-third of all software used in K-12 grades in this country is illegal (Salvador, 1994). This is a significant problem. Some misguided users blame copyright infringement on inadequate budget resources. They fail to recognize copyright violation as the theft that it is. Rampant violations can endanger the profitability and even the continued existence of small producers, many of whom have provided schools with truly innovative and useful software.

Some school districts have established centers for software review where publishers and/or vendors send products. Teachers are invited to visit these centers to review the software. Stringent safeguards are usually in place to assure that illegal copies are not made. The centers provide an excellent opportunity for publishers to display their latest products and for teachers to use software before having to purchase it.

Most large software packages involve a great deal of time to create, and only by getting a fair return on this investment can the companies continue to produce quality materials. The educational community must take the responsibility to handle software in good faith. If a company does send out software for preview, it is usually done under an agreement with the previewer accepting responsibility to see that the product's copyright is protected. If you obtain software from a publisher, make sure you know the return policy before you order. Some software publishers are listed in Appendix O of this text.

### Software Clearinghouses

There are several clearinghouses for the exchange of **freeware,** which is in the **public domain.** These are items that are not protected by copyright and may be duplicated. Clearinghouses often make available **shareware,** software that can be tried out first and then duplicated for a nominal cost.

For example, the Oregon Education Computing Consortium makes both freeware and shareware available to its members. Explore the availability of software exchanges in your area.

## Local User Groups and Electronic Bulletin Boards

Freeware is widely circulated among user groups, simply through exchanging floppy disks. Specific clubs exist for each major brand of computer in most parts of the country. Ask your hardware dealer for a list of local groups. If you do not want to invest the time in a user group or the local groups are not oriented to your needs, another possible source of freeware and shareware is an electronic bulletin board. Hundreds of these services have sprung up across the country and are available by dialing up the service from your computer and modem, choosing the program you want, and retrieving it over the telephone line.

Freeware and shareware exchanges can be major contributors to the spread of computer **viruses.** A virus is a computer program that installs itself in the user's system software or hard disk. It can replicate itself, change the execution of another program, and carry out instructions it contains. Some viruses are rather benign but others have the potential of wreaking major havoc by destroying systems and files on the disk. They are usually spread from computer to computer when users download files or exchange floppy disks.

When might you suspect a virus infection? Suspect a virus if you notice any pronounced change in the way your computer behaves. Do programs take a longer time to open? Do they run more slowly? Does your system suddenly crash? Is there a sudden reduction of hard disk space? Do new error messages appear? Fortunately, **virus protection programs** are available from several publishers. One type prevents viruses from being installed on your hard drive by scanning floppy disks; another repairs your drive by eradicating existing viruses before they can do more damage. With the constant advent of new viruses, virus protection programs are now sold on an annual subscription basis.

## Local Computer Stores

Although local computer stores may not cater directly to the educational market, they may have a small selection of software that could be demonstrated to you. Even some of the software that they carry to meet business and home use can be useful in the classroom. Examine the software and get some ideas on how it might be used. Read the user's guide and any additional material. Run the software. Find out what kind of equipment it will run on, how much internal memory is required, and what additional hardware, if any, is needed to run the software. Keep in mind that the salesperson may know a lot about games but very little about education.

### Computer Magazines and Professional Journals

Computer journals and magazines carry advertisements and critical reviews of a broad range of available products. Read the reviews and look for articles that discuss the kind of software in which you are interested. Be on the lookout for articles that delve into a specific type of program such as word processing and may compare, feature by feature, the leading products. Major technology journals of interest to the library/media specialist and classroom teacher are listed in Appendix P of this text.

### Regional Education Support Groups

Regional educational laboratories, education service districts, institutions of teacher education with resource centers, state departments of education, and computing consortia are actively collecting and reviewing software for the purpose of making this information available to schools for inspection. Visit one of these organizations and review the software they have on hand.

### Other Schools

Heed the old advertising slogan, "Ask the person who owns one." A visit, phone call, or e-mail message to teachers in nearby schools inquiring about software in specific subject areas may yield some valuable information. Ask questions such as, "What software addresses this topic?" "How do you like it?" "Do students find it interesting?" "Is it easy to use?" "Have you had any problems with it?" "Do you know of anything better on the market?" Remember that answers are opinions, however, and that these views may not fit your particular situation. Once you have identified particular software, it is your responsibility to proceed with a systematic evaluation.

### Conferences

Almost all professional education conferences now have vendors displaying software along with the other traditional curriculum materials. Also, many of the conference sessions are devoted to making effective use of software in teaching as it pertains to the interest group of the conference.

## SOFTWARE EVALUATION

We must keep in mind that the fundamental reason for using computer software is to enhance teaching and learning. The fundamental reason for software evaluation is to see if it fits your educational goals. D'Ignazio (1992) states,

Technology has the potential to dramatically improve the performance of teachers and students, and enrich the learning environment. However, in order to produce these outcomes, technology must be used to support the "best practices" for teaching and learning.

Technology must be used by teachers to create a classroom that encourages:

- Heightened student attention, engagement, and enthusiasm for learning
- Inspired teaching
- Students taking responsibility for their learning and for coaching fellow students
- Student authoring, publishing, and presentations
- Cooperative learning
- Problem-solving, critical thinking, questioning, and analysis
- Collaborative inquiry, research, and investigation (pp. 54–55)

When evaluating software, keep some kind of permanent record that describes the product and lists its features and potential applications. Keeping a record of the evaluation serves two purposes. The first purpose is to refine the criteria and guidelines needed to assess the quality and appropriateness of the software. The second is to use the information from the evaluation in the school's electronic resource guides to media available in the school or in the public access catalog of the school library's automated system if the software is purchased.

Some of the criteria for evaluation are general to all software while some of the evaluative criteria are specific to types of software: drill and practice, tutorial, simulation, or tool. The following sections will consider the evaluation process, first according to general criteria, and then according to criteria related to software type.

## General Criteria

Familiarize yourself with the total software package. Read the instructions to the teacher and to the user. Look over the manuals, if available. Pay attention to the organization and layout of the written material.

Run the program following the written or on-screen directions and see if the program leads you through the material in a well-organized fashion. Notice if the program will let you correct mistakes or if it will trap data entry errors. Can you exit the program at any point without difficulty? Is the information accurate? How well are the displays organized?

After you are familiar with the intent of the program, examine the following guidelines, which attempt to address the soundness of the software. The actual worth of the program is determined by the school's curriculum needs. A program can be very good technically but may not develop the needed goals, or it may be of fair technical quality but very good in terms of its approach to subject and content.

Many programs can be used in a variety of settings. Group interaction, whether as an entire class or as a small group of students in a lab setting, can encourage communication and sharing, which leads to a broader range of ideas. Team interaction can occur in either a cooperative or competitive situation. Individual interaction focused on gathering information for a group promotes cooperation and teamwork, enhancing the development of problem-solving techniques. When reviewing software, consider the possible settings in which the program may be used.

Many factors are viewed differently depending on the classification of the software as drill and practice, tutorial, simulation, or one of the construction tools such as word processors and databases. The following general guidelines will help to measure the soundness of a program and to gather information about a piece of software in the drill and practice, tutorial, and simulation formats.

### General Evaluation Guidelines for Educational Software

1. Documentation
   a. Is a manual included?
   b. Are the instructions clear and easy to read?
   c. Are goals and objectives clearly stated?
   d. Are suggested lesson plans or activities included?
   e. Are other resource materials included?
2. Ease of use
   a. Is minimum knowledge needed to run the program?
   b. Are potential errors trapped?
   c. Is text easily readable on the monitor screen?
   d. Can the user skip on-screen directions?
   e. Can the student use the program without teacher intervention?
3. Content
   a. Is the content appropriate to the curriculum?
   b. Is the content accurate?
   c. Is the content free of age, gender, and ethnic discrimination?
   d. Is the presentation of the information interesting and does it encourage a high degree of student involvement?
   e. Is the content free of grammar and punctuation errors?
   f. In a simulation, is the content realistic?
4. Performance
   a. Does the program reach its stated goal?
   b. Is the goal worthwhile?
   c. Does the program follow sound educational techniques?
   d. Does the program make proper and effective use of graphics and sound?
   e. Does the program present appropriate reinforcement for correct replies?
   f. Does the program handle incorrect responses appropriately?

5. Versatility
   a. Can the program be used in a variety of ways?
   b. Can the user control the rate of presentation?
   c. Can the user control the sequence of the lesson?
   d. Can the user control the level of difficulty?
   e. Can the user review previous information?
   f. Can the user enter and exit at various points?
   g. In a tutorial, is the user tested and placed at the proper entry level?
   h. In a tutorial, is there effective remedial branching in the instruction?
   i. In a simulation, can the instructor change random and control factors?
6. Data collection
   a. Is the program's data collection and management system easy to use?
   b. Can student data be summarized in tables and charts?
   c. Is the student's privacy and data security ensured?

## Evaluating the Use of Graphics and Sound

As we contemplate general characteristics in the evaluation of educational software, we must look beyond text as the carrier of the message. The computer as a tool for instruction and learning must first gain a student's attention and then hold that interest to satisfy a curiosity. Addressing the student's interest by using the computer's capabilities of graphics and sound yields the optimum presentation of the software's message in a drill and practice, tutorial, or simulation format. The use of graphics and sound has become so ubiquitous in educational software that it deserves special consideration in the evaluation process.

### Use of Sound

Sound can enhance the learning experience by adding a degree of realism and by holding the user's attention. It can be used as a reward or reinforcement. Sound can help to highlight key concepts. Music and speech synthesis are important factors in some software. Conversely, sound can be distracting in a classroom or in a room full of computers. The ability to turn sound on or off is desirable. If sound is important to the concept being presented, the user should be able to direct it to an external connection rather than to the computer's built-in speaker, to permit the use of headphones.

### Use of Graphics

Learning theorists stress the importance of graphic representation as a means of simplifying complex interactions of verbal and nonverbal communication. A picture contributes an image to be stored in memory for later retrieval. This function is critical to learning.

Graphics included in computer-assisted instruction have the same impact on the student. In a review of visual research, Francis Dwyer (1978) concluded that a moderate amount of realism in a visual results in the maximum amount of learning. Too little realism may not offer enough visual clues, and too much may distract the viewer. Graphics in software are often used to focus student attention. Studies have shown, however, that visual stimuli used to attract attention may not be the most effective in sustaining attention (Dwyer, 1978, p. 156). High-resolution computer graphics offering a moderate degree of realism have the potential to maximize learning. Graphics must support the ideas being communicated without detracting from the instructional objective of the activity. Some very poor programs have been marketed that pair graphic symbols with unrelated text or animate a concept improperly, making the lesson needlessly confusing. These program flaws must be detected in the evaluation process.

The graphic design of text must be considered in combination with visual presentation. Screen layout and design are important in maintaining student attention and interest. The screen should not be overcrowded and should present only one major idea at a time. Animation extends the descriptive impact of the concept being communicated by showing the logical sequence of development.

In reviewing basic math materials found in products of three large commercial software publishers, Francis Fisher (1982) found examples of terrible graphics design, inappropriate use of sound, and other misapplications of computer technology. Although significant improvements have been made since Fisher's initial research, his findings are still applicable as an element of evaluation.

The program in Figure 11–3 responds to a wrong answer with a confusing screen display. What response is the question "How many are there?" supposed to elicit? The number of empty circles? The number of filled circles? The total number of circles? Is it likely that students who cannot add 7 and 2 in the first place will be able to figure out the intended connection between empty circles and the first number in the problem and filled circles and the second number? Such students can and probably will get the answer faster by counting on their fingers than by puzzling over these complicated, poorly organized instructions.

In the right screen of Figure 11–4, the number 2 travels downward, accompanied by musical sound effects. This attention-getter is totally irrelevant to the instruction and serves only to distract some youngsters needlessly.

**FIGURE 11–3**

*Example of confusing screen display*

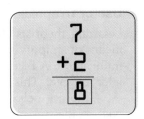

**FIGURE 11-4**
*Inappropriate use of sound*

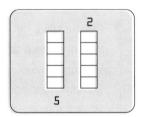 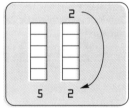

Figure 11–5 illustrates a poor use of the screen area. In the screen to the left, five squirrels have left the box. The two remaining squirrels are located directly above the number 7. The answer box (in which the user is supposed to enter 2) is placed under the five squirrels. The potential confusion here is caused by a designer working against the advantages of the medium. Instead of using the screen space to illustrate the subtraction process plainly in terms of numbers and related squirrel symbols, the designer created a visual juxtaposition of actual minuend with the subtrahend symbolized by the two squirrels and the minuend symbolized by the five squirrels with the intended answer. The screen to the right also has a poorly placed, misleading question that appears to be asking how many are in the box. In evaluating software, be alert for such misuses of graphics capability.

**FIGURE 11-5**
*Example of poor allocation of screen area*

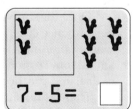 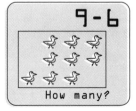

## An Evaluation Instrument for CAI Software

Having familiarized ourselves with general criteria and guidelines for the evaluation of educational software, we must attempt to develop a process for the evaluation of CAI software. A effective instrument is at the heart of a successful process. Just as one set of curricular materials is not expected to meet all the needs of all students, one type of software cannot be expected to address all needs. One "standard" list of criteria will not measure all the necessary elements of good CAI software in the areas of drill and practice, tutorial, and simulation. A reliable list is the set of characteristics that comprise the events of a good lesson in a particular learning situation. A "best fit" happens when the teacher skillfully matches instructional needs with elements in a software program.

An evaluation instrument must provide for the recording of descriptive information about the software being evaluated as well as a listing of

**FIGURE 11–6**
*Descriptive data about CAI
software*

Program title: _____

Vendor name & address: _____

Vendor phone _____    Program cost: _____

Computer and operating system requirements: _____

Internal memory needed: _____    Disk space required: _____

Other required equipment: _____

Content area: _____(e.g., mathematics)_____

Topic: _____(e.g., common fractions)_____

Grade level: _____

Brief description of program: _____

_____

Supplementary materials included: _____

Program goals: _____

Time for estimated program execution in minutes: _____

performance criteria. The descriptive elements listed in Figure 11–6 are presented for your consideration.

Once the software is described, it must be examined and rated against performance criteria. Reflecting on the general evaluation guidelines previously presented, a criterion section could be developed that would examine some common traits as well as allow for the specific characteristics of drill and practice, tutorial, and simulation software to be analyzed.

There is no single correct way to evaluate CAI software. An instrument could be developed that would include only broad guidelines and allow the evaluator considerable leeway in interpreting and applying them. On the other hand, an instrument might have a long list of specifics and a complex scoring system, leaving little to the judgment of the evaluator. Think of an evaluation instrument as a communication device that describes and assesses the value of a given software item. It must convey an accurate impression of the software while being easy and convenient to use. A cumbersome evaluation instrument will be seen as more trouble than its worth to potential evaluators and therefore will be of little use. Four different software evaluation forms are presented for your study in Appendix A of this text. Although all are meant to be used in evaluating drill and practice, tutorial, and simulation software, note the similarities and the differences in their design.

## An Evaluation Instrument for Word Processing

As with previously examined types of software, an evaluation instrument must provide for the recording of descriptive information about the soft-

**FIGURE 11–7**
*Descriptive data about word processors, spreadsheets, and databases*

Program title: _____

Vendor name & address: _____

Program cost: _____

Computer and operating system requirements: _____

Internal memory needed: _____    Disk space required: _____

Other required equipment: _____

Software type: _____ (e.g., word processor) _____

Supplementary materials included: _____

ware being evaluated as well as a listing of performance criteria. The descriptive elements presented in Figure 11–7 are appropriate for word processors, spreadsheets or databases.

Once the software is described, it must be examined and rated against performance criteria specific to word processors. The general categories to be explored would include ease of use, sophistication of features, and usefulness of editing functions. The two most important questions to answer are, "What will it be used for?" and "Who will be using it?" The tasks it will be expected to perform determine which features are most important. The intended user will determine the needed editing functions and relate them directly to the ease of use expected.

### Review of Word Processor Features

The following are some features readily found on a number of word processors currently on the market. The evaluation form that is developed should contain reference to these and perhaps to other features as well.

**column formatting**   Some word processors allow the user to format a page in multiple columns. Columns can be parallel or newspaper-style with text flowing from the bottom of one column to the top of the adjacent one.

**footer**   A footer is a brief message that may include a date, time, or page display that is automatically added to the bottom of each page.

**header**   A header, similar to a footer, can be automatically added to the top of each page.

**help screens**   Help screens present information to the user about the operation of the word processor and its functions as the need arises.

**hyphenation**   The hyphenation feature generates a hyphen at the most appropriate syllable break in a word at the end of a line.

**import**   This feature allows the user to insert graphics or other file types in document.

**index**   An index feature allows a user to mark words that are then automatically copied to an index at the end of the document.

**mail merge**    A feature that allows the merging of data from one file at the proper place in another document.

**outlining**    An integrated outliner allows the user to create an outline of the document and to expand or collapse various levels.

**pagination**    Once a user sets the page length of the document by prescribing top and bottom margins on a specified size of paper, this feature allows a word processor to automatically generate page breaks, indicate them on the screen, number pages, and renumber them when editing is performed.

**preview document**    The better programs allow document editing in this page view and closely approach a WYSIWYG (What You See Is What You Get) state when printed.

**speller**    A spell-checking feature allows the user to compare each word in a document to a known list in the speller's database.

**thesaurus**    A selected word is compared to a list in the thesaurus and a number of synonyms are suggested to avoid undue repetitions.

## Review of Editing Functions

The following are the most often used editing functions and are commonly found in many word processors.

**copy**    The *Copy* command allows the duplication or copying of selected text or graphics to a storage area in temporary memory.

**cut**    This command allows the removal of selected text or graphics to a storage area in temporary memory.

**delete**    The removal or erasure of text can be accomplished in a number of ways. The remaining text is automatically rearranged properly with word wrap and page breaks being taken into account.

**find and replace**    This feature allows the user to find, and if desired, to replace a particular word or phrase by searching for it in the document.

**paste**    This command allows whatever is stored in temporary memory to be duplicated and inserted in the document at the location of the cursor.

Remember that word processing programs are available either as individual programs or as integrated software that may also contain a spreadsheet, file manager, graphics, and telecommunications components. Stand-alone programs are usually more powerful and feature-laden than similar programs that are part of integrated packages. An evaluation form is presented in Appendix B of this text. When examining it, you might find it useful to review the descriptions presented here and in Chapter 3.

## An Evaluation Instrument for Spreadsheets

The descriptive information recorded about the word processing software being evaluated as shown in Figure 11–7 is appropriate to the evaluation of spreadsheets as well. The spreadsheet is a tool uniquely suited to arrange and display data in a matrix of rows and columns. It can store text, values, and formulas that perform a wide range of calculations. The evaluation of spreadsheets should examine both the power and the ease with which the tool may be employed.

## Review of Spreadsheet Features

The following are some features readily found on a number of spreadsheets currently on the market. The evaluation form that is developed should contain reference to these and other features as well.

**cell formatting**    Along with the usual font formats and alignment, spreadsheets often provide a wide range of formats for decimal values, currency, time, and date.

**charting**    Spreadsheets may generate a wide variety of charts such as area, bar, column, line, and pie. Some programs also create pictograms.

**deletes/inserts**    Columns and rows may be able to be deleted or inserted with any affected formulas adjusting automatically.

**display options**    The user may control whether or not gridlines, column and row headings, and values or formulas are displayed.

**filling cells automatically**    Once an entry is made in a cell, spreadsheets usually allow the user to replicate the entry across a row to the right or down a column.

**functions**    Spreadsheets may have 100 or more built-in routines called functions in categories such as business, date, logical, statistical, and mathematic.

**grid labeling**    A convention has emerged in which rows are identified numerically and columns are identified alphabetically.

**page and view formatting**    The user may be able to set forced page breaks and be able to designate the specific area to be printed. The screen should be split into panes or views in order to constantly display the same information at the top or at the left edge. The user should be able to lock the position of rows or columns used as titles and these titles should be able to print on every page in a manner similar to headers and footers.

**protecting data**    The user can usually lock cells in order to protect data or formulas from being changed accidentally.

**sorting**    Ranges of cells may be able to be sorted by rows or by columns. Multiple level or nested sorts are very useful.

Again, it is important to note that spreadsheets are available either as individual programs or as integrated software package. Stand-alone programs are usually more powerful and have a greater number of features than similar programs that are part of integrated packages. An evaluation form is presented in Appendix C of this text. When examining it, you might find it useful to review the descriptions presented here and in Chapter 6.

## An Evaluation Instrument for Databases

The descriptive information recorded about the word processing software being evaluated as shown in Figure 11–7 is appropriate to the evaluation of databases as well. The database manager is a tool uniquely suited to store, access, and organize data in order to display information in an "on-line" screen fashion or as printed reports. It can store text, values, and formulas that perform a wide range of calculations in a record and effectively summarize information across a number of records. The evaluation of a database manager should examine both the power and the ease with which the tool may be employed.

### Review of Database Features

The following are some features readily found on a number of database managers currently on the market. The evaluation form that is developed should contain reference to these and other functions as well.

**accuracy control**    Database managers should include the ability to restrict or evaluate data entry to ensure its accuracy (e.g., a number field meant to record a student's GPA and restricted to data entry between 0 and 4 would not allow a decimal to be typed in the wrong place, resulting in an entry of 35.0).

**data entry automation**    Data such as a serial number or the date might be automatically entered when a new record is created. In order to simplify and control data entry, a layout might include checkboxes, pop-up lists, or buttons to be clicked with the mouse rather than requiring data always to be entered through the keyboard.

**field definition**    Fields should be able to be defined as text, number (value), calculation, and summary. Some programs include other fields such as date and time.

**file linkage**    Some flat file managers emulate relational database managers by allowing the user to create links between files so that data can be exchanged automatically.

**finding records**    The user should be able to find records using the Boolean constructs of AND, OR, and NOT as well as the operators $\leq$ (less than), $\geq$ (greater than), and $=$ (exact match).

**layout**    The better database managers allow the user a great deal of control in designing the data layouts (forms or views). Several programs include a number of preformatted layouts along with graphics tools to enhance their appearance.

**sorting**    The user should be able to sort the entire file or a found set of records in ascending or descending order. Multiple-level or nested sorts are very useful. They allow records to be sorted first by the contents of one field (e.g., *Last name*) and then to be sorted by the contents of another field (e.g., *First name*).

As is the case for word processors and spreadsheets, database managers are available either as individual programs or as part of integrated software packages. Stand-alone programs are usually more powerful and more feature-laden than similar programs that are part of integrated packages. An evaluation form is presented in Appendix D of this text. When examining it, you might find it useful to review the descriptions presented here and in Chapter 7.

## SOFTWARE SELECTION

The importance of the use of computer software to locate information is directly proportional to the increase in the amount of knowledge required to function effectively in today's society. Teachers and students are making better use of a greater variety of all forms of media in instruction and learning. Computer software is a resource that can be used by itself or in conjunction with other instructional materials. The increased impact of curriculum materials including educational software dramatically underlines the significance of the evaluation and selection of high-quality materials. Software that may be effective in one setting may not be useful in another, even if it covers the same concepts. It is important to have a process for determining the quality and content of materials with respect to the needs of the student.

Evaluation is used to assess the quality of the software product. Selection takes evaluation a step further by matching quality of the software and its cost to the specific needs of your school. This can be accomplished in several ways. In the case of an inexpensive or highly specific stand-alone program, the individual making the evaluation may complete the process by recommending purchase. When a more substantial purchase is contemplated or the software under consideration may be applicable in a variety of settings, the collective wisdom, experience, and training present in a team of educators may be valuable in order to better analyze collected evaluations and arrive at a decision regarding selection. Individual teacher requests should certainly play a role in shaping a software collection, but requests should be measured against current software availability in the collection. Notice should be given to all subject areas, but the areas of greatest need and use (based on an understanding of a particular school user community) should be emphasized. Decisions will always take into account costs and budgets, software currently in the collection, equipment presently available or needing to be purchased, the number of machines and the number of students per machine, and the computer literacy of the staff. The important issue in each case should be the "best fit" between the needs of students and teachers and the features of the software.

Teachers have the final word on instructional use and must use the characteristics of a good learning situation as the criteria to measure the value of the software package. Since district needs and student characteristics vary, professional judgment on what elements are present or missing in relation to an instructional situation is the only feasible "standard for evaluation." This judgment also determines what elements need to be supplied in the learning environment or what adaptations need to be made to the software.

The selection process requires documentation of decisions made. Software evaluation, selection, and acquisition are closely related and an efficient documentation process should relate to each phase. If a school has an automated library system in place, such a system might well provide the best means of documenting selection decisions. If not, as software is selected, a software inventory database could be designed.

Figure 11–8 suggests data fields in a sample selection screen layout for a software database that would capture relevant information describing

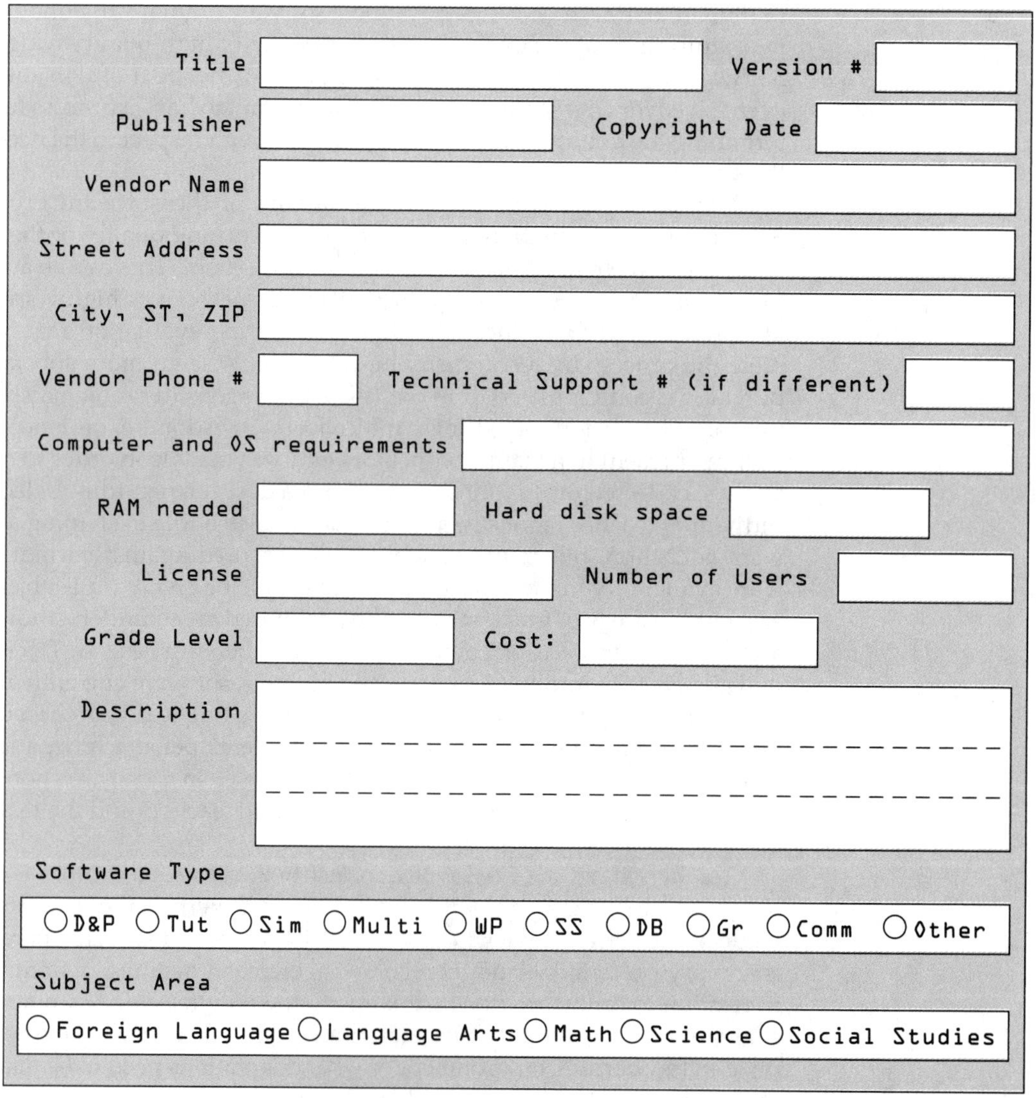

**FIGURE 11-8**
*Selection screen of software database*

software that was selected for purchase. Libraries call information entered at this point the "shelf list record." Data recorded on the descriptive portion of the evaluation form could be entered in the selection screen of the database.

Should you be interested in replicating the record-keeping processes of selection, acquisition, and access described in this chapter, Appendix N of this text contains the complete file description of the software database designed in FileMaker Pro 2.0. You can create this file using either the Macintosh or Windows version of the program and apply it to your own use.

## SOFTWARE ACQUISITION

After the software is selected for purchase, some of the data recorded in the selection step could then be used in the acquisition phase and later to facilitate student and teacher access to information about the software and to promote the software's use. A sample acquisition screen layout is presented as Figure 11–9. Data in the shaded boxes would have been recorded at the time of the selection. The *P.O.#*, *Purchase Date*, and *Shipping* fields would be entered as the software was ordered. The computer would calculate the total cost.

Before sending the order, the person doing the purchasing might wish to do some cost comparisons, remembering that the price along with the quality of service provided by the vendor is the true determiner of value. A consideration of vendor service should include timeliness of delivery, customer's right to return products that do not perform as expected, willingness to demonstrate software, and technical support by telephone. Should a different vendor be chosen, the *Vendor Name* and the *Address* fields of that particular software record would be edited.

Purchase considerations might include deciding whether to buy a single copy, multiple copies (often called a lab pack), or a site license that would grant unlimited use at one location. When purchasing lab packs or a site license, the necessary number of manuals should also be ordered.

## SUSTAINING A SOFTWARE COLLECTION

As indicated in Figure 11–10, the process of supporting a collection can be thought of as the three functions necessary to sustain a viable and effective collection of software: (1) inventory, (2) maintenance, and (3) access. These three functions might differ very little from those applied to all other print and nonprint formats of instructional materials in the school library.

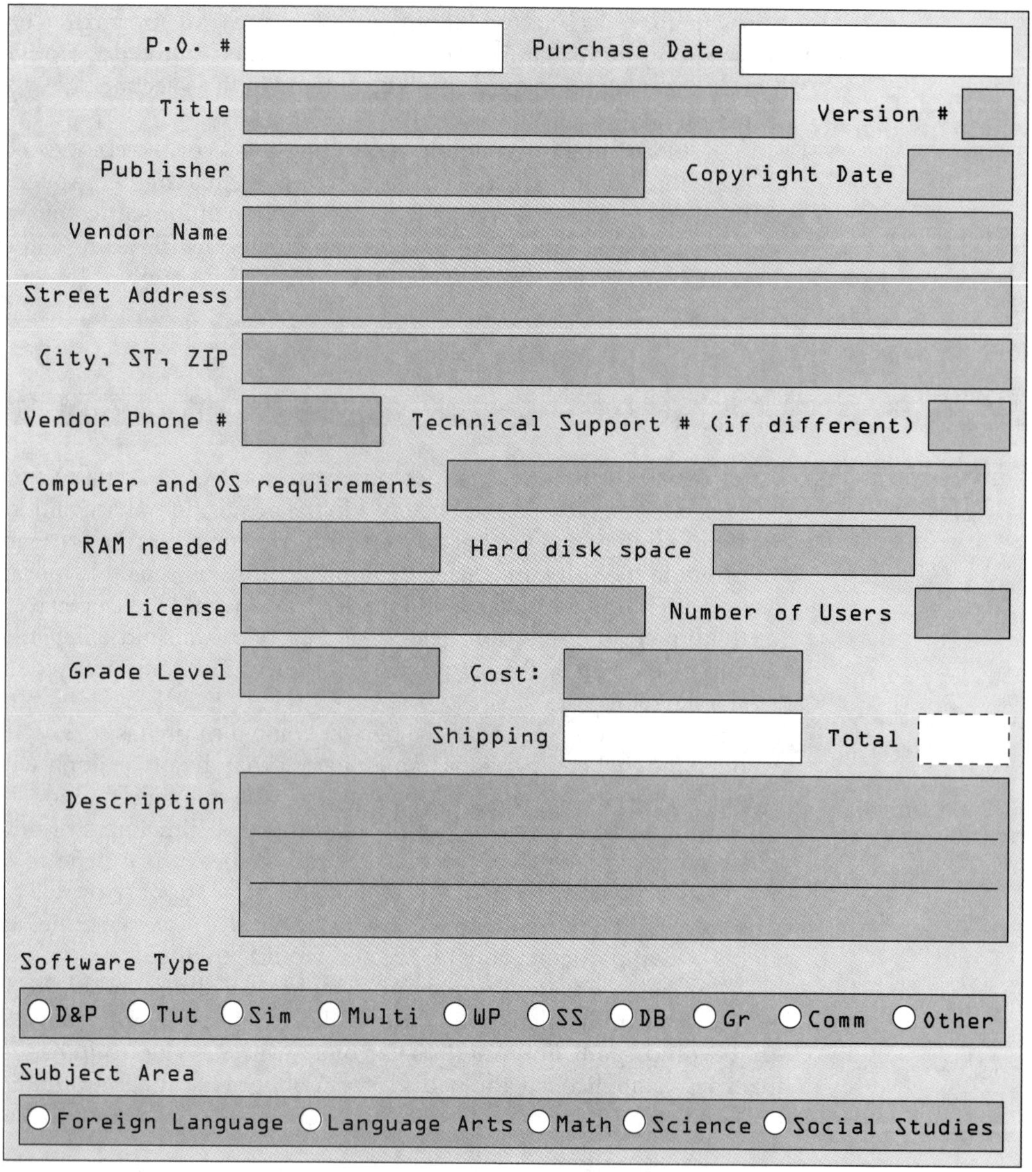

P.O. #   [          ]          Purchase Date   [          ]

Title   [                              ]          Version #   [    ]

Publisher   [                    ]          Copyright Date   [    ]

Vendor Name   [                              ]

Street Address   [                              ]

City, ST, ZIP   [                    ]

Vendor Phone #   [        ]          Technical Support # (if different)   [    ]

Computer and OS requirements   [                    ]

RAM needed   [        ]          Hard disk space   [        ]

License   [                    ]          Number of Users   [    ]

Grade Level   [        ]          Cost:   [        ]

Shipping   [          ]          Total   [    ]

Description   [                              ]

Software Type

○ D&P   ○ Tut   ○ Sim   ○ Multi   ○ WP   ○ SS   ○ DB   ○ Gr   ○ Comm   ○ Other

Subject Area

○ Foreign Language   ○ Language Arts   ○ Math   ○ Science   ○ Social Studies

**FIGURE 11–9**
*Acquisition screen of software database*

## Software Collection Inventory

School librarians use the term *shelf list* to denote the inventory they maintain of books, films, videos, kits and all other forms of media. This concept should be extended to computer software. It makes very little sense to treat the inventory of software in a manner different from other formats.

**FIGURE 11–10**
*The process of supporting*
*a collection*

Granted, physical access to software is different and it doesn't circulate in a manner similar to some other formats. However, its intellectual access requirements are identical. It should be found by searching the library's automated system or card catalog.

Once software has been ordered and received from the vendor, it should be verified against the purchase order, checked to see that it runs properly, and marked for ownership. Backup disks should be copied for archival purposes and must be stored in a secure place and not circulated. The software should then be cataloged and classified to ensure the intellectual access recently mentioned and then entered into the school's software inventory or into the library's shelf list or automated system.

The main purposes of maintaining a software inventory are accountability and control. The expenditure of public funds demands a reasonable accounting. Current and future selections should be compared against the content and scope of the current collection. An effective inventory will identify software location in order to facilitate its circulation and maximize its use.

Building on the software database designed to record selection and acquisition data, Figure 11–11 shows shaded boxes that already contain data. Cataloging and classification yield the *Call #* and *Topics* fields in the specific subject areas. The *School ID #*, if any, will be assigned and *User Location* data identifying where the software will be housed permanently or on a long-term basis are now added to the record of each software item being inventoried.

The entire software collection need not be housed in one central location; in fact, it might be more effective if the collection were dispersed to locations in close proximity to greatest potential use as long as one centralized catalog of holdings is maintained to provide ease of access by everyone. Some software would undoubtedly reside in the library media center and in the computer lab while other software would be better housed in the science lab or the foreign language classroom. Care needs to be taken that teachers understand that the software purchased by the school is for the use of all teachers and students, not just those in a particular classroom.

Circulation of software is somewhat different from that of other library media materials. Circulation systems in school libraries are sophisticated programs designed to handle a high volume of materials being checked in and out. Software circulation, on the other hand, tends to be of a very low volume and of infrequent occurrence. Often copies are legitimately loaded onto hard disk drives or file servers. Software is often checked out on a long-term basis to locations of greatest potential use in

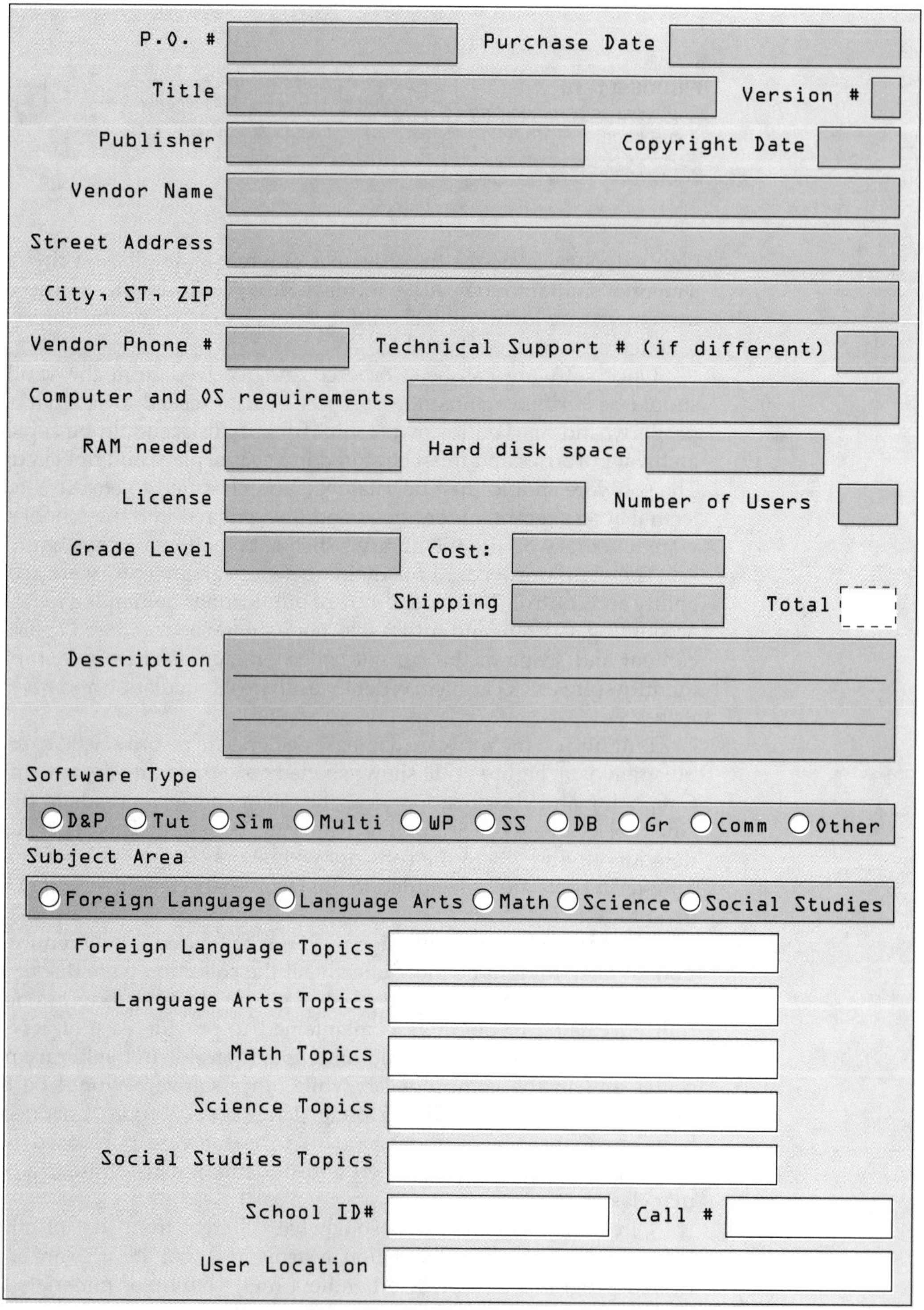

**FIGURE 11-11**
*Inventory screen of software database*

the school. Teachers and students, however, do not generally check out software to take home since the legal number of copies must be controlled.

The concept of computer software circulation is really one of inventory. Effective inventory control dictates that software records be centralized in one location to minimize needless duplication and to facilitate sharing among teachers and instructional programs. In a large setting, centralized cataloging of software also provides a reference source for future acquisitions.

## Software Collection Maintenance

Collection maintenance is essential to sustain currency, relevance, and balance in a software collection. It's easy for a collection to become unnecessarily large and cumbersome as software is added and none is discarded. As well-designed and more effective software is acquired, older software in the collection should be replaced. The collection should be weeded periodically to remove software that is dated, functioning poorly, or has not been used for a long period of time. Maintenance of the software collection should be approached as both an ongoing and a periodic process. An ongoing assessment of the software collection will reveal dated, faulty or cumbersome materials that are no longer effective, prompting their removal and a search for replacement products. Periodically, the entire collection should be assessed so that it can be examined as a whole and any changing needs addressed.

Unique problems are encountered when a significant portion of the collection may be loaded on hard drives or on a central file server. Who has the responsibility to decide what software is placed on hard drives? This should not be left up to individual users. Many schools, lacking full-time computer coordinators, have assigned this task to the library media specialist. In many parts of the country the word *technology* has not only crept into this person's job description but has been made part of his or her professional title. It follows, then, that this person should also be responsible for periodically purging software that has become outdated or has fallen into disuse. It is also important to monitor version numbers of software. Usually as software upgrades are purchased old versions are removed from use to simplify the situation for the users. New versions are backward-compatible with prior ones. Launching the new version and opening a file created by a previous one usually results in the file being updated to the new version.

To make the best use of budget resources, assure compatibility, and simplify staff training needs, a school will often decide to support only one word processing, spreadsheet, and database program. The choice is often to support an integrated package such as ClarisWorks or Microsoft Works.

## Software Collection Access

Collection access has as its goal the matching of the software and the user in as effective and efficient a manner as possible. Many schools have installed sophisticated library automation systems. Software records should be entered into these systems. This would provide one central point for information to be retrieved for all print and nonprint formats. If a school does not have a library automation system or chooses not to enter software records, a further refinement of the database begun at the selection stage might be effective.

At this stage all of the information has been entered in the software database. The task now is to retrieve information by doing a search (Find) on any field present in Figure 11–12. The sample access screen layout presented contains only that information judged relevant to the user. Individual software items can be located with all pertinent information displayed on the screen. A software catalog may be organized by subject area and specific topics and printed as a hard copy.

The responsibility for collection development often rests with the school library media specialist. It is this person's obligation to promote the collection's effective use by teachers and students. This can be done by circulating or posting memos featuring particular software, especially new

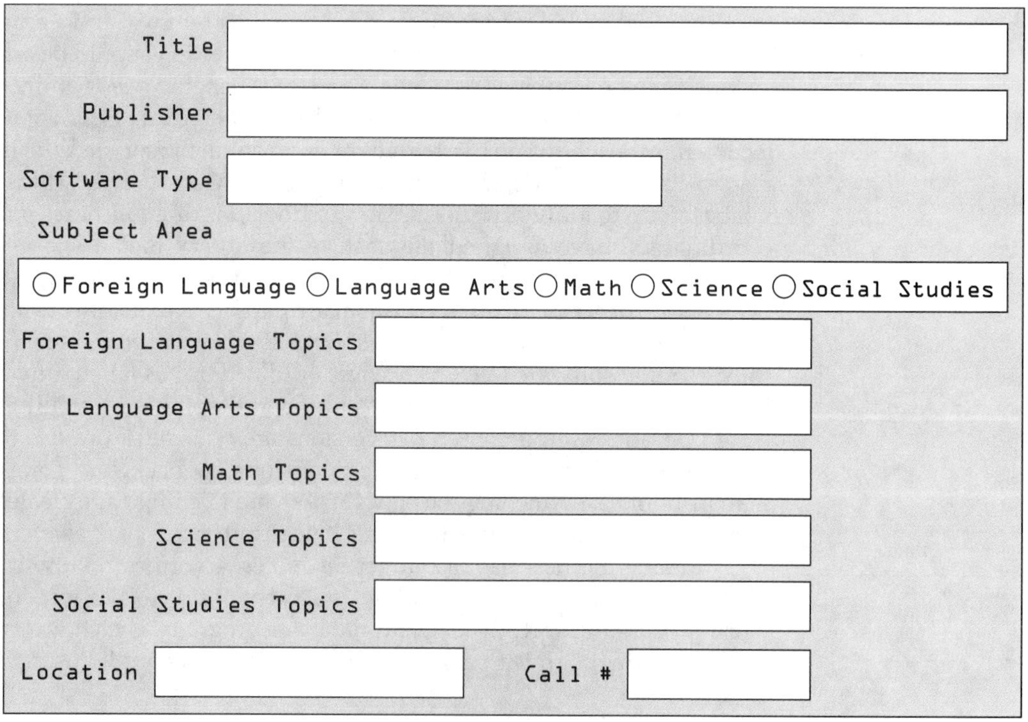

**FIGURE 11–12**
*Access screen of software database*

acquisitions. Bibliographies pertinent to specific topics or events might be posted. One-on-one consulting relative to an individual's need is perhaps the most effective way of ensuring good use of the collection.

## Summary

Collection management describes the processes and procedures by which libraries acquire materials to meet the information needs of teachers and students. The term is well suited to describe the responsibilities and activities related to the evaluation, selection, acquisition, processing, organization, maintenance, promotion, and effective use of computer software.

The process of software selection consists of finding sources along with product information and reviews, evaluating the product, and then selecting the product for adoption in a given setting. One "standard" list of evaluative criteria will not measure all of the necessary elements of good software. An instrument to evaluate software must allow the recording of both descriptive and evaluative information. It is a communication device that describes and assesses a given software item. It must convey an accurate impression of the software while itself being easy and convenient to use. Information from the completed evaluation form could be included in the public access catalog of the school library's automated system or stored in another database format.

When evaluating word processors, spreadsheets, and databases, the general categories to be explored include ease of use, sophistication of its features, and usefulness of its functions. The tasks it will be expected to perform determine which features are most important. The intended user will determine the needed functions and relate them directly to the ease of use expected.

Once software has been ordered and received, it should be verified against the purchase order, checked to see that it runs properly, and entered into the school's software inventory. Backup disks should be copied for archival purposes and must be stored in a secure place and not circulated. Effective inventory control dictates that software records are centralized in one location to minimize needless duplication and to facilitate sharing among instructional programs. Centralized records also provide a reference source for future acquisitions.

Effective collection maintenance preserves currency, relevance, and balance in a software collection. As more effective software is acquired, it should often replace older software in the collection. The collection should be weeded periodically to remove software that is dated, functioning poorly, or has not been used for a long time. The process of collection assessment allows you to base acquisitions on the quality of the material and with an eye to complementing the existing collection.

Collection access has as its goal matching the software and the user in as effective and efficient a manner as possible. For those schools that have installed sophisticated library automation systems, software records should be entered. This would provide one central point for information to be retrieved for all print and nonprint formats. If a school does not have a library automation system or chooses not to enter software records, a specific software database might be effective.

The school library media specialist or whoever is responsible for collection management should promote the software collection's effective use by teachers and students. This can be done by circulating or posting bibliographies and memos featuring particular software, especially new acquisitions. Personal attention related to an individual's need is perhaps the most effective way of ensuring good use of the collection.

## Chapter Exercises

1. Review the sample evaluation forms in Appendix A. Develop your own form for the evaluation of software in the area of drill and practice, tutorial, and simulation.
2. Locate advertisements for a popular computer program. Compare the ad to a review of the program. Is the ad misleading? What functions does the ad highlight? What does the review say about these functions?
3. Analyze a review of a computer program (drill and practice, tutorial, or simulation) to determine the basis on which the program was evaluated. Does the review clearly indicate the evaluative criteria?
4. Locate several reviews of the same program. Compare them and discuss areas of agreement and disagreement.
5. Using a published review of a program, fill out the form you designed as a result of your study of the sample evaluation forms in Appendix A. Are there items on your form that cannot be answered from the review?
6. Run a program and evaluate it using the form you designed. Comment on the process of reviewing. Was it frustrating or rewarding? How long did it take you to evaluate the program thoroughly?
7. Using a published review of a spreadsheet, fill out the appropriate evaluation form found in Appendix C. Are there items on the form that cannot be answered from the review?
8. Using a published review of a database management program, fill out the appropriate form found in Appendix D. Are there items on the form that cannot be answered from the review?
9. Run a word processor and evaluate it using the form found in Appendix B. Comment on the process of reviewing. How long did it take you to evaluate the program thoroughly?
10. Determine the evaluative system used by two different magazines or journals that publish software reviews. In each case, who does the re-

viewing? Is the review based on student use of the program? Describe strengths and shortcomings of both magazines' reviewing systems.

11. While there are ideal ways to evaluate and acquire software, what constraints do you see in a school situation that might interfere with carrying out the process in an optimum way?

12. You have just acquired a new software program at your school. Describe how you would promote its use.

## Glossary

**collection management**   The processes and procedures of evaluation, selection, acquisition, processing, organization, and maintenance of computer software or other materials.

**freeware**   Software available without charge.

**public domain**   Not protected by copyright; may be duplicated.

**shareware**   Software available at minimal charge, with payment usually on the honor system.

**virus**   A potentially damaging program that surreptitiously installs itself in the user's system software or hard disk. Viruses are often spread when users download files or exchange floppy disks.

**virus protection programs**   Software that prevents viruses from being copied to your hard drive and/or repairs your drive by eradicating existing viruses before they can do more damage.

## Notes & Suggested Readings

Barba, R. H. (1990, May). Examining computer configurations: Mini labs, *The Computing Teacher*, 8–13.

D'Ignazio, F. (1992, August/September). Are you getting your money's worth? *The Computing Teacher*, 54–55.

Dwyer, F. M. (1978). *Strategies for improving visual learning* (pp. 33, 156). State College, PA: Learning Services.

Fetner, C., & Johnson, K. (1990, March/April). Selecting software—Who me? *The Computing Teacher*, 12–15.

Fisher, F. D. (1982, Summer). Computer assisted education: What's not happening. *Journal of Computer-Based Instruction, 9*(1), 19–27.

Maddux, C. D. (1991, October). Integration versus computer labs: An either/or proposition? *Educational Technology, 31*(1) , 36–40.

Maxwell, J. R., & Lamon, W. E. (1992, August/September). Computer viruses: Pathology and detection. *The Computing Teacher*, 12–15.

Powell, N., & Bushing, M. (1992). *Collection assessment manual*, (4th ed.). Lacey, WA: Western Library Network.

Salpeter, J. (1993, September). The multimedia encyclopedias face off. *Technology & Learning, 14*(1), 30–38.

Salvador, R. (1994, September). Copyright & wrong. *Electronic Learning*, *14*(1), 32–33, 86.

Wedman, J. F. (1986, November). Making software more useful. *The Computing Teacher*, 11–14.

# 12

# ISSUES AND TRENDS IN INFORMATION TECHNOLOGY

As you have progressed through this text, various issues have undoubtedly surfaced in your thoughts. You may have wondered about copyright from both a legal and ethical perspective—Can I copy software I purchase? You may have questioned the impact that computer access has on student achievement—Do kids who come from homes that can afford a personal computer have an unfair advantage over kids from homes that don't? Are computers best used by the bright kids? Why are there so few girls enrolled in high school computer classes? Are computers a "male thing"? How can computers serve the students with special needs?

This chapter will address these concerns and hopefully provoke more thoughts as you reflect on your increasing knowledge and skill at using the computer. The issues may have no easy answers, but we owe it to ourselves and to our students to examine the issues seriously and strive toward some resolution.

We find ourselves in the midst of a powerful reform movement that is restructuring education significantly in this country. Chapters 9 and 10 recognized that teaching is in a transition phase and that both behaviorist and constructivist perspectives must be recognized and understood. What role might the computer play in school restructuring? Much will depend on you and teachers like you who recognize the potential of the computer as an intellectual tool.

Along with school reform, a number of trends dealing with technology's impact on schools are becoming apparent. The following trends seem to be emerging and very likely will assert themselves in the twenty-first century:

1. Private enterprise will play a more prominent role in schools and will hasten the infusion of technology. This will occur as private enterprise tar-

gets education as a lucrative market, developing better and more powerful computer and video software and installing no-cost or low-cost technology in the schools that will be funded by advertising revenues. It will also occur as private enterprise develops partnerships with schools to provide funding and increased opportunities for job training and career development.

2. Multimedia will show significant growth as a tool for supporting students' construction of their knowledge. This will occur as teachers increasingly develop a comfort level with interactive computer technology. It will occur along with a paradigm shift *from* teachers defining what students should learn and students memorizing what they read or are told, *to* teachers facilitating and coaching students as they learn and students constructing their own meanings and solutions to problems (Cowart & Schalock, 1994).

3. Optical technology will become the storage medium of choice and will be accessible over networks. The low cost, durability, and random access characteristics of optical media such as CD-ROM make it a winner. The technology will continue to improve, providing better compression/decompression techniques and a faster data transfer rate. Publishers will have to work out problems with fee structures for networked products simultaneously accessible by large numbers of users.

4. Libraries will become automated information centers. Public and school libraries will continue to provide recreational reading, viewing, and listening but will also provide outstanding electronic reference services by using networked CD-ROM encyclopedias and databases with provisions to dial in from home computers. Libraries will provide high-level telephone support to reference questions and direct access to the Internet.

5. Telecommunications will become a major factor for delivery of information to the school and to the home. This will increase home schooling opportunities but it will also change the nature of the classroom to support the paradigm shift mentioned above and many others as well.

This chapter will close with a look at past, present, and future trends in information technology and a slightly whimsical but engaging look at a school of the future. This is indeed an exciting time to be a teacher and a learner. Who dares to teach, must never cease to learn!

## Advanced Organizers

1. Do those who have home access to a computer have an unfair advantage over those who do not?
2. Do students who attend schools in affluent neighborhoods have an unfair advantage over those who do not?
3. Is there a inherent gender bias linked with computer technology?

4. How can I strive toward gender equity in computer use?
5. What is legal and ethical use of software?
6. What can the computer provide to students with special needs?
7. What are some of the current and future trends in information technology?

## COMPUTER ACCESS AND EQUITY

What if you gave your students an essay to write and some wrote in pencil, some typed, some used a typewriter with a correcting ribbon, and some wrote the essay on a computer using a word processor complete with spell checker, full dictionary, thesaurus, and grammar checker? You would, of course, expect the products to be different regardless of the individual students' skills and aptitudes. Why? Because of the tools used. The essay prepared in pencil would probably have a number of erasures. You might well find some correction fluid applied to the typed essays. Those typed using a correction ribbon would certainly present a good appearance. However, the essays prepared on the computer with full control over all elements of the font have the potential of presenting the best appearance. Not only will they appear the best, but they should also be free of typing and spelling errors. They also will probably make the best use of words. Why couldn't the students using pencils and typewriters use a dictionary and thesaurus? They could, of course. Doing so, however, would add a considerable amount of time and effort beyond that spent by the students on the computers. The conclusion to be drawn is that the computer is a significant tool in the writing process!

The student writing an essay on a computer is at a distinct advantage. If you consider all of the various types of computer software through which the computer can extend the user's capability, you see that the use of this tool has a significant impact. Equal access to that tool is then a serious concern. We currently have a class of "haves" and a class of "have nots," those with good access to computers and those without.

There are schools in more affluent neighborhoods or with staff possessing grant-writing expertise that are well equipped with computers. They have a reasonably high ratio of computers to students. The computers are located in individual classrooms, in a library media center, and in open computer labs available before, during, and after school hours. Students can search for information, practice skills and concepts, and create their own products.

However, because of a scarcity of resources, apathy toward technology, or lack of leadership, other schools have a paucity of computers and a poor selection of software. Students at these schools are deprived of the richness of resources found elsewhere. After visiting a number of schools in various parts of the country, Charles Piller (1992) stated,

Computer based education in poor schools is in deep trouble. . . . Although some affluent schools also have lackluster computer-based learning programs, students from these schools usually enjoy supportive, well educated families that supplement school-based training with home computers. Federal surveys suggest that whites are about three times as likely to have computers at home as are African Americans or Hispanics; affluent students are nearly four times as likely as poor students.

Recent estimates of computer availability in U.S. homes range from 25 percent to 33 percent. This means that up to one-third of students have access to a computer at home. It stands to reason that most of these homes are reasonably affluent. Among the most common reasons given for purchasing a home computer is to assist in the education of children. A recent contact with a leading educational software publisher revealed that the volume of their sales to the home market was significantly greater than that to schools. Unfortunately, some home computers turn into simple game machines with very little software to help the children learn. Students with access to a home computer having a word processor and other productivity software constitute an elite group, one with a distinct advantage that over two-thirds of the student population does not enjoy. This variability of access should influence a teacher's expectation when it comes to the quality of product prepared by the students.

Differences in achievement for students with and without access to home computers exist. Allen and Mountain (1992) report that in their study of inner city black children with access to computers and an on-line service, one of the primary factors in increased test scores appeared to be whether the children perceived themselves as "haves" or "have nots." A different study by Nichols (1992) suggests that higher achievement scores for students with access to home computers might be the result of those children having an increased desire to succeed. Regardless of the reason—higher self-esteem, higher motivation, or simply more powerful tools with which to work—students with computers tend to achieve higher outcomes.

How can access be improved? Teachers in schools with inadequate computer resources could demand access to such an important educational tool. They should make the administration, the school board, and community groups aware of the need. Teachers in schools with reasonable computer resources should work toward making the computers available with an acceptable measure of security and supervision outside of normal school hours to students, parents, and community groups.

## GENDER EQUITY

Gender equity should be a continuing cause of concern to us as educators. Computer usage suffers from an inherited gender bias that holds that math and science are not "feminine things." Although efforts to remedy this bias are certainly under way, it is difficult to overcome the fallacy that girls cannot excel in math and science. This bias has its roots in the seventeenth century when inventions in science and technology began to be made not by aristocrats but in the monastic environment of the universities, which were under the control of the male-dominated political and religious forces of the time. The elite created an aura of a quasi-priesthood of science and technology and erected barriers to keep others, primarily women, out (Noble, 1992). From that point until the mid-twentieth century, women were basically told that math and science were not for them.

It is interesting to note the equal participation of boys and girls in computer literacy and application activities in the elementary and middle level grades. Girls and boys appear to be equally enthusiastic when it comes to using the computer. As students move into high school, stereotypes exert themselves. Girls continue to refine word processing skills and other business (read "clerical") skills while boys overwhelmingly populate the computer science classes. High school girls tend to develop negative attitudes regarding computers (Kirk, 1992).

Studies have shown that males do not necessarily outperform females in computer courses (Massoud, 1991). In spite of this evidence, some teachers demonstrate gender bias. The more difficult computer class assignments tend to be given to the boys, who therefore receive more personal attention and time from the teacher.

In a typical school computer lab, computers are usually available on a first come, first served basis. With more students than computers, the more aggressive students usually get them. Males have a tendency to be more aggressive.

*How should we as teachers strive to promote gender equity in our classrooms? What actions must we take to affirm this goal?*

Many boys spend countless hours playing video games as preadolescents and gravitate toward the use of computers. Recreational software tends to be loud, flashy, violent, and based on competitive win/lose situations. Even educational software has at times exhibited some of these characteristics. Females tend not to be drawn to this type of software and, therefore, spend less time at the computer as an enjoyable diversion.

Parental encouragement is another factor influencing gender bias. Parents often envision their sons in scientific or technical careers and encourage them to take computer science classes and attend computer camps. Parents are more likely to buy computers for use by their sons than their daughters. Boys get the message that spending time at a computer is a worthwhile activity.

How should we as teachers strive to promote gender equity in our classrooms? What actions must we take to affirm this goal? We should go out of our way to praise girls' accomplishments on the computer. We must be sure to include them in any special computer-based projects. We should include girls' names in computer examples we give. We should encourage girls to consider careers involving computer use beyond standard clerical applications. We must provide more female role models by inviting women who are computer scientists or who make extensive use of the computer in their professions to speak to our classes. We must continually examine our own actions and guard against any subtle, even unintentional, actions we might take that would in any way diminish interest or discourage girls from interacting with the computer in a meaningful way.

## STUDENTS WITH SPECIAL NEEDS

Students with special needs have often been called "at risk." Who are these at-risk students? They are students who are in danger of dropping out of school. Factors that contribute to this potential risk include "low teacher expectations, lack of motivation, academic difficulty, and lack of meaningful experiences" (Poirot & Canales, 1994). Students who are potentially at risk are sometimes thought of as learning disabled, culturally and linguistically different, or yes, talented and gifted.

Good teachers have always tried to individualize their instruction even when dealing with thirty students in a classroom. They have attempted to know each student as an individual, to recognize strengths and weaknesses, and to identify different learning styles. Record-keeping demands were always the bane of individualized instruction. The computer has now provided the means of meeting those demands through the application of easy to use yet powerful database software.

As we seek to recognize the differences in our students, particularly those with special needs, we should review the literature dealing with individuality. Howard Gardner (1983) described seven intelligences: linguistic, logical-mathematical, spatial, musical, bodily-kinesthetic, interpersonal, and intrapersonal. Reflecting on these intelligences and seeking to create a computer environment supportive of all students, Eichleay and Kilroy (1993–94) suggest types of software appropriate to each intelligence.

Not all students will react alike to the same piece of software. A study of Figure 12–1, adapted from Eichleay and Kilroy (1993–94, p. 39), will suggest ways in which a variety of software can be applied to meet the needs of different learners.

As the restructuring of U.S. education progresses, many paradigm shifts will occur. One such shift is that schools will move *from* students with special needs being separated from their regular classmates for instruction, *to* educational programs and practices that have as their aim "full inclusion from the child's perspective, that is, where a teacher adapts the learning environment to meet the diverse needs and backgrounds of the children being taught" (Cowart & Schalock, 1994). Another shift will be that schools will move *from* being organized on a grade-by-grade and course-by-course basis, *to* being organized to accommodate developmental levels of learners. The computer has a significant role to play in both of these changes.

**FIGURE 12-1**

*Seven intelligences and software types*

Adapted with permission from "Hot Tips for Inclusion with Technology" by K. Eichleay and C. Kilroy, December/January, 1993–94, *The Computing Teacher,* 21(4), pp. 38–40.

| Intelligence | Type of Software |
|---|---|
| Linguistic | Word processors, word games, software with speech output, crossword puzzle generators, books on CD-ROM |
| Logical-mathematical | Spreadsheets, databases, problem-solving software, computer programming, Logo, strategy game formats |
| Spatial | Graphic production, 3-D modeling, mazes and puzzles, Logo, maps, charts and diagrams, multimedia |
| Musical | Song creation, music concepts/ skills, story and song combinations, recording music, singing, or rhymes with a microphone |
| Bodily-kinesthetic | Alternative input devices, keyboarding/word processing, science and math with manipulatives and probes, programs that let the user move objects on the screen |
| Interpersonal | Telecommunications, interactions with characters in simulations and adventures, programs about social issues, group participation/decision-making programs, two or more player games |
| Intrapersonal | Tutorial, self-paced games played against the computer, self-awareness/self-improvement–building programs |

## Students with Disabilities

Structuring a suitable learning environment for a physically challenged student requires providing the appropriate learning tools to achieve sensory and communication compensation. Research indicates that technology "can be adapted for use by disabled students and can result in higher achievement and improved self-image" (Kober, 1991). Assistive devices of all kinds that provide visual, aural, or tactile support greatly extend the capabilities of impaired students to use the computer effectively. The computer-based Kurzweil Reading Machine scans printed documents and converts text into electronic speech. Speech synthesizers, speech recognition devices, image magnifiers, specially designed keyboards with exchangeable overlays, and a variety of switches have made the computer a tool useful to the physically impaired.

A student with a learning disability often harbors feelings of inadequacy. As computers have become increasingly user-friendly, they offer that student a chance to be in control, a chance to excel. One day, while vis-

*The computer can help to remove barriers that students with disabilities may encounter.*

iting my son's high school, I observed a remarkable sight—"exceptional children," working as computer lab assistants, helping the "normal" students as they encountered difficulties. I assure you those lab assistants exhibited a very positive self-concept.

Computers are patient tutors and provide simulated environments in which mildly handicapped and learning disabled students can work. Malouf (1991) mentions the limitation of errors, the unhurried pace, the repetition of missed items, and the provision of remedial feedback as characteristics of good computer software that meets the needs of handicapped students. Problems develop for the exceptional child when these same characteristics are not found in the classroom.

## Bilingual/ESL

The computer is a valuable tool in teaching written and spoken communication to students who are culturally and linguistically different. The computer's engaging visual feedback is appealing. Graphics software allows the students to express themselves in ways reflective of their own culture. The right software transforms the computer into a patient tutor that allows students to make mistakes and to proceed as slowly as necessary in each individual case. Other software creates a microworld in which a student responds and practices newly acquired language skills. A word processor using a standard typeface or a special typeface such as Kanji might allow the students to express themselves in their native language and to teach their classmates a few words and expressions in that language.

Some tutorial, drill and practice, and simulation software is now becoming avaiable in non-English-language versions. The most commonly available languages at this time are Spanish, French, and German. Some software allows the user to toggle between English and a second language. Some of the Discis™ interactive storybooks distributed on CD-ROM allow the selection of English or another language and include the ability to have the words showing on the screen read to the user. Spell checkers, dictionaries, and thesauruses are now available in other languages for a number of word processors.

Cooperative learning strategies appear to work well with children who are culturally or linguistically different by integrating them into small groups and then facilitating their integration into the class as a whole. The computer is a tool that lends itself well to a number of cooperative learning strategies.

Students on the Hoopa Indian Reservation spent a year constructing a dictionary in their native language of the plants and animals indigenous to their area (Berney & Keyes, 1990). The project proved to be a challenge for them since their native language was an oral, not a written language. The computer, with its graphics capability, afforded them a concrete experience.

## Talented and Gifted

It is important to acknowledge that even children who are recognized as talented and gifted may be at risk. Boredom, slow pace of instruction, lack of challenge, lack of recognition of a sometimes unique learning style—any and all of these factors may contribute to the talented and gifted child being at risk of dropping out of school or of getting far less out of school than might be possible. Enter the computer! A tool with which to experiment and test hypotheses. A tool with which to analyze information and draw conclusions. A tool with which to express oneself by drawing as well as by writing. A tool with which to explore a wide, wide world!

The computer has many times been called the ultimate individualized instruction tool. The disabled and the gifted represent the opposite ends of an ability continuum. A case can be built supporting computer use as a means of reaching individual students at either end of the scale. Both types of students will derive satisfaction from constructing a worthwhile product as evidence of their creativity and knowledge.

Gifted students are often inquisitive and usually academically uninhibited. When introduced to computer programming, they often develop a high degree of problem-solving skills and abilities. These skills often stand them in good stead in other disciplines.

Talented and gifted children often have difficult social adjustments to make because of their superior intellectual abilities. They are sometimes viewed by other students as uninteresting, overly academic, and with few social skills. They sometimes view other students in uninteresting, unchallenging, and flighty. The computer, once again used wisely as part of

*Computers provide endless opportunities for students to express their creative abilities. This student created a multimedia piece for a school report.*

a cooperative learning strategy, can provide a positive social experience and help in the development of interpersonal skills. Note that to build interpersonal skills Figure 12–1 suggests telecommunications software, programs that contain interactions with characters in simulations and adventures, programs about social issues, group participation/decision-making programs, and games that involve two or more players.

When selecting tutorial, drill and practice, or simulation software for use by talented and gifted students a few considerations should be kept in mind:

1. Software should reflect the interest level of the student.
2. Reading level and level of difficulty must be appropriate.
3. The student should be able to control the pace of the program.
4. The student should be able to exit at any point and resume at that point later.

## SOFTWARE COPYRIGHT

Software falls into three categories: freeware, which is available without charge and is said to be in the public domain; shareware, which authors allow you to try out at no charge with the expectation that if you like it and decide to keep and use it, you will send them some modest payment; and commercial software protected by copyright, which you purchase the right to use.

You don't buy software, you purchase a license for its use. This is somewhat of a novel concept. A publisher makes software available for use under certain conditions. The buyer purchases the right to use it and, therefore, must abide by the conditions imposed. Those conditions are designed to assure the creators profit from their intellectual work and are protected by the Copyright Law of 1978 and the Computer Software Copyright Law of 1980. Under this protection, the copyright holder has the exclusive right to duplicate the work or to derive other software from it; in short, to reap any financial reward from the distribution of the software.

### Software Piracy

As stated in Chapter 11, the Software Publishers Association claims that one-quarter to one-third of all software used in K–12 grades in this country is illegal (Salvador, 1994). Part of this significant problem is rooted in ignorance, a lack of understanding of what software use is allowed under the law. Part of it is a willful disregard of the law based on inadequate budget resources or sometimes on a contempt engendered by what is viewed as excessively high cost. In fact, the cost of developing quality software is quite high and producers have a right to an equitable return on their investment. Copyright protects this right.

The most common reasons why educators make illegal software copies are: ignorance of the law, the high cost of software, lack of school funds to purchase software, and the desire to preview software before purchase (Rice, 1991). Copyright infringement, regardless of cause or motivation, is unacceptable. Unrestrained violations of copyright can seriously endanger small producers who are often a source of truly innovative educational software. A flagrant disregard of the law sends entirely the wrong message to students. Some schools, in order not to mislead students, circulate only disks with original program labels or those with clear statements regarding site licenses. Many schools post notices regarding software copyright in their computer labs and in the library media center.

The Software Publishers Association (SPA) and schools throughout the country are attempting to educate teachers about copyright, what is allowable use, and what is infringement. The SPA distributes a free booklet called *Software Use and the Law* that belongs in every school library or computer lab. Even lacking a thorough understanding of the law, an ethical question to ask might be, "Am I depriving the publisher or creator of this software from legitimately earned income?" An ethical stance rather than a legalistic one may be more effective to take with students. The concept of illegal copying and stealing must be linked. Teachers as role models must demonstrate legal and ethical use of software.

### Software Licensing

Understanding that you don't buy software but that you license its use under certain conditions from a publisher, the following might serve as a guide to your legal as well as ethical use of programs in your school.

### Copying Software

The copyright laws give a user the right to make one backup copy of legally purchased software for archival purposes if one is not included. This copy may not be treated as a second circulating copy, but used only in the event of damage to the original copy. Copying the manual and accompanying support materials is not allowed unless specifically permitted.

### A Stand-Alone License

Stand-alone licenses are either single-user or single-machine licenses. A single-user license allows use by the individual person registered as the software purchaser. The purchaser may install it on more than one machine (e.g., a desktop computer and a laptop computer) as long as no one else can use the software on another machine at the same time as the purchaser. A single-machine license is more restrictive. It allows the installation of the software on only one machine.

### Volume Agreements

Many publishers are willing to offer volume discounts on stand-alone licenses. These are often called lab packs and are for a specific number of copies. An equal number of manuals may or may not be supplied. The agreement may allow the copying of manuals and/or brief guides, or may require their purchase.

### A Network License

A network license allows software to be installed on a file server. The license may specify the number of computers that are allowed to access the software simultaneously.

### A Site License

A site license, as the name implies, allows the copying of software to be used at one location. According to the specific license, that site may be a computer lab, a school building, or an entire school district. Publishers are sometimes willing to take an institution's needs into account and to negotiate licenses when they consider the quantities to be significant.

### Compliance

Computer labs for years have provided students a place to bring software, primarily games, from home and exchange copies with their friends. Teachers must explain copyright rules to students and the potential consequences of infringement to themselves as well as to publishers. Rules of conduct must be posted and student use of computers must be closely monitored to discourage illegal copying.

School districts have formulated policies regarding software copyright. The Connecticut State Department of Education (1991) suggested a model school district policy on copyright that includes the following guidelines: the inclusion of copyright education as part of library information skills instruction; the provision of copyright workshops for school district personnel; the inclusion of sections dealing with copyright in faculty and student handbooks; the posting of copyright reminders on duplicating equipment; and the insistence that faculty and staff act as role models in complying with the copyright law.

## TECHNOLOGY AND THE SCHOOL OF THE FUTURE

### Yesterday

As schools have gradually adopted the use of computers and related technology, they have undergone some degree of change. These are best examined as eight trends experienced by schools that have adopted the use of computers. According to Allan Collins (1991) they include the following:

1. A change from whole-class to small-group instruction.
2. A move from lecture to coaching.
3. A move from working with better students to spending more time working with weaker students.
4. A shift toward students becoming more engaged in their learning.
5. A change to assessment based on products and outcomes.
6. A shift from a competitive to a cooperative atmosphere in the classroom.
7. A shift from all students attempting to learn the same thing at the same time, to different students learning different things at their own rate.
8. A move from an emphasis on verbal thinking to the integration of visual and verbal thinking.

## Today

The advent of the twenty-first century, coupled with the social and economic struggles of the present, has thrust educational and school reform from the theoretical realm of educators into the public arena. Legislators, business people, parents, and other taxpayers are demanding fundamental changes from schools, teachers, and administrators. Each has a unique interpretation of what these changes should be and how they will best occur. Businesses have created, funded, and are managing for-profit schools, some within the public school system. School choice is an issue that has

*The many uses of the computer empowers students to express themselves and use new tools to achieve their goals.*

been the subject of both political rhetoric and informed debate. Some parents advocate more government support of home schooling, while others expect help from the school system with child care, parenting advice, and social services. Taxpayers are dissatisfied with the performance of public schools in relation to the amount of tax money spent. Significant changes in the whole structure of the educational system and our philosophies of education and learning are occurring.

In order for schools to change, there will have to be a philosophical shift in the public's perception of education. Often the public's perception is based on what education was like, rather than the reality of what it is like today or the potential of what it can be. This creates a vision that looks to the past instead of looking forward into the future. Technology provides a turning point for that shift, as its influence pervades so much of our daily lives. It also provides the tools educators need to implement change now.

## Tomorrow

Any lasting changes will need to be preceded by a vision of what future learning environments will be like. What will be the expectation placed on the learner? What will be the role of the teacher? What will be the physical structure of the learning environment? How will library media centers fit into this new environment? How will technology affect learning?

The basic curriculum will change as schools focus on information and thinking skills, and the use of tools such as computers, optical disk storage and retrieval systems, holograms, and virtual reality simulations becomes the norm rather than the exception. Teaching methods will change as these tools are incorporated. Instructional materials will reflect the tools being used in learning. Expectations and outcomes will be different for children, teachers, parents and administrators. The physical structure and internal organization of the school will certainly differ as these changes are assimilated.

The amount of time children spend in school will become more flexible as technology provides new tools and inspires new teaching and learning methods. Networking will allow students to work at multiple sites while interacting with the class or the teacher. As students begin taking more responsibility for their own learning, the pace of that learning will have a more natural rhythm dictated by the individual student's needs instead of an imposed districtwide schedule. Some students may choose to work in the early morning, at night, or on weekends. Even younger children may choose to work on an absorbing project for extended lengths of time rather than having the day segmented into predetermined bits of learning.

Technology will provide students with access to information and the tools to produce substantial work. Each student will have a computer available at school. This may be in the form of a personal computer workstation, shared terminal for database and networking access, or portable computer. The computers would all have networking capabilities and be linked by a worldwide network to teachers, parents, homes, databases, electronic bulletin boards, library and information centers, and other people all over the world.

The most exciting use of technology by the students of the future will be the production of meaningful work. Students will write, illustrate, publish, program, and create models, movies, music, stories, poetry, artwork, and other products of research and learning. They will utilize integrated technologies involving optical disks, computers, multimedia, virtual reality, and holographic imaging. Given access to information and technology, the skills to use them, and the freedom to learn and explore, children will be able to produce work that is barely imaginable to adults today.

Schools are under pressure to provide more than just a limited-use building with a single mission. Taxpayers complain about expensive buildings and equipment that are virtually deserted for up to a fourth of the year, and are only available during school hours for the rest of the year. Teachers find themselves unable to teach academics when children are more in need of a nurse, counselor, social worker, or parent. The school of the future will have to address those needs. A multiple-use neighborhood facility combining education with the traditionally separate fields of child care, health care, social services, and fitness center will more successfully meet the needs of the children and the community. Professionals in each of those fields would staff the facility, working as a team to provide the best possible environment for children and their parents.

Few school patrons would deny the essential nature of pencils, paper, and books in a school. They are the tools and resources children use to learn, explore, and apply new ideas and concepts, communicate with others, express themselves artistically, and produce work. These materials will be important components in education far into the future. Yet technology provides us with powerful tools that serve the same educational purposes and allow us to achieve even more. Why not integrate technology's tools so completely that they become indispensable as well?

Today's information technologies provide us a glimpse into our educational future. They are serving as a catalyst for school reform. With the thought that innovations in technology allow us to dream about the potential of tomorrow's education, I will close with the following story told by Melanie Wallis (1994), an elementary school library media specialist, as she looks into the future.

---

The school day had already begun when the small group of visitors entered the building. They are teachers who had come to observe Community School, an elementary school which had received many awards and accolades for innovative teaching. The school manager greeted them near the entrance.

"Welcome to our school. We'll begin with a tour of the facility, and I'll try to fill you in on aspects of our program as we go."

The manager led the teachers down a short hallway and paused at the intersection of a larger one branching off in both directions. "One difference between our school and traditional schools is that Community School has redefined the role of the principal. As school manager, I oversee the condition and use of the facility; serve as the chair of the personnel committee; coordinate scheduling; facilitate the professional, paraprofessional, and clerical staff; and work as a liaison to parents and the community through our site council. Educational leadership is provided by a team consisting of the information technologist, the lead teachers and the child-care director.

"Here we are at the hub of our school—the information technology center."

The group entered a very large octagonal room through an archway. In the middle of the room was a low, octagonal desk. The center was lined with smaller rooms, computer stations, bookshelves, and a sunken stage with an interactive 3-D wall screen. Children and adults were working, conversing and reading individually and in small groups around the room. There was a purposeful hum of activity.

"The technology center is our pride and joy," beamed the manager. "We believe that we couldn't get along without it. You'll notice the smaller rooms off to your left. Those are our production rooms, used for various projects our learners are working on. We have multimedia capabilities, including sound recording, animation, video, and holographic imaging. Two of the rooms have virtual reality stations for interaction and production. Virtual reality has been the most popular feature of the technology center for quite some time." The manager chuckled. "It's all we can do to get the parents out at closing time."

The visitors walked past the production rooms toward the stage, where a class of older children was viewing the construction of a space dome on the wall-sized 3-D imaging screen. The manager turned toward the visitors.

"If you'll look toward the far side of the room, you'll see our book stacks, which includes our optical disk collections as well. Although some people would have us dispense [with] books altogether, we obviously disagree. We like to give the kids lots of experiences with the books so they're exposed to a medium that encourages them to use their imagination."

The visitors noticed a few computer stations next to the book stacks. The manager explained that those were primarily used as backup stations. Once learners enter the Intermediate Unit of the school, they are each issued laptop computers at the beginning of the school year that connect to an infrared network throughout the school campus for online information searching and satellite downlinks. The information technology center is also connected to the Regional Information Center, through which it accesses the Worldwide Info Network. From the classrooms, their homes or the school, students and adults could communicate with people or databases at information centers around the world. The school provides the necessary equipment for those students' families who are without personal information terminals.

A woman approached them from the computer stations. "Hello, I'm the Information Technologist. The manager told me you were coming and were curious about our program. I'm in charge of this center, which serves the children and staff as well as their parents and other members of the community. My staff consists of two information specialists, a technician, and several assistants. The information specialists and I work with the lead teachers to develop curriculum and plan appropriate learning opportunities for the children. I also coordinate the community outreach program and the volunteer program. Since we're open 12 hours each day except for Sunday, it takes quite a few people to keep things operating smoothly!" She looked up as another group of children entered the center. "You'll have to excuse me. Here comes the robotics team I'm scheduled to work with."

The manager spoke. "Let's walk out to the classroom area, while I address scheduling." They exited the center through the same doorway they had entered. "As the director mentioned, we are open from 7:00 A.M. until seven at night. Students are scheduled for a core block of time during the mornings and afternoons which they spend working with their core teacher, working on cooperative team investigations, individualized learning modules, and individual investigations and projects. Enrichment and extension classes are scheduled before and after their core, or they may schedule individual work time with their teacher, mentor or in the technology center. Lunch and snacks are provided, and of course, the students get daily recreation and fitness time!"

The manager continued talking as the tour group walked down the hallway which encircled the Information Technology Center. "The technology center is the largest room in our school and you probably noticed that it was eight-sided. This surrounding hallway opens into eight wings radiating from the center. You entered the building through the smallest wing which houses the administrative component. Flanking the administrative wing are the community health center and the childcare facility. Both have their own independent directors who coordinate with me.

"The health center has a separate entrance, and serves the entire community as well as the school. It is a primary care unit fully staffed with physicians and nurses. One feature which benefits us is the KidsKare area. It's a group of rooms, each decorated with a different theme, for kids who are contagious. It gives parents an option on those days when their child can't be at school, but isn't sick enough to need to be home in bed. Children can even keep up with their classrooms' activities with two-way interactive video!

"The adults on staff at the care unit are also integrated into our educational program as mentors, volunteers, and resource people. Several groups of children have done fascinating research projects about aspects of the clinic and its operation. They spent up to a week observing and even participating in the clinic's routines as part of their fact-gathering stage.

"If you'll look to your left, you'll see the childcare facility which includes infants through age six and directs a portion of the before and after school program. The childcare center's mission is to provide a broad range of developmentally appropriate activities to stimulate and encourage curiosity, creativity, and critical thinking skills. They also provide parenting classes on subjects such as discipline and nutrition." The visitors were able to catch a glimpse of brightly painted walls and children's artwork before the manager ushered them on.

"Here is our community gym and fitness center. The students have priority during the day, but it is heavily used by the entire community. Fitness specialists instruct the children and plan daily activities. Each child's progress is carefully monitored and the program is adjusted accordingly. The specialists even use virtual reality to help the kids master new skills—that really keeps them motivated!"

The manager checked his watch. "It's almost lunch time. The wing directly opposite us, on the other side of the technology center, houses our cafeteria and food preparation facilities. That wing also has our auditorium and the music practice rooms." He grinned as he motioned the visitors on. "We'll be getting to that side of the building at just about the right time!"

The group of visitors was now standing with their backs toward the second archway into the Information Technology Center, having gone halfway around the building. Directly in front of them, and to the left and the right were the three classroom wings of the school. Between each of the radiating wings were windows and doorways opening onto gardens.

"I see you've noticed our horticulture laboratory, more commonly referred to as 'The Gardens,' " the manager said, following the gazes of a number of the group. "Plots of land are provided for students and their families, as well as for student groups. It's been quite a success!

"Now, I'd like to tell you about our educational program. We serve 450 full-time students, and another 200 children who come part-time or are home-schooled and connected to our network. The three wings are organized by the ages and learning characteristics of the children. The Early Childhood Unit to your left is for four- through seven-year-olds. The focus for them is on socialization, verbal communication, cooperative skills, and the exploration of objects and ideas. No formal reading or writing is taught, but the foundation is firmly established through developmentally appropriate activities. When a child shows competence in the focus areas, and demonstrates that he or she is moving into the concrete operations stage of development, they are moved to the Primary Unit."

The visitors followed the school manager down the hall of the Primary Unit. Doorways on each side opened into rooms of various sizes. Some had tables and chairs, with a few students desks in groups or scattered singly about. Other rooms had couches and kid-sized rocking chairs. Each room contained several computer stations with multimedia capabilities. Children and adults were busily occupied in each of the rooms with a variety of activities. A teacher was making notes on his pen-based personal digital assistant. The manager commented, "The PDAs sure help teachers jot down anecdotal records and progress information as they interact with the learners. That information is sent over the infrared network and stored in the student's permanent file."

The manager stopped to show the group some of the children's work displayed in the hallway. "The children in this unit focus on developing their reading, writing, speaking and critical thinking skills. The fundamentals of mathematics are taught using manipulatives and problem-solving activities. We strive to develop the whole child here, including ample time for the arts. That's one reason the extended day is so beneficial for everyone."

He smiled and nodded at an adult in one of the rooms. "Each of our units is headed by a lead teacher, supported by the full and part-time teachers, along with assistants and volunteers. The children in the Primary Unit range in age from six to nine years. As in the other units, they are assigned to one core teacher with whom they spend most of their time. They stay with that same teacher for two to three years, although they also are instructed by the other teachers for various projects. The teachers work together as a team to evaluate each child and determine the best educational program. The children are in mixed age groupings which change according to the activities throughout the day."

The group exited the Primary Unit, proceeding to the next wing. The children they now saw were older, but equally involved with a variety of activities and projects. The manager continued his presentation. "The children are moved at their own rate into the Intermediate Unit, which includes ages nine to twelve. One of the main criteria for moving into the Intermediate Unit is the ability of the child to set goals and work without as much direct adult supervision. The focus of this unit is helping the child move from concrete operations to formal operations. Critical thinking and problem solving skills are applied to all areas of the curriculum. Students are encouraged to investigate a broad range of topics and ideas, develop areas of expertise and present their findings to their peers. We expect students to do more than just reporting others' research. They also design and carry out their own scientific investigations, and apply their learning to new situations. By the time they leave us, they are quite capable of structuring their own learning! We strive to teach them skills in learning to last a lifetime."

The group of teachers continued down the hall toward the cafeteria. The manager stopped them before they went in. "Our tour is officially over. Enjoy your lunch, and feel free to observe in the classrooms during the afternoon. I hope you'll be taking back some useful information to your own schools." (pp. 2–9)

## Summary

Students using computers are at a distinct advantage in that they use a tool that can extend their capabilities. Some schools are well equipped with a high ratio of computers readily available and others are not. Whites are about three times as likely to have computers at home as are African Americans or Hispanics; affluent students are nearly four times as likely as poor students. Students with access to a home computer having a word processor and other productivity software constitute an elite group with a distinct advantage that over two-thirds of the student population does not enjoy.

While there is fairly equal participation between boys and girls in computer application activities in the elementary and middle level grades, as students move into high school boys overwhelmingly populate the computer science classes. Parents are more likely to buy computers for use by their sons than by their daughters and encourage boys to take computer science classes and computer camps. Teachers must continually guard against any subtle actions that would in any way diminish girls or discourage them from interacting with the computer in a meaningful way.

Students with special needs are often at risk of dropping out of school. These students are sometimes thought of as learning disabled, culturally and linguistically different, or talented and gifted. As the restructuring of U.S. education progresses, educational programs and practices will have as their aim "full inclusion from the child's perspective" and schools will be organized to accommodate the developmental levels of learners. Structuring a suitable learning environment for a physically challenged student requires providing the appropriate learning tools to achieve sensory and communication compensation. A student with a learning disability often harbors feelings of inadequacy. As computers have become increasingly user-friendly, they offer that student a chance to be in control and a chance to excel. Computers are patient tutors and provide simulated environments in which mildly handicapped and learning disabled students can work.

The computer is a valuable tool in teaching written and spoken communication to students who are culturally and linguistically different. Graphics software allows the students to express themselves in ways reflective of their own culture. Other software creates a microworld in which a student responds and practices newly acquired language skills. A word processor might allow students to express themselves in their native language. Some software is now becoming available in non-English-language versions with the user allowed to toggle between English and a second language.

Boredom, slow pace of instruction, and lack of challenge may contribute to the talented and gifted child being at risk of dropping out of school. The computer can be used as a tool with which to test hypotheses; to analyze information and draw conclusions; to express oneself by drawing as well as by writing; and to communicate around the world. Talented and gifted children often have difficult social adjustments to make because of their superior intellectual abilities. The computer, used wisely as part of a cooperative learning strategy, can provide a positive social experience and help in the development of interpersonal skills.

Copyright infringement is unacceptable. A flagrant disregard of the law sends entirely the wrong message to students. An ethical stance rather than a legalistic one may be more effective to take with the students. The concept of illegal copying and stealing must be linked. Teachers as role models must demonstrate legal and ethical use of software. Copyright laws give a user the right to make one backup copy of legally purchased software for archival purposes. Copying the manual and accompanying support materials is not allowed unless specifically permitted. Stand-alone licenses include single-user and single-machine licenses. Volume discounts are often offered on stand-alone licenses. A network license allows software to be installed on a file server with the number of computers allowed to access the software simultaneously usually specified. A site license allows the copying of software to be used at one location.

The advent of the twenty-first century has thrust educational and school reform into the public arena. Businesses have created, funded, and are managing for-profit schools, some within the public school system. In order for schools to change, there will have to be a philosophical shift in the public's perception of education. Technology provides a turning point for that shift, as its influence pervades so much of our daily lives. Any lasting changes will need to be preceded by a vision of what future learning environments will be like. The basic curriculum will change as schools focus on information and thinking skills, and the use of tools such as computers, optical disk storage and retrieval systems, holograms, and virtual reality simulations becomes the norm rather than the exception. Teaching methods will change as these tools are incorporated. Instructional materials will reflect the tools being used in learning.

Technology will provide students with access to information and the tools to produce substantial work. The computers will be linked by a worldwide network to teachers, parents, homes, databases, electronic bulletin boards, library and information centers, and other people all over the world. The most exciting use of technology by the students of the future will be the production of meaningful work. Students will write, illustrate, publish, program, and create models, movies, music, stories, poetry, artwork, and other products of research and learning. They will utilize integrated technologies involving optical disks, computers, multimedia, virtual reality, and holographic imaging.

The school of the future will be a multiple-use neighborhood facility combining education with the traditionally separate fields of child care, health care, social services, and fitness centers and will more successfully meet the needs of the children and the community. Professionals in each of those fields would staff the facility, working as a team to provide the best possible environment for children and their parents.

## Chapter Exercises

1. Do a bibliographic search in the library on the topic "Computer Access: In School and at Home." Select only articles written in the last four years. Using a word processor, write a report on the issues of at least two double-spaced pages using a 10-point serif typeface. Cite references and include a bibliography. Your name followed on the next line by the course number and name must be in the top left corner of the first page. The title must be centered on a line, in a 12-point sans serif typeface, and in boldface.

2. Do a bibliographic search in the library on the topic "Computers and Gender Bias: Cause and Effect." Select only articles written in the last four years. Using a word processor, write a report on the issues of at least two double-spaced pages using a 10-point serif typeface. Cite references and include a bibliography. Your name followed on the next line by the course number and name must be in the top left corner of the first page. The title must be centered on a line, in a 12-point sans serif typeface, and in boldface.

3. Examine vendor catalogs and locate three programs, in at least two different subject areas, that employ a language in addition to English.

4. Locate available graphics software. Make three different 8 and one half-by 11-inch signs to be placed in the computer lab reminding students of copyright rules.

5. Using a draw program, draw a floor plan of your school of the future. Label each space as to its function.

6. Read the story at the close of the chapter. Identify three things that already exist or will soon be commonplace in schools. Identify three things that you do not believe will soon be found in schools. Explain your reasoning.

# Notes & Suggested Readings

Allen, A. A., & Mountain, L. (1992, November). When inner city black children go online at home. *The Computing Teacher, 20*(3), 35–37.

Bauch, J. P. (1990, Summer). The transparent school: A partnership for parent involvement. *Educational Horizons, 68*(4), 187–189.

Berney, T., & Keyes, J. (1990). *Computer writing skills for limited English proficiency students.* Brooklyn, NY: Report to the New York City Board of Education.

Bracey, G. (1992, September). Healthy environment: Why some teachers use computers better than others. *Electronic Learning, 12*(9), 12.

Collins, A. (1991, September). The role of computer technology. *Phi Delta Kappan,* 28–36.

Connecticut State Department of Education, Hartford. (1991). *Learning resources and technology. A guide to program development.* (ERIC Document Reproduction Service Number ED 338 223).

Couch, J. D., & Peterson, A. J. (1991, February). Multimedia curriculum development: A K-12 campus prepares for the future. *T.H.E. Journal,* 94–98.

Cowart, B., & Schalock, D. (1994). *Concepts, practices, and research pertaining to Oregon's new design for schools.* Monmouth, OR: Teaching Research Division, Western Oregon State College.

D'Ignazio, F. (1991, February). The teacher explorer center: Providing techniques and training in multimedia instruction. *T.H.E. Journal,* 90–93.

Eichleay, K., & Kilroy, C. (1993–94, December/January) Hot tips for inclusion with technology. *The Computing Teacher, 21,* 38–40.

Garner, H. (1983) *Frames of mind: The theory of multiple intelligences.* New York: Basic Books.

Gould, K. (1991, November). Indiana's high-tech elementary school. *Principal, 71*(2), 11–13.

Kirk, D. (1992, April). Gender issues in information technology as found in schools: Authentic/synthetic/fantastic. *Educational Technology, 32*(4), 28–31.

Kober, N. (1991). *What we know about mathematics teaching and learning.* Washington, D.C.: Council for Educational Development and Research.

Lewis, P. (1991, November). The technology of tomorrow. *Principal, 71*(2), 11–13.

Malouf, D. B. (1991, Spring). Integrating computer software into effective instruction. *Teaching Exceptional Children*, 54–55.

Massoud, S. L. (1991, July). Computer attitudes and computer knowledge of adult students. *Journal of Educational Computing Research, 7*(3), 269–291.

Nichols, L. M. (1992, August). Influence of student computer-ownership and in-home use on achievement in an elementary school computer programming curriculum. *Journal of Educational Computing Research, 8*(4), 407–421.

Noble, D. E. (1992). *A world without women: The Christian culture of modern science.* New York: Knopf.

Norris, C. A. (1994, February). Computing and the classroom: Teaching the at-risk student. *The Computing Teacher, 21* (5), 12–14.

Parette, H. P., Hourcade, J., & VanBiervliet, A. (1993, Spring). Selection of appropriate technology for children with disabilities. *Teaching Exceptional Children,* 18–22.

Pearson, K. (1994, September). Empowering teachers for technology. *The Computing Teacher, 22*(1), 70–71.

Piller, C. (1992, September). Separate realities. *Macworld, 9*(9), 218–231.

Poirot, J. L., & Canales, J. (1993–94, December/January). Technology and the at-risk—An overview. *The Computing Teacher, 21*(4), 25–26, 55.

Rice, R. L. (1991, November). *Behavior, opinions, and perceptions of Alabama public school teachers and principals regarding unauthorized copying and use of microcomputer software.* Paper presented at the annual meeting of the Mid-South Educational Research Association, Lexington, KY. (ERIC Document Reproduction Service Number ED 340 703)

Salpeter, J. (1992, May/June). Are you obeying the copyright law? *Technology and Learning, 12*(8), 14–23.

Salvador, R. (1994, September). Copyright & wrong. *Electronic Learning, 14*(1), 32–33, 86.

Speziale, M. J., & LaFrance, L. M. (1992, November). Multimedia and students with learning disabilities: The road to success. *The Computing Teacher, 20*(3), 31–34.

Vlcek, C. (1993, March). Copyright policy development. *Tech Trends,* 13–14.

Wallis, M. (1994). A future learning environment. Unpublished report, Western Oregon State College.

# Appendixes

## SOFTWARE EVALUATION

The information in the following form is descriptive of software being evaluated. The form is to be used in conjunction with the seven sample evaluation forms that follow (Appendixes A through D) and is meant to be attached to them.

---

Program title: _____ Version: _____

Publisher: _____

Vender name and adddress: _____

Sales phone #: _____ Technical support #: _____

Program cost: $_____ License cost: $_____ # Users: _____

Computer and OS requirements: _____

RAM needed: _____ Hard disk space required: _____

Other required equipment: _____

Drill & Practice: _____ Tutorial: _____ Simulation: _____ Multimedia: _____

Content area: _____ Specific topic(s): _____

Grade level: _____

WP _____ SS _____ DB _____ Graphics _____ Other _____

Supplementary materials included: _____

Special features: _____

_____

---

### Evaluation Form #1: Educational Software

The following is a checklist to refresh your memory regarding important aspects of computer software. Read the entire list before evaluating the software, then check the appropriate items after using the software. Use the summary evaluation section to record your overall impressions of the program.

*General Criteria Applicable to All Categories*

_____ 1. Content is accurate

_____ 2. Content is appropriate to meet goalS

_____ 3. Instructions are clear

_____ 4. Program executes reliably

_____ 5. Program is easy to use

_____ 6. Format is interactive

_____ 7. High level of interest maintained

_____ 8. User establishes the pace

_____ 9. Progression in levels of difficulty

_____10. Handles incorrect responses appropriately

_____11. Reinforces/rewards user appropriately

_____12. Teacher able to modify the content

_____13. Keeps records of student progress

_____14. No age, gender, or ethnic discrimination

_____15. Sound can be controlled

_____16. Computer used effectively

_____17. Has suggested activities

_____18. Support materials are effective

_____19. Program is cost effective

*Additional Criteria Specific to Tutorial Programs*

_____1. Variety in presentation

_____2. Logical, sequential concept development

_____3. Frequent testing

_____4. Positive reinforcement

_____5. Conditional branching

_____6. Limits frequency of incorrect responses

*Additional Criteria Specific to Simulations*

_____1. Clear directions

_____2. Appropriate graphics

_____3. Simple keyboard/mouse use

_____4. Realistic situation for role playing

_____5. Results predicated upon user input

Summary Evaluation (E = excellent, VG = very good, G = good, F = fair, P = poor):

| | | | | | |
|---|---|---|---|---|---|
| Appropriateness | E | VG | G | F | P |
| Performance | E | VG | G | F | P |
| Documentation | E | VG | G | F | P |
| Ease of use | E | VG | G | F | P |
| Overall rating | E | VG | G | F | P |

Recommend for purchase?_____

Comments: _____

_____

Evaluator's name: _____

### Evaluation Form #2: Educational Software

The following is a checklist regarding important aspects of computer software. Read the entire list before evaluating the software, then mark a "+" for each item present and adequate after using the software. Count the number of "+" and mark the number of stars in the rating section to record your overall impression of the program.

*General Criteria Applicable to All Categories*

| | |
|---|---|
| _____ 1. Content is accurate | _____11. Reinforces/rewards user appropriately |
| _____ 2. Content is appropriate to meet goals | _____12. Teacher able to modify |
| _____ 3. Instructions are clear | _____13. Keeps records of student progress |
| _____ 4. Program executes reliably | _____14. No age, gender, or ethnic discrimination |
| _____ 5. Program is easy to use | _____15. Sound can be controlled |
| _____ 6. Format is interactive | _____16. Computer used effectively |
| _____ 7. High level of interest maintained | _____17. Has suggested activities |
| _____ 8. User establishes the pace | _____18. Support materials are effective |
| _____ 9. Progression in levels of difficulty | _____19. Program is cost effective |
| _____10. Handles incorrect responses appropriately | |

*Additional Criteria Specific to Tutorial Programs*

_____1. Variety in presentation

_____2. Logical, sequential concept development

_____3. Frequent testing

_____4. Positive reinforcement

_____5. Conditional branching

_____6. Limits frequency of incorrect responses

*Additional Criteria Specific to Simulations*

_____1. Clear directions

_____2. Appropriate graphics

_____3. Simple keyboard/mouse use

_____4. Realistic situation for role playing

_____5. Results predicated upon user input

**Rating Criteria**

Count number of "+" on form for both general and specific category guidelines. Mark rating line with appropriate number of stars.

| | |
|---|---|
| **** | = 22 or more |
| *** | = 18–21 |
| ** | = 14–17 |
| * | = 13 or less |

Comments: _____

_____

_____

Evaluator's name: _____

**Rating:** _____

The following is a checklist to refresh your memory regarding important aspects of computer software. Read the entire list before evaluating the software, then mark yes or no by the appropriate items after using the software. Record your overall impressions of the program.

---

**Interaction**

_____1. User can stop and reenter later

_____2. User can see score at any time

_____3. User can select level of difficulty

_____4. Program can set level through testing

_____5. User can review past mistakes

_____6. User proceeds at own pace

_____7. Testing occurs periodically during program

_____8. Program can have more than one user

**Content**

_____ 1. Appropriate subject matter

_____ 2. Appropriate for grade level suggested

_____ 3. No age, gender, or ethnic discrimination

_____ 4. Can reteach principles

_____ 5. Meets objectives—teaches what it should

_____ 6. Applicable to more than one subject

_____ 7. Presents accurate information

_____ 8. Program is interesting

_____ 9. Program is involving

_____10. Program is realistic

_____11. Program is educationally sound

**Format**

_____1. Clear documentation

_____2. Written instructions are short and concise

_____3. Program uses reinforcement

_____through sound

_____through graphics

_____through written text

_____4. Program uses graphics appropriately

_____5. Program format is consistent with objectives

_____6. Program makes full use of computer's ability

**Cost Effectiveness**   Is program worth the cost? _____

**General Remarks:** _____

**Recommend for purchase?**_____        **Evaluator's name:** _____

Evaluation Form #4: Educational Software

The following is a checklist regarding important aspects of computer software. Read the entire list before evaluating the software, then circle the score from 5 to 0 by the appropriate items after using the software. Each item has a multiplier to place a relative value on that characteristic. Multiply the score you circled by the given multiplier. Add the extended scores and record the total as your overall impression of the program.

---

**Rating 5 = agreement, 0 = disagreement**

**Content**
5 4 3 2 1 0 ×5= _____ Content is accurate
5 4 3 2 1 0 ×5= _____ Content has educational value
5 4 3 2 1 0 ×5= _____ Free of age, gender, or ethnic bias

**Instructional Quality**
5 4 3 2 1 0 ×4= _____ Purpose is well defined
5 4 3 2 1 0 ×4= _____ Achieves its defined purpose
5 4 3 2 1 0 ×4= _____ Learner controls rate of presentation
5 4 3 2 1 0 ×3= _____ Presentation is clear and logical
5 4 3 2 1 0 ×3= _____ Support materials are effective
5 4 3 2 1 0 ×2= _____ Appropriate level of difficulty
5 4 3 2 1 0 ×2= _____ Graphics and sound are used effectively
5 4 3 2 1 0 ×2= _____ Feedback is effective
5 4 3 2 1 0 ×1= _____ Stimulates creativity
5 4 3 2 1 0 ×1= _____ Support materials are comprehensive

**Technical Quality**
5 4 3 2 1 0 ×5= _____ Appropriately uses computer capabilities
5 4 3 2 1 0 ×4= _____ Information displays are effective
5 4 3 2 1 0 ×3= _____ User can easily and independently operate program
5 4 3 2 1 0 ×3= _____ Reliable in normal use

**Total score** _____

**Excellent** = 270+   **Very good** = 269–224   **Good** = 223–168   **Poor** = 167–112   **Unacceptable** = 111–

**General Remarks:** _____

_____

_____

**Recommend for purchase?** _____

**Evaluator's name:** _____

Once the software is described, it must be examined and rated against performance criteria specific to word processors. Read the entire checklist before evaluating the software, then enter your rating score from 3 to 0 and the importance (weight) to you. The weight is a multiplier to place a relative value on that criterion.

|  | Rating (3–0) | Weight (3–1) |
|---|---|---|
| **Documentation** | | |
| The manual is designed for easy reference with table of contents, tabs, and an index | ‾‾ | ‾‾ |
| Quick reference card is useful | ‾‾ | ‾‾ |
| The instructions are clear and easy to read | ‾‾ | ‾‾ |
| The tutorial is effective | ‾‾ | ‾‾ |
| **Ease of Use and Support** | | |
| Minimum learning time required to run the program | ‾‾ | ‾‾ |
| Context-sensitive help screens are effective | ‾‾ | ‾‾ |
| Support (3 = free, unlimited; 2 = toll call; 1 = limited time) | ‾‾ | ‾‾ |

**Features and Functions**

Rate these criteria with:
3 = excellent implementation
2 = adequate implementation
1 = poor implementation
0 = missing
Use a weight value of:
3 = very important
2 = somewhat important
1 = not important

*Total the rating column and the weight column. Multiply the rating total by the weight total to get the raw score. Multiply the weight total by 3 to get the possible score. Divide the raw score by the possible score to get a percentage.*

| | Rating | Weight |
|---|---|---|
| Cursor control | ‾‾ | ‾‾ |
| Block moves | ‾‾ | ‾‾ |
| Column formatting | ‾‾ | ‾‾ |
| Find and replace | ‾‾ | ‾‾ |
| Header and footer | ‾‾ | ‾‾ |
| Hyphenation | ‾‾ | ‾‾ |
| Index | ‾‾ | ‾‾ |
| Mail merge | ‾‾ | ‾‾ |
| Outlining | ‾‾ | ‾‾ |
| Preview | ‾‾ | ‾‾ |
| Spelling checker | ‾‾ | ‾‾ |
| Dictionary | ‾‾ | ‾‾ |
| Grammar checker | ‾‾ | ‾‾ |
| Thesaurus | ‾‾ | ‾‾ |
| Split screen | ‾‾ | ‾‾ |
| Undo last move | ‾‾ | ‾‾ |
| Undo last delete | ‾‾ | ‾‾ |
| WYSIWYG screen | ‾‾ | ‾‾ |

**Rating and Weight Totals:** ‾‾ ‾‾
Raw (rating total × weight total) score: ‾‾
Possible (3 × weight total) score: ‾‾
**Percentage (raw/possible score):** ‾‾

**Recommend for purchase?** _____

_____

**Evaluator's name:** _____

**Evaluation Form #6**

Once the software is described, it must be examined and rated against performance criteria specific to spreadsheets. Read the entire checklist before evaluating the software, then enter your rating score from 3 to 0 and the importance (weight) to you. The weight is a multiplier to place a relative value on that criterion.

|  | Rating (3–0) | Weight (3–1) |
|---|---|---|
| **Documentation** | | |
| The manual is designed for easy reference with table of contents, tabs, and an index | _____ | _____ |
| Quick reference card is useful | _____ | _____ |
| The instructions are clear and easy to read | _____ | _____ |
| The tutorial is effective | _____ | _____ |
| **Ease of Use and Support** | | |
| Minimum learning time required to run the program | _____ | _____ |
| Context-sensitive help screens are effective | _____ | _____ |
| Support (3 = free, unlimited; 2 = toll call; 1 = limited time) | _____ | _____ |

**Features and Functions**

Rate these criteria with:
  3 = excellent implementation
  2 = adequate implementation
  1 = poor implementation
  0 = missing
Use a weight value of:
  3 = very important
  2 = somewhat important
  1 = not important

*Total the rating column and the weight column. Multiply the rating total by the weight total to get the raw score. Multiply the weight total by 3 to get the possible score. Divide the raw score by the possible score to get a percentage.*

| | Rating | Weight |
|---|---|---|
| Sufficient matrix size | _____ | _____ |
| Flexible import/export features | _____ | _____ |
| Adequate data entry safeguards | _____ | _____ |
| Adequate cell protection | _____ | _____ |
| Useful math & date/time functions | _____ | _____ |
| Useful statistics functions | _____ | _____ |
| Useful financial functions | _____ | _____ |
| Adequate cell format control | _____ | _____ |
| Adequate column/row size controls | _____ | _____ |
| Good page and view format controls | _____ | _____ |
| Print area controls | _____ | _____ |
| Fast nested ascend/descend sorts | _____ | _____ |
| Flexible header and footer | _____ | _____ |
| Split screen | _____ | _____ |
| Powerful graph generator | _____ | _____ |
| Sufficient number of graph types | _____ | _____ |
| WYSIWYG preview | _____ | _____ |
| Automatic save | _____ | _____ |
| **Rating and Weight Totals:** | _____ | _____ |
| Raw (rating total × weight total) score: | _____ | |
| Possible (3 × weight total) score: | _____ | |
| **Percentage (raw/possible) score:** | _____ | |

**Recommend for purchase?** _____

_____

**Evaluator's name:**_____

Evaluation Form #7

Once the software is described, it must be examined and rated against performance criteria specific to file or database managers. Read the entire checklist before evaluating the software, then enter your rating score from 3 to 0 and the importance (weight) to you. The weight is a multiplier to place a relative value on that criterion.

| | Rating (3–0) | Weight (3–1) |
|---|---|---|
| **Documentation** | | |
| The manual is designed for easy reference with table of contents, tabs, and an index | ___ | ___ |
| Quick reference card is useful | ___ | ___ |
| The instructions are clear and easy to read | ___ | ___ |
| The tutorial is effective | ___ | ___ |
| **Ease of Use and Support** | | |
| Minimum learning time required to run the program | ___ | ___ |
| Context-sensitive help screen are effective | ___ | ___ |
| Support (3 = free, unlimited; 2 = toll call; 1 = limited time) | ___ | ___ |

**Features and Functions**

Rate these criteria with:
  3 = excellent implementation
  2 = adequate implementation
  1 = poor implementation
  0 = missing
Use a weight value of:
  3 = very important
  2 = somewhat important
  1 = not important

*Total the rating column and the weight column. Multiply the rating total by the weight total to get the raw score. Multiply the weight total by 3 to get the possible score. Divide the raw score by the possible score to get a percentage.*

| | Rating (3–0) | Weight (3–1) |
|---|---|---|
| Sufficient file and record size | ___ | ___ |
| Relational/lookup capability | ___ | ___ |
| Flexible import/export features | ___ | ___ |
| Data entry automation | ___ | ___ |
| Adequate data entry safeguards | ___ | ___ |
| Adequate password protection | ___ | ___ |
| Flexible layout design | ___ | ___ |
| Flexible report definition | ___ | ___ |
| Powerful graphics tools | ___ | ___ |
| Useful math & date/time functions | ___ | ___ |
| Useful statistics functions | | |
| Import into picture fields | ___ | ___ |
| Supports AND, OR, NOT and range, exact, and wildcard searches | ___ | ___ |
| Nested ascend/descend sorts | ___ | ___ |
| Adequate speed in searches & sorts | ___ | ___ |
| Reports allow subtotals/totals | ___ | ___ |
| WYSIWYG report preview | ___ | ___ |
| Automatic save | ___ | ___ |
| **Rating and Weight Totals:** | ___ | ___ |
| Raw (rating total × weight total) score: | ___ | |
| Possible (3 × weight total) score: | ___ | |
| **Percentage (raw/possible) score:** | ___ | |

**Recommend for purchase?** _____

_____

**Evaluator's name:** _____

## CARE AND HANDLING OF FLOPPY DISKS

- Do not place a disk on a dirty or greasy surface.
- Keep disks away from liquids or excessive chalk dust.
- Do not store disks in direct sunlight or next to a heater. Protect them from extremes of temperature.
- Keep all magnets away from disks. Do not place a disk on a TV or monitor. The picture tube's magnetic field may destroy the information stored on the disk.
- Do not retract the metal shutter on a $3\frac{1}{2}$ inch microdiskette or touch any exposed disk surface.

## TROUBLESHOOTING GUIDE

Never plug or unplug anything inside a computer with the power turned on. If you must reach inside the computer, touch the power supply before you touch any other component.

- No light on the screen
  Is the computer turned on? Is the monitor turned on?
  Check the contrast and brightness controls.

- No image on the screen
  Check the cable connecting the computer and the monitor.

- Double letters on the screen
  Commonly called key bounce. Identify the faulty key(s).
  Individual keys may be replaceable on some keyboards.
  Refer the problem to a technician.

- Printer does not operate
  Is the printer turned on?
  Is the printer "on-line," in a mode ready to receive data?
  Check the connecting cable.
  On the Macintosh, make sure you have selected the printer in the *Chooser*.
  Refer to the printer manual and run a self-test. If the test is unsatisfactory, refer the problem to a technician.

Most other problems should be referred to a competent technician. Be careful not to do anything that would void your warranty.

- Select a suitable typeface to enhance readability and the expression of your words.

- Use sans serif typefaces for headlines or titles. Used sparingly they have a simplicity that commands attention. Large amounts, such as in body text, are difficult to read. Sans serif typefaces are best used in a large size.

- Use serif typefaces for body text. The decorations on the letters help to guide the reader's eye movement from one letter to the next, thereby helping the reader to perceive words rather than letters.

- Use ornate text for special visual effects.

- Avoid mixing typefaces within a document except for a distinct purpose.

- Select a letter size appropriate to the message and its intended impact. Consider that not all output is intended for $8\frac{1}{2} \times 11$ inch paper. Consider the optimum viewing distance and the medium (e.g., a minimum of 18 point size should be used for overhead transparencies).

- Use style (plain, bold, italic, outline, shadow, underline) for emphasis.

- Use two letter spaces between sentences.

- Allow plenty of space around a block of text. A block of text takes up space so be sure to consider it in your overall design.

## BASIC RULES FOR DESIGNING OVERHEAD TRANSPARENCIES

- Use landscape (horizontal) rather than portrait (vertical) orientation for your layout.

- Lettering must be at least 1/4 inch high (18 point) and should be simple, bold, and easy to read. This will allow the projected screen image of the text to be viewed comfortably from the rear of a typical classroom.

- Lettering and drawings should fill most of the overhead frame leaving enough blank or unoccupied space to emphasize the design elements.

- Color should be used where appropriate. Different colors can be used to highlight key words by separating the components of the transparency into two masters and printing them in different colors of thermal film.

- Text should be kept to a minimum and should present only an outline or key points rather than specific details. Remember that this is an ephemeral medium in that once a projector is turned off, the projected information is gone. Significant text and detail require a printed hard copy in the hands of the students.

- Divide complex topic into "overlay cells" so that the concept may be presented in a logical sequence. "Overlay" transparencies allow items to be added in a progressive fashion to develop the finished product or complete idea.

## SELECTION GUIDELINES FOR CHARTS AND GRAPHS

**Line graphs** are ideal for displaying *a continuous event or trends over time* (e.g., growth or decline over time). The rise and fall of the line on a graph easily portrays the fluctuations in value. Multiple trends can be compared simultaneously by plotting more than one line on the graph.

**Area graphs** are variations of line graphs that are successful at depicting *amount or volume.* A line is plotted and the area below it is filled in with a selected pattern. Each data set creates a band or area with each area being stacked on the preceding one. These graphs can be eye-catching, but since they show cumulative results they can be more difficult to understand.

**Column graphs** (vertical columns) and **bar graphs** (horizontal bars) present *changes in a dependent variable over an independent variable* and are excellent ways of comparing multiple variables to a common variable (e.g., different performances during the same time frame). However, they lack the same feeling of continuity displayed by a line graph. At times column graphs and line graphs can be combined effectively to present both discrete and incremental views of the data. More elaborate graphs adding another variable can be created by stacking the columns/bars.

**Pie charts** are the ideal way to display *part-to-the-whole relationships or percentages.* The size of each slice shows that segment's share of the entire pie. A segment (pie slice) may even be dragged away from the center for emphasis and the chart displayed in three dimensions.

# GUIDELINES FOR EFFECTIVE PRESENTATION GRAPHICS

- Begin and end your presentation with a blank screen.
- Use generous margins to help focus attention on content.
- Use a single background or frame to unify the presentation.
- Limit yourself to two or three colors on one screen.
- Use bright colors to emphasize important points.
- Use color contrasts effectively (e.g., yellow on blue is highly visible, while red on black is barely readable).
- Limit yourself to two typefaces in one presentation.
- Use an attention-grabbing title screen.
- Use single words and short phrases on the screen to focus attention on the details provided orally.
- Use all uppercase letters only in major headings and make them a slightly larger size.
- Place headings at the same location in successive screens.
- Use dingbats (bullets, check marks, or other symbols) to organize lists.
- Use drop shadows and gradient fills for interesting visual effects.
- Use transition effects (wipes and dissolves) that create a graceful style and help your audience to follow your train of thought.
- Check carefully for spelling/typing errors.

Network Communication Etiquette

- Compose all but brief messages off-line to minimize network traffic.

- Limit each message to one topic and keep it succinct.

- Use subject headings that are very descriptive.

- Reply promptly to messages received.

- When replying, restate enough of the message to clearly identify context.

- Delete messages once you have read them.

- Don't be vulgar or offensive.

- Don't criticize ("flame") others on the network.

- Supply clues if you are intending to write using humor, irony, sarcasm, or emotion. Your intent may not be obvious to the reader. Using all uppercase in a word or phrase SHOUTS. Try :-) for a sideways smile or ;-) for a wink.

- Use a signature footer that includes your name, school, and e-mail address.

- Practice safe communications. Don't spread viruses! Check downloaded executable files.

- Consider yourself a guest on the system and behave accordingly.

## ACCESS POLICIES AND PARENT/GUARDIAN CONSENT FORM

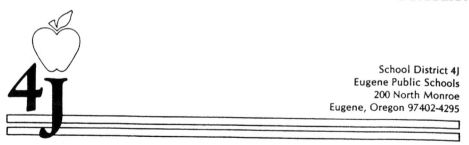

School District 4J
Eugene Public Schools
200 North Monroe
Eugene, Oregon 97402-4295

August 1, 1994

The district has a computer-based communications network known as 4JNet that may be accessed by secondary students with the written consent of a parent and sponsoring teacher. The purpose of this letter is to explain the network and its services so that you will be able to decide if you wish to give permission for your son or daughter to have access.

**ELECTRONIC MAIL:** Within the 4J network your student would be able to communicate via electronic mail (e-mail) with anyone else in the system. Most 4J staff members are on the network.

**LIBRARY ACCESS:** Our network has a direct connection to the library catalogs at the Eugene Public Library and the University of Oregon's Knight Library. With this access your student would be able to browse through the collections at either library.

**INTERNET ACCESS:** The Internet is an international network-of-networks, the communication and information highway you have heard about. Through 4JNet, your student would have access to Internet which means access to hundreds of libraries, databases, and computer services from all over the world. The Internet consists of over 10,000 computer networks in over 50 countries, making it a very diverse source of information and opinion. Your son or daughter would also receive an Internet address allowing communication with any of an estimated 25 million network users all over the world.

**Whereas we accept the responsibility of preparing students for the future by providing them with an opportunity to learn how to use this global information network, it is important that you understand why we require your permission before we allow your son or daughter to have access to Internet. The Internet does not control or in any way monitor the content of material on the network. Thus, your son or daughter may gain access to "adult" material that is extremely objectionable. While we certainly don't teach students how to find this material, it is impossible for us to prevent them from discovering it on their own given the way Internet is structured. If this reality is unacceptable to you as a parent, please do not sign the application form.**

Included with this letter are three important documents:

- An application for your son or daughter to read and sign (on the back of this letter), agreeing to follow the district's policies and guidelines for use of the network. The application requires your signature and the signature of a sponsoring teacher before the student can have access to the network. The application must be renewed each year and kept on file at school.
- A copy of the district's policy statement titled Accessing 4JNet.
- A copy of the district's OnLine Etiquette Guide.

Please feel free to contact Jack Turner (687-3329) in our Computing and Information Services department if you have questions.

Sincerely,

*Margaret Nichols*

Margaret Nichols
Superintendent

## Student Application for A 4JNet Account
### Student application must be renewed each academic year

**1)** *Student Section*

Student Name _____    Grade _____

School _____

I have read the *Accessing 4JNet* Policy Statement and *Online Etiquette* guidelines, and agree to abide by their provisions. I understand that violation of the provisions stated in the policy may constitute suspension or revocation of network access and related privileges, and could lead to disciplinary action as specified in the District's *Student Rights and Responsibilities Handbook.*

Student signature _____    Date _____

∞ ∞ ∞ ∞ ∞ ∞ ∞ ∞ ∞ ∞ ∞ ∞ ∞ ∞ ∞ ∞ ∞ ∞ ∞ ∞ ∞ ∞ ∞ ∞ ∞ ∞ ∞ ∞ ∞ ∞ ∞ ∞ ∞ ∞ ∞ ∞ ∞ ∞ ∞ ∞ ∞ ∞ ∞ ∞ ∞ ∞ ∞

**2)** *Sponsoring Teacher*

I agree to sponsor the above student and to supervise his/her responsible use of the network as defined by the *ACCESSING 4JNet* Policy and *Online Etiquette* guidelines while in school. (Please refer carefully to Guideline III with the student before agreeing to sign.)

Teacher's Signature _____    Date _____

∞ ∞ ∞ ∞ ∞ ∞ ∞ ∞ ∞ ∞ ∞ ∞ ∞ ∞ ∞ ∞ ∞ ∞ ∞ ∞ ∞ ∞ ∞ ∞ ∞ ∞ ∞ ∞ ∞ ∞ ∞ ∞ ∞ ∞ ∞ ∞ ∞ ∞ ∞ ∞ ∞ ∞ ∞ ∞ ∞ ∞ ∞

**3)** *Sponsoring Parent or Guardian*

I have read the *ACCESSING 4JNet* Policy and *Online Etiquette* guidelines for 4JNet. I will monitor my student's use of the network and his/her potential access to the world-wide Internet, and will accept responsibility for supervision in that regard if and when my child's use is not in a school setting. I give my permission to issue an account for my student and certify that the information contained on this form is correct.

Signature of Parent or Guardian _____

Home Address _____

Date _____    Home Phone number _____

∞ ∞ ∞ ∞ ∞ ∞ ∞ ∞ ∞ ∞ ∞ ∞ ∞ ∞ ∞ ∞ ∞ ∞ ∞ ∞ ∞ ∞ ∞ ∞ ∞ ∞ ∞ ∞ ∞ ∞ ∞ ∞ ∞ ∞ ∞ ∞ ∞ ∞ ∞ ∞ ∞ ∞ ∞ ∞ ∞ ∞ ∞

This Space Reserved for CIS Network Manager

- Assigned UserName: _____

- Assigned Password: _____

# ACCESSING 4JNet
## The Eugene School District's Electronic Network

Technical Note: *While it is true that most users currently gain access to the network by using their VAX accounts, there are other ways to access the 4JNet without coming through a VAX account. (For example anyone can now access the Eugene Public Library by typing EPL at the UserName prompt, even though they do not have a VAX account.) And as use of the Internet increases, so too will access to our 4JNet without needing an assigned account. Consequently this document is concerned with the larger issues involved with accessing the network(s), and not just with 4JNet account holders.*

### MISSION STATEMENT
A primary purpose of 4JNet is to support and enhance learning and teaching by providing electronic communications and sharing information resources across the school district.

### SPONSORING NETWORKS
4JNet is a constituent part of NSFNET and NorthWestNet. Users of 4JNet are bound by the statements of purpose and acceptable use policies of these networks, summarized as follows:

1. The purpose of NSFNET (National Science Foundation Network) is to support research and education among academic institutions in the United States by providing access to unique resources and the opportunity for collaborative work. All network use must be consistent with this purpose. Activities in direct support of this purpose (e.g. professional development, administrative communications, grant applications, new product announcements) are acceptable. All for-profit activities and extensive personal business activities are unacceptable.
2. The purposes of NorthWestNet are to promote research, education, and economic development by providing access to network communications, computing, and electronic information systems and services. Membership in NorthWestNet conveys the right to access NorthWestNet facilities and network services for research and educational purposes. All use of NorthWestNet network services and facilities shall be consistent with the mission of NorthWestNet. All use shall be intended to facilitate the exchange of information, intellectual property, and services to promote research, education, and technology diffusion, and otherwise be consistent with the broad objectives of NorthWestNet.

### NETWORK ACCESS
The following people are entitled to use 4JNet:

1. All 4J employees.
2. Secondary students when under the supervision of a sponsoring educator and parent. (It is our intention to extend 4JNet access to elementary students when resources permit; meanwhile they can have access to the network via Classroom Accounts arranged by their teacher.)
3. Others who request Guest Accounts form 4J CIS (Computing and Information Services). These requests will be granted on a case-by-case basis as needs and resources permit.

### GENERAL POLICY AND GUIDELINES
It is a general policy that 4J network facilities (referred to here as '4JNet') are to be used in a responsible, efficient, ethical, and legal manner in accordance with the mission of Eugene School District 4J and the purposes of NSFNET and NorthWestNet. Users must acknowledge their understanding of the general policy and guidelines as a condition of receiving a 4J account or using the networks.

Failure to adhere to this policy and its guidelines below may result in suspending or revoking the offender's privilege of network access by the CIS Network Administrator.

**GUIDELINE I:** Acceptable uses of the network are activities which support learning and teaching. Network users are encouraged to develop uses which meet their individual needs and which take advantage of the network's functions: electronic mail, conferences, bulletin boards, data bases, and access to Telnet and FTP resources.

**GUIDELINE II:** Unacceptable uses of the network include:

1. Violating the conditions of the Student's Rights and Responsibilities policy dealing with students' rights to privacy;
2. Using profanity, obscenity, or other language which may be offensive to another user;
3. Reposting personal communications without the author's prior consent;
4. Copying commercial software in violation of copyright law; and
5. Using the network for financial gain or for any commercial or illegal activity.
6. Users must avoid spreading computer viruses. Always virus-check downloaded files. Deliberate attempts to degrade or disrupt system performance will be viewed as criminal activity under applicable state and federal law.

**GUIDELINE III:** Sponsors of student accounts are responsible for teaching proper techniques and standards for participation, for guiding student access to appropriate sections of the network, and for assuring that students understand that if they misuse the network they will lose their accounts. Particular concerns include issues of privacy, copyright infringement, e-mail etiquette, computer viruses, and intended use of Telnet resources.

**GUIDELINE IV:** The person in whose name an account is issued is responsible at all times for its proper use. Users should change their passwords frequently.

# TELECOMMUNICATIONS RESOURCES

## Commercial Services Vendors

**America Online**
8619 Westwood Center Dr.
Vienna, VA 22182
800–827–6364

**CompuServe**
5000 Arlington Center Blvd.
P.O. Box 20212
Columbus, OH 43220–9922
800–848–8990

**Dialog Information Services**
3460 Hillview Avenue
Palo Alto, CA 94304
800–334–2564

**GEnie**
GE Information Services
P.O. Box 6403
Rockville, MD 20850
800–638–9636

**Prodigy**
445 Hamilton Avenue
White Plains, NY 10610
800–776–3449

## Educational Networks

**AT&T Learning Network**
P.O. Box 4012
Bridgewater, NJ 98807–4012
800–367–7225

**FrEd Mail**
Al Rogers
P.O. Box 243
Bonita, CA 91902
619–475–4852

**GTE Educational Services**
SpecialNet
8505 Freeport Pkwy., Suite 600
Irving, TX 75063–9990
800–659–3000

**K12 Net**
Janet Murray
Wilson High School
1151 SW Vermont St.
Portland, OR 97219
503–280–5280 x 450

**National Geographic Kids Network**
National Geographic Society Educational
    Services
P.O. Box 98019
Washington, D.C. 20090
800–368–2728

### A Sample of USENET Groups

The following are a few USENET bulletin boards that might be of interest to educators.

| Address | Description |
|---------|-------------|
| misc.forsale | A posting of items for sale |
| misc.forsale.computers | Computers listed for sale |
| sci.edu | Discussion of science education topics |
| sci.environment | Discussion of environmental issues |
| sci.math | Discussion of math topics |

### A Sample of FTP Sites

The following are a selected few sites of interest to educators. In each case, enter "anonymous" as your user name and your Internet address as the password unless otherwise directed.

| Address | Response | Description |
|---------|----------|-------------|
| ames.arc.nasa.gov | cd pub/space | NASA information including photos |
| ftp.bio.indiana.edu | {none} | Files for science teaching |
| ftp.unt.edu | cd library | List of libraries connected to the Internet |
| ftphost.nwnet.net | cd nic/nwnet/ user-guide | K-12 telecomputing information |
| hydra.uwo.ca | {none} | Files for school librarians |
| pilot.njin.net | cd pub/ftp-list/ directory/ftp.list | List of Internet FTP sites |
| ra.msstate.edu | cd pub/docs/history | Files concerning the study of history |
| simtel20.army.mil | {none} | DOS software |
| sumex-aim.stanford.edu | {none} | Macintosh software |
| wuarchive.wustl.edu | {none} | Macintosh and DOS freeware |

### A Sample of World Wide Web Servers

The following World Wide Web servers were recommended by Don E. Descy, an associate professor at Mankato State University.

| Address | Description |
|---------|-------------|
| URL:http://www.cisco.com/cisco/ edu-arch.html | Cisco Education Catalog |
| URL:http://hillside.coled.umn.edu | Hillside Elementary School, Cottage Grove, MN |
| URL:http://www.elvis.msk.su | Russia |
| URL:http://web.msu.edu/vincent/ index.html | Vincent Voice Library at Michigan State University |
| URL:http://rs560.cl.msu.edu/weather | Weather maps, satellite pictures, movies |

## A Sample of LISTSERV Lists

LISTSERVs go into and out of existence. The following is a sample of a few that were available at the time of publication of this book. Since these are BITNET addresses, add .bitnet as a suffix to each address.

| *Address* | *Title* |
|---|---|
| AACE-L@AUVM | Association for the Advancement of Computing in Education |
| BIOPI-L@KSUV1 | High School Biology Teachers |
| CHEMED-L@UWF | Chemistry Education |
| DTS-L@IUBVM | Dead Teachers Society Discussion list |
| EDINFO-L@IUBV1 | Educational Information |
| ETDIR-L@UBV1 | Educational Technology Research |
| FINEART@RUTVM1 | Fine Arts Discussion list |
| GENED-L@ULKYVM | Discussion of General Education topics |
| GEOGRAPH@FINHUTC | Geography |
| GEOLOGY@PTEARN | Geology Discussion list |
| HEALTH-L@IRLEARN | International Discussion on Health Research |
| HYPERCRD@PURCCVM | HyperCard Discussion list |
| I-IBMPC@UIUCVMD | IBM PC Discussions |
| INTECH-L@ULKYVM | Instructional Technology Discussion |
| KIDSPHERE@PITTVMS | International list of kids and their teachers |
| LM_NET@SUVM.ACS.SYR.EDU | School Library Media Teachers |
| MACAPPLI@DARTCMS1 | Usage Tips about Macintosh Applications |
| MEDIA-L@BINGVMB | Media in Education |
| MUSIC-ED@UMINN1 | Music Education |
| NCPRSE-L@ECUVM1 | Reform discussion list for Science Education |
| PCSERV-L@UALTAVM | Public Domain Software Servers |
| PDUSIG@UIUCVMD | PC User's Group Public Domain and Utilities SIG |
| PHYS-L@UWF | Forum for Physics Teachers |
| QUALRSED@UNMVMA | Qualitative Research in Education |
| RUSSIA@INDYCMS | Russia and Her Neighbors |
| T321-L@MIZZOUL | Elementary Science Teaching |
| TAG-L@NDSUVM1 | Talented and Gifted Education |
| WX-NATNL@UIUCVMD | National Weather Summary |
| XCULTINS@UNMVMA | Effects of Culture on Instructional Design |
| 9NOV89-L@DBOTUI11 | Events Around the Berlin Wall |

# SOFTWARE DATABASE

| Field Name | Field Type | Formula/Entry Option |
|---|---|---|
| Title | Text | |
| Version # | Text | |
| Publisher | Text | |
| Copyright Date | Number | Range: 1985. . .2010 |
| Vendor Name | Text | |
| Vendor Street Address | Text | |
| City, ST, ZIP | Text | |
| Vendor Phone # | Text | |
| Technical Support Phone # | Text | |
| Computer / OS | Text | |
| RAM Needed | Text | |
| Hard Disk Space Needed | Text | |
| Software License | Text | Value List: |
| | | Single User |
| | | Multiple User |
| | | Site License |
| Number of Licensed Users | Number | |
| Cost | Number | |
| Grade Level | Text | Value List: |
| | | Pri |
| | | Int |
| | | MS |
| | | HS |
| | | Fac |
| Program Description | Text | |
| Type of Software | Text | Value List: |
| | | Drill & Practice |
| | | Tutorial |
| | | Simulation |
| | | Multimedia |
| | | Word processor |
| | | Spreadsheet |
| | | Database |
| | | Communication |
| | | Other |

| Field Name | Field Type | Formula/Entry Option |
|---|---|---|
| Subject Area | Text | Value List: |
| | | Foreign Language |
| | | Language Arts |
| | | Math |
| | | Science |
| | | Social Studies |
| Language other than English | Text | Value List: |
| | | French |
| | | German |
| | | Japanese |
| | | Spanish |
| Purchase Order # | Text | |
| Purchase Date | Date | |
| Shipping Cost | Number | |
| TOTAL | Calculation | = Cost + Shipping |
| Foreign Language Topics | Text | Value List: |
| | | Conversation |
| | | Culture |
| | | Grammar |
| | | Vocabulary |
| Language Arts Topics | Text | Value List: |
| | | Capitals |
| | | Consonants |
| | | Literature |
| | | Paragraphs |
| | | Prefix |
| | | Punctuation |
| | | Reading |
| | | Sentence Structure |
| | | Spelling |
| | | Suffix |
| | | Vowels |
| | | Writing |
| Math Topics | Text | Value List: |
| | | Addition, Simple |
| | | Addition, 2 place |
| | | Addition, > 2 place |
| | | Subtraction, Simple |
| | | Subtraction, 2 place |

| Field Name | Field Type | Formula/Entry Option |
|---|---|---|
| Math Topics | Text | Value List (continued): |
| | | Subtraction, > 2 place |
| | | Place Value |
| | | Multiplication, Simple |
| | | Multiplication, > 1 digit multiplier |
| | | Division, Simple |
| | | Division, > 1 digit divisor |
| | | Fractions |
| | | Decimals |
| | | Story problems, Simple |
| | | Story problems, Complex |
| | | Time |
| | | Money |
| | | Pre-algebra |
| | | Algebra |
| | | Geometry |
| | | Trigonometry |
| | | Calculus |
| Science Topics | Text | Value List: |
| | | Astronomy |
| | | Biology |
| | | Chemistry |
| | | Earth Science |
| | | Geology |
| | | Physical Science |
| | | Physics |
| Social Studies Topics | Text | Value List: |
| | | American History |
| | | Geography |
| | | Government |
| | | Economics |
| | | Mapping |
| | | Regions |
| | | World History |
| School ID # | Text | |
| Call # | Text | |
| User Location | Text | |
| Inventory Value | Summary | = Total of Cost |
| Average Age | Summary | = Mean of Copyright Date |

**Notes:**

| | |
|---|---|
| Copyright Date | This field is prescribed as a number in order to be able to calculate an average. The range is limited to years that would be reasonable numbers (e.g., 1985 to 2010). |
| Software License | As with other fields in this database, a value list is suggested to ensure data entry consistency. Controlling the data entry will facilitate doing searches later on. |
| Inventory Value | A summary field that can reveal the value of the entire holdings represented in the database. It may also be used to show the value of any portion (e.g., MS, Simulation, Science, or Physics) of the database. This could yield useful assessment information. |
| Average Age | A summary field that can reveal the average age (based on copyright, not purchase date) of the entire holdings represented in the database. It may also be used to show the average age of any portion (e.g., MS, Simulation, Science, or Physics) of the database. This also could yield useful assessment information. |

**Broderbund Software**
17 Paul Drive
San Rafael, CA 94903
800–521–6263 (sales and customer service)
415–492–3500 (technical support)
Policies: 30-day preview, 60-day return,
90-day replacement, unlimited support.

**Claris Corporation**
Box 58168
Santa Clara, CA 95052
408–727–8227 (sales and customer service)
800–735–7393 (technical support—
recorded answers to frequently asked
questions)
408–727–9054 (technical support—
Macintosh)
408–727–9004 (technical support—
Windows)
Policies: Unlimited support, on-line support (Claris CR@aol.com).

**Compton's New Media**
Division of Encyclopedia Britannica
2320 Camino Vida Roble,
Carlsbad, CA 92009
800–862–2206 (sales and customer service)
619–929–2626 (technical support)
Policies: 30-day return, unlimited support.

**Davidson & Associates**
P.O. Box 2961, Torrance, CA 90509
800–545–7677 (sales and customer service)
800–545–6141 (technical support)
Policies: 3-day money-back guarantee,
unlimited support.

**Discis Knowledge Research**
90 Sheppard Avenue East, Seventh Floor
Toronto, Ontario M2N SW9, Canada
800–567–4321 (sales and customer service)
800–567–4321 or 904–886–7273 (technical
support)
Policies: Unlimited guarantee, unlimited
support.

**Grolier Electronic Publishing**
Sherman Turnpike
Danbury, CT 06816
800–356–5590 (sales and customer service)
800–356–5590 (technical support)
Policies: 30-day money back guarantee,
unlimited support.

**Intellimation**
P.O. Box 1922, Cremona Drive
Santa Barbara, CA 93116
800–346–8355 (sales and customer service)
800–346–8355 (technical support)
Policies: 30-day money back guarantee,
unlimited support.

**Microsoft Corporation**
One Microsoft Way
Redmond, WA 98052
800–426–9400 (sales and customer service)
206–454–2030 (technical support)
Policies: 90-day money-back guarantee,
unlimited support.

**Minnesota Educational Computing
Corporation (MECC)**
6160 Summit Drive North
Minneapolis, MN 55430
800–685–6322 (sales and customer service)
800–685–6322 (technical support)
Policies: 30-day money-back guarantee.

**Optical Data Corporation**
30 Technology Drive
Warren, NJ 07059
800–524–2481 (sales and customer service)
800–524–2481 (technical support)
Policies: 30-day money-back guarantee.

**Sunburst Communications**
P.O. Box 100
Pleasantville, NY 10570–0100
800–321–7511 (sales and customer service)
800–321–7511 (technical support)
Policies: 45-day preview, 100% lifetime
replacement, 1 year money-back guaran-

tee, unlimited support, on-line support (sunburst4@aol.com).

**Tom Snyder Productions**
80 Collidge Hill Road
Watertown, MA 02172
800–342–0236 (sales and customer service)
800–342–0236 ext. 255 (technical support)
Policies: 30-day preview, 100% lifetime money-back guarantee, on-line support (chiptsp@aol.com).

**Voyager Company**
1351 Pacific Coast Highway
Santa Monica, CA 90401
800–446–2001 (sales and customer service)

914–591–5500 (technical support)
Policies: 30-day money-back guarantee, unlimited support.

**ZTEK Company**
P.O. Box 1055
Louisville, KY 402012
[ZTEK is a reseller as well as a publisher. It provides support for all of its products.]
800–247–1603 (sales and customer service)
800–247–1603 (technical support)
Policies: 30-day money-back guarantee, unlimited support, on-line support (ZTEK@applelink.apple.com).

## Free or Inexpensive Software

**Boston Computer Society**
Three Central Plaza
Boston, MA 02108

**Center for Math Literacy**
San Francisco State University
1600 Holloway Ave.
San Francisco, CA 94132

**CONDUIT**
P.O. Box 388
Iowa City, IA 52244

**FreeSoft Co.**
10828 Lacklink
St. Louis, MO 63117

**Free Ware**
P.O. Box 862
Tiburon, CA 94920

**Lawrence Hall of Science**
MCEP, University of California
Berkeley, CA 94720

**The Learning Center**
College of Education
Northern Illinois University
DeKalb, IL 60115

**Micro-Ed**
P.O. Box 24156
Minneapolis, MN 55424

**National Public Domain Software**
1533 Avohill Drive
Vista, CA 92083

**North Central Regional Library**
Software Mail Order Department
238 Olds Station Road
Wenatchee, WA 98801

**Queue Inc.**
Five Chapel Hill Drive
Fairfield, CT 06432

**SOFTSWAP**
San Mateo County Office of Education
333 Main Street
Redwood City, CA 94063

# TECHNOLOGY JOURNALS AND MAGAZINES

The following magazines and journals contain software reviews as well as "how to" articles. A selection of these would form the core of an excellent collection of periodicals for a school library. The author's favorite, *Learning and Leading with Technology*, formerly *The Computing Teacher*, is of consistent high quality with practical articles founded on a sound theory base.

**CD-ROM Professional**
462 Danbury Road
Wilton, CT 06897

**Classroom Computer Learning**
5615 West Carmel Rd.
Cicero, IL 60650

**Computers in the Schools**
Haworth Press
10 Alice Street
Binghamton, NY 13904

**Learning and Leading with Technology**
International Society for Technology in Education
1787 Agate St.
Eugene, OR 97403–1923

**Ed-Tech Review**
Association for the Advancement of Computing in Education
P.O. Box 2966
Charlottesville, VA 22902

**Educational Technology**
Educational Technology Publishing
140 Sylvan Ave.
Englewood Cliffs, NJ 07632

**Educators' Tech Exchange**
Edutech, Inc.
P.O. Box 51760
Pacific Grove, CA 93950

**Electronic Learning**
P.O. Box 2041
Mahopa, NY 10541

**Information Technology and Libraries**
50 East Huron Street
Chicago, IL 60611

**Journal of Educational Computing Research**
Baywood Publishing
26 Austin Avenue
Amityville, NY 11701

**Learning**
Box 2580
Boulder, CO 80322

**Library Hi-Tech Journal**
Pierian Press
P.O. Box 1808
Ann Arbor, MI 48106

**Macworld**
Macworld Communications Inc.
501 Second Street
San Francisco, CA 94107

**Media & Methods**
1429 Walnut Street
Philadelphia, PA 10102

**New Media**
P.O. Box 1771
Riverton, NJ 08077–9771

**PC World**
PC World Communications Inc.
555 DeHaro St.
San Francisco, CA 94107

**Teaching and Computers**
P.O. Box 2040
Mahopac, NY 10541

**Technology & Learning**
Peter Li, Inc.
2451 East River Rd.
Dayton, OH 45439

**The Computing Teacher**
International Society for Technology
in Education
1787 Agate St.
Eugene, OR 97403–1923

The following are primarily review journals:

**Booklist**
50 East Huron St.
Chicago, IL 60611

**The Digest of Software Reviews**
301 West Mesa
Fresno, CA 93704

**EPIE Micro-courseware Profiles**
EPIE and Consumer's Union
Box 839
Water Mill, NY 11976

**Library Software Review**
520 Riverside Avenue
Westport, CT 06877

**School Library Journal**
Box 13706
Philadelphia, PA 19101

**School Library Media Quarterly**
50 East Huron St.
Chicago, IL 60611

**Whole Earth Review**
P.O. Box 27956
San Diego, CA 92128

**Wilson Library Bulletin**
900 University Avenue
Bronx, NY 10452

## ASSOCIATIONS PROMOTING THE USE OF TECHNOLOGY

The following national and international associations contribute valuable information to their members' professional development through publications and conferences. The reader is encouraged to find statewide associations that would contribute as well.

**Association for Computing Machinery (ACM)**
1133 Avenue of the Americas
New York, NY 10036
212–265–6300

**Association for Development of Computer-Based Instructional Systems (ADCIS)**
Western Washington Computer Center
Bellingham, WA 98225
206–676–2860

**Association for Educational Communication and Technology (AECT)**
1126 16th Street NW
Washington, DC 20036
202–833–4186

**Association for Educational Data Systems (AEDS)**
1201 16th Street NW
Washington, DC 20036
202–833–4100

**International Society for Technology in Education (ISTE)**
1787 Agate Street
Eugene, OR 97403
503–686–4414

# Index